AGhC/ 71

Alex

October 1974

University of Leeds.

PORTRAIT OF PAUL

PORTRAIT OF PAUL

By

E. W. HUNT

John James Pantyfedwen Professor of Theology
St. David's College, Lampeter

LONDON
A. R. MOWBRAY & CO LTD

© *A. R. Mowbray & Co Ltd 1968*

Printed in Great Britain by
Alden & Mowbray Ltd
at the Alden Press, Oxford
6278

SBN 264 65523 0

First published in 1968

UXORI CARISSIMAE HUNC LIBRUM DEDICO

ACKNOWLEDGEMENTS

The thanks of the author and publishers are due to the following for permission to quote extracts:

Basil Blackwell & Mott Ltd., *He that Cometh* by S. Mowinckel; T. & T. Clark, *Commentary on Romans, I.C.C.*, by W. Sanday and A. C. Headlam, *The Christian Doctrine of Man* by H. W. Robinson, and *Bible Studies* by A. Deissmann; Constable Publishers, *Objections to Roman Catholicism* by M. Goffin; Gerald Duckworth & Co. Ltd., *Conscience and Christ* by H. Rashdall; Faber & Faber Ltd., *God was in Christ* by D. M. Baillie; William Heinemann Ltd., *Battle for the Mind* by W. Sargant; Hodder & Stoughton Ltd., *Commentary on Romans, M.N.T.C.*, by C. H. Dodd and *Commentary on 1 Corinthians, M.N.T.C.*, by J. Moffatt; Longmans, Green & Co. Ltd., *The Rise of Christianity* by E. W. Barnes; Thomas Nelson & Sons Ltd., *Christ in the Theology of St. Paul* by L. Cerfaux; Routledge & Kegan Paul Ltd., *The Jewish World in the Time of Jesus* by Ch. Guignebert; S.C.M. Press Ltd., *Introduction to the Theology of the New Testament* by Alan Richardson. *On Paul and John* by T. W. Manson, and *Studies in the Acts of the Apostles* by M. Dibelius; S.P.C.K., *Paul and Rabbinic Judaism* by W. D. Davies; Mrs. N. P. Williams, *The Ideas of the Fall and Original Sin* by N. P. Williams.

Should any acknowledgement have been omitted inadvertently, then this oversight will be rectified in subsequent editions if brought to the attention of either the author or the publishers.

CONTENTS

PREFACE

I HAVE written this book primarily to comply with the request of some of the four hundred students who have listened to my lectures on Paul of Tarsus during the last fifteen years, that I should commit my words to print. Although it is concerned with a country that has been extensively and intensively explored and mapped by many eminent cartographers, we should not forget that

> he that made us with such large discourse,
> Looking before and after gave us not
> That capability and god-like reason
> To fust in us unus'd.

Therefore, although I owe a debt to the many scholars whose names are listed in its bibliography and to whom in grateful acknowledgment I genuflect (figuratively, not literally), this book is the fruit of my own scrutiny of the evidence. In short, 'an ill-favoured thing' it may be, but it is 'mine own.' I am no σπερμολόγος !

Lest I should be accused of having left undone the things that I ought to have done, I must add six points. First, in spite of the findings of mechanical gadgets I am not persuaded that Paul was not the author of ten of the thirteen Epistles traditionally attributed to him, and also of certain fragments in the other three— the Pastoral Epistles. Secondly, I am inclined to hold that the author of the Acts of the Apostles was a more reliable historian than some scholars think. The arguments generated in Tübingen one hundred and thirty years ago, and resurrected from time to time, have been effectively answered by Lightfoot, Ramsay, Harnack, Streeter, and W. L. Knox. I find myself in complete accord with the eminent contemporary classical scholar who states that 'for Acts the confirmation of historicity is overwhelming' and that 'any attempt to reject its basic historicity even in matters of detail must now appear absurd' (A. N. Sherwin-White, *Roman*

Society and Roman Law in the New Testament, p. 189). Thirdly, the translations of most of the Hebrew, Greek, and Latin passages that I have quoted are my own. Fourthly, in transliterating Hebrew words I have followed the system recommended by the *Journal of Semitic Studies*. Fifthly, let no-one think that my quotations from English Literature, whether they are captions or are in the text, are 'merely corroborative detail, intended to give artistic verisimilitude to an otherwise bald and unconvincing narrative.' More often than not they sum up succinctly and elegantly what I am trying to say. Lastly, it is a pleasure to thank those who have helped me: the Reverend P. M. K. Morris, Mr. F. Newte, and Mr. G. Eatough, of St. David's College, Lampeter, and the Reverend A. A. Macintosh of St. John's College, Cambridge, for some valuable suggestions; Mr. R. C. Rider (the Sub-librarian of St. David's College, Lampeter) and the staff of Llyfrgell Genedlaethol Cymru for their kindness; the Pantyfedwen Fund for a grant towards the cost of publication; Mr. Mark Williamson for his help in reading the proofs; and last but not least my amanuensis, Ruth Burke, for taxing her eyesight in deciphering my handwriting.

E. W. HUNT

St. David's College,
    Lampeter.

Feast of the Transfiguration
    of Our Lord, 1967.

SIGLA

Ant.	Josephus, Antiquities
BASOR	Bulletin of the American Schools of Oriental Research
Beginnings	The Beginnings of Christianity, ed. F. J. Foakes Jackson, K. Lake, etc.
B.J.	Josephus, Wars of the Jews
BKW	Bible Keywords
BNTC	Black's New Testament Commentaries
BRL	Bulletin of the John Rylands Library
CNT	Commentaire du Nouveau Testament
EGT	Expositor's Greek Testament
ERE	Encyclopaedia of Religion and Ethics
ET	Expository Times
GEL	W. Bauer, Greek-English Lexicon of the New Testament, translated by W. F. Arndt and F. W. Gingrich
GGNT	J. H. Moulton, W. F. Howard, and N. Turner, Grammar of New Testament Greek
GNTG	G. B. Winer, Grammar of New Testament Greek
HDB	Hastings's Dictionary of the Bible
HJP	E. Schürer, The History of the Jewish People in the Time of Jesus Christ
HTR	Harvard Theological Review
IB	Interpreter's Bible
IDB	Interpreter's Dictionary of the Bible
ICC	International Critical Commentary
ITNT	A. Richardson, Introduction to the Theology of the New Testament
JRS	Journal of Roman Studies
JTS	Journal of Theological Studies
MGLNT	G. Abbott-Smith, Manual Greek Lexicon of the New Testament
MNTC	Moffatt New Testament Commentary
NCHS	S.P.C.K. New Commentary on Holy Scripture
NLC	New London Commentary
NTS	New Testament Studies
PCB	Peake's Commentary, 1962 edn.

PL	Patrologia Latina
RE	Religious Encyclopaedia
RHR	Revue de l'Histoire des Religions
TNTC	Tyndale New Testament Commentaries
TWNT	Theologisches Wörterbuch zum Neuen Testament, ed. G. Kittel
VGT	J. H. Moulton and G. Milligan, Vocabulary of the Greek New Testament
WC	Westminster Commentaries

PORTRAIT OF PAUL

I

OVERTURE

'Where shall I begin, please your Majesty?' he asked.
'Begin at the beginning,' the King said gravely; 'and go on till you come
to the end; then stop.'
LEWIS CARROLL, Alice in Wonderland, Chapter 12

There's a divinity that shapes our ends
Rough-hew them how we will.
SHAKESPEARE, Hamlet, Act 5, Scene 2

UNTIL comparatively recent times biographers of Paul of Tarsus and interpreters of his writings have been wont to begin their works with a detailed account of his life before his conversion to Christianity. For example, in a life of Paul published in 1919 the author devoted approximately nine thousand words to the subject,[1] while six years later Dr. Glover, in the first two chapters of what will always rank as a literary *chef d'œuvre*, exceeded that total by roughly six thousand words.[2] Now the pendulum has swung to the other extreme: we are informed by some of our more sceptical New Testament scholars that we know next to nothing about the apostle's pre-conversion days.[3] We are reminded of the reply given by Viola alias Cesario to Duke Orsino's question. 'What's her history?' asks the Duke; to which Olivia's page answers: 'A blank, my lord.'[4] It is true that those earlier biographies contained many pages of unwarranted conjecture and doubtful inference; but that does not mean that during the first act of the drama of Paul's life the stage is shrouded in

---

[1] D. Smith, *The Life and Letters of St. Paul* (London, 1919), pp. 17–44.
[2] T. R. Glover, *Paul of Tarsus* (London, 1925), pp. 5–46.
[3] E.g. J. Munck, *Paul and the Salvation of Mankind*, Eng. tr. F. Clarke (London, 1959) pp. 11–12; and J. Knox, *Chapters in a Life of Paul* (London, 1954), pp. 74–6.
[4] Shakespeare, *Twelfth Night*, Act 2, Scene 4.

1

complete obscurity. The seeker can find in his primary source—
the Pauline Epistles—the data which, augmented with evidence
culled from the Acts of the Apostles and illuminated by statements
in other writings, both canonical and extra-canonical, will enable
him to paint some kind of picture of Paul as he was on the eve
of his conversion.

First, it is as certain that Paul belonged to the chosen race as it
is that Shakespeare was an Englishman and Abraham Lincoln
was an American. Yet, significantly, in informing the recipients
of his letters of that fact he never calls himself a 'Jew.'[1] Why is
this? The name would have been an accurate description of him
because, although originally it had meant a member of the tribe
of Judah, it had since the return of the exiles from Babylon been
applied to every member of the Hebrew race.[2] On the other
hand, he may have been reluctant to apply to himself an appella-
tion that more than any other had always served to emphasize
the distinctness of the Hebrews from the Gentiles, because as a
Christian he believed that in the new race, the new humanity,
to which he belonged, all racial and national distinctions had been
abolished (Rom. 10. 12; Gal. 3. 28; Col. 3. 11).[3] Nevertheless,
although in his Epistles he does not explicitly call himself a 'Jew,'
he leaves us in no doubt that he is one. 'I am an Israelite, a
descendant of Abraham, a member of the tribe of Benjamin'
(Rom. 11. 1). 'Are they Hebrews? So am I. Are they Israelites?
So am I. Are they Abraham's descendants? So am I.' (2 Cor.
11. 22). 'Circumcised when eight days old, I belong to the Israelite
race and the tribe of Benjamin. I am an Aramaic-speaking Jew,
descended from Aramaic-speaking Jews ('Εβραῖος ἐξ 'Εβραίων)
(Phil. 3. 5). These categorical assertions disclose four facts. First,
Paul was a Jew by birth:[4] he was a descendant of Abraham,

[1] According to Acts 21. 39 he told Claudius Lysias, the military tribune in Jerusalem,
and according to Acts 22. 3, a Jerusalem crowd, that he was 'a Jew.'
[2] Josephus, *Ant.* 11.5.7. Cf. F. J. Foakes Jackson, *The Life of St. Paul* (London, 1926),
pp. 27–8.
[3] *V. inf.*, pp. 126–7, 140.
[4] We are forced to confess our ignorance of the precise date of Paul's birth. The author
of Acts informs us that he was 'a young man (νεανίας)' at the time of Stephen's death
(Acts 7. 58); but this shred of evidence becomes less valuable than it appears when we
realize how vague a word νεανίας is. In the Oxyrhyncus Papyri, which, like the NT

who had, like all Jewish male infants, been circumcised when he was eight days old. There is, therefore, no truth in the scurrilous tale attributed by Epiphanius, Bishop of Salamis from A.D. 367 to 403, to the Ebionites, that Paul was born a Gentile, came to Jerusalem, was converted to Judaism because he aspired to the hand of the high priest's daughter, and when he was not allowed to marry her, became the bitter enemy of the Jews and all things Jewish.[1] As the bishop says, all this is nonsensical. Nor—this is the second inference from Paul's descriptions of himself—were his parents converts to Judaism. The designation 'Israelite' implies that they 'were not grafted into the covenant people, but descended from the original stock.'[2] Thirdly, Paul was a $'Εβραῖος ἐξ 'Εβραίων$: in contrast with the majority of his fellow Jews of the Diaspora Paul belonged to a family that had continued to use the old vernacular language, Aramaic.[3] That he spoke it fluently is evidenced by the statement in Acts 21. 40 (whose authenticity there is no reason to doubt) that he addressed the crowd in that tongue as he stood on the stairs of the Antonia Fortress in Jerusalem. Lastly, this same phrase $'Εβραῖος ἐξ 'Εβραίων$ may imply also that his ancestors originally hailed from Palestine.[4] His reference to his membership of the tribe of Benjamin may well imply the same; for its members boasted that alone of the patriarchs its progenitor was born in the land of promise (Gen. 35. 17).

books, were written in the Koine, νεανίας is applied to a youth of seventeen years of age (VGT, p. 423); but according to GEL (p. 536) it is used of men of between twenty-four and forty years of age. If GEL is right, if (as I am inclined to do) we accept C. H. Turner's date for Paul's conversion, viz. A.D. 35 (art. 'Chronology of the NT', HDB, Vol. 1, p. 424. Cf. D. Guthrie, New Testament Studies, The Pauline Epistles, London, 1963, p. 278), and if (as Acts seems to indicate) that event occurred very soon after Stephen's death, then Paul was born some time between 5 B.C. and A.D. 11. Some writers appeal to the word πρεσβύτης in Philemon 9, but it does not mean 'old man'; it means 'ambassador,' the vowel υ and the diphthong ευ being interchangeable in the Koine (VGT, p. 535).

[1] Epiphanius, Haereses, 30.16.25.
[2] J. B. Lightfoot, Saint Paul's Epistle to the Philippians (London, 1888), p. 146.
[3] V. inf., p. 21.
[4] Cf. the tradition in Jerome's writings (de Vir. Illust., 5 and ad Philemon, 23) that Paul was born in Gischala near the Lake of Gennesareth in Northern Galilee, and that when the village was captured by the Romans, he emigrated with his parents to Tarsus. Although this must be an anachronism, since the Romans took Gischala about seventy years after Paul's birth, it may enshrine the truth that his ancestors originally came from there. Cf. M. Goguel, who rejects Jerome's statement as worthless (The Birth of Christianity, Eng. tr. H. C. Snape, London, 1953, p. 206 n.) and J. K. Klausner, who reads too much into it (From Jesus to Paul, Eng. tr. W. F. Stinespring, London, 1944, p. 304).

If this is true—that Paul's forbears were Palestinian Jews—the tradition of speaking Aramaic had probably been handed down in his family, in which event he learnt it in his home in Tarsus.

Secondly, if Paul was born a Jew, it seems a reasonable inference that his early education followed the normal Jewish course. This race into which he was born certainly understood the vital importance of systematic instruction of the young. 'Our chief care is to educate our children well,' wrote Josephus;[1] and (with the substitution of the word 'race' for the phrase 'people of this country,' and of the word 'it' for 'this country') he would no doubt have endorsed what one of the most celebrated of the sons of Abraham told the British House of Commons nineteen centuries later: 'Upon the education of the people of this country the fate of this country depends.'[2] Indoctrination of the Jewish child began in his home; indeed, almost from the time when he was still 'mewling and puking in his nurse's arms.' As Philo avers, Jewish children were taught to believe in God 'so to speak, from their very swaddling clothes.'[3] Josephus endorses that statement when he says that Jews learn the laws from their very first consciousness, and that thereby they are engraved on their minds.[4] It was, he claims, a policy that accorded with the wish of the great Moses himself, who had commanded that 'children should learn the most important laws, because this is the best knowledge and the cause of prosperity.'[5] The goal of Jewish education was knowledge of the Torah. As Jewish scholars have repeatedly pointed out, this word is not, as many Christian writers have understood it, synonymous with the word 'law.' The cause of this error was the LXX translation of *tôrāh*—*νόμος*. The Hebrew word *tôrāh* is derived from the verb *yārāh*, which means 'to throw lots' and then 'to direct' and 'to teach.' Thus *tôrāh* means 'direction,' 'instruction', 'teaching'; and since the Exile, when the law-books had been combined with the narratives of the early history of the Hebrews in one book, the name had been given to the Pentateuch. Certainly it contained laws, but

---

[1] *c. Apion*, 1. 12.   [2] Benjamin Disraeli on 15th June, 1874.
[3] *Legatio ad Cajum*, par. 31.   [4] *c. Apion*, 2. 18.   [5] *Ant.* 4. 8. 12.

'the legalistic element, which might rightly be called the Law, represents only one element of the Torah.'[1] This same name of *tôrāh* had come to be applied also to the oral expositions of the written Torah supplied by the scribes, which were considered by the Pharisees to be as authoritative as the written Torah. These oral traditions of the elders were of two kinds corresponding to the two divisions of the written Torah: *Hᵃlākhāh* (guidance), explanations of the laws, with detailed authoritative guidance for obeying them; and *Haggādhāh* (narrative), interpretation of the narratives, with practical, homiletic, and imaginative exegesis of them. At this point it is important to refer to a significant development in the Jewish attitude to the Torah, which had begun *c.* 200–180 B.C. with the writing of the book that is called 'Ecclesiasticus' in the Vulgate and in the English translations of the Apocrypha, but whose title in Greek MSS. is *Σοφια Ιησου υιου Σειραχ*, *The Wisdom of Jesus the Son of Sirach*. Ben-Sira, a Sadducean scribe, identified the Torah with Wisdom (Ecclus. 15. 1; 19. 20; 21. 11; 24. 23), already eulogized by the Jewish author of Proverbs (Prov. 8–9). Ben-Sira explicitly says: 'All these things (i.e. Wisdom) are the book of the covenant of the Most High, the Law which Moses commanded as an heritage for the assemblies of Jacob' (Ecclus. 24. 23). Ben-Sira's successor, the unknown author of *The Wisdom of Solomon*, taught the Jews that Wisdom, i.e. knowledge of the Torah, was the most valuable prize of life, to be preferred to rank, wealth, health and beauty. 'She is to men a treasure that does not fail and those who use it obtain friendship with God, being commended to him by gifts which they through discipline present to him' (Wisd. 7. 14). Wisdom teaches soberness, understanding, righteousness and courage, and 'there is nothing in life for men more profitable than these' (Wisd. 8. 7). There is no doubt that the Jews of Paul's day, not only of the Diaspora but also of Palestine, accepted this identification of the Torah with Wisdom.[2]

---

[1] S. Schecter, *Some Aspects of Rabbinic Theology* (London, 1909), p. 117. Nevertheless as it was the major part of it, we are, except in certain contexts, justified in treating the two as synonymous.

[2] W. D. Davies, *Paul and Rabbinic Judaism* (London, 1948), p. 170. On Paul's knowledge of the Book of Wisdom *v. inf.*, *pp*. 24, 95, 226.

Thus knowledge of the Torah, the end of Jewish education, meant knowledge of the Divine Wisdom.

As Joesphus indicates, the teaching given in the Jewish home was divided into two parts. Moses had ordered Jewish parents 'to teach their children to behave according to the laws that, growing up with the laws, they might not break them nor have the excuse of ignorance; and to know the deeds of their ancestors that they might imitate them.'[1] It will be readily seen that these two divisions of the domestic curriculum correspond in fact to the two elements of the Torah, the legal and the historical.[2] As Professor Findlay puts it, Jewish education 'sought to combine instruction on the positive truths of the ancestral faith with preparation for the practical duties of life.'[3] No doubt the first words that Paul of Tarsus was made to learn by heart were those of the Jewish credo, the $\check{S}^e ma^c$: 'Hear, O Israel, Yahweh our God is one Yahweh' (Deut. 6. 4). Furthermore, with his passionate conviction that he belonged to Yahweh's chosen race and that Yahweh was operating in history, his father would almost certainly take care that the events recorded in the Jewish annals were indelibly stamped on his son's memory. The Jewish paterfamilias related Yahweh's marvellous actions that 'the generations to come might know them, even the children who should yet be born, who should arise and tell them to their children, that they might set their hope in God, and not forget the works of God, but keep his commandments' (Ps. 78. 6–7. Cf. Deut. 32. 7). Especially would the infant Paul learn of the most momentous occurrence in Hebrew history, the mighty act of deliverance from the Egyptian oppressors, and of its sequel, the donating of the sacred Torah to Moses (Deut. 6. 20–5); and if there was any danger that he might forget those events, there was always the annual domestic ceremony of *Pesaḥ*, Passover, the Feast of Unleavened Bread, whose purpose was to remind him of them (Exod. 12. 26–7; 13. 14–16). There were, also, the objects in every Jewish home to keep the Torah ever before the child. At every turn Paul would see these

---

[1] *c. Apion*, 2, 26.   [2] *V. sup.*, p. 5.
[3] G. G. Findlay, art. 'Paul,' HDB, Vol. 3, p. 646.

symbols. At the four corners of the *śimlāh*, the outer garment of the Jew (called the *ἱμάτιον* in the NT), he would see the *ṣîṣîth*, the hyacinth blue or white woollen tassels (the *κράσπεδα* of the NT), which were meant to remind the wearer of the commandments of Yahweh (Deut. 22. 12; Num. 15. 37–8). Attached to the right-hand post of the door of his home he would observe the *mᵉzûzāh*, the small cylinder containing a parchment on which was written the *Šᵉmaʿ* (Deut. 6. 4–9; 11. 13–21). Every day except the Sabbath and a holy day he would notice that before morning prayer his father strapped a small box to the upper part of his left arm and another round his forehead; they were the *tᵉphillîn* (the *φυλακτήρια* of the NT), the cases containing the parchments on which were inscribed four passages from the OT (Exod. 13. 1–10, 11–16; Deut. 6. 4–9; 11. 13–21). All this Paul would see and hear in his home.

The second stage in his education would begin at the age of six or seven, when he began to attend the *bêth hassêpher*, the elementary school attached to the synagogue.[1] As the name 'House of the Book' indicates, the curriculum was the study of the Torah. Since presumably Paul attended a synagogue school in his birthplace, Tarsus, the version of the scriptures that he studied was the Septuagint, the Bible of the Jews of the Diaspora, written in Greek, which had for them authority equal to that of the original Hebrew text. In his Epistles there is abundant evidence—he quotes it approximately one hundred times and alludes to it almost as often—that he was steeped in the Greek version of the OT. As Deissmann says, Paul was a 'Septuagint Jew.'[2] It was probably during this, the second, stage in his education that he learnt a trade. As a rabbinical apophthegm probably current in Paul's day shows, the Jews discouraged idleness. It runs: 'He who does not teach his son a trade teaches him to be a thief.'[3]

---

[1] Although we may doubt the Talmudic tradition that these schools were instituted by Simeon ben Shetach in 75 B.C., it is almost certain that they existed in Paul's day. *Vide* E. Schürer, HJP, Div. 2, Vol. 2, pp. 48–50.

[2] G. A. Deissmann, *St. Paul*, Eng. tr. L. R. M. Strachan (London, 1912), p. 101. On Paul's OT quotations *vide* E. E. Ellis, *Paul's Use of the Old Testament* (Edinburgh, 1957).

[3] *Tosephta Kiddushin*, 1. 11, ed. M. S. Zuckermandel (Pasewalk, 1880). On the use of later rabbinical sources *vide* W. D. Davies, *Paul and Rabbinic Judaism*, pp. 3–4.

According to Acts 18. 3 the trade that Paul learnt was the manu-
facturing from goats' hair of the most important staple of his
native Cilicia, viz. a fabric called *cilicium*, from which tents,
carpets, and shoes were made.[1]

Recapitulating, then, in the first place we can be certain that
Paul was born a Jew; and secondly, we are justified in inferring
that his early education followed a normal course. Thirdly, if we
are to believe Acts, he received more advanced education in Jerusalem. At puberty the Jewish male became a *bar miṣwāh*, 'a son
of commandment';[2] and it was then that boys who were to
become professional scribes, i.e. students and expounders of the
Torah, were sent for training to a *bêth hammidhrāš*, 'a house of
interpretation,' a college or theological college so to speak, where
the most erudite rabbis taught. According to Acts 22. 3 Paul
claimed that he had been trained in the famous college in Jerusalem presided over by Gamaliel.[3] The historicity of this statement
has been questioned on four main grounds, and the theory of one
of those who believe it to be unhistorical is that the author of
Acts fabricated it to serve one of his purposes in writing his
work, viz. to show how Jerusalem was the place where the
transition from Judaism to the faith that fulfilled it, Christianity,
took place.[4] To what do these objections amount? First, it is
pointed out that in his Epistles Paul never mentions that he was
'educated at the feet of Gamaliel.' John Knox argues that if this
had happened, the apostle would have mentioned it in Romans
11. 1, 2 Corinthians 11. 22, Galatians 1. 14, and Philippians 3. 5
as a proof of the zealous orthodoxy of his pre-conversion days.[5]
Yet we cannot be sure of this, and in any case where is the evidence that Gamaliel was a pillar of orthodoxy? On the contrary,

[1] On the meaning of σκηνοποιός *vide* VGT, p. 577; F. F. Bruce, *The Acts of the Apostles*
(London, 1951), p. 343; and *Beginnings*, Vol. 4, p. 223.
[2] Not necessarily at twelve years of age as Lk. 2. 42 states. *Vide* E. Schürer, HJP, Div. 2,
Vol. 2, p. 52.
[3] The most celebrated colleges were in Jerusalem. Josephus mentions two that drew
large numbers of pupils in the days of Herod the Great (B.J. 1.33.2; Ant. 17.6.2).
[4] For these arguments *vide* C. G. Montefiore, *Judaism and St. Paul* (London, 1914),
pp. 58–129; A. Loisy, *Les Actes des Apôtres* (Paris, 1920), pp. 284–91; and J. Knox, *Chapters
in a Life of Paul*, pp. 34–5.
[5] J. Knox, *ibid.*

he seems—as we shall see, this is one of the facts used in the second objection—to have been one of the more liberal Jewish teachers. Besides, it is doubtful whether the name of Gamaliel would have had much significance, if any at all, for the Christians of Rome, Corinth, Galatia, and Philippi. The second objection is that such an intransigent, intolerant man as Paul could not have been a pupil of the liberal, tolerant Gamaliel. This is even less convincing than the first objection, for the obvious reason that not every pupil models himself upon his teacher. Particularly would this seem to be true in this instance: from what we know of Paul's personality he was much more likely on highly controversial points to adopt opinions antithetical to those of his teacher.[1] In the third place, it is pointed out that Paul's account in his Epistles of Jewish teaching concerning the Law is 'so gross a caricature of anything which he could have learnt from Gamaliel.'[2] The answer to this objection is that 'Paul's own conversion and all his subsequent experience proved to him that the constant Jewish error was to seek salvation by "works of the Law," and the contrast between faith and works became almost an obsession with him.'[3] The fourth and last objection is that the use of the verb ἀνῆλθον in Galatians 1. 17, and again in the next verse, implies that Paul had never visited Jerusalem before his conversion. This argument has been refuted by H. G. Wood, who shows that the word can be translated 'I returned,' and his conclusion is that it 'affords no ground for supposing that Paul had never been in Jerusalem before.'[4] Thus, the outcome of our examination of these objections is that, with Klausner, we believe that Paul did sit 'at the feet of Gamaliel.'[5] Although he had been born a Diaspora Jew, he was trained to be a scribe in the capital of Jewry itself by one of the most famous Jewish teachers of the day. This Gamaliel,[6] Rabban Gamaliel, is described by Luke as 'a Pharisee,

[1] Cf. H. St. J. Thackeray, *The Relation of St. Paul to Contemporary Jewish Thought* (London, 1900), p. 10.
[2] K. Lake and H. J. Cadbury, *Beginnings*, Vol. 4, p. 279.
[3] C. S. C. Williams, *Comm. on Acts* (BNTC) (London, 1957), p. 243.
[4] *Jesus in the Twentieth Century* (London, 1960), p. 161.
[5] J. Klausner, *From Jesus to Paul*, p. 309.
[6] The name means 'recompense of God.'

a member of the Sanhedrin, a doctor of the Law, who was highly respected by all the people' (Acts 5. 34). He may have been a grandson of the celebrated Hillel, the founder of the more liberal of the two Pharisaic schools. So highly honoured was he that he was the first of seven rabbis to be accorded the honorific title of 'Rabban' (our Rabbi). Like Hillel he was, as we have said, comparatively liberal: he taught that Jews ought to give the Hebrew greeting 'Peace be with you' to Gentiles; that there should be no divorce proceedings without a wife's knowledge; that penurious Gentiles ought to be allowed to gather gleanings after the harvest as poor Jews were; and that soldiers on active service should not be required to keep the more rigorous rules of Sabbath observance. Another example of his liberalism was his penchant for reading Greek literature, and it may have been from his lips that Paul heard the Greek tags that he quoted later in life (Acts 17. 28; 1 Cor. 15. 33).[1] Gamaliel was as wise as he was liberal. We have an example both of his sagacity and of his liberalism in his attitude towards the followers of Jesus. When the Sanhedrin was intent on putting them to death, he advised caution on the ground that if the movement was of human origin, it would collapse; but that if it was divinely inspired, it was bound to flourish, and that therefore in condemning the Nazarenes, the Sanhedrin might be opposing God himself (Acts 5. 33–9). Obviously Gamaliel's premise was the Pharisaic doctrine that God was controlling events, from which it followed that men must leave all to him. Such an attitude breeds tolerance. Like another sage nineteen centuries later Gamaliel believed that 'we can never be sure that the opinion that we are endeavouring to stifle is a false opinion; and if we were sure, stifling it would be an evil still.'[2] It was literally at the feet of this shrewd teacher that Paul was taught, for 'the pupils sat on the ground during the instruction of the teacher, who was on an elevated place.'[3] As

[1] V. inf., p. 71.
[2] J. S. Mill, On Liberty (The World's Classics, Oxford, 1912), p. 24.
[3] E. Schürer, HJP, Div. 2, Vol. 1 ,p. 326.

the Mishna so picturesquely puts it, the pupil was able 'to powder himself with the dust of the rabbi's feet.'[1]

What doctrines did Paul and his fellow-students imbibe during their period of training in Jerusalem? The answer can be given quickly and succinctly: those of Pharisaism. Here we have the third characteristic of the pre-conversion Paul. He was born a Jew; he was indoctrinated with Judaism; and he was trained to be a Pharisaic scribe. Many years after his student days in Jerusalem he described himself as having been a Pharisee where the Torah was concerned (Phil. 3. 5);[2] a few years later he told the Sanhedrin: 'I am a Pharisee, the son of Pharisees' (Acts 23. 6); and likewise shortly afterwards he informed King Herod Agrippa II: 'As a Pharisee I lived according to the principles of the strictest party in our religion' (Acts 26. 5). It has been suggested that the phrase 'the son of Pharisees,' which he used in his speech to the Sanhedrin, should be interpreted literally, i.e. his parents belonged to the Pharisaic party.[3] More probably it means that he had been a pupil of Pharisaic rabbis, the chief of whom was Gamaliel.

The origin of the name of this party whose pedagogues trained Paul, and of which he became a zealous member, has been the subject of prolonged discussion and the question is still *sub judice*. The Greek word is the translation of the Hebrew word *p^erûšîm* and the Aramaic *p^erîšîn*, both of which mean 'separated ones.' It is uncertain whether the Pharisees themselves adopted the name or whether their enemies bestowed it on them.[4] What is certain, however, is that they called themselves *h^abhērîm*, neighbours, associates, or comrades. The bond that united them in their *h^abhûrôth* (societies, associations, or fellowships) was scrupulous adherence to the written Torah and the oral tradition. This fact provides us with a clue to the significance of the name 'separated ones.' From what or from whom were the Pharisees separated? Various answers have been given to this question: they separated themselves from the Gentiles, the priesthood, sin, ceremonial

---

[1] *Sayings of the Jewish Fathers*, ed. C. Taylor (Cambridge, 1877), p. 28.
[2] On the date of Philippians *vide inf.*, p. 148 n. 4.
[3] J. Klausner, *From Jesus to Paul*, p. 312.
[4] *Vide* G. F. Moore, *Judaism* (Oxford, 1927–30), Vol. 1, pp. 60–2.

defilement, or the *'am hā-'āreṣ*, 'the people of the land.' Since the main *raison d'être* of the Pharisaic fellowships was the preservation of the strict observance of the Torah, both written and oral, the most reasonable of these answers is that the comrades separated themselves from those Jews who failed to observe it, those known as the *'am hā-'āreṣ*.[1] Originally this designation, even as it was used by the Pharisees, had no derogatory meaning. It was the customary description of the labouring and peasant classes, the common people, the masses; but eventually it came to be applied to 'the bad Jew, the man who could not recite the *Shᵉma*, nor the morning and evening prayers, who did not wear the ritual fringes (*zizith*) on his garment, who omitted to don the phylacteries (*tefillim*) necessary to proper devotion, who ate without first washing his hands; the man who, having a son, neglected to teach him the Law, or, having property, did not pay his tithe to Yahweh—in a word, a non-practising Jew.'[2] It is to this class that the Evangelists are referring when they speak of 'sinners,' with whom they link the *publicani*, the tax-collectors (Mk. 2. 15–16 = Mt. 9. 10–11 = Lk. 5. 30; Mt. 11. 19 = Lk. 7. 34; Lk. 15. 1). It was to this class that, as their attitude to the Torah shows (e.g. Mk. 2. 18 = Mt. 9. 14 = Lk. 5. 33; Mk. 7. 1 ff. = Mt. 15. 1 ff. Cf. Lk. 11. 37 ff.; etc.), Jesus and his disciples belonged. The attitude of the Pharisees to the *'am hā-'āreṣ* is summed up in one word—contempt: they were the untouchables of Judaism.[3] The mentality of the Pharisee in Jesus' parable of the Pharisee and the Tax-collector was probably typical of most members of his party. When he spoke of 'other men,' he almost certainly had in mind the *'am hā-'āreṣ*. It seems reasonable to believe that as a zealous Pharisee Paul held this same opinion, and it was no doubt one cause of his bitter hostility to the Nazarenes, who originated from the untouchables, a class that, according to the Pharisees, merited nothing but scorn on account of their failure to observe the Torah, which Pharisaism believed to be sacrosanct.

[1] E. Schürer, HJP, Div. 2, Vol. 2, pp. 20 ff.
[2] Ch. Guignebert, *The Jewish World in the Time of Jesus*, Eng. tr. S. H. Hooke (London, 1939), p. 207.
[3] E. Schürer, HJP, Div. 2, Vol. 2, pp. 24–5.

In that last clause we have the quintessence of Judaism, of which the Pharisees were the exemplars. The Torah was 'all that God has made known of his nature, character and purpose and of what he would have men be and do.'[1] The Torah, identified with the Divine Wisdom, was thought to be infallible.[2] This doctrine became the be-all and the end-all of Paul's life, and it is significant that even after his conversion, when he had become convinced that the observance of the Torah was not the path to salvation, he could still speak of it in laudatory language (Rom. 3. 2; 7. 12, 14; 15. 4). Yet although the Torah was divinely inspired, it was not too sacred to be interpreted. So the Pharisees believed; and their scribes spent a vast amount of time and energy on expounding it, laying great stress on the need for accuracy and scrupulosity of exposition. It was one characteristic of the Pharisees, said Josephus, himself one of their number, that they seemed 'to interpret the law accurately.'[3] These interpretations, viz. the *Hᵃlākhāh* and the *Haggādhāh*, the oral traditions to which we have already referred, had come to be regarded as equally infallible with the written Torah.[4] Indeed, in their enthusiasm for hermeneutics some of them, as Jesus said, went so far as to put the oral tradition before the scripture itself (Mk. 7. 8). 'Words of Soferim (i.e. scribes) are akin to words of Thorah [*sic*] and more beloved than words of Thorah, for (Cant. 1. 2), "Thy Love is better than wine (sc. of the Thorah)"';[5] and 'it is more culpable to teach contrary to the precepts of the scribes, than contrary to the Thorah itself'[6] were two rabbinical pronouncements. Yet in insisting that the interpretation of scripture was vitally important, were they not the progressive party of Judaism, and were not their rivals, the Sadducees, with their belief that only the written word was binding, the obscurantist bibliolaters? By interpreting the Torah the Pharisees adapted it to new conditions and developed

---

[1] G. F. Moore, *Judaism*, Vol. 1, p. 263.
[2] Nevertheless, there is no evidence that the beliefs about the Torah that are expressed in some of the more extravagant dicta of later rabbis (e.g. Akiba and Simeon the Just) were current as early as Paul's time.
[3] B.J. 2.8.14. *Vita* 38.   [4] *V. sup.*, p. 5.
[5] *Sayings of the Jewish Fathers*, ed. C. Taylor, p. 119.
[6] Quoted by E. Schürer, HJP, Div. 2, Vol. 2, p. 12.

an exegesis by which a basis for new doctrines and laws could be found. As a twentieth-century Jew puts it, the Pharisaic belief in progress 'enabled the immutable Torah, which is self-sufficient for all time, to adapt itself to the varying conditions of each age without the loss of continuity.'[1] Thus as a Pharisee Paul learnt to believe that the Torah was the infallible, unalterable word of God. At the same time he learnt that every scribe had the right to interpret the Torah and make it suitable for new conditions, which is precisely what he did after his conversion, when he adapted it to the new situation created by the advent of Jesus, in order to prove that he was the Messiah, not only of the Jews, but of all mankind.[2]

From his study of the Torah Paul assimilated two fundamental doctrines each of which can be summed up in one word: expectation and election. The first—expectation—is an implication of the prevailing doctrine of the OT, that God was sovereign ruler of the universe and was controlling events. Jesus himself inherited this theocratic conception, which became, as Professor T. W. Manson says, 'a dominant factor in his life.'[3] The central tenet of his teaching was the Rule of God. On that same belief the Pharisees laid tremendous stress. Josephus tells us that they 'attribute everything to Fate (εἱμαρμένη) and God.'[4] Yet although God was sovereign ruler of the universe, man had free-will. The Pharisees taught that although 'in each action Fate co-operates, to act rightly or otherwise rests, indeed, for the most part with men'.[5] This explained why, although God ruled the universe, he was ruler only *de jure*. When would he be ruler *de facto*? Here we have the eschatological expectation: the Pharisaic answer to the question was that he would assuredly intervene to establish his reign one day, 'the Day of Yahweh.' Modern scholars who write on Jewish eschatology are at pains to point out that it is

[1] H. M. J. Loewe, in *Judaism and Christianity*, ed. W. O. E. Oesterley (London, 1937), Vol. 1, p. 107.
[2] *V. inf.*, p. 70.
[3] T. W. Manson, *The Teaching of Jesus* (Cambridge, 1963), p. 160.
[4] B.J., 2.8.14. The word εἱμαρμένη is a Hellenization.
[5] *Ibid.*, cf. *Ant.* 13.5.9; 18.1.3.

complicated because 'the fact is that there was no single and generally accepted view of the national future, but shifting combinations unified by the conviction that God would eventually vindicate his rule.'[1] Consequently Guignebert issues the caveat that 'in approaching the subject it is necessary to resist the temptation of making definite statements and of over-systematization.'[2] Nevertheless, if we accept the opinion that most of the apocalypses of the first century B.C. and the first century A.D. came from Pharisaic circles,[3] it is possible, in spite of the bewildering diversity of detail, to outline the main eschatological beliefs of the Pharisees in the days when Paul was one of their number. In the first place, common to all the apocalypses is the division of history into epochs, the present age (*'ôlām hazzeh*) of sin and grief, and the coming age (*'ôlām habbā'*), when Yahweh will rule and men will be righteous and happy. In some of these writings (e.g. 1 En. 91–104, 2 En., 2 Bar., and 4 Ez.) we have three ages: this age; the Messianic Age, which will be temporary, lasting for a millennium (2 En. 32. 2—33. 2) or 400 years (4 Ez. 7. 28); and the age to come, when Yahweh will reign for ever. Secondly, before the age to come dawns, there will be a period of unprecedented distress and wickedness, the time of the Messianic woes. Thirdly, it is in the apocalypses that the figure of the Messiah *qua* Messiah appears for the first time. This word 'Messiah' (Heb. *māšîᵃḥ*, Aram. *mešîḥā'*), which merely means 'anointed,' is applied by OT writers to patriarchs, priests, prophets, the whole people of Israel, kings (including even an alien ruler, Cyrus of Persia), and the Servant figure of Deutero-Isaiah, but never to a coming deliverer.[4] Although the prophets expected the advent of an ideal king of David's line who would act as Yahweh's delegate in establishing and maintaining his rule (Am. 9. 11; Mic. 5. 2, 4; Is. 9. 6–7; 11. 1 ff.; 16. 5; 37. 35; Jer. 23. 5; Ezek. 34. 23; 37. 24 f.; Zech. 12. 7 ff.), they never called him 'the

[1] G. H. C. Macgregor and A. C. Purdy, *Jew and Greek: Tutors unto Christ* (London, 1959), p. 100.
[2] Ch. Guignebert, *The Jewish World in the Time of Jesus*, p. 122.   [3] *Ibid.*, p. 134.
[4] Th. C. Vriezen, *An Outline of OT Theology* (Oxford, 1960), pp. 352–3; H. H. Rowley, *The Faith of Israel* (London, 1956), pp. 187–8.

Messiah.' According to R. H. Charles, the earliest extant work
in which the word occurs as a *terminus technicus* is the apocalyptic
work known as the Similitudes of Enoch, dated by him *c.* 94–79
B.C. or 70–64 B.C..[1] The author applies it to that apocalyptic figure
created by his lively imagination, the pre-existent, superhuman
Son of Man, who would descend from the heavens to establish
his own rule, which was also Yahweh's (1 Enoch 62 and 69)[2].
The first person to use it as a description of the expected ruler of
Davidic lineage who would liberate the Jews from their oppressors
and set up a Jewish kingdom was the unknown zealous Pharisee
who a short time after Pompey's invasion of Palestine and capture
of Jerusalem in 63 B.C. wrote the Psalms of Solomon (17. 36;
18. 6, 8).[3] Thus there were two main conceptions of the Messiah,
the apocalyptic Son of Man and the Davidic king, and of the two
it was probably the latter that the majority of Pharisees preferred
in the days of Paul.[4]

The fourth component of Pharisaic eschatology was the belief
that the dead would be revivified (Acts 23. 8; Josephus, BJ 2.8.14;
Ant. 18.1.3). It was the *ḥᵃsîdîm*, the forbears of the Pharisees,
who first created this hope, the earliest statement of it being
found in a resistance tract written by one of their number *c.* 165 B.C..
The passage runs: 'And many of those who sleep in the dust of the
earth shall awake, some to everlasting life, and some to shame and
everlasting contempt' (Dan. 12. 2).[5] Thereafter there developed
a fair amount of speculation about the resurrection. First, there
was the question what form the resurrection body would take.
Probably the majority of Jews believed that the physical organism
would be raised from the grave to be reunited with the soul. To
understand this statement we should bear in mind that the Jews
'could only conceive of man in his totality, as the vital union of

[1] *The Book of Enoch* (Oxford, 1893), p. 136.
[2] The Son of Man figure in Dan. 7 is not an individual, but a personification either of
Israel or Israelites loyal to the Torah.
[3] Although this work contains some features of prophecy, it is correctly classified as an
apocalyptic writing.
[4] Ch. Guignebert, *The Jewish World in the Time of Jesus*, pp. 141, 143.
[5] Is. 26. 19 is earlier than Daniel; but it is almost certainly a figurative description of the
restoration of the nation. *Vide* G. F. Moore, *Judaism*, Vol. 2, pp. 295–7. Moore thinks
that the Daniel passage also refers to 'the renascence of the people.'

flesh and soul. . . . A truly living being was always an embodied spirit, soul and body having been created by God for a mutual interdependence, and being therefore incapable of genuine life apart from one another.'[1] Death consisted in the dissolution of this unity, the separation of flesh (Heb. *bāśār*, LXX usually *σάρξ*) from soul or life (Heb. *nepheš*, LXX mostly *ψυχή*), the former being buried and the latter descending to Sheol, the underworld. At the resurrection the two elements would come together again, the flesh being raised from the dust and the *nepheš* from Sheol. It is this view that is expressed in such passages as 2 Maccabees 7. 10–11 and 2 Baruch 50. 1–4. Others there were who, finding it difficult to believe that the corruptible, physical body could be reanimated, conceived the notion of its metamorphosis into another and a far more glorious organism (1 En. 62. 15; 108. 11, 12; 2 Bar. 51. 10). It is to these that H. St. John Thackeray refers when he writes: 'The more spiritually minded of Jewish thinkers in the time of St. Paul were familiar with the conception of a transfigured resurrection body.'[2] A third group, very small in number, accepted the view held by some Greeks that the body perished, but that the soul was naturally imperishable and would live immortally in a disembodied state. The obvious example of this conception is to be found in the comparatively well-known passage, Wisdom 3. 1–4: 'But the souls of the righteous are in the hand of God, and there shall no torment touch them. In the sight of the unwise they seemed to die; and their departure is taken for misery, and their going from us to be utter destruction; but they are in peace. For though they be punished in the sight of men, yet is their hope full of immortality.' Which of these was the Pharisaic view? It is not entirely inconceivable that some Pharisees held the third view, the Greek view of the immortality of the disembodied soul; for in his later account (written *c.* A.D. 94) of their beliefs Josephus informs us that the sect believed that 'souls have an immortal vigour,'[3] and since he makes no mention of any kind of body, his description could easily be interpreted as

[1] Ch. Guignebert, *The Jewish World in the Time of Jesus*, pp. 109, 118.
[2] *The Relation of St. Paul to Contemporary Jewish Thought*, p. 118.   [3] *Ant.* 18.1.3.

the Greek doctrine of the immortality of the soul; on the other hand, this may be an inaccurate description, due to Josephus's penchant for Hellenization. Whether it was the view of the Pharisee of c. A.D. 94 or not, it was certainly not the view of his predecessor of twenty years earlier; that is, if we can trust Josephus's earlier account of Pharisaic beliefs, written A.D. 77. There he informs us that the Pharisees believed that souls were incorruptible, and that 'the souls of good men are removed into other bodies,'[1] which sounds like the second of the views described above. Yet we cannot be certain that this was Pharisaic teaching during Paul's days in Jerusalem half a century earlier. All we know is that before he wrote 1 Corinthians, he had accepted the second view;[2] but whether this acceptance went back to his Pharisaic days we cannot say.

Other variations of belief concerning the resurrection related to which groups of men would be raised. Some apocalyptic writers taught that all Jews would be raised, the righteous to enjoy the bliss of the Age to Come and the sinful to suffer punishment (Dan. 12. 2; 1 En. 22; 1 En. 51. 1. ff; others said that righteous Jews alone would be raised (1 En. 61. 5; 1 En. 90. 33; 1 En. 91. 10; 2 Bar. 50 1-6; Pss. Sol. 3. 16; 13. 9); and yet others, that all men would be raised (4 Ez. 7. 32). It is probable that the writers of all these passages belonged to the Pharisees or their predecessors, which makes it impossible to say which view was the normative Pharisaic view. Again, we should be reluctant to rely too much on Josephus, who in both accounts says that the Pharisees believed that the souls of the righteous alone would be raised, the souls of the wicked being detained in Sheol to receive retributive punishment.[3]

The other main tenet that Paul assimilated from the study of the Torah was that Israel was Yahweh's elect people. It is one of the salient doctrines of the OT writers, this doctrine of election. It is expressed *in nuce* in Deuteronomy 7. 6: 'For you are a people sacred to Yahweh your God; Yahweh your God has chosen you to be his prized possession out of all nations on the face of the

---

[1] B.J., 2.8.14.   [2] 1 Cor. 15. 35 ff. *V. inf.*, pp. 152 ff.   [3] Josephus, *ibid.*

earth' (cf. Deut. 14. 2; Lev. 20. 26). Those words contain the essence of the b^erîth, a word that is invariably translated 'covenant,' which implies that it was a bargain, a compact between Yahweh and Israel; i.e. if at any time either party violated its terms, it was within the right of the other to declare the agreement and the partnership at an end.[1] It is difficult to see how this view is borne out by the OT where the b^erîth is not an agreement, but the divine arrangement. It is, as the LXX rightly translates it, a διαθήκη, a disposition made by Yahweh, not a συνθήκη, a contract between equal parties. As Kautsch points out, 'the religious b^erîth always stands primarily for a Divine order or arrangement which takes its rise without the co-operation of man or, to be more precise, of the people of Israel, and yet is unconditionally binding upon the latter.'[2] What was its purpose? The purpose for which Yahweh had chosen Israel was not to glorify herself, but to serve him, not only by obeying his commandments, but also by revealing him to other nations and bringing them to acknowledge him as their God. Even in the earliest stratum of the Pentateuch, the Yahwist epic, 'there is implied the thought that Abraham's faith and that of his descendants will give to Israel a universal significance.'[3] In a frequently quoted verse Yahweh informs Abraham: 'All the nations of the earth will bless themselves in thee' (Gen. 12. 3).[4] This concern for the welfare of other races is developed in the writings of many of the prophets, who predict that the Gentiles will, if they accept the faith of the Hebrews, participate in the Golden Age (Is. 2. 2 ff.; Mic. 4. 2 f.; Jer. 3. 17; Zeph. 3. 9–10; Zech. 8. 22–3, etc.). The highest point of all is reached in the writings of the unknown prophet Deutero-Isaiah, who emphasizes that it is Israel's mission to proclaim her faith to the Gentiles and to be Yahweh's servant in this matter (Is. 42. 6; 43. 10; 45. 22; 49. 6; etc.). Yet side by side with this solicitude for the Gentiles, there arose the tendency to regard them

---

[1] W. O. E. Oesterley and T. H. Robinson, *Hebrew Religion* (London, 1930), p. 140.
[2] E. Kautsch, art. 'The Religion of Israel,' HDB, extra vol., p. 630.
[3] H. H. Rowley, *The Faith of Israel*, p. 183.
[4] On the correct translation of this statement *vide* H. H. Rowley, *The Biblical Doctrine of Election* (London, 1950), pp. 65–6.

as hostile to Israel and Israel's god. Although it is found as early as *c.* 600 B.C. (Hab. passim.), this opinion did not grow until after the Babylonian exile, when Ezekiel, Nehemiah, and Ezra put a fence around Israel, separating her from the rest of mankind. What happened to the Gentiles was not her concern. Later this indifference turned to bitter hatred under the savage treatment meted out to the Jews by Antiochus IV Epiphanes and thereafter by the Roman conquerors of Palestine. Deutero-Isaiah's noble ideal had been lost and nationalism prevailed. In Paul's day the normal attitude of the sect to which he belonged and of most other Jews towards Gentiles was that they would either be destroyed (Pss. Sol. 17. 24–7; 4 Ez. 12. 33; 13. 37–8, 49) or if they were spared, be Israel's slaves (Pss. Sol. 17. 32; 1 En. 90. 30; 2 Bar. 72. 4–6. Cf. Ps. 72. 11; Is. 14. 2; 66. 12–14, 18–20; Zech. 14; Dan. 7. 14). What some extremist Pharisees thought of the Gentiles in the first century A.D. is summed up thus: 'Thou hast said that they are nothing and that they are like spittle and thou hast likened the abundance of them to a drop on a bucket' (4 Ez. 6. 56). The world had been created for the benefit of Israel alone, and Gentiles were ciphers (4 Ez. 6. 55–9. Cf. 2 Bar. 48. 20). Yet there were signs that other Pharisees did not live comfortably with this doctrine. Even the same 4 Ezra showed some feeling of grief over the destruction of the Gentiles (4 Ez. 7. 72–3); and it was no doubt this emotion that led some Pharisees to make some efforts to save the Gentiles by trying to convert them to Judaism: if we are to believe Matthew 23. 15, there was vigorous proselytizing in the days of Jesus, and as the evidence shows, it was fairly successful.[1]

To sum up, the chief doctrines imbibed by Paul from his Pharisaic teachers were that the Torah was infallible; that God was the sovereign ruler of the world, who would certainly establish his sovereignty, inaugurating the Age to Come through the agency of the Messiah; that the dead would be raised; that the

---

[1] W. L. Knox, *St. Paul and the Church of Jerusalem* (Cambridge, 1925), p. 120 n.; F. J. Foakes Jackson and K. Lake in *Beginnings*, Vol. 1, pp. 164 f.; K. Lake *ibid.*, Vol. 5, pp. 74 f.; and E. Schürer, HJP, Div. 2, Vol. 2, pp. 291 f., 297 f.

Jews were God's chosen covenant-people; and that the Gentiles, with whom the Pharisees lumped their Jewish opponents (the sinners or transgressors of the Psalms of Solomon), the *'am hā-'āreṣ* and the Samaritans, were doomed either to destruction or enslavement unless they accepted Judaism. To these beliefs one other, less important, must be added: that Yahweh had at his behest angelic messengers. The words of Daniel 7. 10, 'A fiery stream issued and came before him: a thousand thousands ministered to him; and ten thousand times ten thousand stood before him,' are a summary of the angelology of the apocalypses. Likewise evil possessed its own host, led by Satan; and indeed, demonology had come to assume 'a much greater importance in Jewish belief than the angelology.'[1]

One other important gift that his Jerusalem teachers probably bestowed on Paul was a knowledge of the Hebrew language. Although, as we have seen, in his youth he learnt to read the Jewish Scriptures in the Greek version, now and then the quotations from the OT in his Epistles seem to be derived from the original Hebrew (e.g. Rom. 10. 15; 11. 35; 1. Cor. 11. 22). Also relevant here is his description of himself as a Ἑβραῖος (2 Cor. 11. 22; Phil. 3. 5). As we have previously suggested, it primarily means that he was an Aramaic-speaking Jew; it may contain the further implication that he could read Hebrew.

Paul of Tarsus was, then, first and foremost 'a one-hundred-per-cent Jew.'[2] He was born a Jew; his parents were Jews by birth; his ancestors had come from Palestine; his early education was probably that which every Jewish boy was given; he was trained to be a doctor of the Law in Jerusalem; he was steeped in the ways and doctrines of the Pharisaic party, of which he became a zealous member; and he spoke Aramaic and understood Hebrew. In short, Pharisaic Judaism is the design on the obverse side of the coin. What do we find on the reverse side? According to some, perhaps the majority, of the students of Paul, the answer

---

[1] Ch. Guignebert, *The Jewish World in the Time of Jesus*, p. 101.
[2] The description is T. W. Manson's, *On Paul and John* (London, 1963), p. 12.

is Hellenism. There is no doubt that Paul was a Jew to the core. To what extent was he a Greek as well? In the first place, he spoke the Κοινὴ διάλεκτος, the Greek in common use, which was chiefly Attic with an admixture of Ionic and other dialects,[1] and which had become the lingua franca of the Roman Empire. It was a language that Paul, born a Diaspora Jew in Tarsus, must surely have known from boyhood, in which was written the version of the Jewish Scriptures that he read, the Septuagint, in which he wrote his Epistles, and which he used in his conversations with Gentiles (Acts 21. 37). Like approximately thirty per cent of the population of Wales he was bilingual, speaking both Greek and Aramaic equally fluently. In this connection it is important to notice that the Semitisms in his Greek are secondary.[2] The opinion that the Greek of his Epistles (or for that matter, of most of the NT) is Hebraic and therefore a debased language, vastly inferior to what is known as 'Classical Greek,'[3] was given its quietus by the researches of Deissmann, J. H. Moulton, and W. F. Howard.[4] The Greek that Paul learnt and used was neither Hebraic Greek nor Classical Greek, which by the first century A.D. survived only as an artificial language in the writings of pretentious epigoni who, despising the Koine, thought to gain a literary reputation by using classical Attic.[5] It was not in this mummified language that Paul wrote, but in a living tongue, full of vitality, original, and appealing. Those same epithets are applicable to the language of his speeches as they are recorded in

---

[1] On the origin of the Koine vide J. de Zwaan, Beginnings, Vol. 2, p. 32.

[2] V. inf., pp. 245–8.

[3] By this term I mean the Greek spoken and written until the time of Alexander the Great.

[4] GGNT, Vol. 2. Yet it dies hard; e.g. H. J. Schoeps, Paul, Eng. tr. H. Knight (London, 1961), p. 36. Nevertheless, as more recent scholarship has emphasized, it is probably true that in their exuberance Deissmann and Moulton went to the extremes of 'grammatical anti-Semitism.' A more balanced view is that while no-one can now dispute that the Greek of the NT is the Koine, it has its idiosyncrasies, engendered partly by the influence of the LXX and partly by the new, the Christian, situation. Whether this justifies us in calling it 'Biblical Greek,' as some are doing, is questionable. On the whole subject vide N. Turner, art. 'The Language of the New Testament', PCB, pp. 659–62; GGNT, Vol. 3, also by N. Turner; and C. F. D. Moule, An Idiom-Book of New Testament Greek (Cambridge, 1963), Chapter 1; and on Paul's Semitisms v. inf., pp. 245–8.

[5] G. Thomson, The Greek Language (Cambridge, 1960), p. 36.

Acts, although it is more polished than the Greek of his Epistles.[1]

For some scholars a knowledge of the Greek language is the sum total of Paul's indebtedness to Hellas. The outstanding example of this school of thought is Schweitzer, who after thirty-six pages of discussion concludes with the judgement that 'Paulinism and Greek thought have nothing, absolutely nothing, in common.'[2] We find it difficult to see how anyone can still maintain this position. The amount of Stoicism and Platonism, together with echoes of Greek poetry and drama, to be found in Paul's writings and speeches, whilst it is not enormous, is by no means negligible.[3] The question that concerns us here is whether or not he acquired any of his Hellenistic ideas before his conversion to Christianity or not. In their eagerness to prove that he did, some scholars have laid stress on the undeniable fact that Tarsus, his birthplace (Acts 22. 3) and early environment,[4] was dominated by Stoicism;[5] but although many Jews of the Dispersion eagerly imbibed Hellenistic ideas,[6] there is no evidence to show or suggest that the youthful Paul belonged to their number. Where and when, then, did he acquire them? It is erroneous to imagine that

---

[1] On the authenticity of the speeches *v. inf.*, pp. 65–7.

[2] A. Schweitzer, *Paul and his Interpreters*, p. 99. Cf. C. A. A. Scott, *Christianity according to St. Paul* (Cambridge, 1961), pp. 3–5.

[3] *V. inf.*, pp. 71, 85, 167–8, 222. Also the illuminating article by E. B. Howell, 'St. Paul and the Greek World,' *Greece and Rome*, 2nd series, Vol. 11, No. 1 (March, 1964), pp. 7–29.

[4] Although he does not mention it in his Epistles, there is no reason to question his assertions, recorded in Acts, that he was born in, and was a citizen of, Tarsus, 'a city not without distinction (οὐκ ἀσήμου πόλεως),' as he proudly described it to Claudius Lysias in a phrase that is often quoted by grammarians as a choice example both of meiosis and litotes. The Greek adjective ἄσημος means literally 'without a mark.' Paul was claiming that his birthplace was not, to use a phrase of American origin, a one-horse little town, but a famous city. Assuredly he had every reason to be proud of it. No-one could justifiably utter the kind of derogatory remark that Mrs. Elton made about what is now regarded as the second city of the United Kingdom: 'One has no great hopes from Birmingham. I always say there is something direful in the sound' (Jane Austen, *Emma*, The Chawton Edition, London, 1948, p. 272). Tarsus had many σήματα to display to the world. The question is whether or not any of them played a part in helping to mould Paul's personality. As to Paul's Tarsian citizenship, we do not know how he gained it. Was it bestowed on one of his ancestors when Antiochus IV Epiphanes colonized the city in 170 B.C. or when Mark Antony made it a libera civitas *c.* 42 B.C.?

[5] E.g. W. M. Ramsay, art. 'Tarsus,' HDB, Vol. 4, pp. 685–7.

[6] *Vide* J. Klausner, *From Jesus to Paul*, pp. 25 ff., E. Schürer, HJP, Div. 2, Vol. 3, pp. 156 ff., R. H. Pfeiffer, *History of NT Times* (New York, 1949), pp. 181 ff., and W. W. Tarn, *Hellenistic Civilization* (London, 1930), pp. 188–208.

he was entirely cut off from Greek influence while he was being trained in Jerusalem, for, as Schürer says, 'Hellenism had, notwithstanding the rising of the Maccabees, gained access in no inconsiderable measure into Palestine even before the commencement of the Roman period.'[1] Indeed, there is some evidence to show that it had infiltrated into rabbinic teaching,[2] in which connection it is important to notice that Rabban Gamaliel is associated with this Hellenization of Judaism,[3] and it may well be that Paul heard expressions of it dropping from his tutor's lips. Thus there is much to be said for the view of W. L. Knox that his knowledge of Stoicism and Platonism was imparted to him by his rabbinic training.[4] It is possible also that it was during this same period of his life that he read that product of Hellenistic Judaism, the Book of Wisdom, which contains Stoic and Platonic ideas. We have but to consult two detached notes in the ICC Commentary on Romans to be convinced that Paul knew and used this work.[5] Yet although he may have imbibed a certain amount of Hellenism through the media of his rabbinic training and a reading of the Book of Wisdom, and although he may even have been sympathetic to it,[6] his descriptions of himself as he was in the days before his conversion (Acts 22. 3; 26. 4–5; Gal. 1. 14; Phil. 3. 5–6) imply that he would hardly have contaminated himself by accepting heathen ideas.[7]

Taking stock, then, we see that, first, Paul was steeped in Judaism; and secondly, that he had some knowledge of Hellenism. Thirdly, it is customary to call him a Roman as well. Is the epithet justifiable? In the first place, according to Luke he claimed

---

[1] E. Schürer, HJP, Div. 2, Vol. 1, p. 30. Cf. D. E. H. Whiteley, *The Theology of St. Paul* (Oxford, 1964), pp. 5–8.

[2] W. D. Davies, *Paul and Rabbinic Judaism*, 6–8; W. D. Stacey, *The Pauline View of Man* (London, 1956), pp. 27–8.

[3] *V. sup.*, p. 10.

[4] W. L. Knox, *St. Paul and the Church of the Gentiles* (Cambridge, 1939), pp. 30 ff.; *Some Hellenistic Elements in Primitive Christianity* (London, 1944), p. 31.

[5] W. Sanday and A. C. Headlam, *op. cit.* (Edinburgh, 1900), pp. 51–2; 267–9.

[6] S. G. F. Brandon, *The Fall of Jerusalem and the Christian Church* (London, 1957), pp. 61–2.

[7] There is evidence that some Diaspora Jews who had a knowledge of Hellenism abhorred it, (*vide* S. G. F. Brandon, *ibid.*, p. 62). Perhaps Paul was among them. On the other hand, there may have been a tension between his fanatical Pharisaism and what he knew of Hellenism. *V. inf.*, pp. 29–30.

to possess Roman citizenship (Acts 16. 37; 22. 27; 25. 11). The question remains whether this is historical or not. Although in his Epistles he never states that he is a Roman citizen and although this picture, painted in Acts, of Paul as a Roman citizen suits one of the author's purposes, viz. to convince the Roman authorities of his day that Christianity is not a political menace, the only ground for doubting whether Paul was a Roman citizen is his own statement in 2 Corinthians 11. 25 that on his travels he had been flogged by the lictors three times,[1] a punishment that, according to the ancient Valerian and Porcian laws and the more recent *lex Julia de vi publica*, it was illegal to inflict upon a Roman citizen who exercised his right of *provocatio* (appeal to Caesar). Several conjectures have been produced in the effort to dispose of this doubt: there may have been occasions when Paul refrained from demanding his rights and allowed himself to be flogged; or during the beating that he and Silas received at Philippi (Acts 16. 22–3) perhaps he protested, but could not be heard by the authorities for the uproar; or there were arbitrary Roman magistrates who disregarded the *lex Julia de vi publica*, punishing Roman citizens *ultra vires*.[2] We realize that these conjectures are unnecessary when we read a recent work which shows that in Paul's day exceptions to the law were made, allowing a provincial magistrate to flog even a Roman citizen for certain minor offences, e.g. contumacia, deliberate disobedience to a magistrate's order. He was not, however, allowed to administer this punishment until the prisoner had been tried and convicted.[3] In the light of this evidence it will be readily seen that the ground of Paul's objection to the flogging that he and his companions received at Philippi and to the threat of a flogging at Jerusalem (Acts 22. 24–5) was not that Roman citizens could not legally be flogged (for he surely must have known that they could be flogged for certain offences), but that he (and at Philippi his companions as well)

[1] Luke reports only one of these floggings, that administered at Philippi (Acts 16. 22–3).
[2] Josephus mentions one of these magistrates, Gessius Florus, who became the Procurator of Judaea in A.D. 64 or 65 (B.J., 2.14.9). Cf. Cicero, *In Verrem*, 5. 62.
[3] A. N. Sherwin-White, *Roman Society and Roman Law in the New Testament* (Oxford, 1963), pp. 71–6.

had, as he said, not been tried and sentenced (ἀκατακρίτους Acts 16. 37; 22. 25). We have, then, no reason to doubt the record of Acts that Paul was a Roman citizen (Acts 16. 37; 22. 27; 25. 11). With Cicero he proudly asseverated, 'Civis Romanus sum.'[1] The proof that he had inherited his citizenship is to be found in his statement (the authenticity of which there is no cogent reason to doubt) to the Roman military tribune Claudius Lysias that he had been born free, unlike Lysias himself, who had bought his citizenship (Acts 22. 27–8). It is impossible to say when or under what circumstances Paul's family had acquired this prized privilege. One of his ancestors may have been among those Tarsians to whom Pompey the Great granted it as a reward for helping him to bring order to Cilicia after he had conquered it in 66 B.C.[2]

Secondly, had he any command of Latin, the official language of the Empire, used in legal, administrative, and military circles? J. H. Moulton suggests that he may have addressed the people of Lystra in that tongue, a conjecture that is not so far-fetched as it may sound.[3] After all, every Roman citizen was expected to know some Latin; for did not the Emperor Claudius deprive a Greek of his citizenship because he was ignorant of the language?[4] Paul may well have been learned in the Latin tongue. More important is the question how far he assimilated before his conversion those Roman ideas that we find in his Epistles. Here we are in even worse case than we were when we discussed Hellenistic influence on his thinking. We can conjecture that the youthful Paul may have been impressed by that inescapable universalism whose foundations had been laid by Alexander's policy of spreading the language and culture of Hellas, and whose magnificent superstructure had been erected by Imperial Rome; and also may have partially realized even then, as he did fully in his later years when he was travelling up and down the Empire, that it was the universal *Pax Romana* that enabled men to journey in safety along a network of roads made by these same Romans with such

---

[1] *In Verrem*, 5, 57.   [2] W. M. Ramsay, *The Cities of St. Paul*, p. 205.
[3] GGNT, Vol. 1, p. 233.   [4] Suetonius, *Claudius*, 5.16.2.

expertness that many of them still remain even to this day, and to sail seas on which, before Pompey exterminated the pirates, no mariner could be certain of reaching his desired haven.

One fact that emerges from this sketch of Paul's life before his conversion is that he was richly endowed. Yet like many who appear to have all that life can give them he had for many years been a discontented, unhappy man. He himself describes in an autobiographical fragment in Romans 7 both the nature, and the source, of his wretchedness. It sprang from his efforts to comply with the demands of the Jewish Law. He had become fanatically devoted to Pharisaism and its teachings: indeed, none of his contemporaries could equal his zeal for Judaism (Gal. 1. 14). Yet obedience to the Law, far from bringing him peace of mind, made his life more and more intolerable by maintaining a tension within him. Paul gives a poignant account of the pitiable state to which the internal conflict between the wish to keep the precepts of the Torah and his own selfish desires had brought him. There are those who demur to this interpretation of Romans 7. 7–25.[1] Their main argument is that Paul's description of himself in Philippians 3. 6 as having been 'blameless where the righteousness that consists in obedience to legal precepts was concerned' proves that in Romans 7. 7–25 he could not possibly have been giving an account of his own experience. There is, however, no inconsistency. What Paul meant in Philippians 3. 6 was that externally he had omitted to observe none of the commands of the Torah, however minute, and that therefore according to human, i.e Pharisaic, standards he was blameless. The word ἄμεμπτος (blameless) is derived from μέμφεσθαι, a verb that 'applies to sins of omission.'[2] In Romans 7. 7–25, on the other hand, he is describing, not external actions, but the internal struggle within

[1] It is untrue to say that the opinion that Rom. 7. 7–25 is autobiographical 'has been generally abandoned' (J. Munck, *Paul and the Salvation of Mankind*, p. 11); e.g. it is accepted by T. W. Manson, *On Paul and John*, p. 40. With Dodd we would add that Paul means it to be a generalization from his own experience (*Comm. on Rom.*, MNTC, London, 1932, p. 104).

[2] J. B. Lightfoot, *St. Paul's Epistle to the Philippians*, p. 304. Cf. M. R. Vincent, *Comm. on Philippians and Philemon*, ICC (Edinburgh, 1897), p. 99; J. N. Sanders, *The Foundations of the Christian Faith* (London, 1950), p. 121.

his personality between his sincere wish to keep the Law and his
desires. The sin that conquered him was lusting. He could fulfil
all the external requirements of the Law; but within him there
were these inordinate desires. Wistfully he recalls his childhood
days before the Torah taught him the difference between right
and wrong. It was a blissful state. 'Heaven lies about us in our
infancy.'[1] It is a time when:

> regardless of their doom,
> The little victims play!
> No sense have they of ills to come
> Nor care beyond today.[2]

(How Paul would have endorsed those lines of Wordsworth and
Gray!). Yet ere long:

> Shades of the prison-house begin to close
> Upon the growing boy.[3]

There came the rude awakening when, probably at the age of
thirteen, Paul comprehended the full meaning of the Law,
especially the last commandment of the Decalogue, 'Thou shalt
not lust (οὐκ ἐπιθυμήσεις)'; i.e. every kind of excessive desire
was contrary to the Divine Law. Thus for the first time he became
fully conscious of the power of sin. 'When I learnt the commandments,
sin sprang to life' (Rom. 7. 9). For this service he was
grateful to the Law. He would not have known what lusting
(ἐπιθυμία) was if the Law had not ordered him not to lust
(Rom. 7. 7. Cf. 3. 20). For all that, it was a miserable moment
in his life because 'Sin found a base of operations in me through
the commandment of the Law, and the result was all kinds of
lusting in me' (Rom. 7. 8). The devastating consequence for him
was, so he thought, a forfeiture of immortality. 'Sin sprang to
life and I died' (Rom. 7. 9). (It would seem that Paul had in
mind the Genesis 3 myth, mistakenly taking it to mean that a
consequence of Adam's sin was the loss of his own immortality

---

[1] Wordsworth, *Ode on the Intimations of Immortality*, line 66.
[2] Gray, *Ode on a Distant Prospect of Eton College*, lines 51–4.
[3] Wordsworth, *ibid.*, lines 67–8.

and that of all his descendants.)[1] Thus began the second stage in
Paul's life, during which he tried as strenuously as he could to
please God and find peace of mind by obeying the Law. As he
told the Philippians, he omitted none of the prescribed legal
observances (Phil. 3. 6). Yet it was all in vain because he was a
creature of unredeemed human nature (σάρξ). As it is used by
Paul here (Rom. 7. 18, 25,) this word σάρξ means the inherited
human nature, which, having been corrupted, rebels against the
dictates of the Law.[2] Thus he was in a continual state of conflict:
there raged within him a battle between his reason, which
approved of the Law, and his corrupted human nature, which
always prevailed. He wanted to do right, but was unable to do it.
'The good which I want to do, I fail to do; but the evil that I do
(viz. lusting) is contrary to my wish' (Rom. 7. 19).[3] How much
agony this had caused Paul is seen in his *cri de cœur*: 'Miserable
wretch that I am! Who will rescue me from this my unredeemed
personality doomed to death?' (Rom. 7. 24). The flames of this
agitation within his soul may have been fanned if there was a
clash between the exclusiveness of his intransigent Pharisaism and
the cosmopolitan ethos of the Hellenism with which he had come
in contact in the teaching that he had received from the rabbis,
for although his zeal for Judaism prevented him from openly
accepting Greek ideas, they must have entered his mind and may
well have conflicted subconsciously or even consciously with his
extreme Pharisaic beliefs.[4] The answer to this problem and also to
the problem where to find liberation was to be supplied by his
conversion.

We have completed our study of Paul's life before his conversion to Christianity. The finished product of this period was a
zealous Pharisaic rabbi, possessing Roman citizenship and some
knowledge of Hellenism. At the same time there was this malaise

---

[1] For a further discussion of this point, *v. inf.*, p. 95.   [2] *V. inf.*, pp. 88-9.
[3] The exegetes draw our attention to Ovid's similar experience: 'Video meliora pro-
boque; deteriora sequor.' Quoted from *Metamorphoses*, 7. 20 by C. H. Dodd, *Comm. on
Rom.*, MNTC, p. 113.
[4] W. D. Davies is certain that he was troubled by this tension. Hellenism attracted
him; but 'the very fascination of Hellenism would make him more intensely aware of
his Judaism' (*Paul and Rabbinic Judaism*, p. 66).

within him, springing first from the consciousness of being unable
to live strictly according to the ordinances of Judaism and thus to
secure for himself a sense of pardon and liberation from an unbearable bondage, and secondly, possibly from a conscious or subconscious clash between his Judaism and the Hellenistic ideas that
he had encountered. A description of how his problems were
solved will be the subject of the next chapter.

2

VITAL VOLTE-FACE

I say, the acknowledgement of God in Christ
Accepted by thy reason, solves for thee
All questions in the earth and out of it.
ROBERT BROWNING, *A Death in the Desert*, ll. 474–6

OF ALL the red-letter days in the ecclesiastical calendar one of the most significant is 25th January, when annually the Church bids her sons and daughters recall one of the turning-points of history, the conversion of Paul of Tarsus to Christianity. How strange it is that the painters, the poets, the dramatists and the composers have largely neglected the occurrence that is so vividly described in Acts! We have Murillo's arrestingly realistic masterpiece in the Prado, Camuccini's altarpiece in St. Paul's Without-the-Walls, and Caravaggio's curious painting in the Church of Santa Maria del Popolo at the foot of the Pincian Hill, but what others are there of note?[1] Mankind would not be the poorer if some Nativity and Crucifixion pieces had not been created; it would almost certainly be the richer if Leonardo, Pinturicchio, Raphael, Giorgione, or Andrea del Sarto, 'the faultless painter,' had depicted the event. When we turn to the poets, we find a similar disregard of it. There are Keble's 'The Conversion of St. Paul,' which, although it has some merit, can scarcely be called one of the most inspiring poems in *The Christian Year*, and Ellis Roberts's gem, 'O Ryfedd hir amynedd Duw'; but there is little else worthy of commendation. The dramatists have taken even less notice of it. Is it that they have been fearful lest they should not do the theme justice? As to musical compositions with this leitmotiv Mendelssohn's dramatic oratorio *St. Paul*, the first that he wrote, stands alone. Yet without the conversion of Paul the movement that had begun at Pentecost might well, after surviving for a brief period as a Jewish heresy, have dissolved, leaving behind it only

---

[1] I do not include Michelangelo's fresco in the Capella Paolina because it can scarcely be called a notable example of his art.

a memory of an idealistic visionary named Jesus of Nazareth. As H. G. Wood puts it, 'the spirit of Jesus was liberated from the hard shell of Judaism only when a converted Pharisee learned to count the traditions of his fathers as dross, that he might win Christ and be found in him.'[1] In fine, as a result of his conversion Paul 'made the free development of Gentile Christianity possible.'[2]

It is not, however, with the consequences of this seminal event that we are at the moment concerned: our immediate task is to consider the question: What caused Paul of Tarsus to forsake Judaism and become a Christian? One answer is that his conversion was caused by divine intervention, having no natural cause or causes. No doubt this would have been Paul's own answer. Interpreted literally, the relevant statements in his Epistles appear to mean that and nothing else. One moment he was a fanatical Pharisaic Jew, relentlessly persecuting Christians; the next moment God was delighted ($\epsilon\upsilon\delta\acute{o}\kappa\eta\sigma\epsilon\nu$) to reveal his Son to him and he became a Christian (Gal. 1. 13–16). As in the case of the other apostles and many other Christian believers, this revelation took the form of an appearance of the risen Lord Jesus Christ to him (1 Cor. 9. 1; 15. 8). It was an experience in which he felt himself seized ($\kappa\alpha\tau\epsilon\lambda\acute{\eta}\mu\phi\theta\eta\nu$) by Christ (Phil. 3. 12). The wording of every one of these statements suggests that Paul believed his conversion to have been a supernatural happening. This conclusion is confirmed when we scrutinize his speeches in Acts 22 and 26, which, even if they do not give us his *ipsissima verba*, are probably a fair summary of what he said.[3] As in Galatians 1. 13–16, Paul is at great pains to portray himself as the erstwhile deadly foe of Jesus and his followers, who was suddenly and unaccountably changed into the Nazarene's devoted follower when he underwent a shattering experience in the environs of Damascus. He sees the blindingly brilliant flash of light that indicates the divine presence and he hears the voice of Jesus addressing him from the sky. Substantially the description of the occurrence given by Luke is the same (Acts 9. 1–9); and our

---

[1] *Jesus in the Twentieth Century* (London, 1960), p. 164.   [2] *Ibid.*
[3] On the authenticity of Paul's speeches in Acts *v. inf.*, pp. 65-7.

conclusion is that it is all intended to show that Paul's conversion was a bolt from the blue, the work of the Christian *deus ex machina*.

To those who have been nurtured in modern scientific historiography this explanation of the event (which is no explanation, but is tantamount to saying that it is inexplicable) is unacceptable. As Richardson says, 'to assert that something is inexplicable would negate the very assumption upon which historical thinking is founded, namely, that every historical happening is part of an unbroken sequence of historical causation.'[1] The modern historian, as Troeltsch showed in what is one of the outstanding articles in the *Encyclopaedia of Religion and Ethics*,[2] adopts 'a purely scientific attitude to facts,' seeking to explain every event in terms of a causality that is immanent in the 'unspeakably complex yet altogether coherent whole' that we call the history of mankind. There is, therefore, no room in his scheme for supernatural interventions or invasions *ab extra*. The place where for the most part the historian discovers the causes of historical events is the human personality: in short, historical causation is 'almost exclusively a matter of psychological motivation.' Natural phenomena like earthquakes and weather conditions sometimes perform a causative function, but it is secondary to that of human motives. In his efforts to find and describe those motives the historian is guided by the principle of analogy. As Troeltsch puts it, 'on the analogy of events known to us we seek by conjecture and sympathetic understanding to explain and reconstruct the past,' for 'we discern the same process of phenomena in operation in the past as in the present.' In short, what Troeltsch means is that innately and essentially man is the same yesterday, today, and for ever. The instincts (or as some would prefer to call them, impulses or drives), emotions, and desires of our ancestors, whether proximate or remote, are no different from our own; therefore the historian finds the explanation of their actions in his own motives and those of his contemporaries. To quote a more recent historian,

---

[1] A. Richardson, *History, Sacred and Profane* (London, 1964), p. 216.
[2] E. Troeltich, art. 'Historiography,' *op. cit.*, ed. J. Hastings (Edinburgh, 1937), Vol. 6, pp. 716–723.

'In the last analysis, whether consciously or no, it is always by borrowing from our daily experiences and by shading them, where necessary, with new tints that we derive the elements which help us to restore the past.'[1] To this we would add the views of that disciple of Croce, R. G. Collingwood. In a posthumous work he makes a distinction between what he calls 'the outside' and 'the inside' of historical actions. By the former he means 'everything belonging to it which can be described in terms of bodies and their movements'; by the latter he means 'that in it which can only be described in terms of thought.' It is the historian's task to investigate both parts. The method that he uses is to think himself into the action, in other words to find out what the agent was thinking. Once he has made that discovery, he understands the event: he knows what its cause was or causes were. As Collingwood puts it, 'when he knows what happened, he already knows why it happened.'[2] In an earlier work, after stressing that every human action 'is the free and deliberate act of a conscious and responsible agent,' he had analysed what causes the agent to perform it into two elements: the *causa quod*, 'a situation or state of things known or believed by the agent in question to exist'; and the *causa ut*, 'a purpose or state of things to be brought about,' i.e. an intention.[3]

Using this method advocated by Troeltsch, Bloch, and Collingwood, in an attempt to discover the cause or causes of the conversion of Paul of Tarsus, the historian makes the preliminary assertion that the event caused was (to repeat Collingwood's phrase) 'the free and deliberate act of a conscious and responsible agent.' (Whether Paul himself would have questioned that statement or not is beside the point here.[4]) Then, having established

---

[1] M. Bloch, *The Historian's Craft*, Eng. tr. P. Putnam (Manchester, 1954), p. 44.

[2] *The Idea of History* (Oxford, 1946), pp. 213–14.

[3] *An Essay on Metaphysics* (Oxford, 1940), pp. 290–5. For a criticism of Collingwood's theory of history *vide* E. H. Carr, *What is History?* (London, 1962), pp. 20–1.

[4] One fundamental belief of the Pharisees, and indeed of all Jews except the Sadducees, that Paul did not shed when he became a Christian was that as God was sovereign Lord of history and, therefore, ultimately responsible for every event, all that happened was predetermined (*V. sup.* p. 14). Thus, in Gal. 1. 15 he says that his conversion had been predestined from his birth. At the same time, there was (this appears to contradict the doctrine of predestination) another Pharisaic doctrine that he retained after his conversion:

Paul's responsibility for his own actions in becoming a Christian, we ask: What were the thoughts that led him to make this decision? This means, if we adopt the method advocated by Collingwood, that we try to find, first, the *causa quod* of his conversion, the situation that he believed to exist, and then its *causa ut*, his intention in changing his beliefs. It is obvious that the *causa quod* was the conviction that Jesus, who had been crucified and buried, had, as his followers were claiming, been raised from the dead; a conviction grounded on Paul's belief that he had seen the risen Lord. Writing to the Christians of Corinth twenty years after his conversion, he stated that the risen Christ had appeared to him even as he had appeared to the other apostles and many other Christians (1 Cor. 15. 8); and earlier in the same Epistle he had asked his converts the rhetorical question: 'Have I not seen our Lord Jesus?' (1 Cor. 9. 1), which, beginning as it does with the adverb οὐχί, demands, like the Latin nonne, a categorical affirmative for an answer.[1] It was in this vision that God had disclosed his Son to him (Gal. 1. 16). It was this vision 'that convinced him (a) that he was in touch with a living and exalted person and (b) that that person was identical with Jesus of Nazareth.'[2] The lacunae in Paul's own references to the vision in

that man had free will. It is true that nowhere in his Epistles does he explicitly state that man has free will; but it is obvious that the whole of his soteriology ultimately depends on the hypothesis that man is responsible for his own actions. Therefore, presumably he would have agreed that it had been of his own free will that he had deliberately turned his back on Pharisaic Judaism and decided to become a Christian.

[1] It is highly improbable that as some (e.g. J. H. Moulton, art. 'The Gospel according to Paul,' *Expositor*, 8th series, No. 2, July, 1911, p. 16; W. M. Ramsay, *The Teaching of Paul in Terms of the Present Day* (London, 1913), pp. 21–30; and J. Klausner, *From Jesus to Paul*, p. 435) have held, Paul was referring here to an occasion or occasions on which he had seen Jesus in the flesh. The context, which is an assertion of his claim to be a genuine apostle, shows that he is speaking of the risen Lord. It is significant that he does not use the name 'Jesus' by itself here, which is his normal practice when he is referring to the historical Jesus (e.g. 1 Thess. 4. 14; 2 Cor. 4. 10–12; Phil. 2. 10); he speaks of him as 'our Lord Jesus,' i.e. the Jesus whom we Christians acknowledge as Lord, the living Jesus. We should notice, too, that he uses the perfect tense (ἑώρακα), the aktionsart of which denotes 'what began in the past and still continues' (GGNT, Vol. 1, p. 109). Would Paul have used this tense if he had been referring to an occasion when he had seen the man Jesus? Surely he would have written εἶδον. In using the perfect tense he is emphasizing that the Jesus whom he has seen is the Jesus who can still be seen at the time of writing, the risen Lord. It is true that he uses the aorist (ὤφθη) in 1 Cor. 15. 8; but the context shows that there he is emphasizing the particular past action, and therefore the punctiliar tense is correct.

[2] T. W. Manson, *On Paul and John*, p. 13.

D

his Epistles, viz. the time, the place, and the circumstances, are filled up by Luke with his own narrative of the event (Acts 9) and the two accounts of it that are reported by him as having been given by Paul himself (Acts 22 and 26). Scholars have discussed, still discuss, and will no doubt continue to discuss whether these accounts are historical or not. Some have reached the conclusion that they must be rejected as unhistorical on the grounds that it is impossible to reconcile them with Paul's auto-biographical fragment in Galatians 1. 11–17;[1] but as H. G. Wood has pointed out, their arguments are by no means unassailable, and his judgement is that 'if we do not accept the stories in Acts of the event on the road to Damascus, and the martyrdom of Stephen, as history, we shall have to invent for ourselves stories of the same character, which seems to me a work of supererogation.'[2] This supposed discrepancy apart, the historian grants that there is nothing in the accounts themselves that he cannot swallow as intrinsically improbable except the notion of a supernatural inter-vention. He is unwilling to concede that as probably both Luke and (if we accept his speeches in Acts 22 and 26 as substantially accurate) Paul himself believed, Jesus literally spoke from a superterrestrial realm situated far beyond even Appleton layer F_2 of the ionosphere and that the sudden dazzlingly brilliant flash (which was possibly lightning)[3] indicated his presence. What the historian maintains is that the sound of Jesus' voice was heard and his presence perceived in Paul's imagination and nowhere else.[4] In any case, whether we believe that the presence of Jesus was objective or subjective, and indeed, whether we accept the accounts in Acts as historical or not, the truth that we have already established on the basis of the evidence in the Pauline Epistles remains intact: that the *causa quod* of Paul's conversion was his belief that he had seen Jesus. It is Paul's thought, his belief,

---

[1] E.g. J. Knox, *Chapters in a Life of Paul*, pp. 35–6.

[2] *Jesus in the Twentieth Century*, pp. 161–2. Cf. S. G. F. Brandon, *The Fall of Jerusalem and the Christian Church*, p. 58.

[3] The verb περιαστράπτω used in Acts 9. 3 and 22. 6 is cognate with ἀστράπη, the usual Greek word for 'lightning.'

[4] According to Acts 9. 7 Paul's companions heard the voice, but saw no-one; but in Acts 22. 9 Paul himself denies that they heard the voice, but says that they saw the light.

his conviction that the historian emphasizes. Indeed, Paul himself seems to do the same in Galatians 1. 15-16: Ὅτε δὲ εὐδόκησεν ... ἀποκαλύψαι τὸν Υἱὸν αὐτοῦ ἐν ἐμοί. In the first place, the most plausible translation of the preposition ἐν is 'within,' i.e. God disclosed his Son within his personality[1]: whatever else it may have been, his vision of the risen, living Lord was a mental one; it represented a belief. Secondly, this interpretation of the passage does not rest only upon this translation of the preposition: there is also the meaning of the verb ἀποκαλύπτω, which 'denotes a disclosure of something by the removal of that which hitherto concealed it, and especially, a subjective revelation to an individual mind.'[2]

Having found the *causa quod* of Paul's conversion, we turn to the *causa ut*. The *causa quod* alone could not have caused him to transfer his allegiance from Judaism to Christianity; if Collingwood is right, there must also have been a *causa ut*. What was Paul's intention in becoming a Christian? A remark by J. A. C. Brown supplies the clue to the answer: 'Obviously, conversion is based upon mental conflict and a feeling of inadequacy, otherwise there would be no point in changing one's beliefs.'[3] As Oscar Wilde puts it, 'Discontent is the first step in the progress of a man or a nation.'[4] We have already referred, when we were describing Paul's life before his conversion, to the twofold tension within him.[5] First, there was his unavailing struggle to keep the Law. Paul was a man painfully conscious of his own guilt (no doubt some psychologists would call it a guilt-complex). The prize that he was striving to gain was that peace of mind which a sense of pardon brings to those who find the burden of their sins intolerable. Where could he find the power to liberate him from the thraldom of sin, to save him from his unredeemed self, which

[1] J. B. Lightfoot (*Comm. on Gals.*, *in loc.*) thinks that ἐν is instrumental, i.e. Paul is referring to God's action of revealing his Son to mankind in and through Paul.
[2] E. de W. Burton, *Comm. on Gals.*, ICC (Edinburgh, 1921), p. 50. We should remember, too, that the verb ὁράω in 1 Cor. 9. 1, like the English verb 'to see,' is applied to mental as well as to optical vision.
[3] *Techniques of Persuasion* (London, 1963), p. 224.
[4] *A Woman of No Importance*, Act 2.   [5] *V. sup.*, pp. 29-30.

would, if it remained unliberated, die?[1] The Torah had proved to be a broken reed, incapable of freeing him from his bondage. He had been taught to believe that it was infallible, but his experience, described in Romans 7, had given the lie to that belief. Judaism, with all the benefits that it conferred on its votaries—the sense of belonging to God's chosen covenant-people, the Temple cultus, the divinely given Torah, the Messianic expectation (Rom. 9. 4–5)—did not after all point the way to the liberation, the salvation, that Paul was craving. What was the true and living way? Coupled with this dissatisfaction with the Torah there was possibly some clash between Paul's Pharisaism and the Hellenistic ideas that, even if he would not accept them, had entered his mind. Was God, as the strict Pharisees to whom Paul belonged (Gal. 1. 14; Acts 22. 3; 26. 5) taught, interested only in Jews, and more particularly in those Jews who meticulously observed the Law? Would he save them alone? Or was this narrow exclusivism wrong? Was God perhaps solicitous about the welfare of the ʿam hā-ʾāreṣ and even that of the Gentiles?

With the discovery of the *causa quod* and the *causa ut* of Paul's conversion the historian's task comes to an end. Yet it leaves one vital question unanswered: What led to the *causa quod*; the conviction that Jesus had been raised from the dead and was still alive? As we have seen, prima facie the statements in Paul's Epistles and Acts indicate that Paul himself and Luke believed that its source was a supernatural vision of the risen Lord Jesus; but if, as the historian maintains, it was merely a mental vision, the acceptance of an idea, what was its cause then? Did Paul attain to this mental conviction by a process of ratiocination, or was it an intuitive illumination? When we try to answer these questions, we find ourselves hamstrung by the paucity of the evidence; on the face of it Professor Munck is right when he emphasizes that the accounts in the NT of Paul's vision do not know of any preparation for it.[2] Yet to argue that there was no preparation for it is a *non sequitur*. What, then, led to the acceptance of this

[1] *V. sup.*, p. 28.   [2] J. Munck, *Paul and the Salvation of Mankind*, pp. 11–13.

belief that Jesus was still alive? It is at this point that the psychologists appear on the scene and have their say, advancing their
hypotheses in an attempt to explain the phenomenon of conversion. One such theory that has attracted much attention is that
while conversion is often sudden, inasmuch as there comes a
moment when the direction of a man's life is changed, there is
always in such cases a period of what William James called 'subconscious incubation' or 'subconscious or subliminal cerebration.'[1]
In the two lectures of his celebrated classic, *The Varieties of
Religious Experience*, devoted to the subject of conversion,[2] he
makes only three direct references to Paul's conversion[3] although
he describes it as the most eminent of all instantaneous conversions; but much of his account of the mechanics of conversion
may seem to some to be relevant to what happened to Paul. The
basis of his theory is that every man has different groups of ideas
and aims. Ordinarily his interest passes quickly from one group
to another; but sometimes one group dominates his thoughts and
his life and becomes what James calls 'the habitual centre of his
personal energy,'[4] while the other groups are relegated to the
subliminal part of his mind. At this point James appeals to Starbuck's account of conversion.[5] In the mind of the candidate for
conversion there are two main ideas: his sinful condition and the
ideal that he wants to attain, and in the majority of cases it is the
former that is the dominant idea in the mind, while the latter is in
the subconscious. Conversion takes place when the ideal displaces
the sense of sinfulness as the habitual centre of personal energy.
This happens in either of two ways. Some men, the once-born,
reach the desired state of righteous living consciously, voluntarily,
and gradually, building a virtuous character over a period of time.
In James's terminology, what is in the subliminal region gradually
becomes central, replacing the sense of sinfulness. Others—and
it is with these that James is chiefly concerned—attain the ideal by
self-surrender. Obsessed with their sin, they struggle with it, and

[1] *The Varieties of Religious Experience* (London, 1902), p. 207.
[2] *Op. cit.*, Lectures 9 and 10.
[3] *Ibid.*, pp. 217, 236 n., 251. Also on p. 171 he mentions Paul's 'discordant personality.'
[4] *Op. cit.*, p. 196.   [5] E. D. Starbuck, *The Psychology of Religion* (London, 1901).

the more they struggle, the worse their plight grows. The cause of this is that they are still concentrating on their sinfulness: it is still the centre of their personal energy. Their conversion comes either when through exhaustion they cease to struggle with their sin or when the ideal, which has been incubating in the subconscious, 'having reached the due degree of energy, bursts through all barriers and sweeps in like a sudden flood.'[1] James describes these conversions, which take place 'often amid tremendous emotional excitement or perturbation of the senses,' as 'the most striking and memorable cases, the cases of instantaneous conversion to which the conception of divine grace has been most peculiarly attached.'[2] It seems hardly necessary to add that it is among these conversions that James includes Paul's. Can we reasonably describe Paul's conversion in these terms? If we accept the view that Romans 7. 7–25 is a description of Paul's state of mind before his conversion, it can be argued that his own sinfulness was the habitual centre of his personal energy. He was obsessed with it (the word 'sin' occurs fourteen times in Romans 7. 7–25), concentrating all his powers on the struggle to conquer it. Can we say also that the state of righteousness, the ideal, to which he wished to attain, was on the periphery of his thinking? Such statements as: 'I delight in the law of God in my inmost self' (Rom. 7. 22);[3] and: 'In the practice of Judaism I was surpassing many of my Jewish contemporaries, being extremely zealous in maintaining the traditions of my ancestors' (Gal. 1. 14) suggest that the Torah was as much a focus of his thinking as was his sense of guilt.[4] Yet close scrutiny of Romans 7. 7–25 shows that of the two it was the latter that was the more prominent. One of the central ideas of the passage is that the Law's only value had been to disclose to Paul the true nature of sin and his own sinfulness, and obviously it was this which dominated his mind, leading him to cry in despair, 'Miserable wretch that I am! Who will rescue me from this situation in which my personality is doomed

---

[1] *The Varieties of Religious Experience*, p. 216.   [2] *Ibid.*, p. 217.
[3] Can we interpret 'in my inmost self' as 'in my subconscious'?
[4] There are sixteen references to the Torah in the passage.

to die?' (Rom. 7. 24). We can say, then, that thus far Paul's pre-conversion state conforms to the pattern described by James. Furthermore, we have only to read the account of Stephen's death, Paul's persecution of Christians, and his experience near Damascus to agree with James that the conversion moment came amid great emotional excitement and perturbation of the senses. The point at which, as he himself admits in a footnote,[1] his explanation signally fails is that the idea of the way of life to which Paul was converted was not that of the righteousness that comes from the observance of the commandments of the Torah at all, but of a way of liberation from sin entirely new to him, that which comes from faith in Jesus Christ. Admittedly he knew what that way was before his conversion; but his savage attack on those who were proclaiming it shows that the idea that it was the true way did not exist anywhere in his mind, not even subconsciously. There are those who try to show that it did, and this brings us to another explanation of Paul's conversion, put forward by R. H. Thouless, who builds his hypothesis on Jungian psychology. Like Jung (and James) Thouless thinks that the idea to which the subject is converted already exists in the subliminal region. Although conversion is 'the outbreak into consciousness of something, such as a body of belief, which seems to have had no previous period of development in the mind,' it has been there all the time, but (it is here that Jung and Thouless differ from James if we except his footnote) the subject has been repressing it as 'painful, immoral, or otherwise displeasing to consciousness,' and it becomes so weak that it rises to the surface as something apparently new. Approaching Paul's conversion from this angle, Thouless believes that he had a repressed Christian complex, which he loathed and resisted until it came to the surface and conquered him.[2]

Our comment on this explanation of Paul's conversion is that it goes much too far in asserting that he had already subconsciously

---

[1] *The Varieties of Religious Experience*, p. 236.

[2] R. H. Thouless, *Introduction to the Psychology of Religion* (Cambridge, 1924), pp 188–91. Is this the meaning of the words, 'It is hard for you to kick against the goads' (Acts 26. 14)? Cf. S. Cave, *The Gospel of St. Paul* (London, 1928), p. 40.

accepted the Christian claim; that, in the words of Jung, he 'had unconsciously been a Christian for a long time.'[1] The evidence on which it is based—his fanatical persecution of the Nazarenes—suggests no more than that he was uncertain of himself. We do not need the psychologists to tell us that persecution arises from the fear in the breast of the persecutor that his own creed may be false and that that of his victims may enshrine the truth.

> Who lights the faggot?
> Not the full faith, but the lurking doubt.

We have already suggested that Paul was dissatisfied with Judaism before he ever came in contact with the Nazarenes. What were his thoughts as he listened to the ideas that they were disseminating? Here it is important to notice that it was the kerygma of 'the Hellenists' (Acts 6. 1), those converts who were Diaspora Jews and whose first language was Greek, not that of 'the Hebrews' (Acts 6. 1), the members of the Palestinian Church, whose first language was Aramaic, that he heard. In spite of the teaching of Jesus the Hebrews had not broken free from the shackles of Judaism, worshipping in the Temple regularly (Acts 2. 46; 3. 1, 8) and expecting the return of Jesus the Messiah to consummate his kingdom (Acts 3. 19–21), in which there would be no room for the Gentiles.[2] The Hellenists, however, whose mouthpiece was Stephen, were proclaiming that the crucified, risen Jesus, Messiah and Lord, had, as he himself had claimed, superseded both Torah and Temple, thus abolishing the distinction between Jews and Gentiles.[3] To Paul's ears this was blasphemy. The man Jesus was no Messiah, but accursed, meriting the death which according to the Torah, carried a curse with it (Deut. 21. 23).[4] Likewise Stephen deserved to die (Acts 8. 1), as did all those who thought as he did. Accordingly, like a wild beast,[5] Paul embarked on a ruthless persecution of 'the Way,' thus disclosing

---

[1] C. G. Jung, *Collected Works*, 18 vols. (London, 1953–), Vol. 8, p. 307.
[2] Unless they became Jews, in which case they ceased to be Gentiles.
[3] On the Hellenists *v. inf.*, pp. 51–2.
[4] Later Paul himself quoted this verse (Gal. 3. 13).
[5] The Greek word ἐλυμαίνετο in Acts 8. 3 is used of mangling by wild animals.

'the lurking doubt' in his mind, but not the subconscious conviction that the Nazarenes were right.

Another psychological theory (more recent than those that we have examined), which claims to explain how Paul the persecutor was persuaded to join those whom he was persecuting, interprets it in Pavlovian terms. Pavlov and his disciples maintain that like a dog a man can be conditioned to hate what he loves and to love what he hates. His set of behaviour patterns can be replaced by another that completely contradicts it. For this change to take place intolerable strains must be imposed upon him. He 'may first have to have his emotions worked upon until he reaches an abnormal condition of anger, fear, or exaltation. If this condition is maintained or intensified by one means or another, hysteria may supervene, whereupon the subject can become more open to suggestions which in normal circumstances he would have summarily rejected.'[1] It is after periods of intense stress that 'he may adopt new beliefs or patterns of behaviour, as a result of illuminations bursting upon the mind suddenly and with great intensity.'[2] William Sargant, the Behaviourist from whose book we have been quoting, gives us a Pavlovian analysis of the conversion of Paul, which he describes as 'the most striking and momentous individual conversion . . . in the history of the early church.'[3] What made Paul highly suggestible was his violent anger towards Christians. He was in this state when he made the journey to Damascus. There followed what the Behaviourists call 'a state of transmarginal inhibition,' by which they mean a condition of total collapse, in which Paul was no longer able to respond to stimuli normally. At this point 'hallucinations and an increased state of suggestibility appear to have supervened.' Other inhibitory manifestations are reported, viz. blindness and complete loss of appetite, which weakened him still further and made him still more suggestible. He was in this condition when three days later Ananias of Damascus brought him relief from his distress and put new ideas into his mind. His sight returned, he was baptized, he

---

[1] W. Sargant, *Battle for the Mind* (London, 1959), p. 33.
[2] *Ibid.*, p. 80.   [3] *Ibid.*, p. 106.

was given food, and finally he was indoctrinated by the Christians of Damascus.[1]

It would have been strange if there had been no attack on this explanation.[2] Our own criticism of it is threefold. First, there is a fundamental difference between Paul's experience and that of the dogs which Pavlov stimulated with an electric current, or that of rats in a maze, or that of the bomb-shocked war-time patients to whom Sargant administered drugs. The dogs, the rats, and even Sargant's patients were at the mercy of stimuli, whereas Paul was free. According to Sargant, his stimulus was anger. If it was, then it was induced and controlled by himself. He was free to let his anger continue or to rid himself of it. Pavlov's dogs, the rats, and Sargant's patients, once the process of stimulation began, lost control of themselves and were controlled by others. This point is well put in another way by Jarrett-Kerr when he says that 'human beings not only "behave" but also have inner beliefs or convictions about what their behaviour is meant to be. When these beliefs or convictions are themselves part of the activity itself, then to analyse the activity abstracted from the beliefs is to fail to analyse it.'[3] A second criticism is tersely summed up by J. A. C. Brown: 'We are going to be seriously led astray if we are induced to believe that the mind under stress can be wiped clean like a slate and new patterns imposed upon it which have no bearing upon what has gone before.'[4] It was one virtue of the theories of William James and Thouless that they emphasized the continuity of a man's thinking; in Paul's case the idea of the Messiahship and Lordship of Jesus had existed in his mind for some time before he accepted it as the truth. Thirdly, there is no evidence to show that Paul was indoctrinated by Ananias or anyone else. He himself says that he neither received the gospel from, nor was instructed by, any human being; it came to him through the agency of (διά) a revelation of Jesus the Messiah,

[1] *Ibid.*, pp. 105–6.
[2] The most detailed that I know is *Conversions Psychological and Spiritual*, by D. M. Lloyd-Jones (London, 1959).
[3] M. Jarrett-Kerr, *The Secular Promise* (London, 1964), p. 62.
[4] *Techniques of Persuasion*, p. 226.

i.e. his vision. This does not mean that he had no knowledge of the Christian gospel before his experience near Damascus. He knew its content only too well and persecuted those who were propagating it. What Paul means in Galatians 1. 12 is that it was his vision that convinced him that what the Nazarenes were saying was true. This is not to say that his conversion took place there and then, at the split second of his experience. His vision was not his conversion, but its *causa quod*, its efficient cause. In this connection Sante de Sanctis pointed out in his comprehensive study of conversion that 'it is not the event itself, but rather the conscious reflection that immediately follows, which determines the change, that is, the conversion, properly so called.'[1] Paul himself tells us when and where he reflected on his experience: immediately after it he went to Arabia (Gal. 1. 17), a vague name that could be applied to any district east of the Jordan as far as Babylon. Obviously he went into the waste places away from the company of men to meditate on his vision and its implications before taking action. There is no more satisfactory summary of the conclusions that he reached than that in W. D. Davies's article 'The Apostolic Age and the Life of Paul' in Peake's Commentary: (1) Paul was convinced of the reality of the risen Lord; (2) in persecuting Christians he had been persecuting their Lord (Acts 9. 4), for the Lord and his followers were united, forming one corporate body;[2] and (3) he must proclaim the good news to the Gentiles.[3]

We have completed our analysis of Paul's conversion from the historian's point of view, and we have examined psychological theories in so far as they are relevant to the historical treatment of the subject. What has the theologian to say about it? If he is a literalist, he believes that the event was caused by supernatural intervention. The risen Jesus, who literally rose from the tomb, dwells in the heavenly places, from which he speaks to Paul. Similarly he addresses Ananias when he orders him to approach

---

[1] *Religious Conversion*, Eng. tr. W. H. Augur (London, 1927), p. 65.
[2] An idea that became one of the central themes of Paul's theology. *V. inf.*, pp. 113 ff., 132 f., 183-4.
[3] *Op. cit.*, pp. 873-4.

Paul (Acts 9. 10). At the opposite pole stand those liberal theologians (now regarded by many as old-fashioned) to whom the
concept of supernatural intervention in the natural order is just
as unacceptable as it is to the historian when he speaks as a historian. They see the world as a place in which all that happens
conforms to natural laws; in short, their thinking is based on the
principle of the uniformity of nature. Therefore accounts in the
New Testament of supernatural events must be rejected either as
inventions of the writers or exaggerations of normal happenings.
The accounts of Paul's conversion could fall into either of these
categories. Thirdly, there are the existentialists, to be in whose
ranks is to be à la mode. Like the liberal theologians they accept
the scientific view of the uniformity of nature. The protagonist
of this cause is Bultmann, the publication of whose first essay on
myth in the NT was one of the most significant moments in the
history of theology.[1] Bultmann stated that the world-view of the
NT writers was mythical, or, to use Macquarrie's phrase, 'a
museum of antiquities.'[2] One of the fundamental mythical conceptions is that of supernatural intervention in the natural world,
including human affairs. Like all the other mythical conceptions
this has no longer any place in the modern world.[3] Therefore we
cannot accept the notion that Jesus literally spoke to Paul on the
Damascus road. The voice and the bright light denoting the
divine presence in the Acts stories of the apostle's conversion are
mythical ideas and in a scientific age no longer acceptable. Yet
Bultmann does not jettison them as entirely valueless. They are
valuable, but only if we interpret them existentially; i.e. for what
they tell us about the being of man. The question that Bultmann
always puts to himself when he reads the Bible (his *Fragestellung*)
is: What does it say to me about man's existence?[4] In short, his
approach is anthropological. Accordingly he describes Paul's

[1] Art. 'New Testament and Mythology' in *Kerygma and Myth*, ed. H. Bartsch, Eng. tr.
R. H. Fuller (London, 1953).
[2] J. Macquarrie, *An Existentialist Theology* (London, 1955), p. 165.
[3] 'It is impossible to use electric light and the wireless and to avail ourselves of modern
medical and surgical discoveries, and at the same time to believe in the New Testament
world of daemons and spirits.' R. Bultmann, *op. cit.*, p. 5.
[4] *Kerygma and Myth*, p. 192.

conversion as his reaching a new understanding of himself.[1]
Before his conversion Paul was in a state of what Heidegger calls
Angst, anxiety. Then he heard the kerygma of the Hellenistic
Church, which faced him with the question whether the risen
Jesus was the expected Messiah. This raised a doubt about the
efficacy of the Torah (on which he had so long relied), which in
turn led him to question his understanding of himself. Was he
willing to acknowledge in the Cross God's judgement upon his
understanding of himself, i.e. God's condemnation of his striving
after justification by fulfilling the works prescribed by the Law?
At first he gave a negative answer to this question; then he
changed it to the affirmative, and this constituted his conversion.
Bultmann sums it up thus: 'He surrendered his previous understanding of himself, i.e. he surrendered what had up to then been
the norm and meaning of his life, he sacrificed what had hitherto
been his pride and joy (Phil. 3. 4–7).'[2]

'Quot homines, tot sententiae.' Terence's observation is an
apposite comment on this chapter. If we ask which opinion is the
most plausible, the answer is that every one of them contains
some truth. Whichever of them any individual Christian accepts,
all Christians, whether they are literalists, liberals, or existentialists,
cannot deny that the immanent God was operating in the whole
process of the conversion of Paul. He was active in the chain of
events that led to it; in the *causa ut*, Paul's longing for a cure for
the malaise caused by his dissatisfaction with Judaism, and, above
all, in the *causa quod*, his mental vision of the risen Lord. Even if
we think of this vision as merely subjective, we can still say that
God was at work in it. We can say of Paul's mental encounter
with Jesus the Messiah what Shaw's Joan of Arc said when she
was refuting Robert de Beaudricourt's suggestion that her voices
were bogus because they came from her imagination: 'That is
how the messages of God come to us.'[3] The divine power was
active, too, in what in our opinion led to this conviction: the

---

[1] *Theology of the NT*, Eng. tr. K. Grobel, 2 vols. (London, 1952), Vol. 1, p. 188.
[2] R. Bultmann, *Theology of the NT*, Vol. 1, pp. 187–8.
[3] G. B. Shaw, *St. Joan*, Scene 1.

behaviour of those whom Paul was persecuting. Although it is impossible to prove it, it is hard to believe that the conduct of Christians under persecution had no effect on their persecutors. Indeed, unless we believe that it had, the history of mankind becomes purposeless;

> a tale told by an idiot,
> Full of sound and fury, signifying nothing.[1]

It was not merely their readiness to sacrifice themselves for their beliefs—indeed, some of them fled from Jerusalem at the onset of persecution (Acts 8. 1)—but far more their love of those who were killing them. The outstanding example of this attitude was Stephen, whose conduct at his martyrdom, was a facsimile of that of Jesus himself. His prayer, 'Lord, do not hold this sin against them' (Acts 7. 60), reminds us of the words of the dying Jesus, 'Father, forgive them' (Lk. 23. 34). Stephen was following the injunction of him who had ordered his followers to love their enemies and pray for their persecutors (Mt. 5. 44), and who practised what he had enjoined. The emulation of their Lord by Christians was seen by Paul; and it is surely significant when we are considering the possible effect of the conduct of those whom he was persecuting on Paul's mind that Luke links Stephen and Paul closely. Hard upon the martyrdom of the one there follows the conversion of the other; and it would seem that Luke intended to show that there was a close link between the two events. Also in this same connection it is not without significance that Paul himself later in life remorsefully referred to the shedding of the blood of Stephen the martyr and of his own part in the killing (Acts 22. 20). Ehrhardt's comment succinctly epitomizes this argument: 'St. Paul's career takes its origin from the first execution of a Christian witness.'[2] In all this the divine activity was operating; and after his experience on the Damascus road it continued to operate in the necessary ministrations of Ananias and his fellow-Damascenes and in the mind of Paul as he contemplated his experience, in the solitary places.

---

[1] *Macbeth*, Act 5, Scene 5.
[2] A. Ehrhardt, *The Framework of the New Testament Stories* (Manchester, 1964), p. 72.

To those who might object that this description of the immanent divine activity seems to lose sight of God's transcendence,
we reply that his transcendence lies in the fact that when we have
said all that we can say about his immanent activity, there is still
much that transcends our understanding. After all the ingenious
theorizing, there is in the conversion of Paul a residuum that we
cannot explain. What we are saying has been expressed nowhere
more adequately than in a recent collection of essays: 'Surely all
revelation of a transcendent God must, without exception, in the
nature of the case, be filtered through the human intellect and
human understanding, coloured by the imagination of the
recipient, and distorted by language not fitted to express it.'[1]

[1] M. Goffin in *Objections to Roman Catholicism*, ed. M. de la Bedoyere (London, 1964),
p. 40.

3

APOSTLE

Blessed is he who has found his work; let him ask no other blessedness.
CARLYLE, Past and Present, Book 3, Chapter 9

THE conversion of Paul solved the two problems that were troubling him. First, the acceptance of Jesus as Messiah and Lord was the answer to his quest for that liberation in which salvation consists; and secondly, it showed him what the place of the Gentiles was in the scheme of things. As we have seen, by and large the party that had nurtured him had a low opinion of Gentiles: they would have no part in the Messianic kingdom, but would either be destroyed or subjugated by the Jews unless they were converted to Judaism.[1] To their credit or their discredit (whichever way we look at it) there were those Pharisees who felt sufficient concern for Gentiles to proselytize them energetically (Mt. 23. 15).[2] Paul himself, being one of the more zealous members of the party, may well have been among the proselytizers. Perhaps his words in Romans to his imaginary Jewish objector reflect his own pre-conversion attitude to Gentiles in this matter: 'You are convinced that you are a guide to the blind, a light to those in darkness, an instructor of the foolish, a teacher of infants, because you possess in the Torah the embodiment of knowledge and truth' (Rom. 2. 19–20). Then came his encounter with Christianity, and 'there can be little doubt that in principle the question of 'universalism' was decided for Paul in the fact of his conversion.'[3] It is important to emphasize once again that it was the kerygma of those Christians who had been Hellenistic Jews that Paul heard before his conversion, not that of the Judaeo-Christian body, which, to judge by Peter's speeches, thought of Christianity as a reforming movement within Judaism,

[1] *V. sup.*, p. 20.   [2] *Ibid.*, p. 20.
[3] C. H. Dodd, *The Meaning of Paul for Today* (London, 1958), p. 52.

50

which still worshipped in the Temple, and which expected the establishment of a Jewish kingdom by Jesus the Messiah when he returned to earth, with no room in it for Gentiles. Obviously these 'Hebrews,' as Luke calls them, had failed to understand the message of him whom they were proclaiming as Messiah and Lord. They had not realized that unfermented wine should not be poured into worn skins nor a new patch sewn on a threadbare cloak; i.e. that there could be no compromise between Jesus and Judaism, whose legalism, cultus, and narrow nationalism were obsolete. They had not comprehended that their Lord, the revolutionary of Nazareth, had replaced legalism with love, the ancient cultus with an entirely new kind of cultus, and nationalism with universalism. Fortunately for the future of Christianity the Hellenists had grasped the intention of Jesus. Their views are expressed in Stephen's long speech, recorded in Acts 7, which was intended to show that the Torah and the Temple had been super-seded by Jesus.[1] Since 'the Jewish form of worship with its legalistic set-up from which it could not be separated created a gulf between Jews and Gentiles and placed the latter beyond the reach of the covenant with God,'[2] the implication of its abolition, which Jesus himself had prophesied, was that the good news of God was meant for Gentiles as well as for Jews. Thus it was the Hellenists who opened the way for the wholesale proclamation of Christianity to the Gentiles. The pioneering step towards the admission of Gentiles into the Church was taken when as a result of the persecution of the Hellenists in Jerusalem the Gospel was proclaimed to Samaritans by Philip, like Stephen, one of the seven Hellenists originally appointed to 'serve tables' (Acts 6. 3); for although the Samaritans had some Jewish blood in them, no strict Jew regarded them as anything but aliens (Lk. 9. 52–3; 10. 29–37; 17. 18), and therefore on a par with Gentiles. Soon afterwards this same Philip converted and baptized a proselyte of the gate in the person of an Ethiopian (Acts 8. 38–9) who because he was a

---

[1] On the various interpretations of Stephen's speech *vide* C. S. C. Williams, *Comm. on Acts*, BNTC (London, 1957), pp. 100–2.
[2] M. Goguel, *The Birth of Christianity*, p. 175.

E

eunuch could never belong to Israel (Deut. 23. 1). Slowly the drawbridge giving access to the citadel of the Church was being lowered. At last it reached the ground, spanning the moat, when after the persecution that began with Stephen's martyrdom some Cypriot and Cyrenian Hellenists fled to Syrian Antioch and began to proclaim the Gospel to Gentiles who were not even proselytes of the gate, Gentiles having no connection whatsoever with Judaism (Acts 11. 20).[1] What was the reaction of the Jerusalem Church to this departure? According to Luke the apostles sent Peter and John to Samaria to investigate Philip's activities, which they confirmed by praying that his converts might receive the Spirit as they themselves had done at Pentecost and by imposing their hands on them in rabbinical fashion. This suggests, as Brandon says, that they believed themselves to be remedying 'some defect which was still deemed to exist in the Samaritans' membership of the Church after their baptism by Philip,'[2] which implies the claim to control the Church. Still more important for us here is that this action shows that the Jerusalem Church gave its approval to the propagation of the Gospel among non-Jews. A still more serious step from its point of view was taken when one of its leaders himself baptized Cornelius, the Roman centurion of Caesarea, and his household (Acts 10. 48), who, even though he was a proselyte of the gate, was a Gentile. When Peter's action was called in question by the Jerusalem Church, he justified it by attributing it to divine guidance, which convinced his fellow-Jews (Acts 11. 1–18). Thus even the Jerusalem Christians had come to admit that the Hellenists were right in proclaiming the Gospel to Gentiles. Yet these efforts, however successful, were only isolated; and a bold policy was needed. Who was to initiate it? The Hellenists seem to have lacked a leader after the death of Stephen. Furthermore, as subsequent events showed, Peter was unsuitable for the task. Although he had converted, baptized,

---

[1] There is a v.l. here: Ἑλλήνιστας (Greek-speaking Jews) or Ἕλληνας (Greeks, i.e. Gentiles). The former is probably the better attested reading, but it is meaningless. There is a contrast with Ἰουδαίοι (see the previous verse). The author's point is that this was a new departure. Moreover the καί ('also' or 'even') demands Ἕλληνας.

[2] S. G. F. Brandon, *The Fall of Jerusalem and the Christian Church*, p. 128.

and even repeatedly sat at table with, Gentiles (Gal. 2. 12), this last action being tantamount to a declaration that the Law was not binding on him, and although he had convinced the Jerusalem Christians that Gentiles and Jews were on the same footing in the eyes of God (Acts 11. 17–18), he later changed his mind from fear of the Judaizers, who were willing to admit Gentiles only on condition that they became Jews by submitting to the rite of circumcision (Gal. 2. 12). It was obvious that this unstable man, a movable stone rather than an immovable rock, was not fitted to lead the mission to the Gentiles. The one man who could cope with the situation, the man to lead and organize the evangelization of the Gentiles on a large scale, was in his home-town, Tarsus, to which city Barnabas, the emissary sent by the Jerusalem ecclesia to investigate the events in Syrian Antioch, travelled to bring him back to Antioch to begin his career (Acts 11. 25). Thus it was that these two, Paul and Barnabas, were specially commissioned by the Antiochene Church to begin the first large-scale campaign among the Gentiles (Acts 13. 1–3).

This was the moment for which Paul had been waiting. It was for this very purpose that he had been converted. He had discovered, or (as some, including Paul himself, prefer to put it) God had disclosed to him, his *métier*. In his potted autobiography he says that God converted him in order that he might 'proclaim the good news about his Son among the Gentiles' (Gal. 1. 16); and before the amanuensis allows the ink on his stylus to become dry, the apostle dictates the words, 'I was entrusted with the announcement of the good news to the uncircumcised' (Gal. 2. 7). Similarly in the very first sentence of his Epistle to the Christians in Rome he asserts that the purpose of his conversion was 'to promote obedience to the faith among all the Gentiles for the sake of Jesus Christ' (Rom. 1. 5). Later in the same Epistle, using a sacerdotal metaphor with that imaginative beauty frequently found in his writings, he describes himself as 'a priest of Jesus Christ among the Gentiles in the service of the good news of God, whose aim is to present the Gentiles, consecrated by the Holy Spirit, as an acceptable offering' (Rom. 15. 16). Then there are the references to this same apostolic calling in the opening salutations of six of his Epistles (Rom., 1 and 2 Cor., Gal., Col. and Eph.), and in certain other places in them (Rom. 11. 13; 1 Cor. 4. 9; 9. 1; 15. 9; 1 Thess. 2. 6); and also in Acts 9. 15; 22. 15; 26. 17.

Yet Paul's belief that the main sphere of his evangelistic activity was the Gentiles did not stop him from proclaiming the Gospel to the members of his own race. Indeed, all three accounts of his conversion emphasize that he has been called to evangelize Jews as well as Gentiles (Acts 9. 15; 22. 15; 26. 17), which harmonizes with his statement that his dearest wish is that his own race should be converted (Rom. 10. 1); and it was to this end that, whenever he thought it necessary to the advancement of the Christian cause, he was prepared to live like a Jew (1 Cor. 9. 19–20; Acts 16. 1–3; 21. 20–6).[1] Here we are faced with the problem of the apparent inconsistency of this picture with Galatians 2. 7–9, where Paul tells his converts that by a concordat with the leaders of the Jerusalem Church it was agreed that they should be responsible for the mission to the Jews, while he and Barnabas should take charge of the evangelization of the Gentiles. Yet is this what the passage means? The agreement was ἵνα ἡμεῖς εἰς τὰ ἔθνη (sc. ἐλθώμεν or εὐαγγελίσωμεθα or κηρύξωμεν), αὐτοὶ δὲ εἰς τὴν περιτομήν (sc. ἔλθωσι or εὐαγγελίσωνται or κηρύξωσι). We are indebted to Burton for pointing out that Paul uses neither the simple dative case (ἔθνεσι), which after the understood verb would have denoted the persons addressed, nor πρός governing the accusative, which 'with words denoting persons individually or collectively denotes personal approach or address,' but εἰς, which, governing personal designations, means 'to and among.' Thus the phrase εἰς τὰ ἔθνη means 'to and among the Gentiles,' i.e. in Gentile territory, and εἰς τὴν περιτομήν means 'to and among the Jews,' i.e. the Jerusalem apostles were to preach in Jewish territory, namely Palestine.[2] In fine, the division of spheres was territorial, not racial; and therefore Paul and Barnabas preached to all men in Gentile lands, whether they were Jews or Gentiles.

[1] E. de W. Burton, *Comm. on Gals.*, ICC (Edinburgh, 1921), pp. 96–8.
[2] *V. inf.* pp. 96, 99.

It would have been strange if Paul had not proclaimed the Gospel to Jews. In the first place, although he regarded himself as the leader of the Gentile mission and his leadership was acknowledged by the Jerusalem Church, 'the synagogue would naturally be the base of any missionary enterprise to the Gentiles, because of the number of adherents from among the latter that most synagogues seemed to have, and it may be urged that this entirely accounts for Paul's practice of first approaching the synagogue.'[1] In short, the soil most likely to be fertile was the proselytes of the gate attached to the synagogues. In the second place, irrespectively of tactical considerations, Paul believed that although his main work lay with the Gentiles, it was God's will that he should first evangelize Jews. Did he not say that the proclamation of the Gospel was 'God's powerful agency to bring to salvation all who have faith, first in order of precedence the Jews, and then the Gentiles' (Rom. 1. 16)? Commenting on this verse, C. H. Dodd remarks that it 'is in the first instance a simple matter of historical fact. The Gospel had been offered to the Jews by Jesus. And that, Paul thought, indicated that it was the will of God that they should have the first chance of accepting it.'[2] This is probably the meaning of the words of Paul and Barnabas to the Jews of 'Pisidian' Antioch: 'It was necessary (sc. because it is God's will) that the word of God should be spoken to you first' (Acts 13. 46).[3] Accordingly if there was a synagogue in a town or city that he visited, he made a bee-line for it on arrival. It happened thus in Salamis (Acts 13. 5), 'Pisidian' Antioch (Acts 13. 14), Iconium (Acts 14. 1), Thessalonica (Acts 17. 1), Athens (Acts 17. 17), Corinth (Acts 18. 4), and Ephesus (Acts 19. 8) (cf. his similar action at Rome, Acts 28. 17).

There is still one other difficulty to be faced concerning the range of Paul's apostolic activities. We have argued that it was from the moment of his conversion that Paul was convinced that the gospel ought to be proclaimed to the Gentiles and that together

---

[1] W. D. Davies, *Paul and Rabbinic Judaism*, p. 68.
[2] C. H. Dodd, *Comm. on Roms.*, MNTC, p. 9.
[3] For an examination of this difficult verse *v. inf.*, pp. 56-7.

with Barnabas he was appointed to begin this task. How can we square this with the words of the two apostles recorded in the second part of that *crux criticorum* Acts 13. 46, which prima facie state that what caused them to turn to the Gentiles was the repudiation of their message by the Jews? Furthermore, Paul's words to the Jews in Corinth (Acts 18. 6) and in Rome (Acts 28. 25–8) have the same implication. In the first place, it is possible that all three statements were created by the author of Acts in order to show that the Jews were to blame for their own rejection by God; but if he did invent the words, he is inconsistent, for they conflict with his narratives of Paul's conversion, which state that Paul was convinced by his conversion experience that he was to lead the mission to the Gentiles (Acts 26. 17. Cf. 22. 15). Of course, it is equally possible that this latter picture is the author's own creation, and that the words of Paul in Acts 13. 46, 18. 6, and 28. 25–8 are authentic. This still leaves unexplained, however, the statements in Paul's own writings, in which he asserts that from the time of his conversion he was convinced that he was called to evangelize the Gentiles.[1] One suggestion is that it was only in retrospect that he saw that this had been God's purpose for him from his birth and that it began to be fulfilled at his conversion (Gal. 1. 15–16). We suggest another solution. The English versions render the conjunction ἐπειδή in Acts 13. 46 'since,' 'because,' or 'as,' i.e. it introduces a causal clause; it can, however, bear the meaning (as it usually does in Classical Greek) 'when now,' 'after that'; i.e. introducing a purely temporal clause (cf. Luke 7. 1). The primary meaning of ἐπεί is 'when' and δή is merely a particle whose function is to emphasize the word to which it is attached. If we accept this meaning for ἐπειδή, the translation reads: 'It was necessary that the word of God should be spoken to you first; when now you repudiate it and consider yourselves unfit to possess eternal life, see! we turn to the Gentiles.' Thus in the second part of the statement Paul and Barnabas were emphasizing that the Jews must be given the first chance of hearing the Christian proclamation. This interpretation

---

[1] *V. sup.*, pp. 53–4.

receives support from Acts 18. 6 and 28. 25–8. When Paul is rejected by the Jews in Corinth, he says: 'Your blood be on your own head; from this moment (ἀπὸ τοῦ νῦν) I, who am guiltless, shall go to the Gentiles (sc. in Corinth).' Similarly, after informing the Jews in Rome that they are like their ancestors, who refused to listen to God's words in the days of Isaiah, he tells them that the Gentiles would listen to him. In neither instance is there any suggestion that he would not have preached to the Gentiles if the Jews had accepted his teaching. Lastly, the quotation from Isaiah 49. 6 in Acts 13. 47 implies the conviction that he had been appointed to evangelize the Gentiles irrespectively of any other circumstances, e.g. his rejection by the Jews. Thus our contention is that Paul was convinced by his conversion that his life's work was to be an apostle to the Gentiles, but that it was essential that wherever he found Jews he should preach to them first.

Yet however firmly Paul himself was convinced that his apostleship was genuine, there were many who denied that it was. Of their identity there can be very little doubt; the evidence of the Galatian, Corinthian, and Roman Epistles shows that they were representatives of the Jerusalem Church, who probably included Peter, and who, in spite of the agreement with Paul described in Galatians 2, stirred up trouble in the churches that he had founded. With the casus belli we are not concerned now. All that we need to say is that Paul's opponents were still trying to impose conditions on the admission of Gentiles to the Church. It was their persistent opposition to his apostolic authority that provoked him to emphasize it again and again and also to write some of his more pungently polemical passages. On what did he base his claim to be an apostle? Unlike any one of the Twelve he could not reply that he had heard, with his own ears, words of the earthly Jesus that announced to him his appointment to the apostolate (Mk. 3. 14–19 = Lk. 6. 13–16. Cf. Mt. 10. 1–4); nor could he claim to be eligible for membership of the post-Resurrection apostolate, since he lacked one of the two essential qualifications for it; he had not been a follower of Jesus from the beginning of the Lord's ministry (Acts 1. 21–2). He did, however, possess the

other qualification: he was convinced that he had seen the risen
Lord (1 Cor. 9. 1; 15. 8) and therefore was able to testify to the
reality of the Resurrection (Acts 1. 22). Yet to possess the qualifications for apostleship was not enough; before a man could be an
apostle, he must be divinely appointed to it. Thus, when the
eleven apostles chose a successor to Judas, they used the ancient
Jewish method of ascertaining the divine will: they cast lots (Acts
1. 26. Cf. 1 Sam. 14. 41) and believed that it was God himself
who had chosen Matthias. Paul had no need of any such indication that the source of his apostleship was divine. In the greeting
with which he begins nearly every one of his Epistles and elsewhere (Gal. 1. 15–16; 2. 7–8) he insists that his call to apostleship came to him direct from God and Jesus, Messiah and Lord.
Yet as his Corinthian correspondence shows, he must have
thought that however powerful was his conviction that God had
appointed him to be an apostle, his position would be greatly
strengthened if he could produce some objective evidence to
support his claim. His authority in Corinth was endangered by
the arrival there of certain Jewish Christians (2 Cor. 11. 22) who
had received letters of recommendation from someone in authority (2 Cor. 3. 1), almost certainly the leaders of the Judaizing party
in Jerusalem,[1] and who were claiming to be true Christians
(2 Cor. 10. 7; 11. 23) and apostolic delegates (2 Cor. 11. 5, 13;
12. 11). According to Paul they were proclaiming a different
kind of Jesus (2 Cor. 11. 4), i.e. their picture of the historical Jesus
differed from Paul's. It would seem that they were depicting him
as 'a Christ who would return in glory to vindicate none but
Jews, and those who had been by circumcision incorporated into
their nation; a Christ who would judge men by their obedience
to the Mosaic law, and so had died for nothing.'[2] The controversy between Paul and his opponents waxed hot. They launched
an assault on his character, accusing him of being no true apostle,
but a morally weak creature ruled by his unredeemed nature

---

[1] There is no evidence to show that they belonged either to the Cephas faction or the
Christ party, both of which were in being before they arrived (1 Cor. 1. 11–12).
[2] H. L. Goudge, *Comm. on 2 Corinthians*, WC (London, 1927), p. 113.

(κατὰ σάρκα) (2 Cor. 10. 2). As proof of this they levelled several particular charges against him; his letters, in which he had attempted to discipline his converts, sounded bold enough, but his actions were ineffectual (2 Cor. 10. 10); he refused to accept maintenance from them, which presumably implied to them that he lacked humility (2 Cor. 11. 7–12; 12. 13); he had embezzled some of the money that had been collected in Corinth for the Palestinian Christians (2 Cor. 12. 16); he proclaimed not Jesus, but himself (2 Cor. 4. 5); and finally, he was a madman (2 Cor. 5. 13) and an impostor (2 Cor. 6. 8). In the face of this multiform challenge to his apostolic authority in an ecclesia that he himself had founded he asserted the genuineness of his commission with some vehemence. How passionate he felt is shown by the salvos of invective with which he enfiladed the position of his adversaries. These 'super-extra apostles,' as he sarcastically calls them twice (2 Cor. 11. 5; 12. 11), are bogus, practising deceit (2 Cor. 11. 13). They profess to be Christ's apostles, but in reality they are apostles of Satan (2 Cor. 11. 14–15). Paul can rebut their charges *seriatim*. 'By their fruits you will recognize them' was the Dominical test of a teacher's genuineness (Mt. 7. 16); and it is Paul's too. The genuineness of his apostleship is proved by his conduct. First, in reply to the accusation that he has written strong letters but has taken no action, thus showing himself to be a moral coward, he says that they will discover whether he is a moral coward or not when he comes to Corinth (2 Cor. 10. 11). Then there was the charge that he had refused to accept maintenance from the Corinthian Church. Already in an earlier letter he had pointed out that although in accordance with the principle enunciated by Jesus himself (Mt. 10. 10 = Lk. 10. 7) he had a right to maintenance from the Corinthian Church, he would rather die than avail himself of it (1 Cor. 9. 3–15). He knew what was in the minds of the suspicious Corinthians! Now he justifies his conduct on the ground that he has no wish to be burdensome to them. Nor did it spring from pride, for he had willingly accepted the gifts offered him by other churches, e.g. the Church in Macedonia (2 Cor. 11. 8–9). He cannot refrain from contrasting his own behaviour in this particular with the exploitation of the Corinthian Christians by his Judaizing opponents (2 Cor. 11. 20). In rebuttal of the charge of embezzlement he points out that it was collected by Titus and some other anonymous Christian[1] (2 Cor. 8. 18–21; 12. 17–18), the implication being that Paul could not have embezzled it. As for the accusation that he has been proclaiming himself, he denies it: he has proclaimed 'Christ Jesus as Lord, and ourselves your slaves for Jesus' sake' (2 Cor. 4. 5). In short, he is neither a madman nor an impostor. They have but to examine his record. In his dealings with his fellow-men he has always been ruled by sincerity and disinterestedness (2 Cor. 1. 12). To substantiate his claim still further he catalogues his tribulations as evidence that he has suffered in the service of Jesus (2 Cor. 11. 21–33). Flagellations at the hands of both Jews and Romans, imprisonment, stoning, shipwreck, exposure, drowning, attacks by bandits, treachery, sleeplessness, hunger, thirst, incessant toil—all these he has faced in Messiah's service. He could have added to his list the sacrifice of those Jewish privileges which he enumerates in Philippians 3. 4–6. As he had already said, his life was like sacrificial incense offered to God, with its sweet fragrance (2 Cor. 2. 15). All the time, like Jesus he was being betrayed to death; and thus in his own life he has tried to reproduce the Passion of Jesus (2 Cor. 4. 10–11. Cf. Rom. 8. 36; 1 Cor. 15. 31). It was by this life of endurance, afflictions, necessities, distresses, and the rest, as well as by the purity of his conduct and his evangelistic activity, that he commended himself to men (2 Cor. 6. 4–10). Had any of those who were questioning his apostolic authority suffered as much?

Besides his conduct, which he considers to be above suspicion, and his sufferings, there are other proofs that he is a *bona fide* apostle. He can appeal to his mystical, ecstatic experiences, one of which he describes in 2 Corinthians 12. 1–4. Fourteen years before the time of writing he had been transported into the highest

[1] He may have been Luke the doctor; but this conjecture does not rest on the words, 'whose praise in the gospel is spread through all the churches' (2 Cor. 8. 18), which do not refer to the third Gospel as the B.C.P. Collect for St. Luke's Day suggests, but to his evangelistic work.

spiritual realm or (as he calls it) 'paradise' to hear secrets that he has no right to disclose to a living soul. The sensation was indescribable: he was not sure whether his body belonged to him or not. So exhilarating was the experience that he was given some ailment, what he calls his 'stake for the flesh, a messenger of Satan'—to prevent him from becoming too proud (2 Cor. 12. 7).[1] He has one final item of proof, which the men of Corinth them- selves have seen: the mighty, wonderful deeds (σημείοις τε καὶ τέρασιν καὶ δυνάμεσιν) that he has performed in their city (2 Cor. 12. 12). What these deeds were it is impossible to say because the details of Paul's sojourn in Corinth supplied in Acts are meagre, the author devoting a mere eighteen verses to them (Acts 18. 1–18). Paul's word σημεῖα includes all his achieve- ments, σημεῖα, τέρατα, and δυνάμεις. He is probably using it in the sense in which it is used many times in the NT, i.e. the signs of a divinely conferred authority,[2] in this instance that of an apostle. The words τέρατα and δυνάμεις are customarily used to describe actions that NT writers, including Paul himself, would have considered supernatural or miraculous. In the brief account in Acts of Paul's doings in Corinth there is no mention of any such happenings. Perhaps Paul counted the establishment of the church in the city his mightiest achievement (δύναμις) there. Reading between the lines, we can infer that the proclamation of the gospel in a city where the chief deity was Aphrodite, who was worshipped by her votaries not only with their lips but in their lives, and where the Jewish population vigorously opposed him (Acts 18. 6, 12–13), was an uphill task. At the beginning of his ministry in the city 'many of the people of Corinth listened, believed, and were baptized' (Acts 18. 8); but its continuation demanded great endurance (2 Cor. 12. 12). This brings us to Paul's last argument in support of the genuineness of his apostle- ship: the Corinthian Church was his creation, 'his own handi- work' (1 Cor. 9. 1). He was the skilled master-builder (σοφὸς

---

[1] It is impossible to pin-point the vision. *Vide* A. D. Nock's suggestion that it occurred during the thirteen or fourteen years that he spent 'in parts of Syria and Cilicia' (Gal. 1. 17), *St. Paul* (London, 1938), pp. 88–9.

[2] For references *vide* MGLNT, p. 405.

ἀρχιτέκτων) who had laid the foundation of the church in Corinth (1 Cor. 3. 10); he was the gardener who had planted the seed of Christianity there (1 Cor. 3. 6); he was the only father of the Corinthian Christians, who had begotten them again, his children and his alone (1 Cor. 4. 15); and because they had accepted the gospel proclaimed by him and because they loved him, they were his letter of testimonial, written by the Spirit of God on Paul's heart, coming from Christ, and plain for all to see and read (2 Cor. 3. 1–3).[1] Paul sums this point up with his metaphor of the seal: the Corinthian Church is the seal of his apostleship (1 Cor. 9. 2), i.e. his seal or signet (σφραγίς) which authenticates his apostolic authority.

As we read Paul's impressive description of his credentials, his conduct, his sufferings, and his achievements, we ask ourselves whether or not he is a braggart. Yet he himself realized that he was boasting, and indeed more than once called himself stupid (ἄφρων) for doing so (2 Cor. 11. 1, 17; 12. 11). Moreover, he admitted that it was not in accordance with the teaching and example of Jesus (2 Cor. 11. 17); but he felt himself driven to use this weapon (2 Cor. 12. 1, 11), distasteful though it was, to combat what he considered to be the slanders of his opponents. Are we convinced by Paul's attempt to justify his boasting? The truth is that it is an example of the argument used not only by charlatans and knaves but also by others besides Paul who have been canonized, that the end justifies the means. The conclusion of the matter is that Paul's boasting is not consonant with the example of him whom he acknowledged as Lord. It is egocentric, and no amount of apologizing can vindicate it. Its sole value is that it serves to show us that Paul fell short of the dominical pattern. In fact, it might have been used by his opponents as an argument against his claim to be a genuine apostle. 'Quod magnificum referente alio fuisset, ipso qui gesserat recensente vanescit.'[2]

---

[1] The metaphor is somewhat involved.
[2] Pliny the Younger, *Letters*, 1, Ep. 8. Later another did recount Paul's sufferings (Acts 14. 19; 16. 22; 20. 18–21; 27).

Paul of Tarsus, then, was convinced that he was a Christian apostle equal in rank to the original twelve, sent by God primarily, but not exclusively, to evangelize the Gentiles. How high his opinion of his apostolic authority was is demonstrated by another of his metaphors. In his letter to Philemon Paul describes himself as 'a legate (πρεσβύτης or πρεσβευτής) of Jesus the Messiah' (Philem. 9). Similarly, to the Corinthians he writes: 'We act as legates (πρεσβεύομεν) of the Messiah' (2 Cor. 5. 20); and in Ephesians he says that he is 'carrying out his legatine functions (πρεσβεύω) even though he is shackled with a chain' (Eph. 6. 20). The metaphor is derived from the Roman system of provincial government, with which Paul could not avoid being familiar. As our translation indicates, the noun πρεσβευτής is the Greek version of *legatus*, and the verb πρεσβεύω means 'to perform the functions of a *legatus*.' This last sentence demands elucidation. Since 27 B.C. the provinces of the Roman Empire had been divided into two groups; senatorial, those administered by the Senate through their representatives, the proconsuls; and imperial, those ruled by the Emperor through his deputies, the *legati Augusti pro praetore*.[1] Paul had personal experience of the administration of both kinds of province. He was born and bred in an imperial province, Syria—Cilicia—Phoenice; received his higher education in another, Judaea; and travelled in several others, Galatia, Pamphylia-Lycia, and Cappadocia, as well as in his native province. The senatorial provinces which he visited were Cyprus, Asia, Macedonia, and Achaia. He had personal encounters with two pro-consuls—Sergius Paulus, whom he converted, and the shrewd Gallio—and two *legati* of procuratorial rank—Claudius Felix and Porcius Festus. His long excursus in Romans 13 reflects his admiration and respect for the imperial Government, which was not surprising when we remember that he himself was a Roman citizen and that on several occasions imperial authority intervened to save him from physical harm and even death (Acts 18. 12–17; 21. 30–36; 23. 23–35; 25. 4–5; 27. 43). It was to this conceptual realm that he went when he

[1] L. Homo, *Roman Political Institutions*, Eng. tr. M. R. Dobie (London, 1929), p. 216.

was seeking a metaphor to convey to his readers his conception of his apostolic authority. He thought of himself as one of the representatives of that *imperium* he so much admired; it was the *legatus Augusti pro praetore* that he had in mind when he called himself Christ's πρεσβευτής. He could have found no more pregnant metaphor, for the *legatus* was the embodiment of the full imperium of the Emperor himself. Whatever he said, the voice was the Emperor's; whatever he did, his actions were the Emperor's. Thus his authority was both comprehensive and supreme. Within his province he was the highest civil official, the commander-in-chief of the armed forces, and the supreme judge. There is not one of Paul's letters in which we fail to hear Christ's *legatus* enforcing his ruler's *imperium*. He spoke with Christ's voice (2 Cor. 13. 3) and acted with Christ's authority. As God's legatus he knows and declares the secret purpose of his emperor (1 Cor. 2. 1); he is fully acquainted with the mind of Christ (1 Cor. 2. 16); his activity (πνεῦμα) is God's (1 Cor. 7. 40);[1] he gives orders as one who is to be trusted (1 Cor. 7. 25); the tradition that he hands on is derived from the Lord himself (1 Cor. 11. 23); he knows the Lord's instructions (1 Cor. 9. 14); and the authority behind all this was given him by the Lord (2 Cor. 10. 8; 13. 10). It is by virtue of this legatine authority that he gives a series of ethical imperatives (Rom. 12. 3 ff.; Gal. 5. 13 ff.; Eph. 4. 1–3; 4. 25—6. 9; Col. 3. 12 ff.; etc.), wields the disciplinary rod (1 Cor. 4. 21—5. 5; 2 Thess. 3. 4), makes *ex cathedra* casuistical pronouncements on matters that perplex the Lord's subjects, like matrimony (1 Cor. 7. 1–16, 25–40), the consumption of food consecrated to heathen idols (1 Cor. 8. 1–13), behaviour at the Lord's Supper and Christian meetings (1 Cor. 10. 16–33; 11. 2–34), and the right use of the χαρίσματα given by the Spirit (1 Cor. 12. 1–31; 14. 1–40), and urges his converts to follow his own example since he follows the Lord's (1 Cor. 11. 1; Phil. 3. 17). Finally, it is as Christ's legatus in command of his emperor's legions that he issues military orders for the campaign against evil (Eph. 6. 10–20; Phil. 1. 27).

---

[1] On the meaning of πνεῦμα v. inf., pp. 112-13.

When we turn to the Acts of the Apostles, we hear Paul proclaiming by word of mouth the good news of the sovereign
whom he represents. As God's *legatus* he is under constraint to
announce the good news of saving emancipation (1 Cor. 9. 16).
To that end Christ had sent him out (1 Cor. 1. 17), and he would
have been wretchedly unhappy if he had not carried out his
mission (1. Cor. 9. 16). This raises the frequently discussed question whether Paul's nine speeches (Acts 13. 16–41; 14. 15–17;
17. 22–31; 20. 18–35; 22. 1–21; 24. 10–21; 26. 2–23, 25–7; 27. 21–6;
28. 17–20) are authentic or not. Nowadays there are very few
scholars who would maintain that the author is reporting them
in full and verbatim; but this does not mean that we must go to
the other extreme and agree with those who, obsessed with
Formgeschichte, believe that he fabricated them. Typical of this
school of thought is Professor John Knox, who states that they
'are largely, if not wholly, the composition of the author';[1] a
belief that prevents him from falling into what he evidently
regards as the grave error of 'citing any of Paul's words in Acts
as though they were the apostle's own.'[2] The evidence that leads
him to this conclusion is that 'both in idea and in literary style the
speeches resemble, not Paul's work, with which we are fortunately
in a position to compare them, but Luke's.'[3] In the same camp we
have that giant of the *Formgeschichte* school and one of its creators,
Martin Dibelius, for whom the trumpets sounded on the other
side far too soon. With formidable erudition he agonized to
show how to a large extent Luke followed the method of the
ancient Greek historians, which is explained by one of the most
celebrated of their number in a frequently discussed passage.[4]
According to Dibelius's interpretation of his words, Thucydides
meant that the speeches in his work did not consist of *ipsissima
verba*, but were, on the basis of the general purport of what had been
said (ξύμπασα γνώμη τῶν ἀληθῶς λεχθέντων), which the historian
knew either from his own recollection or from reports given to
him by others, composed by him to fit various historical situations

---

[1] J. Knox, *Chapters in a Life of Paul*, p. 23.
[2] *Ibid.* [3] *Ibid.* [4] Thucydides, *Historiae*, 1. 22.

that he was describing.[1] Dibelius tries to show that likewise Luke
put speeches into the mouth of Paul and others to illuminate and
emphasize the epoch-making events that he was describing.[2] In
addition, we must remember, says Dibelius (ever true to the
credo of *Formgeschichte*), that unlike the ancient Greek historians
Luke's chief motive in writing Acts was propagandist. (Form
Critics cannot forget the *sitz im leben*!) 'Luke tells a story, but,
while doing so, he is also preaching;' he uses the method of the
ancient historians of composing speeches 'not only to illuminate
the situation but also to make clear the ways of God; he did not
desire to testify to the capabilities either of the speaker or of the
author, but to proclaim the gospel.'[3] The content of his compositions is the kerygma of the time when he was writing, *c.* A.D. 90.[4]
The conclusion of the matter is that as we read Acts, we are to
'ignore completely the question of historicity.'[5]

What shall we say to these things? As always, Dibelius argues
impressively and cogently; but in one place he shows symptoms
of uneasiness; 'I should like to say: "if we deny the historicity of
these speeches," but we cannot go so far;'[6] we must ignore it but
not deny it! The truth is that Dibelius begins with the *a priori*
dogmatic presuppositions of the *Formgeschichte* school, which
eventually lead to historical scepticism.[7] He introduces the
description of the method of the Greek historians to bolster up
his case, which however impressive it may sound to some cannot
be shown to have any relevance to the matter. In any case,
before we compare Luke's method of writing with that of Thucydides, it would be as well to know what the latter was. As
C. S. C. Williams has pointed out[8] and as Dibelius himself
admits,[9] Thucydidean scholars disagree with one another over the
meaning of the passage by which Dibelius and others set such

[1] M. Dibelius, *Studies in the Acts of the Apostles*, Eng. tr. M. Ling (London, 1956),
pp. 140–2.
[2] *Ibid.*, pp. 150–64.   [3] *Ibid.*, pp. 151, 183.   [4] *Ibid.*, p. 165.
[5] *Ibid.*, p. 164.   [6] *Ibid.*, p. 164 n.
[7] Yet he says that we must *not* use the *Formgeschichte* approach in our criticism of Acts!
Ibid., p. 4.
[8] C. S. C. Williams, *Comm. on the Acts of the Apostles*, BNTC (London, 1957), pp. 36–7.
[9] M. Dibelius, *ibid.*, p. 141.

great store. Can any of them tell us with certainty what is the meaning of τὴν ἀκρίβειαν αὐτὴν λεχθέντων or of τὰ δέοντα or of τῆς ξυμπάσης γνώμης τῶν ἀληθῶς λεχθέντων?[1]

Hear the conclusion of the whole matter. In the first place, most of the differences that there are between the theology of the speeches and that of the Epistles can be accounted for by the fact that in the speeches (with one exception—the farewell charge to the Ephesian elders, the thought of which, it is pertinent to observe, accords with that of the Epistles), Paul is speaking to the unconverted, whereas in the Epistles he is addressing the converted. How insignificant are the differences, and how great the similarities between the two, was eruditely demonstrated more than half a century ago by Dr. Maurice Jones.[2] Secondly, it must be conceded that the language and style of the speeches differ from those of the Epistles; but to say that Luke 'was giving at least the gist of what was really said on various occasions'[3] is not sufficient. We return to Maurice Jones for what we believe to be the most plausible hypothesis; while the speeches 'betray considerable proofs of editing on St. Luke's part, in the way of summarizing, many expressions and phrases being undoubtedly Lucan, the utterances are, in the main, those of the Apostle' and 'through the major portion of their contents we are listening to the voice of St. Paul himself.'[4] A similar opinion seems to be held by a more recent NT scholar, who at the end of a discussion of the speeches in Acts writes; 'St. Luke was inclined to transpose into direct speech material which he possessed in form of historical reports; but . . . he was loth to invent speeches freely.'[5]

No doubt it will not have escaped notice that we have avoided

[1] One classical pundit interprets the passage as meaning that Thucydides intended to report the speeches as accurately as possible, and that they are to be treated as substantially historical. A. W. Gomme, *A Historical Commentary on Thucydides* (Oxford, 1945), Vol. 1, pp. 140–8.
[2] *St. Paul the Orator* (London, 1910), pp. 52–7, 75, 101–3, 147–51, 152, 193–4, 209, 238–40, 268–72. Cf. C. S. Dessain, art. 'The Acts of the Apostles,' *A Catholic Commentary on Holy Scripture* (Edinburgh, 1953), pp. 1019–20.
[3] F. F. Bruce, *The Acts of the Apostles* (London, 1951), p. 21.
[4] M. Jones, *St. Paul the Orator*, p. 17.
[5] A. Ehrhardt, *The Framework of the New Testament Stories* (Manchester, 1964), p. 88.

F

describing Paul's speeches as 'sermons.' The reason is that the word has disagreeable associations for many of us: to the twentieth-century mind it suggests the

> Weekly drawl,
> Though short, too long[1]

or Samuel Pepys's 'lazy, poor sermon.'[2] With few exceptions the modern sermon has become a prosaic, pedestrian, *ennuyeux* convention of that most socially respectable of all acts of worship, Anglican Morning Prayer, possessing greater efficacy than any barbiturate; or a breezy, racy half-hour's talk at an evening service. The speeches of Paul, God's apostolic legatus, are as different from the modern sermon as wine is from water. Their first characteristic, often lacking in the modern sermon, is that they are proclamatory. The debt that NT scholarship owes to C. H. Dodd for his immortal contributions to it is incalculable. Of particular importance is the emphasis that he lays on the κήρυγμα in the New Testament.[3] Nor must we forget to mention what Rudolf Bultmann has done, and continues to do; indeed, the word κήρυγμα seems to have become his constant obsession![4] If, when we translate it by the English noun 'preaching,' we see in the mind's eye a pulpit occupied by vicar, rector, or curate, it is time to disabuse ourselves; for the κήρυγμα of Apostolic Christianity was, as the word indicates, a proclamation. Let us continually remind ourselves that it is derived from κηρύσσειν, 'to proclaim as a κῆρυξ, a herald, does.' The κήρυγμα is a heraldic proclamation. When Paul the *legatus* used the verb κηρύσσειν and the noun κήρυγμα, he possibly had in mind another Imperial official, the *praeco*, the State crier, who was the mouthpiece of the magistrate, and therefore of the Emperor himself, proclaiming official orders. As God's praeco he proclaims

---

[1] William Cowper, *Hope*, line 201.

[2] *Diary*, 22nd January, 1660. Preached in St. Bride's, Fleet Street, by a Presbyterian minister named John Herring.

[3] C. H. Dodd, *The Apostolic Preaching and its Developments* (Cambridge, 1936), *passim* and *History and the Gospel* (London, 1938), pp. 161–3.

[4] Cf. Professor R. H. Fuller's story that on Bultmann's birthday his students gave him a huge demythologized Bible that contained only one word, 'Kerygma.' *The New Testament in Current Study*, p. 60.

(κηρύσσομεν) the crucified Christ to the Corinthians (1 Cor.
1. 23). This was his task—to travel proclaiming (κηρύσσων)
God's Rule to all and sundry. The tidings, the content of his
proclamation, was εὐαγγέλιον, good news. 'We proclaimed
(ἐκηρύξαμεν) the good news (εὐαγγέλιον) of God to you,' he
told the Thessalonians (1 Thess. 2. 9), and to the Corinthians he
wrote: 'Christ did not send me to baptize, but to announce good
news' (εὐαγγελίζεσθαι 1 Cor. 1. 17). According to his letters,
the core of the κήρυγμα, the εὐαγγέλιον, proclaimed by Paul
was that Jesus was the Christ, the Son of God (Rom. 16. 25;
2 Cor. 1. 19), crucified (1 Cor. 1. 23; 2. 2), yet not dead, but still
alive, since the κήρυγμα would not have been εὐαγγέλιον but
so much wind, if Jesus had been a dead Messiah (1 Cor. 15. 14).
This coincides with the content of Paul's κήρυγμα as it is reported
in Acts. In 'Pisidian' Antioch the climax of his resumé of the
history of the Jews was his reference to the crucifixion and
resurrection of Jesus the Messiah (Acts 13. 28–31). In the Thessa-
loanian synagogue he expounded the scripture to show that the
Messiah must suffer and rise from the dead (Acts 17. 2–3).
Although in his speech at Athens he made no mention of the
crucifixion, obviously the death of Jesus is implied in his statement
that he has been raised from the dead (Acts 17. 31). In the manner
of his apostolic predecessors Paul concluded his speeches with an
appeal to repent and accept the crucified, risen Jesus as Messiah
and Lord (Acts 13. 38–9; 20. 21; 26. 18–20).

From the content of the κήρυγμα, as proclaimed by Paul, we
turn to its characteristics. In the first place, we notice how
shrewdly the discourses are accommodated to the audiences.
When Paul was addressing Jews, both his terminology and his
method of argumentation were such that would appeal to his
hearers. First, there is the appeal to history. The Jew passionately
believed that God was controlling history, and that he operated
especially in and through the events of the history of Israel, the
elect people. Accordingly we find that Paul gives an outline of
Jewish history from the Exodus to the advent of Jesus to show
that Israel was God's instrument in his preparation of mankind

for that climactic event (Acts 13. 17–25). Secondly, he makes use, as he does in his Epistles, of quotations from the Torah, which every Jew, whether Pharisee, Sadducee, Zealot, or non-partisan, believed to be divinely inspired. There are few books of the OT from which Paul does not quote; and his customary method of using it is summed up in Acts 17. 2–3; in a synagogue in Thessalonica he argued with the Jews on three sabbaths, 'quoting texts of Scripture, which he expounded and applied to show that the Messiah had to suffer and rise from the dead.' To King Herod Agrippa II he pointed out that his gospel was a fulfilment of the prophetic writings, which the king himself, being a Jew, accepted as the truth (Acts 26. 22–3, 27). As Paul himself wrote, 'All the ancient scriptures were written for our own instruction in order that through the encouragement they give us we may maintain our hope with fortitude' (Rom. 15. 4). On the other hand, when he was speaking to Gentiles, there was no point in appealing to the Jewish Scriptures, of which his audience was ignorant. There was, however, a powerful argument appreciated by Gentiles, the argument from natural religion. Of this argument Paul made effective use in his speeches to his audiences at Lystra and Athens. Repelled by the idolatry of the inhabitants of Lystra, who, familiar with the ancient fable of Philemon and Baucis,[1] believed Barnabas and Paul to be Zeus and Hermes and accordingly worshipped them, Paul proceeded to teach them the truth about the one living God.[2] Knowing that they lived close to nature, he argued that the natural processes, viz. the seasons, the harvest, and the rain, showed that there was a beneficent Creator who had made the skies, the earth, and the sea, and who, unlike the gods whom the Lystrans worshipped, was a living reality (Acts 14. 15–17). Addressing another Gentile audience, the Court of Areopagus in Athens, he employed this same argument (Acts 17. 22–31).[3] Because his hearers contained Stoic and Epicurean philosophers,

[1] Ovid, *Metamorphoses*, 8. 719 ff.   [2] Acts 14. 13 says that Paul was the spokesman.
[3] For the spate of books and articles on Paul's *Areopagitica vide* F. F. Bruce, *The Acts of the Apostles*, pp. 353–4 n. The most convincing summary of the arguments in favour of its authenticity that I have seen is in *Ancient Ideals*, by H. O. Taylor (New York, 1900), Vol. 2, p. 317 n.

Paul skilfully used some of their own concepts. God created the world, a proposition accepted by the Stoics, who believed that all things came into existence from God, but not by the Epicureans, who believed that the world came into being accidentally. God is Lord of his creation, the Disposer Supreme; a statement consonant with the Stoic notion of Providence and Fate, but not with the Epicurean concept of fainéant deities. God does not live in man-made temples, e.g. those in Athens; indeed, he needs nothing from men, a statement palatable to Epicureans. He gives all, and in return men can offer him only themselves. God made all mankind from one stock. That would appeal to the Stoics, who stressed the unity of the human race, although they believed that all other races were inferior to the Greeks. The *pièce de résistance* of the speech was to quote two tags from classical authors, 'In him we live and move and have our being,' the fourth line of a quatrain in a poem attributed to Epimenides the Cretan (*flor. c.* 550 B.C.) a Stoic;[1] and, 'for we also are his offspring,' part of a line from the *Phainomena* of Aratus (*flor. c.* 250 B.C.), who like Paul himself was born in Cilicia and like Epimenides was a Stoic.[2] No doubt Paul's ability to quote from Stoic writings suitably impressed his hearers. In the last part of his oration, the specifically Christian part, we have another example of how he adapted his words to his audience: he made no mention of the name of Jesus because he knew that his hearers had already misunderstood the word, thinking that Jesus was another deity whom Paul wished to add to the pantheon (Acts 17. 18). Instead, Paul speaks of him as 'a man of God's choosing' (Acts 17. 31). There are yet other instances of this ability to make his discourse suitable to his hearers. Because the aim of his farewell charge to the Ephesian elders is to strengthen and encourage them in the face of imminent dangers both from outside and inside the Church, he makes an appeal to their knowledge of his own sincerity, service, and suffering in the cause

[1] On the source of this quotation *vide* F. F. Bruce, *The Acts of the Apostles*, p. 359 n. and C. S. C. Williams, *Comm. on Acts*, BNTC, p. 205.
[2] *Phainomena*, line 5. Almost similar words are found in the *Hymn to Zeus*, written by another Stoic poet, Cleanthes.

of the gospel (Acts 20. 18–35). Then there are his apologiae. Standing on the steps leading to the Antonia fortress in Jerusalem, he faces a Jewish mob. How does he begin his speech? Speaking in Aramaic, their native tongue, he shouts, 'I am a Jew of Cilicia, educated in this city at the feet of Gamaliel, instructed according to the strict manner of the law of our forefathers, being zealous for God, even as you all are today; I persecuted this way of life to the death, binding and delivering into prisons both men and women, as also the high priest and the elders can testify' (Acts 22. 3–5). He had already quietened the howling crowd by addressing it in Aramaic; now his emphasis on his Jewish birth and education and his zeal for the faith of his fathers must have affected them deeply. No doubt there was what Leigh Hunt calls 'a pin-drop silence.'[1] Finally, there is the *captatio benevolentiae* at the beginning of his apologiae before Claudius Felix and King Herod Agrippa II. He congratulates himself because he is to plead his cause before a Roman official who, as a result of his long tenure of office, has a thorough knowledge of Judaism, and will therefore understand the issue at stake (Acts 24. 10). The opening gambit of his apologia before Herod Agrippa II is similar. He counts himself fortunate that he is granted the opportunity of making his plea in the presence of one who has a full knowledge of Judaism (Acts 26. 2–3).

Lastly, we should notice the method of argumentation that Paul uses in his speeches and, indeed, in his writings as well. His inferences come from facts, not from assumptions; e.g. we have already referred to his appeal to the facts of history and of nature. Above all, there is the fact of his own experience of the risen Jesus, Messiah and Lord, which was the source of his conversion and his call to be God's legatus and herald, proclaiming the good news of saving emancipation to the Gentiles (Acts 22. 3–21; 26. 4–23).

The whole purpose of this proclamation, and, indeed, of all Paul's legatine activities, is summed up by him in 2 Corinthians 5. 20: 'We are legati representing Christ: it is as if God were

---

[1] *Rimini*, 1, line 144.

appealing to you through us; in Christ's name, we entreat you, be reconciled to God.' In the previous verse he has stated that 'in Christ God was reconciling the world to himself'; and now that Christ has left the earth God's apostolic legati are continuing his reconciling activity. Paul saw mankind as hostile to God and needing to be reconciled to him. Possibly he was thinking of the hostility of the population of some Roman provinces towards the Imperial authority, and the task of the legatus to reconcile them to it. As his statements in Romans 13 indicate, he appreciated the benefits conferred by the universal Pax Romana, whose character is elegantly summed up in three lines of the most celebrated of all Latin poets:

> Tu regere imperio populos, Romane, memento
> (Hae tibi erunt artes), pacisque imponere morem,
> Parcere subjectis et debellare superbos.[1]

Although Paul was a Cilician Jew, he was proud of his Roman citizenship, of belonging to an international commonwealth of nations. It was the task of Paul the Christian legatus to extend the bounds of another international empire, the Regnum Dei, by proclaiming the good news of reconciliation.

Yet although he claimed that the κήρυγμα was good news to some who heard it, there were others who thought it nonsense. To some 'wise' Greeks of Corinth the concept of a crucified Lord was 'sheer folly' (μωρία) (1 Cor. 1. 18), and those who proclaimed it were 'fools' (μωροί) (1 Cor. 4. 10). This was 'a hit, a very palpable hit' because like the Athenians and, indeed, the Greeks in general, the men of Corinth were intellectual snobs, priding themselves on their 'wisdom' (σοφία), their cleverness, intelligence, and erudition. Yet how stupid their wisdom seemed at the foot of Messiah's Cross! 'Jews demand miraculous happenings, Greeks look for wisdom, but we proclaim Messiah—yes, Messiah nailed to the Cross; and though this is a stumbling-

---

[1] Virgil, *Aeneid*, Book 6, lines 851–3. Cf. also '. . . pacatumque reget patriis virtutibus orbem' (Virgil, *Eclogues* 4. 17), which is the superscription of E. V. Rieu's essay on the Messianic Eclogue (Penguin Classics translation, p. 136)—words put into Paul's mouth, on Virgil's tomb, by an unknown Christian poet.

block to Jews and folly to Greeks, yet to those who have heard his call, Jews and Greeks alike, he is the power of God and the wisdom of God' (1 Cor. 1. 22–4). Paul delights in the paradox that God's folly and weakness have brought salvation to man (1 Cor. 1. 25 ff.). The κήρυγμα was plain, straightforward, and simple, and Paul proclaimed it without cleverness or subtlety; yet it convinced the Corinthians by its power (1 Cor. 2. 1–5). From that statement it might be inferred that Paul was anti-intellectual, disparaging human reason, and indeed, such has been the conclusion reached by some of our neo-Lutherans and neo-Calvinists, who enjoy living in a Gilbertian realm of paradoxes, a theological topsy-turvydom, where every activity of human reason is suspect. Yet the κήρυγμα proclaimed by Paul consisted of rational propositions, for Paul was a theologian, propounding certain doctrines. It is this facet of his personality which will be the subject of the next four chapters.

4

THEOLOGIAN

PART I—TYRANNY

High on a throne of royal state, which far
Outshone the wealth of Ormus and of Ind,
Or where the gorgeous East with richest hand
Showers on her kings barbaric pearl and gold,
Satan exalted sat, by merit rais'd
To that bad eminence.

MILTON, Paradise Lost, Book 2, lines 1–6

'ST. PAUL was the first theologian of the Christian Church,' avers Professor Goudge,[1] and many others have said the same. In what sense can he be called a theologian? It would hardly be accurate to describe him as a theologian in the sense that we now give to the word. Theology is a science, dealing 'with the facts and phenomena of religion' and culminating 'in a comprehensive synthesis or philosophy of religion.'[2] It is 'a manifestation . . . of the scientific spirit.'[3] Like the biologist, the physicist, or any other kind of scientist, the genuine theologian uses the scientific method, assembling, sifting, comparing, and classifying the data and finally trying to offer a coherent explanation of them. That was not Paul's method; he did not sit down and deliberately formulate a vast, systematic theological compendium, a Summa Theologica Paulina. His doctrines are scattered throughout documents written *currente calamo* to deal with the diverse problems and needs of newly-founded Christian communities.[4] Thus it is not too much to say that many of his most profound theological statements were ad hoc and might never have been made

---

[1] Art. 'The Theology of St. Paul,' NCHS, Pt. 3, p. 403.
[2] D. S. Adam, art. 'Theology,' ERE, Vol. 12, p. 293.
[3] R. G. Collingwood, *Speculum Mentis* (Oxford, 1924), p. 152.
[4] Cf. Austin Farrer's description of Paul as 'a very unsystematic systematic theologian . . . too impulsive and enthusiastic to put his material in proper order or to standardize his terminology' (*The Glass of Vision*, Westminster, 1948, p. 45).

had it not been for the practical questions that confronted him.
For example, his earlier eschatology was evoked by the fermenta-
tion in the minds of the men of Thessalonica, caused by the
thought that the Day of the Lord was imminent. Again, it was
the scandalous behaviour of some of his Corinthian converts that
occasioned his explanation of the meaning of the Lord's Supper;
similarly it was queries about the resurrection of the dead that
led him to write in the same Epistle his comparatively lengthy
disquisition on the subject. His exposition in Colossians and
Ephesians of the universal sovereignty of Christ was intended to
combat Gnostic speculations rife in Asia Minor. The Christological statements of Philippians 2 arose out of the necessity of
emphasizing his injunction to practise humility. Above all, it
was the Judaizing controversy that caused him to formulate in
Romans and Galatians one of his palmary doctrines, vindication
by faith. Thus we would endorse Bultmann's assertion that
'Pauline theology is not a speculative system.'[1] At the same time,
since his statements are theological interpretations of his experience, since his doctrine is 'simply the direct transcription of his
experience, the pure outflow of his moral and religious life, which
ascending from the depths of his soul into the sphere of the
intellect, there finally expands into its theoretical form,'[2] he may
justifiably be called a theologian.

What is the theological message of the Pauline Epistles? If a
composer were asked to write a musical work that would convey
it, he could do no better than to create a symphony in four movements entitled Tyranny, Liberation, Consummation, and Liberator, every one of them including a motto phrase that expressed
the focal concept of Paul's thinking, namely, the Divine Way to
Freedom.[3] There are those who would demur to that statement,
claiming that Paul's overriding, all-embracing idea is that of

[1] R. Bultmann, *Theology of the NT*, Vol. 1, p. 190.
[2] A. Sabatier, *The Apostle Paul*, Eng. tr. A. M. Hellier (London, 1891), p. 278.
[3] I am reminded of Brahms's First Symphony, which has been described by Julius
Harrison as 'one of the greatest masterpieces of intellectual thought and beauty ever
conceived in symphonic form.' I see it as a representation of the victory of good over
evil.

justification by faith. These are the children of the Protestant Reformation, heirs of that monk of Wittenberg who on the Scala Santa took the first step towards the disinterment of the doctrine and the fragmentation of Western Christendom.[1] There are others, notably Deissman, H. R. Mackintosh, and Schweitzer, who hold that the dominant sentiment in Paul's mind was that of a mystical absorption into the personality of Christ. More recently N. Flew, W. D. Davies, and R. P. Shedd have agreed with Deissmann that the phrase ἐν Χριστῷ is the core of Paulinism, but that what Paul meant by it was not so much a mystical (in the strict sense of the word)[2] union with Christ as the experience of living as a member of Christ's Body, the Church. Finally, there are others, e.g. C. A. A. Scott, Bultmann (who inevitably looks at the question anthropologically), and T. W. Manson, who emphasize that all Paul's thought is controlled by his experience of having found what every man needs and seeks—salvation. No more than a cursory reading of the Pauline Epistles is necessary to reveal that every one of these ideas is prominent therein. The most prominent idea is that of salvation—but we must ask ourselves what precisely Paul meant by the word σωτηρία, which occurs fairly frequently in his Epistles, as does the cognate verb σώζω. As always when we are investigating the meaning of Pauline terms, our first action must be to discover how they are used in the OT. The Hebrew words translated σωτηρία in the LXX—yēša‘, yešûāh, tešûāh—are derived from the stem yš‘ (found only in the niphal and the hiphil). Basically this root means 'to be broad,' 'to become spacious,' 'to enlarge,' and hence in the hiphil 'to deliver,' 'to liberate'; and in that last word we have the pith and marrow of the Hebrew conception of salvation —deliverance, liberation. If we proceed to ask why this is so, we have but to recall that for the Hebrews 'the determinative experience of Yahweh's salvation was the deliverance from Egyptian bondage.'[3] It is, therefore, not surprising to find that

[1] On Luther's pregnant moment of doubt *vide* R. H. Bainton, *Here I Stand* (New York, 1950), p. 51.
[2] The German word 'mystisch' expresses perfectly what is meant.
[3] A. Richardson, art. 'Salvation,' IDB (New York, 1962), Vol. 4, p. 171.

Paul's theology is primarily an exposition of a way of liberation
—a more precise term than 'salvation'—that he himself had discovered, and that he believed to be the one and only way of
liberation for all men and, indeed, for the whole of creation, from
an intolerable slavery.

The first movement of the Pauline symphony, written in a
minor key, would describe the tyranny imposed on creation by
evil in all its forms—sin, suffering, demonic forces, legalism,
corruption and death. As far as man is concerned these manifestations of evil referred to by Paul can be divided into two categories:
those operating outside man's personality and those operating
within it. In this respect the human ego resembles a citadel
besieged by enemies at the gates and undermined by a fifth column
within the walls. The first of the two enemies outside the walls
is the army of evil spirits, whose objective existence Paul never
for one moment doubted. Many years after his conversion he
could describe himself as a Pharisee (Acts 23. 6), and here we have
an example of one of the Pharisaic tenets (Acts 23. 8) that he did
not jettison when he became a Christian, namely the belief that
in the heavens there was an organized realm peopled by angels
and evil spirits, to whom all men, Jews and Gentiles, were in
bondage. They are variously described by him: δαιμόνια,
ἀρχαί, ἐξουσίαι, δυνάμεις, θρόνοι, κυριότητες, οἱ κοσμοκράτορες
τοῦ σκότους, τὰ πνευματικὰ τῆς πονηρίας, and ἄγγελοι[1]
(Rom. 8. 38; 1 Cor. 10. 20–1; 15. 24; Eph. 1. 21; 3. 10; 6. 12;
Col. 1. 16; 2. 10, 15).[2] All these words and phrases are names for
the same beings, the evil demons, the

principalities and powers,
Mustering their unseen array[3]

[1] The word ἄγγελος merely means 'messenger'; and just as there are messengers of
Satan (2 Cor. 12. 7), so there are messengers of God (1 Cor. 13. 1; 2. Cor. 11. 14; Gal. 1. 8;
4. 14; 1 Thess. 4. 16; 2 Thess. 1. 7); therefore Richardson errs when he says that 'there are
no good angels in Paul' (ITNT, p. 209).

[2] I have not included οἱ ἄρχοντες τοῦ αἰῶνος τούτου (1 Cor. 2. 8) in this list because I
believe that it refers to the Roman and Jewish authorities who put Jesus to death. The
word οὐδείς possibly supports my interpretation.

[3] C. Elliott, 'Christian, seek not yet repose.' English Hymnal, 374.

in the celestial places (ἐν τοῖς ἐπουρανίοις) (Eph. 3. 10; 6. 12).
At their head is Satan, whom Paul mentions several times
in his Epistles, both by that name (Rom. 16. 20; 1 Cor. 5. 5; 7. 5;
2 Cor. 2. 11; 11. 14; 12. 7; 1 Thess. 2. 18; 2 Thess. 2. 9), and by
other appellations; the accuser (ὁ διάβολος) (Eph. 4. 27; 6. 11),
the tempter (1 Thess. 3. 5; 1 Cor. 7. 5), Beliar, a word that
probably means 'worthlessness'[1] (2 Cor. 6. 15), the ruler of the
authority of the air (Eph. 2. 2), the serpent (2 Cor. 11. 3), the god
of this age (2 Cor. 4. 4), and the destroyer (1 Cor. 10. 10). Clearly
one conclusion that can be drawn from these names is that Paul
seems to think of the devil as a person and not as an impersonal
force. For the present, Satan the archdemon is the *de facto* ruler
of men, the god whom the majority of them worship (2 Cor.
4. 4) and to whom, therefore, they are in bondage, the enemy of
Christ and his Church, who are engaged in a deadly struggle with
him (Eph. 6. 12 ff.); a struggle that will last until Antichrist, his
representative, launches a definitive assault on the Church at the
end of the current age (2 Thess. 2. 8–9).[2] How does Satan carry
on his campaign against them? What is his strategy, of which
Paul justifiably claims to have some knowledge (2 Cor. 2. 11)?
First, if Paul's 'stake for the flesh' was a bodily ailment,[3] he sees
the hand of Satan in the physical ills that affect men (2 Cor.
12. 7). Furthermore, he brings death to some; for did he not slay
the querulous Israelites in the wilderness (1 Cor. 10. 10)? Secondly,
he detects his activity in the mental blindness of the unconverted
that prevents them from seeing the light of God's good news
(2 Cor. 4. 4). Thirdly, he perceives him at work in the hostility
of the Jews of Corinth that prevented him from visiting his
converts in Thessalonica (1 Thess. 2. 18).[4] Fourthly, idolatry is
another item in his tactics; for the gods of the heathen are nothing
but Satan's subordinate demons incognito, the purpose of their
disguise being to deceive men and to make them their slaves
(1 Cor. 10. 19–21).[5] Fifthly, he is operating even within the

[1] It is a common name for Satan in Test. XII Pat. On its meaning *vide* A. E. Garvie, art. 'Belial,' HDB, Vol. 1, pp. 268–9.
[2] *V. inf.*, pp. 150–2.   [3] *V. inf.*, p. 255.
[4] Cf. W. Neil, *Comm. on* 1 *Thess*, PCB, p. 998.   [5] Cf. Milton, *Paradise Lost*, Book 1.

Church itself. He tempts Christians to satisfy their sexual desires extramaritally (I Cor. 7. 5) and to apostatize under persecution (I Thess. 3. 5). He employs false apostles to masquerade as genuine apostles in order to seduce Christians from their allegiance to Christ (2 Cor. 11. 13–15). Thus are they following the example of their leader, whose first action was to seduce the mother of the human race (2 Cor. 11. 3). Paul even thinks, somewhat naïvely, of Satan's minions as being present at Christian meetings and as liable to ogle Christian women with lustful glances if they omit to cover their hair (1 Cor. 11. 10)![1] Satan's activity is comprehensively described in Ephesians 2. 2 as that which is operating among 'the sons of disobedience,' a Hebraistic phrase that here refers to those who disobey God's commands and includes not only Gentiles but, as Paul proceeds to state (Eph. 2. 3), also Jews.

This brings us to a consideration of the next manifestation of evil, the first of man's enemies residing within the walls of his personality, Satan's fifth column, sin. An evil host, led by Satan, is the chief tyranny that is assailing the citadel from without. Residing inside it there is this other tyrant, sin (Rom. 7. 17, 20), which will, if man allows it, become his lord and master, utterly enslaving him and enforcing obedience on him (Rom. 6. 6, 16–18; 7. 14). If he permits it, sin will, like a despotic monarch, reign over his personality, completely subjecting him to its sway (Rom. 5. 21; 6. 12). As we have seen, in Romans 7. 7–25 Paul describes how he came to know that sin existed, how he longed for deliverance from it and its consequences, how Judaism failed to deliver him, and how at last he found the liberator, Jesus the Messiah.[2] At the same time as he experienced the fact of sin in his own life, he observed it in the lives of other men, both Jews and Gentiles. The Scriptural diagnosis of man's condition expressed in the Psalms was altogether accurate. No man was exempt from this sinful condition. 'All men have sinned and are lacking the

---

[1] It would seem that Paul, like the authors of 1 En. 6 and 7 and 2 Bar. 56. 10 ff., was alluding here to that weird passage, Gen. 6. 1–4, which he took to mean that incontinent angels had insisted on copulating with women whom they found desirable, thus fathering a race of lawless Brobdingnagians.

[2] V. sup., pp. 27–9 and Chap. 2 passim.

divine glory, *sc.* that Adam possessed before he fell' (Rom. 3. 23, cf. Rom. 3. 9; Gal. 3. 22) is Paul's summing-up of the section Romans 1. 18–3. 20. The question is, What did he believe the essential nature of sin to be? In the first place, the abstract noun that he uses most frequently (in all about sixty times) to denote sin is ἁμαρτία, and the verb (from which the noun is derived) that he often uses is ἁμαρτάνω, which in Classical Greek means literally 'to miss the mark,' and hence 'to make a mistake,' 'to fail to carry out a purpose,' 'to hold a wrong opinion,' and, very occasionally, 'to commit a moral wrong.' As Sanday and Head-lam have pointed out, the words mean far more than this in the LXX and the NT. The Hebrew words translated in the LXX ἁμαρτία and ἁμαρτάνω mean 'not a mere defect, the coming short of an ideal, the mark of an imperfect development,' but 'a positive quality, calling forth a positive reaction'; they denote 'a personal offence against a personal God . . . an injury or wound . . . directed against the Holy One whose love is incessantly going forth towards man.'[1]

Secondly, what is the personal offence that man commits against God? As Ephesians 2. 2–3 shows, it consists in his disobedience to God and his obedience to Satan. This implies the existence of divine orders that man is disregarding, rules that he is breaking. God has given men laws, which they contravene, and this is their sin, lawlessness. As St. Thomas Aquinas succinctly puts it, 'Nihil aliud est peccare quam transgredi divina mandata.'[2] When we consider the other terms that Paul uses to denote sin, we see that the statement fully accords with the apostle's teaching. What was it to which the Christians of Rome had yielded themselves in their unregenerate days but ἀνομία, 'lawlessness' (Rom. 6. 19)? What kind of actions does God forgive but lawless deeds (αἱ ἀνομίαι) (Rom. 4. 7)? What is utterly incompatible with righteousness but ἀνομία (2 Cor. 6. 14)? What is the all-embracing characteristic of that representative of Satan, Antichrist, who will lead the final attack on the Church at the end of the age, but

[1] *Comm. on Rom.*, ICC, p. 144.   [2] *Summa Theologica*, 1. 2. q. 72. a. 1.

ἀνομία (2 Thess. 2. 3, 7)?[1] Thus the sinner is he who intentionally flouts God's law. As Barclay says, the word ἀνομία 'stresses the deliberation of sin; it describes the man who well knows the right, and yet who does the wrong.'[2] Three other Pauline terms that convey the notion of lawlessness are παρακοή, παράπτωμα, and παράβασις. The first, which Paul uses to describe the primal sin, the sin of Adam (Rom. 5. 19), is derived from the verb παρακούειν, which originally meant 'to hear imperfectly,' and then in the LXX 'to hear without paying attention.' Thus what Paul means in Romans 5. 19 is that Adam deliberately disobeyed the divine command. The second word, παράπτωμα, derived from the verb παραπίπτειν and applied by Paul to Adam's sin (Rom. 5. 15, 17, 18, 20) and to the sins of men in general (Rom. 4. 25; 2 Cor. 5. 19; Gal. 6. 1; Eph. 1. 7; 2. 5; Col. 2. 13), means literally 'a falling away sideways,' and hence 'a false step,'[3] 'a lapse,' the termination -μα denoting the concrete action of law-breaking. The last of the three Pauline words to convey this same notion of sin as disobedience to the divine command is παράβασις, a *nomen actionis* derived from the verb παραβαίνειν, 'to pass over,' 'to step over a clearly defined line,' and hence in the LXX 'to transgress God's law.' Perhaps the most illuminating comment on the meaning of παράβασις is to be found in a non-Christian writer, 'Est peccare tamquam transire lineas.'[4] Like the other two words it is applied by Paul to Adam's sin (Rom. 5. 14). On the other occasions when he uses the word, he is referring to the breaking of their own Law by the Jews (Rom. 2. 23; 4. 15; Gal. 3. 19), and the same applies to his use of the related word παραβάτης (Rom. 2. 25, 27; and possibly Gal. 2. 18).[5] This serves to emphasize the point that we are making; Paul thought of sin as the breach of the divine law, since to the Jew the Law was the embodiment of knowledge and truth, the expression of God's will (Rom. 2. 18, 20), and, therefore, when he contravened it, he knew that he was sinning. It is, therefore, by law, his own

[1] The reading ἀνομίας is to be preferred to ἁμαρτίας here.
[2] W. Barclay, *The Mind of St. Paul* (London, 1958), p. 192.
[3] This is what it means in Rom. 11. 11–12.
[4] Cicero, *Paradoxa Stoicorum*, 3. 20.   [5] *Vide* J. B. Lightfoot, *Comm. on Gal.*, p. 117.

law, that he will be judged (Rom. 2. 12), just as the Gentile will
be judged by his own law, the law of conscience (Rom. 2. 14–16).
The point that sin is lawlessness is driven home still further by
Paul's statement that without law God keeps no reckoning of sin
(Rom. 5. 13); without law there can be no breach of law (Rom.
4. 15); and if sins, i.e. breaches of law, are committed, as happened
between the time of Adam and the giving of the Jewish Law, then
God does not enter them in the ledger (ἐλλογεῖται) (Rom. 5. 13).
Sin, then, is disobedience to God's law. The Jews have been
guilty of it (Rom. 10. 21; 11. 30), and so have the Gentiles
(Rom. 11. 32); all are disobedient (Eph. 5. 6).

Thirdly, Paul is not so superficial as to inform us that sin is
rebellion against God's command without also showing what the
source of the rebellion is. Its *fons et origo* is self-deification. On
the devil's shield is inscribed the motto, 'Non serviam': he is
convinced that 'it is better to reign in hell, than serve in heaven';[1]
and, obedient to his master's behest, unredeemed man seeks to
make himself God.[2] This is what Paul means by ἀσέβεια (Rom.
1. 18; 11. 26), a word that, as E. R. Bernard correctly points out,
'expresses the insult and blasphemy involved in sin'; i.e. it is the
indifference to, and defiance of, God.[3] Here, in Romans 1. 18–25
we reach the heart of the matter; for in this trenchant passage we
have, as Reinhold Niebuhr says, 'the most classical definition of sin
in the New Testament. . . . The sin of man is that he seeks to make
himself God.'[4] As Paul sees it, the ἀσέβεια of the Gentile world
consists in this: that, although God has made known to it 'his
invisible nature, namely, his eternal power and deity,' in the
things that he has created, it refuses to acknowledge that he is
God, and worships the created thing rather than the Creator
(Rom. 1. 19–20, 25). This is a reference to the ubiquitous idolatry

---

[1] Milton, *Paradise Lost*, 1, 263.
[2] 'Every man would like to be God, if it were possible; some few find it difficult to
admit the impossibility,' wrote Bertrand Russell (*Power. A New Social Analysis*, London,
1938, p. 9). For 'some few' substitute 'a large number.'
[3] Art. 'Sin,' HDB, Vol. 4, p. 532.
[4] R. Niebuhr, *The Nature and Destiny of Man*, 2 vols. (London, 1941), Vol. 1, p. 150.

G

in the Graeco-Roman world, which Paul observed with abhor-
rence (Rom. 1. 23. Cf. Acts 17. 16, 29) and which was (*monstrum
horrendum!*) even being aped by the Jews, who robbed pagan
temples of their images in order to worship them (Rom. 2. 22.
Cf. Acts 19. 37). Now the essential truth concerning idolatry is
that in bowing down before their images the idolaters are worshipping themselves. The Gentile divinities—Jupiter, Mars, Venus,
Juno, Diana, Apollo (to give them their Roman names), and the
rest—represented by the idols, had no objective existence. Like
the good Jew that he was, Paul put it thus: 'We know that "an
idol has no real existence," and that "there is no God but one."
For although there may be so-called gods in heaven or on earth—
as indeed there are many "gods" and "lords"—yet for us there is
one God, the Father, from whom are all things and for whom
we exist, and one Lord, Jesus Christ, through whom are all things
and through whom we exist' (1 Cor. 8. 4–6. Cf. 1 Cor. 10. 19;
Rom. 11. 36; Eph. 4. 5–6; Col. 1. 16; Deut. 6. 4; Is. 44; 45. 5).
The reason why 'an idol has no real existence' is that the divinity
that it represents is merely the projection of the ideas of its
devotees, facets of the human ego. The idolatrous cultus is an
external expression of man's self-deification.

If that had been its only external expression, Paul might not
have been unduly disturbed. There was, however, the immoral
behaviour of the idolaters when they put into practice those
ideas of which their gods and goddesses were the reflection. To
some the tales that tell of the unrestrained promiscuity, sadistic
savagery, base treachery, and ruthless banditry of the Olympians
are heroic; to others, apart from their dreariness, they represent,
not only the self-centred thinking, but also the self-centred
actions, of a society that deified Man.[1] No-one saw this link
between the idolatry that was the cultic expression of self-
deification, and the immorality of the idolaters, more clearly than
Paul of Tarsus; it was 'because they exchanged the truth about
God for a lie and worshipped the creature rather than the Creator'

---

[1] Protagoras's dictum, πάντων χρημάτων ἄνθρωπον μέτρον εἶναι, quoted by Plato in
Theaetetus, 160d, expresses it perfectly.

that 'God gave them up in the lusts of their hearts to impurity, to the dishonouring of their bodies among themselves . . . to a base mind and to improper conduct' (Rom. 1. 24–5, 28). A word that Paul uses to describe the immorality that was the fruit of their idolatrous self-deification is ἀδικία, by which he means man's ruthless disregard for the personality of his neighbour. The several components of ἀδικία are the anti-social vices, what Paul calls τὰ μὴ καθήκοντα (Rom. 1. 28), enumerated in Stoic fashion by him in Romans 1. 29–31 and elsewhere (Rom. 13. 13; 1 Cor. 5. 10–11; 2 Cor. 12. 20; Gal. 5. 19–21; Eph. 5. 3–5; and Col. 3. 5–8.)[1] If, as we read these lists in which Paul ranges over the whole gamut of vice, we wonder whether he is exaggerating, and tell ourselves that we must make allowances for a Jew when he is denouncing the immoral accompaniments of Gentile idolatry, we should do well to remember that Roman satirists like Persius, Petronius, and Juvenal castigated the corruptness of the times just as severely as Paul did; and if we doubt the truth of their strictures on the ground that, like moralists, satirists tend to magnify their target, we have but to read reliable works that deal with the state of society in the Julio–Claudian age to realize that they were not so wide of the mark.[2] Matthew Arnold's frequently quoted description of the epoch accords with the picture painted by the social historians:

> On that hard pagan world disgust
> And secret loathing fell.
> Deep weariness and sated lust
> Made human life a hell.[3]

One last aspect of Paul's criticism of Gentile idolatry remains to be considered. His experience of the Graeco-Roman world had demonstrated to him that intellectual speculation, however profound, did not of necessity destroy superstition and vice.

[1] For a detailed examination of the Greek terms used by Paul v. inf., pp. 203–6.
[2] E.g. L. Friedlander, *Roman Life and Manners under the Early Empire*, Eng. tr. L. A. Magnus, J. H. Freese, and A. B. Gough (London, 1908–13), 4 vols.; H. O. Taylor, *Ancient Ideals*, 2 vols. (New York, 1900), Vol. 2; and M. Grant, *The World of Rome* (London, 1960). On the satirists vide J. W. Duff, *Roman Satire* (Connecticut, 1964).
[3] *Obermann Once More*, lines 93–6.

Approximately a century and a half after Paul had written the Epistle to the Romans one of the most eminent of the Christian Platonists of Alexandria could claim that philosophy was 'God's special covenant with the Greeks as a basis for the philosophy according to Christ.'[1] It is highly unlikely that Paul would have given that statement his unqualified approval; for although, if Acts 17 is authentic, he saw that Greek philosophy had some inkling of truth, he saw also that its speculations (διαλογισμοί)[2] were rendered ineffectual by the idolatry and vice that existed side by side with them without any suggestion of incompatibility. Athens had its full quota of high-minded Stoics and Epicureans, who lived in the rarefied atmosphere of metaphysical discourse, but at the same time the city was cluttered up with idols (Acts 17. 16). It was this idolatry that made Paul write: 'Their misguided minds are plunged in darkness. They boast of wisdom, but they have made fools of themselves' (Rom. 1. 21–2). When he penned that last sentence, he appears to have had in mind the folly and sinfulness of man's self-deification. This interpretation of his words is reinforced by his polemic in 1 Corinthians against the σοφία that regarded the proclamation of the Cross as foolishness. This, however, is not the case, for 'God has made the wisdom of this world look foolish' (1 Cor. 1. 20). How is this? In the first place, the wisdom of Greek philosophy, far from finding God, had resulted in the kind of schisms that were troubling the Church in Corinth (1 Cor. 1. 10 ff.; 3. 3 ff.; 3. 18 ff.). Philosophical speculation was not God's way of saving mankind; his way was the *Via Crucis*, regarded as folly by the philosophers (1 Cor. 1. 18; 3. 19); but the 'divine folly is wiser than the wisdom of men, and divine weakness stronger than man's strength' (1 Cor. 1. 25). The proof of this is plainly evident in the Corinthians' own experience; very few of them possessed intellectual power, yet they had experienced the liberation brought by the good news of the Christ nailed to the Cross, and consequently were enjoying

---

[1] Clement of Alexandria, *Stromateis*, 6. 8.
[2] There is no need to interpret this word in a pejorative sense. In the LXX, as in Classical Greek, it merely means 'cogitations,' 'speculations' (VGT, p. 151).

life in Christ Jesus (1 Cor. 1. 26–31). They had not been saved by subtle arguments, but by the power of the Cross (1 Cor. 2. 1–5). Secondly, intellectual wisdom is transitory: it belongs to an age that is passing (1 Cor. 1. 20; 2. 6; 3. 18). God is bringing it to nothing (1 Cor. 1. 19), as Isaiah had said (Is. 29. 14). Thirdly, and above all, without the Cross intellectual wisdom is sinful, for its tap-root is human pride, and 'there is no place for human pride in God's presence' (1 Cor. 1. 29; 3. 21); pride is a manifestation of self-deification.

Fourthly, to denote human nature corrupted by sin Paul uses the term σάρξ. In its unredeemed condition man's σῶμα is a σῶμα τῆς σαρκός (Col. 2. 11). Properly to understand this important phrase we should bear in mind that the word σῶμα does not mean the physical body, but 'the organic principle which makes a man a self-identical individual, persisting through all changes in the "substance" through which he realizes himself, whether material or non-material.'[1] The nearest English word that conveys this concept is 'personality' or 'self' or 'ego.'[2] Since the unredeemed human σῶμα is a σῶμα τῆς σαρκός, it is a sinful σῶμα (Rom. 6. 6; 8. 3): 'I know that nothing good inhabits my σάρξ' (Rom. 7. 18). To the σάρξ belong the ἐπιθυμίαι (Rom. 13. 14; Gal. 5. 16, 24; Eph. 2. 3), the lustings that activate men to commit the sinful acts subsumed under the headings ἀσέβεια, ἀδικία, and ἁμαρτία. Such a mentality (το φρόνημα τῆς σαρκός) can have but one end—corruption and death (Rom. 8. 6, 13; Gal. 6. 8. Cf. Rom. 7. 5). It goes without saying that the σάρξ is God's enemy (Rom. 8. 7), and those who are ἐν σαρκί cannot please him (Rom. 8. 8). In his analysis in Romans 7. 7–25, of the state of his own personality in its pre-conversion days, Paul shows how the σάρξ was at war with what he regarded as divine law, of which his reason (νοῦς) approved, and how his ego, controlling his will, was ever faced with the choice between obedience to the

[1] C. H. Dodd, Comm. on Rom., MNTC, p. 125. Cf. R. Bultmann, Theology of the NT, Vol. 1, pp. 192 ff.
[2] Neither Hebrew nor Greek has a word that is the exact equivalent of the English word 'personality.' In Greek σῶμα is the nearest to it.

divine law and the lawless lustings of the σάρξ. Even in the converted, who are no longer ἐν σαρκί (Rom. 8. 9) and whose
conduct is therefore not guided by it (Rom. 8. 4, 12), the lingering
σάρξ is still liable to fight against the divine πνεῦμα, which as a
result of their conversion dwells in them (Gal. 5. 16–17).

The view of one school of thought that Paul used this word
σάρξ to connote corrupted human nature because, influenced by
the dualism of Greek anthropology, he believed that the physical
flesh, the soft substance that covers the bones and through which
the blood flows, was innately and essentially 'altogether evil,
altogether unclean, altogether corrupting and productive of
wickedness,'[1] and was in active opposition to a non-physical part
of man, has been ably refuted by more than one scholar, and it
would be superfluous to repeat their arguments here.[2] To quote
the conclusion of one of them, 'The evidence is against the view
that Paul found in the flesh as a physical thing a compelling force
for evil.'[3] As H. W. Robinson and others[4] claim, the key to the
understanding of Paul's doctrine of the σάρξ is to be found in his
development of the meaning of the Hebrew bāśār (= σάρξ in
the LXX) in the later parts of the OT, where it denotes 'man,
or man's essential nature, in contrast with God or with "Spirit,"
to emphasize man's frailty, dependence or incapacity.'[5] W. D.
Stacey summarizes this development thus: 'If σάρξ implied so
much with regard to human differences from the divine, if it
implied so strongly the contrast between the frail and mortal,
and the omnipotent and eternal, it is highly likely that σάρξ will
gather up into its meaning that other great point of difference,

---

[1] J. Klausner, *From Jesus to Paul*, p. 489. Others who belong to this school of thought are
O. Pfleiderer, *Paulinism*, Eng. tr. E. Peters (London, 1877), Vol. 1, pp. 46–7, 278 ff.,
H. J. Holtzmann, *Lehrbuch der Neutestamentlichen Theologie* (Tübingen, 1911), Vol. 2,
pp. 12–14, and W. Bousset, *Die Religion des Judenthums* (Berlin, 1903), p. 386.

[2] For a summary of them *vide* W. D. Stacey, *The Pauline View of Man* (London, 1956),
pp. 176–9; W. D. Davies, *Paul and Rabbinic Judaism*, pp. 18–19; and J. Laidlaw, art.
'Psychology,' HDB, Vol. 4, pp. 165–6.

[3] E. De W. Burton, *Spirit, Soul, and Flesh* (Chicago, 1918), p. 197.

[4] H. W. Robinson, *The Christian Doctrine of Man* (Edinburgh, 1926), pp. 104 ff.;
E. de W. Burton, *Spirit, Soul, and Flesh*, pp. 184–6; W. D. Davies, *Paul and Rabbinic
Judaism*, pp. 18–19; W. D. Stacey, *The Pauline View of Man*, pp. 160 ff.

[5] H. W. Robinson, *The Christian Doctrine of Man*, p. 25. Cf. J. A. T. Robinson, *The
Body* (London, 1952), pp. 11–26.

human sinfulness.'[1] Where this leads in the end is shown by H. W. Robinson's final verdict: 'Paul finds in man's physical nature the *immediate* foe of the higher principle, though this does not, of course, prove that the flesh is the *ultimate* enemy, as is implied when "Hellenistic dualism" is ascribed to Paul. . . . We are entitled to say that the ultimate enemy of the Spirit of God is not flesh, but the Sin of which the flesh has become the weak and corrupted instrument.'[2] Our criticism of this view is that, although admittedly Robinson says that Paul, in accordance with OT usage, thought of the flesh 'as a *psychical* factor in man's nature,'[3] he still appears to limit the meaning of σάρξ to the physical flesh whereas Paul, by attributing to it certain sins that are certainly not carnal, e.g. idolatry, sorcery, enmity, strife, jealousy, anger, self-seeking, dissension, party spirit, and envy (Gal. 5. 20), shows that he is using the word in a far wider sense: it was the most suitable word that he knew to describe corrupted human nature as a whole, including its carnality. In short, he was using the term metonymically as one adjunct of that nature. The answer to the question why it was the most suitable term is to be found in the fact emphasized by Robinson and those who follow him, and referred to above: the use of the term in the later books of the OT to denote man in all his frailty in contrast with God in all his power. Let C. H. Dodd have the last word on the Pauline meaning of σάρξ: 'The flesh is the common stuff of human nature which we inherit' and which is made up of 'the natural instincts as perverted to the ends of sin.'[4]

How was it that humanity found itself in this sorry plight? Paul's answer to this question shows that he followed that Jewish school of thought that linked human depravity with the transgression of Adam as it is described in the Yahwistic compiler's aetiological myth in Genesis. 3.[5] As a scrutiny of this story reveals,

---

[1] W. D. Stacey, *The Pauline View of Man*, p. 160.
[2] H. W. Robinson, *The Christian Doctrine of Man*, pp. 115, 117.   [3] *Ibid.*
[4] *Comm. on Rom.*, MNTC, pp. 112, 125.
[5] Except perhaps for a perfunctory allusion to it in 1 Cor. 11. 10, Paul never refers to the other Yahwistic legend, used by 1 En. and 2 Bar. to explain the origin of human sinfulness, the story of the angels who had sexual intercourse with women (Gen. 6. 1–4).

the writer himself never mentions the sinfulness of Adam's descendants. Cave's caveat should be heeded: the myth 'is to be understood in its own light and not in the light of Milton's *Paradise Lost* or Augustinian and Calvinistic theology.'[1] The Yahwistic writer's purpose was to show that the cause of man's forfeiture of an innocent, carefree, idyllic existence for bondage to drudgery and mortality was his presumptuousness in attempting to seize the knowledge that places him on the throne of the Deity himself, i.e. the knowledge of how to control the universe. Apart from two casual allusions to it in the Apocryphal books (Ecclus. 25. 24 and Wisd. Sol. 2. 23–4), a reference to it in the Book of Jubilees 3. 17–35, and another in the Testaments of the Twelve Patriarchs (Test. Lev. 18. 10–11), the myth was entirely ignored by Jewish writers until certain of the later pseudepigraphic apocalypses (which were probably compiled some time during the closing decades of the first century of the Christian era, thus reflecting opinions current in Paul's day) seized on it as offering them an adequate solution of the problem that was troubling them far more insistently than it had bothered their forefathers: how it was that man had reached his depraved condition. It is clear that these writers treated the story as a historical narrative. For them Adam was the first human being to walk the earth; he disobeyed his Creator's command; and his transgression implicated all his posterity in sin and mortality. Paul himself held this same view, the *locus classicus* being Romans 5. 12–21. Hitherto in our consideration of the subject it has been plain sailing. Now when we proceed to ask how Adam's sin involved his descendants, we encounter difficulties created by ambiguity and obscurity. One of the pseudepigraphic writers, the author of the Slavonic Enoch (or the Book of the Secrets of Enoch), informs us that by their transgression man's first parents brought ruin upon him and caused his infirmity, by which he appears to mean sinfulness and its punishment, existence in the lowest hell (2 En. 41); but he omits to tell us how the one caused the other. A later apocalypse is more explicit: accepting the current Rabbinical doctrine that God

---

[1] S. Cave, *The Christian Estimate of Man* (London, 1944), p. 39.

implanted in Adam the *yēṣer hā-ra'*, the evil inclination or impulse, when he created him,[1] he says that yielding to it, Adam transgressed and 'likewise all who were born of him. Thus the infirmity became inveterate' (4 Ez. 3. 21–2. Cf. 4. 30). Another passage from the same source reads: 'O Adam, what have you done? For though it was you that sinned, the fall (or ruin[2]) was not yours alone, but ours also who are your descendants' (7. 118). It is possible that the writer had in mind the hereditary transmission of an innate weakness that caused Adam's posterity to sin. On the other hand, it may mean no more than that it followed his example.[3] Paul is even less explicit than 4 Ezra; which lack of precision has given Pauline exegetes, ancient, mediaeval, and modern, the opportunity of exercising their ingenuity and causing the shelves of our theological libraries to groan under the weight of theories concerning *peccatum originale*, many of which cannot justifiably be deduced from Paul's language. What, then, does he say in Romans 5? The two salient statements are: δι' ἑνὸς ἀνθρώπου ἡ ἁμαρτία εἰς τὸν κόσμον εἰσῆλθεν (verse 12); and διὰ τῆς παρακοῆς τοῦ ἑνὸς ἀνθρώπου ἁμαρτωλοὶ κατεστάθησαν οἱ πολλοί (verse 19). The first feature of these statements is that the preposition διά followed by the genitive case can mean only 'through the agency of,' i.e. in verse 12 Paul means that Adam's transgression caused sin to enter the world. Secondly, in verse 19 this grammatical construction is repeated, and coupled with it this time there is the verb κατεστάθησαν, the most fitting translation of which, when we consider the forensic context (Rom. 5. 15–19), is—'were made to appear before God the Judge.'[4] Thus what this verse says is that Adam's transgression caused his

---

[1] On the *yēṣer hā-ra'* vide F. C. Porter, *The Yeçer Hara*, in the Yale Bicentenary volume of *Biblical and Semitic Studies*, 1901; N. P. Williams, *The Ideas of the Fall and Original Sin* (London, 1927), pp. 59–70; and W. D. Davies, *Paul and Rabbinic Judaism*, pp. 20–3.

[2] On the meaning of this word vide N. P. Williams, *The Ideas of the Fall and Original Sin*, p. 252, n. 4.

[3] There is yet another possible interpretation, v. inf., pp. 92–3.

[4] It is translated 'were made' in AV, RV, Moffatt, RSV, and NEB; 'were constituted' by Sanday and Headlam (*Comm. on Rom.*, in loc.) and N. P. Williams (*The Ideas of the Fall and Original Sin*, p. 131); and 'were given facilities for' or 'were made apt to' by W. D. Davies, who adds that this means much the same as 'caused' (*Paul and Rabbinic Judaism*, p. 31 n.). The meaning that we prefer is found elsewhere in the *Koine* (VGT, p. 313).

posterity to stand in the dock, indicted of sin. It would seem, then, that Paul thought of Adam's transgression as in some way causally connected with the sinfulness of mankind; but he does not state the precise nature of the causal nexus. To say, as N. P. Williams does, that 'the conception which is struggling for expression in St. Paul's mind is that of a hereditary disease somehow introduced into the human stock by Adam's sin; the "inherited tendency to sin," or "original sin," so called—if a fact—must be conceived as a disease, and medical terminology alone is appropriate in speaking of it,'[1] is to be guilty of reading into Paul's language a pathological metaphor that it does not contain. All that he does is vaguely to connect Adam's sin causally with that of his descendants without giving us the slightest indication of what he considered the nature of the cause to have been.

This omission need not, however, occasion us any regret; for Paul more than makes up for it by showing us a way of interpreting the Adam story far more meaningful than any other because it does not depend upon the historicity of the Genesis 3 narrative. The key to this interpretation is to be found in the OT concept of the solidarity of the human race, which emphasizes the unity of groups, viz. the family or clan, the tribe, the race, and the whole of mankind. So vivid was this concept that the group was thought of as a corporate personality, and some prominent individual who belonged to it, e.g. its founder or leader, as incorporating its essence within himself. Thus he came to be identified with it and was regarded as its representative.[2] There seems to be little doubt, especially in the light of recent investigation of the subject,[3] that when Paul used the term Ἀδάμ, he was thinking of him in this way: for him 'Adam' was both a historical figure and, more significantly, representative man containing

---

[1] *The Ideas of the Fall and Original Sin*, pp. 132, 133.

[2] For a comprehensive treatment of the whole theme *vide* R. P. Shedd, *Man in Community* (London, 1958), pp. 3–89.

[3] E.g. H. W. Robinson, *The Christian Doctrine of Man*, pp. 8, 27–30, 120–1; F. R. Tennant, *The Sources of the Doctrines of the Fall and Original Sin* (Cambridge, 1903), pp. 235 f.; C. H. Dodd, *Comm. on Rom.*, MNTC, pp. 79–80; W. D. Davies, *Paul and Rabbinic Judaism*, pp. 31–2; A. Nygren, *Comm. on Rom.*, Eng. tr. C. C. Rasmussen (Philadelphia, 1949), p. 213; E. Best, *One Body in Christ* (London, 1955), *passim*; A. Richardson, ITNT, pp. 245–9; and R. P. Shedd, *Man in Community*, pp. 108–110.

within himself all humanity.[1] We have but to consider the context of Romans 5. 12 and 19, and couple with it the statements in 1. Corinthians 15. 22 and 45-8, to see that this interpretation of Paul's thought is very plausible. In these passages there is a correspondence between the predicament of unregenerate man, who is described as being 'in Adam' (1 Cor. 15. 22), and the blissful condition of regenerate man, who is enjoying salvation 'in Christ.' Clearly it is an instance of Pauline typology. Sinful Adam, historically the first human being and (what is more important) representative man, is the τύπος of which Jesus the Messiah, the eschatic Adam and also a historical figure, is the ἀντίτυπος (Rom. 5. 14). As all the redeemed are 'in Christ' in the sense that they are united with him to form the Church, the corporate Christ, so all the unredeemed are 'in Adam' in the sense that they are united with him to form the corporate body of unregenerate humanity. It is in this sense that Paul can say that 'all men sinned' (Rom. 5. 12), the verb ἥμαρτον being a constative aorist, summarizing the action:[2] the whole human race, united with Adam, sinned proleptically at that point of time when Adam sinned. It is this thought, and not that of a hereditarily transmitted disease called 'sin,' that lies behind the somewhat obscure passage Romans 5. 13-14, where Paul refers to the death of Adam's descendants before the coming of the law. When there is no law, avers Paul, men cannot be accused of sinning. How, then, can their death, which was the consequence of sin, be explained? They shared Adam's guilt because they were corporately united with him. This whole interpretation of Paul's statements is admirably summed up by Richardson; in sinning, Adam 'typifies the relation of all sinful men to God, who created and loves them. . . . He represents . . . the unity or solidarity of the human race, as created in God's image, yet rebelling against God and asserting its independence of God.'[3]

---

[1] Some of the statements of the pseudepigraphic writers could be plausibly interpreted in this same way; e.g. 4 Ez. 7. 118.

[2] GGNT, Vol. 1, p. 109.

[3] A. Richardson, ITNT, p. 248. When Professor Richardson points out that the Hebrew word 'ādhām is a collective noun meaning 'mankind,' he is repeating what Origen said 1700 years ago (c. Celsum, 4. 40).

Before we leave our consideration of this Pauline passage, we would add a rider to what we have said. Some scholars have argued—on the basis of the supposed synonymity of such Pauline terms as ἁμαρτία, τὸ φρόνημα τῆς σαρκός and ὁ παλαιός ἄνθρωπος with the term the yēṣer hā-ra'—that the apostle held the current Rabbinical theory that human sinfulness was due to the operation of the evil inclination placed by God in man at the Creation.[1] Our criticism of this suggestion agrees with H. W. Robinson's observation that 'Paul does not anywhere reproduce this doctrine.'[2] For Paul it was not God, but Adam (= man) and Adam alone, who was responsible for the human condition. Nevertheless, as Robinson adds, Paul has his own version of the doctrine in Romans 7; and it is here that we find, if we need it, the unifying factor common to Adam and his posterity, a discovery that justifies the assertion that all men are 'in Adam': it is the infirmity of the σάρξ, the unregenerate human nature, prompting Adam and all his offspring to self-deification (which is the very quintessence of sin) that unites them all in one body, one massa peccati (to use Augustine's phrase).[3] If we want to indicate the similarity of the concept of the σαρξ to that of the yēṣer hā-ra', we can call this nature yēṣer hā-ra' if we like, although in view of the associations of the term (more especially the idea that God is the author of evil), it would be advisable not to; better is it to be content with Paul's word σάρξ, which is totally adequate.

Working with and for the tyrant Sin within man's personality there is another oppressor, mortality, which, like sin, is universal (Rom. 5. 12) and originated with Adam's transgression. 'Through the agency of the one man sin entered the world, and through the agency of (διά) sin death (sc. entered the world), and thus death spread to all men because (ἐφ' ᾧ)[4] all men sinned,' wrote Paul (Rom. 5. 12). Again, in verse 15 we read, 'By the transgression of the one man the many (οἱ πολλοί = all mankind)[5] died

---

[1] E.g. W. D. Davies, *Paul and Rabbinic Judaism*, pp. 20 ff.
[2] *The Christian Doctrine of Man*, p. 120.   [3] *ad Simpl.*, 1, q. 2. 16.
[4] *V. inf.* p. 95 n. 1.   [5] *Vide* Sanday and Headlam, *Comm. on Rom.*, ICC, *ad loc.*

(ἀπέθανον),' and finally, in verse 17, 'By the transgression of the one man death reigned through the agency of the one man'. Paul can hardly mean less than that Adam's sin caused, not only human sinfulness, but also human mortality. Here, again, he is going far beyond the meaning of the original story in Genesis. Paul's statement implies that Adam was created with an immortal nature, which he lost by his transgression; the Yahwistic writer implies that Adam was created mortal (Gen. 3. 19), and that by seizing the forbidden knowledge he lost the opportunity of eating the fruit of the tree of life, which would have given him immortality (Gen. 3. 22). It is to the current doctrine of the Sapiential writers (Ecclus. 25. 24; Wisd. Sol. 2. 23–4) and, once again, of the pseudepigraphic apocalypses (4 Ez. 3. 7; 2 Bar. 17. 3; 23. 4) that Paul's teaching on this subject seems to approximate. It was Adam's sin that *caused* human mortality. Yet as in his treatment of the origin of human sinfulness, he does not show how Adam's transgression caused death. What he does give us again is the corporate notion: death is the lot of all men ἐφ' ᾧ ἥμαρτον (Rom. 5. 12). The conjunctional phrase ἐφ' ᾧ cannot mean anything other than 'because'[1] and, as we have already pointed out, the aorist ἥμαρτον is constative,[2] meaning that in the sin of Adam all men sinned corporately. If further evidence is needed, we have another constative aorist in verse 15: ἀπέθανον. All men died when Adam transgressed and as a consequence of his transgression. As we have emphasized previously, the whole passage is a piece of typology, in which Paul contrasts the effects of Adam's sin and those of God's redeeming act in Jesus Christ: the one brought not only sin, but mortality; the other brings salvation and with it ζωή αἰώνιος. Paul sums up what he has been saying, in the concluding verse: ὥσπερ ἐβασίλευσεν ἡ ἁμαρτία ἐν τῷ θανάτῳ, οὕτως καὶ ἡ χάρις βασιλεύσῃ διὰ δικαιοσύνης εἰς ζωὴν αἰώνιον διὰ Ἰησοῦ Χριστοῦ τοῦ Κυρίου ἡμῶν (Rom. 5. 21). The typology is repeated in 1 Corinthians 15. 21–2: 'As in Adam

---

[1] The meaning of ἐφ' ᾧ in Rom. 5.12 is a notorious *crux criticorum*, *vide* Sanday and Headlam, *ad loc.*, and GGNT, p. 107. Cf. N. Turner, *Grammatical Insights into the NT* (Edinburgh, 1965), pp. 116–18.

[2] *V. sup.*, p. 93.

all die, so in Christ will all men be made alive.' Because Adam is corporate, representative man, all men share his mortality as well as his sinfulness. Nor, according to Paul, were corruption and mortality confined to the human part of creation; they pervaded the whole of it, and this calamity, like all the others, Paul traces to the sin of Adam. The passage to which we are referring is Romans 8. 20-2, of which N. P. Williams wrote: 'His explanation of the evil which prevails in Nature is enshrined in words of almost lyrical beauty and power, to paraphrase which would be a profanation.'[1] All created things were subjected to frustration, a purposeless existence, says Paul, not through their own fault, but through Adam's sin. Enslaved by corruption, the whole creation is groaning and travailing in concert with mankind. Clearly Paul has in mind the explanation of the pain, anguish, and death that he sees in Nature, given by the Yahwistic writer in Genesis 3. 17-18 and embellished by the pseudepigraphic writers (e.g. 4 Ez. 7. 11).

Recapitulating and maintaining the metaphor to which we have committed ourselves, we see that inside the walls of the citadel of man his tyrannical enemies are sin, corruption, and death; outside are encamped Satan and his host. With them they have another oppressor of man, legalism, which, according to one modern scholar, Paul regarded as one of their weapons.[2] Whether we agree with this interpretation or not, there is certainly no doubt that Paul had come to see that legalism was a tyranny. Some have thought that his attitude to the Jewish Law was ambivalent in that there were times when he roundly condemned it, and other times when he not only extolled it in his writings, but also insisted on observing it scrupulously and on seeing to it that Jewish Christians did likewise (Acts 16. 3; 21. 26; I Cor. 7. 18).[3] Yet is there this contradiction in his estimate of the Law? It is true that he recoils in horror from the suggestion that it is a form of sin (Rom. 7. 7); more than that, he describes it as 'the oracles of

---

[1] *The Ideas of the Fall and Original Sin*, p. 157.
[2] G. B. Caird, *Principalities and Powers* (Oxford, 1956), Chapter 2.
[3] S. Cave, *The Gospel of St. Paul*, p. 129.

God' (Rom. 3. 2), 'sacred, just, good, and πνευματικός,' i.e. part of the divine activity (Rom. 7. 12, 14); but we must bear in mind that in those statements he was speaking, not of what the Law meant to him at the time of writing, but of what it had been in his experience. In this connection it is significant that in the Greek of Romans 7. 12 there is no verb. It is the English translators, following the Vulgate, who have supplied the present tense of the verb 'to be,' thus giving the impression that Paul was stating his evaluation of the Law as it was operating in his life at the time when he was writing Romans; but the past tense, viz. 'was' or 'has been,' would be more appropriate to the context since the apostle was describing what the Law had meant to him in his pre-conversion Jewish days. 'The Law *was* (or *has been*) sacred, just, and good.'[1] To the objection that he uses the present tense (ἐστιν) in verse 14 (οἴδαμεν γὰρ ὅτι ὁ νόμος πνευματικός ἐστιν) the reply can be made that at this point in his argument he is beginning to generalize from his own experience concerning the conflict taking place in the human personality between the commandments of the Law and man's lower nature, and, therefore, that what he means is that the Law *is* πνευματικός, in the sense that it still plays the role in the life of every man who acknowledges and tries to observe it, that it played in Paul's own life before his conversion. What that role was he makes abundantly clear. The Law had been instituted by God as an afterthought (παρεισῆλθεν) (Rom. 5. 20) 'because of transgressions' (Gal. 3. 19), i.e. to make men conscious that they were sinners (Rom. 3. 20; 4. 15). Thus its function was to act as man's παιδαγωγός (Gal. 3. 24), the tutor who supervised the education and moral upbringing of the son of a Roman household during his nonage.[2] It was, says Paul, using another simile, like the Roman boy's legal guardians (ἐπιτρόπους) and his bailiffs (οἰκονόμους), who managed his household and property (Gal. 4. 1–2). As Paul points out (*ibid.*), thus demonstrating his knowledge of Roman Law, while the heir

---

[1] As Winer comments, 'In the simple language of the NT the form (sc. of εἰμί) to be supplied is always clearly indicated by the context' (GNTG, p. 732).

[2] The παιδαγωγός 'did not merely conduct the boy to school, but had a general charge of him as a tutor in the old sense of the word, until he reached maturity' (VGT, p. 473).

is a minor (νήπιος), his status is that of a slave even though
eventually he will inherit all his father's possessions, and as a slave
he is not his own master, but is under tutelage until he reaches the
age of emancipation.[1] Similarly, before his conversion the
Christian, whether Jew or Gentile, is under authority until he
attains maturity, i.e. until he is converted, the authority of law;[2]
the παιδαγωγός—whose function is to teach him the meaning of
sin (Rom. 3. 20)—the ἐπιτρόπος and the οἰκονόμος, the legal
guardian and the bailiff, to whom, as a slave, he is in subjection.
All this is a reflection of Paul's own experience. He tells us that
he would not have known what sin was had not the Jewish Law
taught him its nature (Rom. 7. 7). Law, however, is, as Paul
discovered, powerless to liberate man from sin and give him a
sense of pardon (Rom. 3. 20; Gal. 2. 16; 3. 11). Indeed, by
forbidding him to perform certain actions it provokes him to
commit sin (Rom. 5. 20; 7. 8); and so Paul can say that 'the power
of sin lies in the law' (1 Cor. 15. 56) and that 'through the agency
of the law sin brings about death' (Rom. 7. 11). Thus the law,
like the oversight of the minor by his tutor, his legal guardian,
and his bailiff, is a form of tyranny: scrupulous observance of
legal enactments, whether those in the Torah or in any Gentile
code, was, as Paul knew from his own bitter experience, bondage
to what he calls τὰ στοιχεῖα τοῦ κόσμου (Gal. 4. 3, 8–9; Col.
2. 8, 20), elementary teaching.[3] Obedience to law, which involves
not only moral duties, but also ritualistic and ceremonial practices
like circumcision and the observance of the feasts and fasts of the
Jewish cultus (Gal. 4. 10; Col. 2. 16–17), is, like the Roman boy's
minority, a rudimentary stage of man's education, which he

---

[1] The Roman heir was emancipated at the age of twenty-five.
[2] The Gentiles had legal codes and also the law made up of the dictates of conscience
(Rom. 2. 14–15).
[3] Exegetes have devoted much time and space to the meaning of this phrase. The
interpretation that we accept is J. B. Lightfoot's (Comm. on Galatians, p. 167). Another
interpretation, suggested by most of the patristic writers and developed by some modern
scholars, is that Paul was referring either to the physical constituents of the cosmos,
especially the celestial bodies, or to the δαιμόνια who were believed to control them
(C. A. A. Scott, Christianity according to St. Paul, p. 31; and D. E. H. Whiteley, The
Theology of St. Paul, pp. 23–5). There are cogent arguments in favour of either interpretation; and it is difficult to accept either in preference to the other. Perhaps our judgement
should be: adhuc sub judice lis est.

leaves behind when he comes of age, i.e. when he becomes a Christian (cf. 1 Cor. 13. 11). There remains the objection that Paul himself observed the Law after his conversion and that he ordered Jewish converts to do the same. Can it be answered satisfactorily? First, there has been a tendency to exaggerate his practical devotion to the Law[1] : after all, Acts mentions only two instances of it (16. 3; 21. 26), and 1 Cor. 7. 18, if it does imply that Jewish Christians must keep the Law, should be interpreted in the context of Paul's conviction that the end of the age was very near. Secondly, he explains in 1 Cor. 9. 19-23 why he keeps the Law: expediency. As W. D. Davies writes, 'The observance of the Law was Paul's passport with Judaism. Had he ceased to be faithful to the former, such a meeting as that of the Council of Jerusalem would have been impossible, because a non-practising Paul would not have been taken seriously'.[2] It was 'for the sake of the Gospel' (1 Cor. 9. 23) that he submitted to what must have been distasteful to him.

This, then, was the predicament in which, according to Paul, whose analysis of the situation was the fruit of his own agonizing experience, humanity, and as far as pain, corruption and death were concerned, the whole of Nature, found itself. He believed that his own *cri du cœur* was being echoed by all men, who like himself had been brought to despair by the tyranny of evil in its various forms—the fear of demonic forces, the oppression of sin, the dread of death, and the burden of legalism: 'Miserable wretch that I am! Who will rescue me from this situation in which my personality is doomed to die?' (Rom. 7. 24). Nor where suffering, corruptibility, and mortality are concerned is evil limited to man: 'We know that the whole creation has been groaning in travail together with us until now' (Rom. 8. 22). Who indeed could deliver it? Without hesitation comes Paul's triumphant reply, once again the product of his experience: 'Thanks be to God that it is achieved through Jesus, our Lord and Messiah' (Rom. 7. 25). How does God achieve it? That question we shall attempt to answer in the next chapter.

---

[1] E.g. W. L. Knox, *St. Paul and the Church of Jerusalem*, p. 152. n. 54.
[2] *Paul and Rabbinic Judaism*, p. 74.

H

5

THEOLOGIAN

PART II—LIBERATION

Done is a battell on the dragon blak,
  Our campioun Christ confountet hes his force;
The yettis of hell ar brokin with a crak,
  The signe triumphall rasit is of the croce.

WILLIAM DUNBAR, On the Resurrection of Christ

To THE first movement, written in a minor key, of our imaginary Pauline symphony we have given the title 'Tyranny.' The second movement, in a major key, we call 'Liberation.' As the title indicates, it describes the operation by which man, and indeed creation as a whole, is freed from the tyranny of evil. Unless he wrote the Epistle to Titus, which is highly unlikely,[1] Paul uses neither the verb λυτρόω, 'to free persons or slaves by payment of a ransom,' nor the noun λύτρον, 'a ransom'; but he does use the noun ἀπολύτρωσις, 'the act of freeing by payment of a ransom' (Rom. 3. 24; 8. 23; 1 Cor. 1. 30; Eph. 1. 7, 14; Col. 1. 14). With these passages we must couple those in which he states that men have been 'bought, sc. out of slavery' (1 Cor. 6. 20; 7. 23; Gal. 3. 13; 4. 5. Cf. Acts 20. 28). The source of the Christian use of this metaphor, which occurs in Hebrews, 1 Peter, Titus, 1 Timothy, and Revelation as well as in the Pauline Epistles, was Jesus himself, who had spoken of the approaching ἀπολύτρωσις, at the end of the current age (Lk. 21. 28) and of his own life and death as a λύτρον ἀντὶ πολλῶν (Mk. 10. 45=Mt. 20. 28), 'a ransom in exchange for the lives of many.'[2] Of this last Paul was entirely convinced. In the life, death, and resurrection of Jesus the Messiah, God had acted to liberate man from slavery to evil

[1] On the authorship of the Pastoral Epistles, *v. inf.*, pp. v, 250 n. 5.
[2] On this *crux criticorum vide* V. Taylor, *The Gospel according to St. Mark* (London, 1962), pp. 444–6.

in all its forms (Rom. 3. 24; 6. 6, 17–18, 20–3; 8. 2; 1 Cor. 1. 30; Eph. 1. 7; Col. 1. 14). Just as Yahweh had freed the Israelites from Egyptian oppression through the agency of Moses in the archetypal act of deliverance, so now he has liberated all mankind from the tyranny of evil through the agency of Jesus the Messiah. The latter action is the antitype of which the former is the type (1 Cor. 10. 1–4).[1] What is more, liberation is not confined to man alone. In Romans 8. 18–25 Paul looks forward to the eventual liberation of all creation, which has been corrupted by Adam's sin and is, therefore, groaning and travailing in its bondage to decay and death. The price of liberation is a high one—nothing less than the death of Jesus the Messiah (1 Cor. 6. 20; 7. 23; 2 Cor. 5. 14–15; Gal. 3. 13; Eph. 1. 7; 2. 13; Col. 1. 20. Cf. Acts 20. 28). Neither Jesus nor Paul says to whom the price of liberation is paid, and it is gratuitous to press the metaphor and speculate about it as later theologians delighted to do.[2]

Although it was this idea of liberation that was foremost in Paul's mind when he was thinking of God's action in saving his creation through the agency of Jesus the Messiah and Lord from evil in all its forms, he supplemented it with other metaphors. First, there is the metaphor of what is usually called 'justification,' the understanding of which demands an examination of the meaning of the words δικαιόω, δικαιοσύνη, δίκαιος, δικαίωσις, and δικαίωμα, all of which occur in the Pauline Epistles. As with most biblical topics nowadays, no student begins from scratch; he has the advantage of the findings of those scholars who have wrestled with the problem of the precise meaning of these terms.[3] He should, however, beware of those who have interpreted them in the light of Western juridical notions, and

---

[1] As scholars have pointed out, whenever Jews used the metaphor of redemption, their minds went back to the Exodus. A. Richardson, ITNT, pp. 218–19. Yet this is the only occasion on which Paul explicitly mentions the event, although as C. H. Dodd says, he had it in mind in Rom. 3. 21–6 and Gal. 3. 23–4. 5 (Comm. on Rom. MNTC, p. 54), to which we would add 1 Cor. 5. 7.

[2] For a criticism of these theories vide Hastings Rashdall, The Idea of Atonement in Christian Theology (London, 1925), passim.

[3] To those mentioned by Sanday and Headlam (Comm. on Roms., ICC, pp. 147–53) I would add the names of Bengel, Gifford, Liddon, Meyer, N. P. Williams, C. H. Dodd, N. Snaith, Karl Barth, C. K. Barrett, and T. W. Manson.

also of those who have laboured strenuously, and still do, to
stretch them on Procrustean beds of various dogmatic systems.
As we have already made plain, it is an axiom of Pauline studies
that in order to comprehend the apostle's terminology the only
satisfactory course to follow is to discover what the words that
he uses mean in his Bible, the Septuagint, and, since he 'frequently
betrays the fact that the meaning of a Greek word used by the
Septuagint translators was determined for him by reference to
the Hebrew lying behind it,'[1] also what their Hebrew equivalents
in the original text mean. This is exactly what scholars have done
in their examination of the *ṣᵉdhākāh* (=δικαιοσύνη=righteous-
ness) group of terms, and although, not surprisingly, there is a
certain amount of disagreement among them,[2] they have reached
certain conclusions that can confidently be described as 'established.' First, it seems to be generally accepted that in the OT
Yahweh's *ṣedheḳ* or *ṣᵉdhākāh* (the two are practically interchangeable) denotes neither a state nor an abstract quality, but
his acts;[3] it is 'a transitive action and a visible manifestation of
Yahweh's being in his relations with men.'[4] Secondly, these acts
are saving, liberating acts; Yahweh's *ṣedheḳ* is what G. von Rad
calls a *justitia salutifera*.[5] This theme—that Yahweh's *ṣedheḳ* is
perceived in his continuous deliverance of Israel—recurs throughout the OT, and is found in what is probably its most ancient
fragment, the Song of Deborah (Jgs. 5. 11); it reaches its peak in
Deutero-Isaiah, where *ṣedheḳ* and *yēša'* are synonymous (Is. 45. 8,
21; 46. 13; 51. 6, 8; 54. 14, 17), and where Yahweh saves the
Gentiles as well as the Jews (Is. 51. 5). Thirdly, this article of
Israelite faith must be considered (as, indeed, all that the OT
contains must) in the light of the *bᵉrîth* and the doctrine of election. *Sedheḳ* 'belongs to the terminology of relationship. He is

---

[1] C. H. Dodd, *Comm. on Rom.*, MNTC, p. 10.
[2] E.g. concerning whether or not the fundamental concept of the Hebrew root *ṣdhḳ*
from which the words represented in the LXX by δικαιόω and its cognates is that of
conformity to a norm. E. Jacob argues that it is (*Theology of the OT*, Eng. tr. A. W.
Heathcote and P. J. Allcock, New York, 1958, pp. 94–5); but J. Skinner (art. 'Righteousness,' HDB, Vol. 4, p. 274) and, more recently, G. von Rad (*OT Theology*, Eng. tr.
D. M. G. Stalker, Edinburgh, 1962, pp. 370–1, 373) argue that it is not.
[3] G. von Rad, *OT Theology*, pp. 372–3; E. Jacob, *Theology of the OT*, p. 95.
[4] E. Jacob, *ibid.*   [5] *OT Theology*, p. 372.

just who does justice to the claims made upon him in the name of relationship.'[1] The relationship between Yahweh and Israel is defined in the *b^erīth*, according to which he has chosen her to be his own peculiar people, and will, therefore, deliver her from the evils that beset her and establish his sovereignty. Israel has no doubt that he is always faithful and loyal to the *b^erîth*, which he himself has created. It is, therefore, not surprising to find that although in the LXX the noun δικαιοσύνη (Yahweh's) mostly represents *ṣedheḳ* or *ṣ^edhāḳāh*, there are rare occasions when it is the translation of '*^emeth*, 'loyalty to obligations' (Is. 38. 19; Dan. 9. 13), and even of *ḥesedh*, 'kindness' (Gen. 32. 10; Exod. 15. 13; 34. 7; Is. 63. 7); and conversely when *ṣ^edhāḳāh* (Yahweh's) is translated ἔλεος, 'mercy' (Is. 56. 1). Thus the makers of the LXX rightly interpreted Yahweh's *ṣedheḳ* in saving Israel as a kind, merciful action, demonstrating his love for his chosen race.[2] Fourthly, the majority of those who have written on the subject of Yahweh's *ṣedheḳ* have stressed its forensic character; Skinner, for example, holds that 'the idea of Divine righteousness is based on legal analogies applied to the relation between Yahweh on the one hand and Israel or mankind on the other.'[3] He is the just judge (Jer. 11. 20; Ps. 7. 11), sitting on his throne and judging the world righteously (Pss. 9. 4, 8; 96. 13; etc.). The twofold function of a judge in Israel was to redress, acquit and vindicate, those who were in the right, and to condemn and punish those who were in the wrong. While both functions were important, the emphasis in the OT is placed on the former; the judge vindicates the innocent, the poor, the oppressed, and the helpless.[4] When they applied this idea to Yahweh, the Hebrews saw his main judicial function as that of vindicating themselves since they were his own peculiar people. For our purposes here it is important to remember that the verb δικαιόω, which Paul uses frequently, is in the LXX the equivalent of the Hebrew verb *hiṣdîḳ*, the hiphil of

---

[1] G. Quell and G. Schrenk, art. 'Righteousness,' BKW, Eng. tr. J. R. Coates (London, 1951), p. 29.
[2] On Israel's *b^erîth* obligations to Yahweh, *v. inf.*, p. 116.
[3] J. Skinner, art. 'Righteousness,' HDB, Vol. 4, p. 273.
[4] Ibid. p. 280.

ṣādhaḳ = 'to be in the right'; therefore δικαιόω = *hiṣdîḳ* means 'to cause someone to be in the right,' 'to put in the right,' and hence 'to give redress to,' 'to acquit,' 'to vindicate.'

These four ideas which constitute the OT doctrine of Yahweh's *ṣedheḳ* = δικαιοσύνη were taken by Paul and transformed by him in the light of his experience of Jesus the risen Messiah and Lord. First, as in the OT, God's δικαιοσύνη is an activity, evident to all in the proclamation of the good news about Jesus the Messiah and Lord (Rom. 1. 17; 3. 21, 25). Secondly, it is a liberating, vindicating action. The good news of God is his dynamic action, whose effect is the salvation of men (Rom. 1. 16). Men are being vindicated (δικαιούμενοι) by means of the redemption or liberation (ἀπολύτρωσις) that comes in Jesus the Messiah (Rom. 3. 24–6).[1] Thirdly, just as Yahweh's vindicating liberation of his chosen people, the Hebrews, was the outcome of the personal relationship with them which he himself had created, viz. the *bᵉrîth*, so now God's vindication of the New Israel is the consequence of a new act of election and a new *bᵉrîth*. This New Israel is the Christian Church, which is not restricted to Jews, but includes Gentiles as well. Christians are children of the new *bᵉrîth* (Gal. 4. 24–6), inheritors of God's promise made to Abraham (Rom. 4. 13, 16; Gal. 3. 29; 4. 28, 31), God's elect people (Rom. 8. 33; 9. 24–6), his chosen remnant (Rom. 9. 27–9; 11.1–7). Thus, as the relationship between Yahweh and the old Israel was a loving relationship, so it is with the relationship between God and the New Israel. He bestows his δικαιοσύνη, his vindication, on Christians as a free gift (Rom. 3. 24; 5. 17; Phil. 3. 9) in the person of Jesus the Messiah (1 Cor. 1. 30), thus demonstrating his love for them.[2] Finally, there is no doubt that Paul, like some OT writers, has in mind the forensic character of God's vindicating action. At the same time there has been a tendency to exaggerate this. In all three passages

[1] Some commentators stress that Paul thinks that vindication comes only in and through the death of Christ. They point to Rom. 3. 25 and 5. 9. We should, however, beware of thinking that Paul isolated the Cross from the rest of Christ's life. He regards it as the climax of his life, that which consummates it.
[2] *Vide* the next point.

(Rom. 5. 15–18; 8. 33–4; 2 Cor. 3. 9) where it is most marked, there is a contrast between the judicial sentence (κρίμα) of condemnation (κατάκριμα) pronounced on guilty man in consequence of the sin of Adam and the free gift (δώρημα or δωρεά) of God's vindicating verdict (δικαίωμα or δικαίωσις[1]), pronounced as a consequence of the work of Jesus the Messiah and Lord, whom Paul in Romans 8. 34 describes as pleading man's cause. The contrast seems to be between the two judicial functions of God as portrayed in the OT: the strictly retributive function—whereby God metes out punishment to those who deserve it, and his vindicating function—whereby he comes to the aid of those in need of it, the oppressed and helpless. Yet in describing the latter, Paul goes far beyond the forensic conception, for God acts more like a loving father, vindicating even sinners, than like a judge. That this was Paul's view is clearly obvious from Romans 4. 5, where he makes the startling statement that God 'vindicates the ungodly,' an action that is 'in plain contradiction of the civil justice which justifies the righteous.'[2] The question is whether or not he vindicates the sinner unconditionally. To that subject we shall return later.[3]

The reconciliation of those at enmity with each other provides Paul with another metaphor in his efforts to describe God's liberating activity. In this connection, the two verbs and the noun that he, and he alone of the NT writers, uses are καταλλάσσω, ἀποκαταλλάσσω (both of which mean 'to reconcile') and καταλλαγή, 'reconciliation.' Paul sees man, before he accepts Jesus as Messiah and Lord, as hostile to God, who reconciles him to himself through the agency of Jesus the Messiah (Rom. 5. 10; 2 Cor. 5. 18–19; Col. 1. 22; Eph. 2. 16). It needs to be stressed that according to Paul it is man who is hostile to God, and not God to man. Contrary to the idea expressed in such passages as 2 Maccabees 1. 4 f., 7. 33 and 8. 29, which speak of God's being reconciled to man, Paul's doctrine is that man is reconciled to

---

[1] The two words are practically synonymous.
[2] G. Quell and G. Schrenk, art. 'Righteousness,' BKW, p. 61.
[3] V. inf., pp. 118 ff.

God. It is man who must change his attitude (the simplest form of the verb—ἀλλάσσω from ἄλλος—means 'to alter,' as in Galatians 4. 20 and 1 Corinthians 15. 51) if reconciliation is to take place. Nevertheless, it is God who takes the initiative, not man; 'God in Christ was reconciling the world to himself' (2 Cor. 5. 19). In Christ, God reconciles sinful man to himself and thus liberates him from the bondage of evil. Nor is this reconciling action confined to mankind: it includes 'all things,' i.e. the whole universe (Col. 1. 20). Once again the source of Paul's thinking is the OT. He has taken the metaphor of reconciliation from the sacrificial procedure of Jewish ceremonial. This is clear from Romans 3. 25, where he states that God sent the Messiah to be a ἱλαστήριον, a word translated in AV and RV 'propitiation,' which implies that an angry God was demanding appeasement. The inaccuracy of this rendering has been conclusively demonstrated by C. H. Dodd, who has shown that the meaning of the verb ἱλάσκεσθαι in the LXX is 'to perform an act by which guilt or defilement is removed, and that the more accurate translation of it is "to expiate".'[1] It does not mean 'to propitiate,' i.e. to change God's attitude to man. As Jacob has pointed out, the Hebrew word of which ἱλάσκεσθαι is a translation, viz. kipper (piel of kāphar) means 'to erase.'[2] In the Hebrew sacrificial system the priest offered the sacrifices to expiate the people's sin, i.e. to erase it and thus rid them of what made them unfit for communion with Yahweh; in contrast, pagan sacrifices were regarded by those who offered them as an appeasement of a wrathful deity. Another important point is that although the Hebrews themselves found the victims and other sacrificial offerings, they believed that it was Yahweh who provided them. It was he who took the initiative, appointing the means of reconciliation because he desired the restoration of fellowship between himself and man. It is this idea that is behind Paul's statement that God has appointed Jesus as the ἱλαστήριον by which man is reconciled to him. There is little doubt that he had in mind specifically the ceremonial of the yôm hakkippûrîm,

[1] C. H. Dodd, Comm. on Roms., MNTC, p. 54. RSV translates ἱλαστήριον 'expiation.'
[2] E. Jacob, Theology of the OT, p. 293.

the Day of Atonement, when there took place the rite of expiation for the transgressions and all the sins of the people of Israel
(Lev. 16. 16). Indeed, it has been suggested that the word
ἱλαστήριον may well mean 'mercy-seat,' the kappōreth, the
ἱλαστήριον ἐπίθεμα (Ex. 25. 17), the cover of the ark in the
Holy of Holies, which was sprinkled with the victims' blood on
the Day of Atonement (Lev. 16. 11 ff.).[1] If this interpretation of
the word is correct, then Paul was thinking of Jesus the Messiah
as the place where the expiatory act by which God and man are
reconciled and man is thus liberated is performed.

At this point we are faced with an objection. We have said
that Paul taught that man was hostile to God and not vice versa.
How is it, then, that he speaks, as he explicitly does several times
(Rom. 1. 18; 2. 5, 8; 3. 5; 5. 9; 9. 22; Col. 3. 6; Eph. 2. 3; 5. 6;
1 Thess. 1. 10; 2. 16; 5. 9), of the wrath of God, thus apparently
implying divine hostility to man? One explanation, first given
more than a century ago by Ritschl and reproduced in a modified
form in our own day by C. A. A. Scott and Alan Richardson, is
that all Paul's references to the ὀργή τοῦ θεοῦ are eschatological.
Ritschl maintained that every time he mentioned the wrath of
God the apostle was speaking of the Day of the Lord, the Day of
Judgement.[2] If Ritschl is right, then Paul believed that God was
not hostile to man; his anger is retributive, judicial, and impartial;
it is the wrath of the judge, who has no resentful feelings towards
the defendant, but is righteously angry because the moral law
has been broken, and inflicts the punishment that justice demands.
Ritschl errs, however, when he says that all of Paul's allusions to
the divine anger refer to the Day of the Lord; in two instances—
Romans 1. 18 and 1 Thessalonians 2. 16—he is speaking of a
present anger. The theme of Romans 1. 18–32 is the sinfulness of
the Gentile world, which had been given the opportunity of
knowing the one true God through conscience and creation, but
preferred idolatry. As a punishment for this deliberate refusal to

[1] On the Day of Atonement vide W. Eichrodt, Theology of the OT, Vol. 1, pp. 130–1, 163 ff.
[2] A. B. Ritschl, De Ira Dei (Bonn, 1859), pp. 16 ff.

acknowledge him God handed the Gentiles over (παρέδωκεν) to every kind of moral depravity, which is a manifestation (ἀποκαλύπτεται) of his wrath. Thus, as the present tense of the verb ἀποκαλύπτω shows, it is operating now. The context of the other passage, 1 Thessalonians 2. 16, is an attack on the Jews of Thessalonica for obstructing the proclamation of the Christian gospel, for which, asserts Paul, the wrath of God came (ἔφθασεν— aorist) upon them; i.e. if Paul is using the tense grammatically, at some point in the immediate past. Thus once again Paul is saying that God's wrath does operate here and now. This is where we turn to the explanation given by C. A. Anderson Scott and Alan Richardson, who agree that Paul thought of the wrath of God as operating in the present, but that it was still eschatological (and therefore by implication judicial) because he believed that the eschaton had begun, that he was living in the last days;[1] in which case God's anger does not contain hostility towards man, but is *always* the retributive, righteous anger of the judge. Yet another interpretation of Paul's statements about the ὀργή τοῦ θεοῦ has been proposed in the effort to remove the idea that he believed that God was hostile to man. It comes from C. H. Dodd and A. T. Hanson, who maintain that Paul used the concept of the wrath of God, 'not to describe the attitude of God to man, but to describe an inevitable process of cause and effect in a moral universe.'[2] Hanson describes it as 'wholly impersonal,' 'a condition of man,' 'a self-operating process.'[3] What are our final comments on these speculations? We believe that the interpretation suggested by Dodd and Hanson is nothing more than a subconscious subterfuge, caused by their laudable reluctance to attribute any weakness of character (of which anger against persons is undoubtedly a sign) to the Christian deity.[4] The statement that 'God handed them over (παρέδωκεν)' to all kinds of sin (Rom. 1. 24,

---

[1] C. A. A. Scott, *Christianity according to St. Paul*, pp. 78–9; A. Richardson, *Introduction to the Theology of the NT*, p. 76.

[2] C. H. Dodd, *Comm. on Roms*. MNTC, p. 23.

[3] A. T. Hanson, *The Wrath of the Lamb* (London, 1957), p. 110.

[4] Ritschl had this same reluctance (*The Christian Doctrine of Justification and Reconciliation*, Eng. tr., H. R. Mackintosh and A. B. Macaulay, Edinburgh, 1900, Vol. 3, p. 233).

26, 28) seems to destroy their case decisively, for it describes a personal action, not an impersonal principle.[1] Admittedly the law of cause and effect operates here as it does everywhere else; sin begets further sin (and frequently illness and disease as well) and thus brings its own punishment;[2] but the stubborn fact remains that Paul describes this as the operation of the divine anger (cf. 1 Cor. 11. 29–30). The only satisfactory solution is that, as Anderson Scott and Richardson maintain, in this passage Paul was speaking eschatologically. As we shall point out later, Romans was written when his thought concerning the final consummation was moving in the direction of an inaugurated eschatology;[3] therefore in Romans 1. 18 ff. he may well have been referring to the retributive anger of God the judge, which he was beginning to display in the present age because the eschaton had started. There still remains 1 Thessalonians 2. 16. It is doubtful, in view of the apocalyptic emphasis of that epistle, whether we can say of that passage what we have said of Romans 1. 18 ff.. When he wrote 1 Thessalonians, the idea of an inaugurated eschatology had not yet swum into his ken; therefore when he wrote, 'God's wrath came upon (ἔφθασεν, aorist) them (sc. the Gentiles) at last,' he must have meant that God's anger was being visited upon sinners in the present age without any reference to the eschaton. On the other hand, as J. E. Frame says, it is possible that the aorist is proleptic,[4] in which event Paul was even there speaking of the retributive wrath of the Last Day. If this is so, then in every instance where he mentions the divine wrath, he is thinking eschatologically: God's judicial, retributive anger will show itself at the final consummation, and since the end-time has already begun, that anger is already manifesting itself in this present age.

---

[1] A. T. Hanson says that 'God gave them up,' is another way of saying, 'they gave themselves up' (as in Eph. 4. 19). On his premise it probably is. Cf. R. V. G. Tasker's remark: 'The wrath of God is an affectus as well as an effectus, a quality of the nature of God, an attitude of the word of God towards evil' (*The Biblical Doctrine of the Wreath of God*, London, 1957, p. 16).

[2] The fact that I differ from Paul, believing that sin produces idolatry, and not the converse, makes no difference to the argument. *V. sup.*, pp. 83–4.

[3] *V. inf.*, p. 163.

[4] *The Epistles of Paul to the Thessalonians*, ICC (Edinburgh, 1912), pp. 113–14.

Yet another metaphor used by Paul to portray the divine liberation of men is that of adoption. We have already referred to it in our discussion of the liberation of mankind from the bondage of legalism.[1] Until he is converted, man, trying to live according to legal requirements, is like the son of the household during his minority; he is treated as a slave. When in due course he comes of age, he is legally adopted into the family, no longer being treated as a slave, but as what he is, a son. Likewise God sent his son, Jesus the Messiah, to bring men adoption ($\upsilon\iota o\theta\epsilon\sigma\iota a$) in order that they might truly 'be his sons, fellow-heirs' of him who is 'the eldest among a large family of brothers,' and so be able to approach their divine Father, freed from the slavery of a life of fear and enjoying 'the liberty and splendour of the children of God' (Rom. 8. 14–17, 20–1, 29; Gal. 4. 4–7).

God in Christ liberates humanity, then, vindicating it by giving it a sense of pardon; reconciling it to himself; providing the means by which its sins are expiated; and adopting its every member as his son. That is a terse statement of Paul's soteriology. The question is, How does God carry on this activity when Jesus is no longer on earth? In the words and works of the historical Jesus God showed men the way of liberation. 'Repent and let God the loving, paternal sovereign rule your lives' was the gist of the message of Jesus; at the same time he gave men their example by living a life ruled by God, i.e. a life of self-sacrifice and service whose inevitable culmination was death. In the end he was put to death; 'ay, there's the rub.' Professor D. M. Baillie says that 'in the early days of Christianity, the question must often have been asked: What can make up to us for the loss of the actual presence of Jesus on earth? How can a precious memory take the place of His presence for those of us who once knew him in the flesh? And how can an old story, given by others at second hand, avail for those of us who never knew him in the flesh at all?'[2] He proceeds to point out that 'the Church was quite clear about the answer. It derived from Pentecost, and

---

[1] *V. sup.*, pp. 97–9.   [2] *God was in Christ* (London, 1961), p. 153.

amounted to this: Christians need not be content with either an old story at second hand, or a precious memory of the past, and those who never knew Jesus in the flesh are at no disadvantage as compared with those who did, because the divine Presence which he brought into the world goes on for ever in the hearts of his people through the Holy Spirit.'[1] This was one of the salient doctrines of Paul's theology; indeed, some would argue that it was the core of it. Jesus of Nazareth had been killed, but his death was not a defeat; it was a victory. In and by his crucifixion he conquered because his πνεῦμα remained in his adherents. In fine, this is one meaning of his resurrection, recalling Bultmann's view that the crucifixion of Jesus and his resurrection are one and the same event, the latter being an interpretation of the former.[2] In 1 Corinthians 15. 45 Paul writes: 'The first man Adam became a living psyche;[3] the last Adam became a life-creating spirit (πνεῦμα), sc. after his resurrection.' In another passage, which has occasioned plenty of debate, we read: 'The Lord is (or means) the Spirit, and wherever the spirit of the Lord is, there is freedom. But we all reflect the glory of the Lord with face unveiled, and so we are being transformed into the same likeness as himself, passing from one glory to another, for this comes from the Lord the Spirit' (2 Cor. 3. 17–18). Attempts, which perhaps arise from the fear of making Paul a binitarian, have been made by some scholars to prove that the first five and the last four words of that quotation do not mean what they plainly say: that the Spirit is identical with the risen ascended Jesus, Messiah and Lord.[4] Finally, we find this same equating of

---

[1] D. M. Baillie, *God was in Christ*, p. 153.

[2] 'Can mention of the resurrection of Christ be anything other than the expression of the significance of the cross?' *Kerygma and Myth*, Vol. 1, p. 44.

[3] It is impossible to find for this word an English equivalent except the anglicized original Greek word ψυχή. A. Robertson and A. Plummer give what seems to be an adequate paraphrase of the word: 'The ψυχή results from the union of the breath of life with a lifeless body.' *Comm. on 1 Corinthians*, ICC (Edinburgh, 1911), p. 373.

[4] This is the view of C. H. Dodd, *The Apostolic Preaching and its Development* (London, 1936), pp. 147; R. H. Strachan, *Comm. on 2 Cor.*, MNTC (London, 1935), p. 88; T. Rees, *The Holy Spirit in Thought and Experience* (London, 1915), pp. 98 f.; and E. Schweizer, *Spirit of God*, Eng. tr. A. E. Harvey (London, 1960), pp. 59–60. Cf. E. F. Scott, *The Spirit in the New Testament* (London, 1923), pp. 180 f; A. E. J. Rawlinson, *The New Testament Doctrine of the Christ* (London, 1926), p. 155 n. C. A. A. Scott, *Christianity according to*

the one with the other in Romans 8. In verses 9–11, *pace* C. K. Barrett,[1] a man's possession of the Spirit of the Messiah and the indwelling of the Messiah within him are two different ways of expressing the same truth, while in verses 26–7 Paul says that the Spirit intercedes for men, and in verse 34 that the risen, exalted Messiah performs the same action. This conclusion that the risen, ascended Christ and the Spirit were one and the same was the consequence of Paul's conversion experience. As G. B. Caird puts it, 'Paul had come to know Christ as a life-giving Spirit' at his conversion, and thereafter 'could never dissociate the experience of the Spirit from his experience of Christ.'[2]

The question is, What does Paul mean by this word $\pi\nu\epsilon\hat{\nu}\mu\alpha$, which, as a concordance reveals, occurs in his writings numerous times, and which is as nebulous as its customary English equivalent 'spirit'? It is possible to assert that the majority of Biblical students know that in the LXX the word $\pi\nu\epsilon\hat{\nu}\mu\alpha$ is the translation of the Hebrew word *rūaḥ* which has the root meaning of air in motion, and which was therefore the usual word for wind and breath; and because breath is closely connected with life and activity, Yahweh's or a man's $\pi\nu\epsilon\hat{\nu}\mu\alpha$ was his person possessing power ($\delta\acute{\nu}\nu\alpha\mu\iota\varsigma$), in action. This is also the basic meaning of the word in the NT. As applied to God, it denotes his creative, active, personal power, observable especially in the words and works of Jesus and after his death in the Christian community. It had been part of the prophetic message that in the period immediately preceding the Day of Yahweh there would be an abnormal activity of his spirit (Is. 32. 15; Jer. 3. 34; Ezek. 11. 19; Joel 2. 28–30). The early Christian community claimed that this was happening just as the Lord had promised (Acts 1. 8); God's $\delta\acute{\nu}\nu\alpha\mu\iota\varsigma$ was being given to its members to enable them actively to testify to the Lordship of the crucified, victorious Messiah

St. *Paul*, p. 258, says that Paul thought of the Spirit and Christ as equivalent but not identical. G. S. Hendry, *The Holy Spirit in Christian Theology* (London, 1957), pp. 22, 24–5, says that Paul identified the two, but distinguished between their spheres of operation, the objective (Christ) and the subjective (the Spirit).
[1] *Comm. on Roms.* BNTC (London, 1957), pp. 158–9.
[2] *The Apostolic Age* (London, 1955), p. 138.

(Acts 2. 14–21). It was left to Paul to develop this primitive pneumatology in the light of his own experience. The πνεῦμα, the activity, of the Church was that of Jesus himself, who was no longer dead, but in this way alive; and it revealed his personality vitally and vividly. Professor Wheeler Robinson sums up the matter thus: 'If, then, there is any truth in the Christian claim to have fellowship with God in Christ, He must be active through His real presence, and present by his real activity. This is what the New Testament means primarily by the Holy Spirit.'[1] God's πνεῦμα or Christ's πνεῦμα—they are one and the same (Rom. 8. 9)—is Christ's corporate personality, the Church, in action. It is perhaps unfortunate that the gender of the Greek noun πνεῦμα is neuter because it tempts us to picture the pneumatic activity of the Church as impersonal, whereas, according to Paul, it is personal (Rom. 8. 14, 26–7), for the Church's power (δύναμις) and activity (πνεῦμα) are those of the Messiah himself: the Church is the living personality of Christ. As Calvin puts it *tout court*: 'He (Paul) calls the Church Christ.'[2] That is what Paul means when he describes the Church as the σῶμα τοῦ Χριστοῦ, the personality of the Messiah (Rom. 12. 4–5; 1 Cor. 6. 15; 10. 16–17; 12. 12–13, 27; Eph. 1. 22–3; 5. 30; Col. 1. 18, 24; 2. 19). That is what Longinus meant in his answers to Procula's questions: 'Do you think he is dead?' 'No lady, I don't.' 'Then where is he?' 'Let loose in the world, lady, where neither Roman nor Jew can stop his truth.'[3] That is what Francis Thompson implied when he wrote:

> And lo, Christ walking on the water
> Not of Gennesareth, but Thames![4]

Much attention has been directed to the *fons et origo* of Paul's concept of the Church as the σῶμα τοῦ Χριστοῦ. Some think that its source was the Jewish idea of the corporate personality, according to which all the members of a body of people are so closely identified with their leader or a prominent figure in their

---

[1] H. W. Robinson, *The Christian Experience of the Holy Spirit* (London, 1962), p. 128.
[2] *Commentary on 1 Corinthians*, on 1 Cor. 12. 12.
[3] John Masefield, *The Trial of Jesus*, Act 3.   [4] *The Kingdom of God*, ll. 23–4.

group that it is not only named after him but also is regarded as his personality.[1] Others hold that the origin of the concept was a metaphor popular in classical circles.[2] Greek and Roman authors, notably the Stoics, compared a body of people, e.g. a commonwealth, to the human body.[3] Yet others, basing their theory on what we would regard as a mistranslation of 1 Corinthians 10. 17, viz. 'Because there is one loaf, we that are many are one body, for we all partake of one loaf,' think that the origin of the concept is to be found in the words of Jesus spoken over the bread at the Last Supper.[4] A fourth suggestion is that in our search we need go no further than the teaching of Jesus himself about 'the Son of Man,' by which he meant not only himself, but himself and his followers united to form one corporate personality. It is pointed out by those who hold this view that although Paul never uses the Greek equivalent of the Hebrew *ben-'ādhām* or the Aramaic *bar-nāšā'* or *bar-'enāšā'*, being 'too good a Grecian to translate *Bar-nasha* by so impossible a phrase as ὁ υἱὸς τοῦ ἀνθρώπου',[5] the teaching of Jesus concerning the Son of Man reappears in the Pauline concept of the Church as the σῶμα τοῦ Χριστοῦ.[6] Of these four hypotheses the second and the third can be dismissed fairly rapidly; the former because, although Paul was possibly familiar with the Stoic metaphor, it was unlikely that it was the source of his idea of the Church as Christ's σῶμα when there was (as we shall see) a doctrine held and taught by Jesus from which it could be derived, and the latter because, as we have pointed out, it is based on a mistranslation of Paul's words. This leaves the last hypothesis and the first; and we believe that the most plausible answer is a combination of both. The immediate origin of Paul's description of the Church as the

---

[1] *V. sup.*, p. 92.

[2] E.g. W. L. Knox, *St. Paul and the Church of the Gentiles*, pp. 161 ff.

[3] Zeno, *ap. Maximus Florilegium*, 6; Seneca, *De Ira*, 2. 31. 7; Epictetus, *Dis.*, 2. 10. 3. Cf. the oration of Menenius Agrippa to the plebs of Rome (Livy; 2. 32. 8), which Shakespeare reproduced in *Coriolanus*, Act 1, Scene 1.

[4] A. E. J. Rawlinson, essay 'Corpus Christi' in *Mysterium Christi*, ed. G. K. A. Bell and G. A. Deissmann (London, 1930), p. 228. On the translation of 1 Cor. 10. 17, *v. inf.*, p. 130.

[5] F. J. Foakes Jackson and K. Lake, *Beginnings*, Vol. 1, p. 380.

[6] A. Richardson, ITNT, pp. 138–9.

σῶμα τοῦ Χριστοῦ was probably the teaching of Jesus about the Son of Man, which consisted of the application by Jesus, not only to himself but to the whole company of his disciples, of the idea in Daniel 7. 13 of the corporate figure of 'one like a son of man' (i.e. a human being), who represented 'the saints of the Most High' (Dan. 7. 18, 22, 25, 27), i.e. a righteous remnant of the Jews. Jesus regarded himself and his disciples as the righteous remnant, the nucleus of the new Israel, the Messianic community.[1] This brings us back to the first of the four hypotheses, for it is obvious that in the Danielic vision, and therefore in the teaching of Jesus concerning the Son of Man, we have a version of one of the basic Hebrew concepts, that of the corporate personality.[2]

In his later epistles we find a development of Paul's doctrine of the Church as the σῶμα τοῦ Χριστοῦ; a man's body must have a head and so must the Church; and that head is Christ (Col. 1. 18; Eph. 1. 22; 4. 15). Using language redolent of medical writings, Paul says that the relationship between the σῶμα τοῦ Χριστοῦ and Christ its head resembles that which exists between the human body and its head. The limbs of the body are framed together (συναρμαλογούμενον) and knitted together (συμβιβαζόμενον) by the ligaments with which the body is equipped (διὰ πάσης ἁφῆς τῆς ἐπιχορηγίας), and the whole apparatus is connected with the head, on which it depends and from which it derives its strength (Eph. 4. 16; Col. 2. 19). If a body without a head is physiologically unthinkable, so is a head without a body. So Paul must have thought; for he offers us the daring, but perfectly logical, statement that Christ is incomplete without his σῶμα. Thus he describes the Church as the πλήρωμα of Christ, that which completes Jesus the Messiah (Eph. 1. 23).[3] This is obviously true

[1] T. W. Manson, *The Teaching of Jesus*, pp. 227 ff. It is more probable that the Son of Man concept came to Christianity from Jewish apocalypses than (as Rietzenstein, Bousset, Bultmann, and others have suggested) from some form of the Indo-Iranian myth of an Urmensch or Primordial Heavenly Man. However, Mowinckel is probably right in maintaining that the Son of Man of the Jewish apocalypses is a variant of the oriental myth. S. Mowinckel, *He that Cometh*, Eng. tr. G. W. Anderson (Oxford, 1956), pp. 420 ff. Cf. D. E. H. Whiteley, *The Theology of St. Paul*, pp. 114–17.
[2] On the relevance of this concept to Paul's Christology, *v. inf.*, pp. 183–4.
[3] On the meaning of πλήρωμα vide J. A. Robinson, *St. Paul's Epistle to the Ephesians* (London, 1907), pp. 255–9; and VGT, p. 520.

I

since Jesus would have ceased to exist except as an obscure reference in a historical record or a vague name that would sooner or
later have faded, had there not been created a band of followers
to perpetuate his πνεῦμα. Even the sufferings of Christ (the
Church has laid such emphasis on the *einmaligkeit* of the Cross
that this seems to us a startlingly bold assertion) are incomplete
without the sufferings of Christians (Phil. 3. 10; Col. 1. 24),
which means that the answer to Cauchon's question, 'Must then
a Christ perish in torment in every age to save those that have no
imagination?'[1] is an affirmative.

The Church, then, is the living σῶμα τοῦ Χριστοῦ, continuing
his liberating activity. She is the Christ, leading men along the
road to liberation from evil. Before they can be liberated, however, they themselves (so Paul says) must accept the proferred
gift of liberation. God takes the initiative in liberating humanity;
but his action cannot be effective unless man co-operates with
him. In Pauline theology this comes out most clearly when the
apostle is describing the saving, liberating action of God in terms
of δικαιοσύνη, although it is present also when he is using the
reconciliation metaphor, since, as we have seen, he makes it clear
that it is man who must change his attitude to God and not
vice versa if they are to be reconciled. Reverting to the use of the
metaphor of ṣedheḳ=δικαιοσύνη in the OT, we recall that
Yahweh's ṣedheḳ is depicted as his liberating vindication of his
people. The relevant question here is this: Did the Jews, and
more particularly the Pharisees of Paul's day, believe that God's
vindication of Israel was unconditional? According to some
statements in their beloved Torah, which they regarded as the
inspired Word of God, it was not. Exodus categorically states
that it is only 'if you will obey my voice and keep my covenant'
that 'you shall be my own possession among all peoples' (Ex.
19. 5). The terms of the bᵉrîth demanded loyalty and obedience
to Yahweh's commandments, and if Israel disobeyed them, then
she would cut herself off from him and suffer dire consequences

---

[1] G. B. Shaw, *St. Joan*, Epilogue.

(Lev. 26. 14 ff.; Deut. 31. 16 ff.; Jer. 11. 3 ff.; 22. 8–9). On the other hand, there was the reluctance of some of the prophets to credit that Yahweh would ever forsake his chosen people (Hos. 11. 8–9; Jer. 31 *passim*; 32. 27 ff.; Is. 49. 15–16; Ezek. 37. 26).[1] Later, this prophetic belief was taken to extremes by some of the apocryphal and pseudepigraphic writers, who asserted that Yahweh could not give up Israel. By the *berîth* he was bound to save his people. 'The planting of them is rooted for ever: they shall not be plucked out all the days of the heaven: for the portion of the Lord and the inheritance of God is Israel' (Ps. Sol. 14. 3) are words written by a Pharisee about sixty years before Paul's birth (cf. Ps. Sol. 9. 17–18; Wisd. Sol. 15. 1–2). This kind of thinking went to the extreme limit of absurdity with the claim that it was for Israel's benefit that God had created the world (4 Ez. 6. 55; Ass. Mos. 1. 11–12). To neither of these views—(*a*) that Israel would be saved only if she fulfilled the demands made on her by the *berîth*, i.e. by keeping the commandments of the Torah; and (*b*) that Israel would be saved no matter what she did—did Paul subscribe. It was in reply to the latter opinion that he wrote Romans 9. 6–29, where his argument, based on the fundamental conception of God's sovereignty, is that God can choose as and whom he pleases. As to the former of the two views, his own experience had taught him that the observance of laws was powerless to save man. 'By deeds commanded by the law no man will be vindicated in his sight' (Rom. 3. 20; Gal. 2. 16; 3. 11). Nor, holding this opinion, was he likely to have much sympathy with an elaboration of the doctrine of vindication by the observance of the Law, which some of his Pharisaic contemporaries held: that a man could add to the merits he had acquired from his scrupulous adherence to legal regulations, by performing charitable deeds, especially almsgiving, regular fasting, and payment of his tithes (cf. Lk. 18. 12), thus laying up for himself a treasure of good works in the sight of God (4 Ez. 7. 77; 8. 33 ff.; and 2 Bar. 14. 12); and if all that

---

[1] Deutero-Isaiah seemed to think that Israel had suffered more than enough for her backsliding: she had 'received of the Lord's hand double for all her sins' (Is. 40. 2).

did not suffice to vindicate him, there were the good deeds of the patriarchs, which were imputed to every good Jew; and that when the Last Day came, every man would be judged by his works: if his good deeds exceeded his transgressions, he would be vindicated; if they did not, he would be condemned. Thus God was as it were an accountant, who would inspect the ledger of every man's life to discover whether he had a credit balance or not. All these views, which Paul surely heard expressed in his pre-Christian days, and one of which, vindication by works commanded by the Law, had been his lodestar, he totally rejected when he became a Christian. He had found a new answer; the right answer (so he believed), to the question, on what grounds is a man vindicated? He is vindicated neither unconditionally nor by keeping the ordinances of the Torah and amassing a measure of good deeds. Certainly God makes demands on sinful man before he vindicates him—to say otherwise would be absurd since it would make God indifferent to a man's attitude. This is why it is misleading to interpret, as some Pauline exegetes have done, Paul's statements about God's δικαιοσύνη, e.g. Romans 4. 5, as if he believed that God forgave sinners without any response from them. To say that God acquits a guilty man even though he is still guilty, i.e. forgives the sinner even though he is still a sinner, and to call it a fiction[1] is not only to make him indifferent to man's behaviour, but also to make him a liar. Before he forgives a man, God requires a response from him. That response is not the performance of the actions enjoined in the Torah, but faith. God's vindicating activity is proclaimed in the good news that Jesus, crucified and risen, is Lord and Christ; it can only be effective if a man has faith. Faith, and faith alone, is the condition on which a man is forgiven (Rom. 1. 17; 3. 28, 30; 4. 3; 5. 1; 6. 9; 9. 30; 10. 6; Gal. 3. 6, 8; Phil. 3. 9). God's action in offering forgiveness to sinful man must, if man is to be liberated from sin and its consequences, be accepted by him. The key quotation cited by Paul (Rom. 1. 17) to support his argument is: Ὁ δὲ

---

[1] W. Sanday and A. C. Headlam, *Comm. on Rom.*, ICC, p. 36.

δίκαιος ἐκ πίστεως ζήσεται (Hab. 2. 4), which he takes to mean that a man is saved as a result of his faith.[1]

What does Paul mean when he speaks of πίστις as a human attitude and response? He answers that question in his references to the faith of Abraham, who 'put his faith in God and it was put down on the credit side (ἐλογίσθη αὐτῷ) as the equivalent of vindication' (Rom. 4. 3; Gal. 3. 6). He is quoting Genesis 15. 6 (LXX), which was a standard proof-text in rabbinical discussions, being used to prove that Abraham's faith consisted in his faithfulness in carrying out proleptically the legal ordinances contained in the Torah.[2] Paul uses it to prove that it did not! Abraham was vindicated, not by performing the deeds enjoined in the Torah, but by his attitude of reliance on God. He simply believed that God would keep his promise to give him an heir and thereby enable him to be the ancestor of many descendants. Thus Abraham's faith was confidence in God's faithfulness, and as such it is the type of which Christian faith is the antitype. The words of Genesis 15. 6 were written, not for Abraham alone, but 'for our sakes as well'; all whose faith resembles his are vindicated (Rom. 4. 23–4). It is the men of faith who are Abraham's true descendants (Rom. 4. 1 ff.; Gal. 3. 7–9). The Torah and circumcision are irrelevant, for Abraham was vindicated before either existed (Rom. 4. 10), the implication of which is that it matters not whether men are Jews or Gentiles where salvation is concerned: all who rely on God in Jesus Christ (Rom. 3. 22, 26), i.e. all who accept as Lord the crucified Jesus, whom they see risen and still alive in the πνεῦμα, the activity of his σῶμα, his corporate personality, the Church, are vindicated (Rom. 10. 9). Patently this

---

[1] The original Hebrew is ambiguous. The context of the words, which are spoken by Yahweh, suggests that the prophet was being informed that in the imminent Babylonian attack on Judah the man who was faithful to Yahweh and the Covenant would be saved. On the other hand, they may mean that he would be saved by Yahweh's faithfulness. This is how the LXX interprets it; to resolve the ambiguity of the Hebrew it inserts μου, 'my faithfulness' (Yahweh is speaking). Some MSS and versions of Rom. 1. 17 give the LXX rendering. If they are right, then Paul was following the LXX and meant that men were vindicated by God's faithfulness. The Qumran commentary on the verse interprets it as meaning both faithfulness in observing the Law and also reliance on a person, The Teacher of Righteousness.

[2] H. St. J. Thackeray, *The Relation of St. Paul to Contemporary Jewish Thought*, pp. 91–7.

decision to trust God involves a radical change of attitude on the part of sinful man. In short, the act of faith includes what is usually termed repentance, which the *Shorter Oxford English Dictionary* defines as 'sorrow, regret, or contrition for past action or conduct.' This definition does not fully convey the meaning of the Greek noun μετάνοια, its cognate verb μετανοέω, and the verb ἐπιστρέφω, as they are used by Paul. Turning to his Bible, the LXX, once again, we find that μετανοέω, which is used to translate the Hebrew *niḥam* (niphal of *nāḥam*),[1] and ἐπιστρέφω, the equivalent of the Hebrew *šûbh*, are virtually synonymous. These verbs are 'used absolutely and generally with the implication of a complete change of character and disposition, a turning away from a whole course of behaviour to a different course of behaviour. . . . It is a turning of the whole man from one way to another, a return to God and his obedience from some other attachment.'[2] This expresses perfectly what Paul means by repentance. For example, he tells his Thessalonian converts: 'You turned (ἐπεστρέψατε) to God from idolatry, to serve a living, genuine God' (1 Thess. 1. 9. Cf. 2 Cor. 3. 16). In a less happy vein he fears lest the Corinthians have not 'repented of' (here the verb is μετανοέω), i.e. have not turned from, their sensuality (2 Cor. 12. 21). The content of the act of faith, then, is a turning from every other allegiance to God and a complete confidence in him. If that prompts us to ask Paul why man should take this step, he tells us, first, that it is God's goodness that should lead us to turn to him (Rom. 2. 4), and if we then ask Paul how he knows that God is good, we hear him say: 'Christ died for us while we were still sinners, and that is God's own proof of his love for us' (Rom. 5. 8), by which he means that God has revealed his very nature in the life, death and resurrection of Jesus. Secondly, still in answer to our question why we should have confidence in God, he replies that Jesus the Lord lived a fully human life and through his crucifixion and resurrection conquered evil once and for all, thus making it

[1] The root of this verb is onomatopoeic: it means 'to pant' or 'to groan.'
[2] T. W. Manson, *On Paul and John*, pp. 58–9.

possible for man to do the same (Rom. 6. 4 ff.; 1 Cor. 15. 20 ff.; Phil. 3. 10–11; Col. 3. 1–4).

This act of faith by which man turns to God by accepting Jesus as Messiah and Lord, does not mean, however, that he achieves complete freedom from evil instantaneously: it is but the first step of the long journey towards that goal. Paul was a convert of long standing when he told the Philippians that he had not experienced his resurrection to the new kind of life all at once (ἔλαβον, aorist) (Phil. 3. 12). Although at his conversion he had been vindicated by virtue of his faith in Jesus the Messiah (Phil. 3. 9), it was no more than the beginning of the race. Using one of his favourite metaphors, drawn from the stadium, in a passage that has served as the theme of many sermons, especially at watch-night services, the apostle describes himself as a runner in a foot-race, straining forward in his effort to reach the winning-post, when he will be awarded the prize (Phil. 3. 12–14). To put it another way, at his conversion a man is like a new-born baby, at the start of his life (1 Cor. 3. 1; Gal. 4. 19). Maturity is his goal (1 Cor. 2. 6; 14. 20; Eph. 4. 14–15); a goal that many years after his conversion Paul had yet to reach (οὐχ ... ἤδη τετελείωμαι) (Phil. 3. 12). The liberation of the convert from sin takes time. If it is to be achieved, he must be completely united with Christ: he must be 'in Christ,' 'in Jesus Christ,' or 'in the Lord.'

We do not wonder that these phrases are associated with the name of Paul, for he uses them no fewer than 164 times. As Deissmann says, 'in Christ' is 'the characteristic expression of his Christianity.'[1] What does Paul mean by being 'in Christ'? Once again we are faced with what T. S. Eliot calls

> the intolerable wrestle
> With words and meanings,[2]

but however irksome it may be, it is a struggle that the theologian, or for that matter anyone else, cannot avoid if he wants to find the truth. It is well known among students of Paulinism that the first scholar to examine with any thoroughness the meaning of

---

[1] G. A. Deissmann, *St. Paul*, p. 128.   [2] *East Coker*, II.

the phrase ἐν Χριστῷ was Deissmann, who came to the conclusion
that it summarized a mystical experience.[1] He put it down to
Paul's 'mystical and prophetic nature,'[2] which led him to realize
that as a result of his conversion experience Christ was in him and
he in Christ.[3] Deissmann describes this personal relationship as
'the most intimate possible fellowship of the Christian with the
living Christ.'[4] It is obvious that Paul thought that by his conversion every individual Christian convert was united with Christ.
Indeed, so closely united are they that the believer's experience is
identical with Christ's own. As Christ did, he undergoes a
crucifixion, burial, and resurrection: it is the execution and burial
of the old unregenerate ego (σάρξ or ὁ παλαιὸς ἄνθρωπος), which
is a death to sin;[5] from which death a new redeemed personality
arises, a new self is put on, and the life which the convert lives
thereafter is no longer his own, but Christ's life within him
(Rom. 6. 3–11; 8. 10; Gal. 2. 20; 5. 24; Phil. 3. 10–11; Col. 2. 12;
3. 1–4). All this sounds beautifully inspiring; but what did Paul
mean by it? Deissmann rhapsodizes about Paul's mysticism, and
in his enthusiasm exaggerates the mystical strain in his thought.
Although the apostle's language concerning the conversion
experience of the Christian and its consequences may be reminis-
cent of the terminology that mystics use to describe the final
stage of the mystic way, the unitive life,[6] there is a world of
difference between Paul's concept of the state of him who is ἐν
Χριστῷ and the mystical idea of union with some nebulous
Absolute. Nor, as Professor W. D. Davies has ably demonstrated,
is it likely that Paul derived it from that leading feature of contemporary mystery cults, the notion of deification.[7] We return

[1] G. A. Deissmann, *Die neutestamentliche Formel 'in Christo Jesu'* (Marburg, 1892).
[2] G. A. Deissmann, *St. Paul*, p. 82.   [3] *St. Paul*, pp. 123 ff.   [4] *Ibid.*, p. 140.
[5] It is certain that Paul included in this death of the self physical death, i.e. if necessary,
martyrdom. So did Jesus (Mk. 8. 34–5 = Mt. 16. 24–5 = Lk. 9. 23–4).
[6] W. R. Inge, *Christian Mysticism* (London, 1925), p. 64.
[7] *Paul and Rabbinic Judaism*, pp. 89–93. The most that Professor Davies is willing to say
is that 'the mysteries quite definitely formed part of the milieu into which Paul brought
his gospel; that Paul undoubtedly would therefore be open to their influence, and that
many of the terms he used would have an undertone of meaning which would strengthen
the appeal of the gospel to the Hellenistic world' (*op. cit.*, p. 98). For an accurate summary
of the beliefs and practices of the mystery cults *vide* G. H. C. Macgregor and A. C. Purdy,
Jew and Greek: Tutors unto Christ, pp. 224–8, 273–90.

to the question, What did the apostle mean by ἐν Χριστῷ? Practical man that he was, he meant something far less vague, far less individualistic, and far less impalpable than some 'flight from the alone to the Alone,' some absorption into the divine. As we have already shown, he identified the ascended, living Christ with the πνεῦμα of Christ,[1] by which he meant the corporate σῶμα of Christ, the Church, in action; therefore, to be ἐν Χριστῷ meant to participate in that πνεῦμα, that activity, as a member of the corporate σῶμα. To be ἐν Χριστῷ is synonymous with being ἐν πνεύματι (Rom. 8. 9). Thus acceptance of the living Christ involved membership of the Church.

This immediately raises the question of Paul's teaching about initiation into membership of the Christian society. It is generally accepted that Paul taught that after a man had been converted, i.e. after the act of faith by which he acknowledged Jesus as Messiah and Lord, he must be baptized with water. His remarks in 1 Corinthians 1. 14–17, especially verse 17, although they were written when he was in a highly emotional state because of the divisions in the Church at Corinth, suggest that there were moments when he did not attach so much importance to the act of lustration as many Christian theologians think; and, indeed, the whole tenor of all his references to it is to emphasize the significance of the ceremony rather than the ceremony itself. In the first place, when a convert was dipped (βαπτίζειν) into the water, the action signified that he was being immersed in Christ (Rom. 6. 3; Gal. 3. 27). When a man accepts Jesus as Lord and Messiah, he is dipped into his personality and is thus united with him. As we have pointed out, Paul thinks that the convert is so closely identified with his Lord that like him he undergoes crucifixion, death and resurrection; a crucifixion of the unredeemed self, a death to sin, a burial of the old self and a resurrection to the new life in Christ. All this, says Paul, is represented by the baptismal ceremony (Rom. 6. 3–4; Col. 2. 12). There seems to be no doubt that he has in mind total immersion, regarding it as a dramatic representation of the convert's experience. The immersion

---

[1] V. sup., pp. 110–16, 183.

represents the death and burial of 'the old unredeemed self with the passions and lusts' (Gal. 5. 24), and the emergence from the water represents the rising to new life.[1] Since the living Christ, into whom the convert is immersed, now exists on earth only as a corporate σῶμα, the Church, baptism is immersion into the Church and its activity (πνεῦμα). 'We were all dipped into one σῶμα' and therefore into the πνεῦμα of that σωμα (1 Cor. 12. 13). This is that immersion into the activity (πνεῦμα) of Christ that had been foretold by John the Baptist (Mk. 1. 8 = Mt. 3. 11 = Lk. 3. 16), and to which the immediate disciples of Jesus had looked forward (Acts 1. 5). The second concept which Paul associates with initiatory immersion is the obvious one—purification. The cleansing property of water is mentioned when he tells the Corinthians that they have washed off for themselves (ἀπελούσασθε) the filth of their past life, and have been dedicated and vindicated (1 Cor. 6. 11). Similarly in Ephesians 5. 26 he tells his readers that the purpose of Christ's self-surrender was to cleanse the Church by washing it ἐν ῥήματι. The obvious interpretation of this passage is that Paul is alluding to baptism, and the ῥῆμα which he mentions seems to be the public profession of faith made by the convert. Romans 10. 9 and 1 Corinthians 12. 3 gives us its complete content: 'Jesus is Lord.'

The idea of immersion in Christ's πνεῦμα is not the only way in which Paul thinks of the convert's first experience of it. Using another aquatic metaphor, he says: 'We were all given a drink (ἐποτίσθημεν) of one πνεῦμα' (1 Cor. 12. 13). At his conversion a man is proferred, and swallows, his first draught of the Spirit. It would seem that Paul has the same picture in mind in Romans 5. 5, where he says that through the gift of his πνεῦμα God's love has been poured out (ἐκκέχυται) in men's personalities (καρδίαις).[2] The bestowal of the πνεῦμα on the Christian at his initiation is described also as a sealing (2 Cor. 1. 22; Eph. 1. 13; 4. 30). The

---

[1] C. A. A. Scott, Christianity according to St. Paul, pp. 117–18; W. F. Flemington, The N.T. Doctrine of Baptism (London, 1948), pp. 59–60; H. G. Marsh, The Origin and Significance of the N.T. Baptism (Manchester, 1941), p. 169.

[2] The perfect tense (ἐκκέχυται) means that an event has taken place in the past and the effect continues. καρδία means the seat of a man's life. MGLNT, p. 230.

verb in these passages, σθραγίζειν, means 'to impress with a seal or signet' for various purposes; viz. to denote ownership, to authenticate a document, and to ensure that goods reach their destination safely. The three passages cited would seem to contain all three metaphors. The πνεῦμα of Christ, i.e. his activity, which the Church continued and which began for its members with their initiation into the corporate σῶμα, was a mark denoting that they belonged to him, that his ownership of them was genuine, and that they would eventually obtain complete liberation. In this last connection Paul uses yet another metaphor when he describes the πνεῦμα as the ἀρραβών, a commercial term meaning the first instalment or earnest-money paid in advance of what will be given fully later (2 Cor. 1. 22; 5. 5; Eph. 1. 14). The πνεῦμα (the activity) that is assigned to the convert to carry on is but the beginning, the first instalment as it were, 'a token payment in guarantee that the whole amount is ultimately due.'[1] Using another metaphor to express the same truth, Paul speaks of the first-fruits (ἀπαρχή) of the πνεῦμα, the first part of the harvest, gathered when a man becomes a Christian (Rom. 8. 23). Eventually he will be given this activity to perform in full measure. Our last word on Paul's metaphors for the bestowal of the πνεῦμα on the Christian at the beginning of his journey is that (with the exception of ἐκκέχυται in Rom. 5. 5) the tense of the verb is in every instance the aorist, which indicates that Paul was thinking of a point in time; i.e. the moment of conversion.

The convert finds himself admitted to the σῶμα τοῦ Χριστοῦ, the Christian society, and thus immersed in the πνεῦμα τοῦ Χριστοῦ, the activity of Christ. What are the characteristics of that society and what is the nature of its activity? If it is the living personality of Christ, then its characteristics and activity are the same as his were: it says what he said and does what he did. Ideally, the corporate personality of Christ as it is described by Paul imitates Christ himself. In the first place, it is a unity. Both 'the God and Father of us all' and the Lord Jesus are each a unity; and so is the Lord's corporate personality, the Christian society

[1] R. H. Strachan, *Comm. on 2 Corinthians*, MNTC, p. 101.

(1 Cor. 10. 17; 12. 12; Eph. 4. 4). Like man's σῶμα it has many functions (1 Cor. 12. 5–6, 14) and like those of man's σῶμα all its various activities are manifestations of the one activity (πνεῦμα) (1 Cor. 12. 4–11). Paul scales the heights when he presses this metaphor (which is in fact more than a metaphor) a stage further in order to show that all the Church's activities are interdependent. The organs of man's σῶμα are dependent on one another. No organ functions in isolation from the others. All of them, whether εὐσχήμονα, ἀσχήμονα, or ἀτιμότερα, are equally important. So interdependent are they that when one suffers, all the others suffer with it, and when one is praised, all the others rejoice with it. Likewise all the functions of the σῶμα τοῦ Χριστοῦ are interdependent and equally important (1 Cor. 12. 15–26).

Since the Christian society is a unity in which all the functions are interdependent and equally important, it is, secondly, a communistic society, a κοινωνία; the κοινωνία of God's Son, Jesus the Messiah and Lord (1 Cor. 1. 9; 10. 16 ff.), having a common activity (2 Cor. 13. 14; Phil. 2. 1). This noun κοινωνία, popular nowadays with many Christians who have not begun to understand what it means, and who would probably be horrified if they did comprehend all its implications, is derived from the verb κοινωνέω, 'to have a share of, to go shares in something with someone.' From the beginning κοινωνία, 'sharing,' had been one of the salient characteristics of the Christian community (Acts 2. 42). Its members shared their possessions: those who had property sold it and handed the proceeds to the common purse, from which disbursements were made to any Christian who happened to be in need of financial aid (Acts 2. 44–5). One example of this primitive Christian communism is cited by Luke: the Cypriot Barnabas realized his land and gave the sum to the apostles (Acts 4. 37). The all-important fact is that this system (if we can call it that) was the outcome of the ἀγάπη by which the Christian society was ruled. Where ἀγάπη sits on the throne, inevitably a communistic, classless society is created. Where God is concerned, there is no προσωπολημψία (Rom. 2. 11; Eph. 6. 9; Col. 3. 25); and therefore in God's Church distinctions of race, status, and sex cease to exist (Rom. 10. 12; Gal. 3. 28; 5. 6; Eph. 2. 13–16; Col. 3. 10–11). The Church is a family whose father is God (Gal. 6. 10; Eph. 2. 19). George Herbert summed up Paul's teaching on this matter when he wrote, 'All equal are within the Church's gate.'[1]

One of the most intensive expressions of the Church's communism (κοινωνία) was the communal meal, which Paul calls 'the Lord's Supper' (1 Cor. 11. 20).[2] As Moffatt finely puts it, 'nowhere else could the local converts enjoy the consciousness of being one in the Lord. There, refined and unrefined, master and employees, mistresses and servants, officials and hucksters, people from the suburbs and from the slums, poor and well-to-do, respectable citizens and reclaimed waifs, all had the opportunity of owning their common debt to the Lord.'[3] Discussion concerning the nature of the archetype of the meal—known as the Last Supper—has been prolonged and profound.[4] Was it, as the Synoptists seem to depict, a Passover meal, or was it a *Kiddûš* eaten on the eve of the Passover to sanctify the imminent feast, or was it some other kind of meal? In our opinion, the most plausible of all the answers given to the question seems to be that it was a *ḥᵃbhûrāh* supper,[5] withal no ordinary one. This term '*ḥᵃbhûrāh*,' says Oesterley, 'means "fellowship," almost "love." . . . The root meaning of this word is a "bond"; then it comes to mean fellowship among men; and *chaber* means a friend.'[6] In the days of Jesus Jews were accustomed to form groups of friends who banded together 'for purposes of special devotion and charity, existing within the ordinary jewish (*sic*) congregations, much like the original "Methodist" societies within the Church

---

[1] *The Temple*, The Church Porch.
[2] Others were hospitality and the collection for indigent Christians, which Paul regarded as extremely important. *V. inf.*, pp. 206–7.
[3] J. Moffatt, *Comm. on 1 Corinthians*, MNTC (London, 1938), p. 159.
[4] For a comprehensive list of the many works on the subject *vide* J. Jeremias, *The Eucharistic Words of Jesus*, Eng. tr. A. Ehrhardt (Oxford, 1955), pp. 177–8. The thesis of this outstanding piece of scholarship is that the Last Supper was a Passover meal.
[5] For a criticism of this theory *vide* J. E. L. Oulton, *Holy Communion and Holy Spirit* (London, 1951), pp. 19–21; and N. Clark, *An Approach to the Theology of the Sacraments* (London, 1956), pp. 47–8.
[6] W. O. E. Oesterley, *The Jewish Background of the Christian Liturgy* (Oxford, 1925), p. 204.

of England before the breach with the Church authorities developed.'[1] These groups ($ḥ^abhûrôth$) used to assemble every week, usually on the afternoon of the day before the Sabbath, and on the eves of feast days, in the house of one of their number to eat a communal meal, every member of the $ḥ^abhûrāh$ contributing his share of the food and the wine. This function was not merely a supper: it was also a business meeting and a social occasion, a time for conversation about any topic of interest to the members of the $ḥ^abhûrāh$. It would seem that Oesterley is right when he says that 'the circle of friends formed by Christ and the Apostles constituted a Chaburah.'[2] Certainly the earliest description of the two most significant moments at the Last Supper, found in 1 Corinthians 11. 23–5 (a description whose source, so Paul claims, is the Lord himself which, we can infer, reached him through the apostolic tradition),[3] suggests that it resembled the $ḥ^abhûrāh$ meals. As the leader of the $ḥ^abhûrāh$ or the head of the house where the meal was being eaten did at the beginning of the meal, Jesus at the Last Supper took a cake of bread, recited over it a grace or blessing of God for the gift of bread, broke it and distributed the pieces among the company; as the leader of the $ḥ^abhûrāh$ or the head of the house did at the end of the meal, Jesus at the end of the Last Supper recited over a cup specially reserved for the purpose and known as 'the cup of the blessing' (1 Cor. 10. 16) another grace or thanksgiving to God (much longer than the first) for his gifts in general, and handed it round to every member of the company.[4] Yet, as we have already mentioned, the Last Supper was not a normal $ḥ^abhûrāh$ meal. The $ḥ^abhûrāh$ of which Jesus was the leader had almost certainly enjoyed many a communal meal; but this meal, the last that he was to share with his intimates on this earthly plane, he invested with a special significance. If, as many modern British NT

---

[1] G. Dix, *The Shape of the Liturgy* (London, 1945), p. 50.

[2] W. O. E. Oesterley, *The Jewish Background of the Christian Liturgy*, p. 172.

[3] As Dom Gregory Dix points out, Paul intended the responsibility for the historical truth of his description of the Last Supper to rest 'ultimately on Peter and those others at Jerusalem who were the only persons who had been present at the supper itself' (*The Shape of the Liturgy*, p. 64).

[4] The texts of the two graces are given by G. Dix, *ibid.*, pp. 52–3.

scholars appear to believe, the Johannine chronology of the Passion story is the correct one, the Last Supper was eaten twenty-four hours before the Passover;[1] therefore it could not have been either a true Passover meal or, pace the suggestion that the cup mentioned in Luke 22. 17 may have been a Kiddûš-cup, a Kiddûš because the Kiddûš took place either at the very beginning of the feast itself or, as some think, on its eve.[2] Mlle Jaubert's hypothesis that Jesus and his disciples followed the old Jewish sacerdotal calendar (as the Qumran sect did), according to which the Passover was kept on the third day of the week,[3] is ingenious but untenable, because, like every other theory that seeks to show that the Last Supper was a Passover of one kind or another, it is invalidated by the stubborn fact that in none of the accounts of the meal is any mention made of the food essential to the Passover feast, the roasted lamb, the unleavened cakes,[4] and the bitter herbs.[5] For the same reason, if for no other, the theory that is was an anticipated Passover must be abandoned. Yet the disciples of Jesus must have been thinking of the imminent feast; as his words and actions showed, Jesus himself interpreted his approaching death and its purpose in terms of this the most important of all the Jewish feasts. Furthermore, although this was the last ḥᵃbhûrāh meal that he ate on earth, it was the first of many such meals that, after he had assumed another form, he would share with his followers both present and future. In fact, he was originating a novel ḥᵃbhûrāh supper, at which he himself would always be present. According to 1 Corinthians and Luke's

---

[1] For the arguments in favour of the Johannine chronology vide W. O. E. Oesterley, The Jewish Background of the Christian Liturgy, pp. 158–72. Cf. V. Taylor, The Gospel according to St. Mark, pp. 664 ff., J. Jeremias, The Eucharistic Words of Jesus, pp. 4–5, and A. J. B. Higgins, The Lord's Supper in the N.T. (London, 1952), pp. 13 ff., who argue in favour of the Synoptic chronology. For an attempt to reconcile the two points of view vide W. Manson, Comm. on St. Luke, MNTC (London, 1930), p. 243.

[2] F. L. Cirlot, The Early Eucharist (London, 1939), pp. 8–9.

[3] A. Jaubert, RHR (1954), pp. 140 ff.; and La Date de la Cène (Paris, 1957), passim.

[4] In all the accounts of the Last Supper the word used for the bread is ἄρτος. If the cakes had been unleavened, surely the Evangelists and St. Paul would have used the word ἄζυμα (sc. λάγανα).

[5] B. Gärtner argues that it was a Diaspora Passover meal, which (so he claims) was eaten without the roasted lamb on the eve of 14th Nisan instead of on the eve of the 15th (John 6 and the Jewish Passover, Lund and Copenhagen, 1959, pp. 47 ff.). Unfortunately the evidence that he produces for his theory is flimsy.

longer text Jesus stated that the meal was to be repeated εἰς τὴν
ἐμὴν ἀνάμνησιν (1 Cor. 11. 24–25; Lk. 22. 19), a phrase that is usually
translated 'in remembrance of me'; but as more than one scholar
has shown, the word ἀνάμνησις does not mean a mere subjective
recollection of Jesus, but an objective action whose purpose was
to re-present his personality in the midst of the Christian society
again and again.[1] In view of these facts—that Jesus had instituted
the meal and promised that he himself would be present whenever it was eaten—the most appropriate name for it was that
which Paul gave it, the κυριακὸν δεῖπνον (1 Cor. 11. 20). The
adjective is derived from the noun κύριος, which Paul uses as a
title for Jesus the Messiah.[2] The Lord's Supper and the Messianic
banquet are proleptically one and the same meal.[3] Thereat the
final words of Jesus the Messiah at the Last Supper come true
(Mk. 14. 25 = Mt. 26. 29 = Lk. 22. 18); for at every Lord's
Supper he is present to drink the new wine of the Kingdom with
the New Israel, the Church.[4]

The inevitable question, which has engendered acrimonious
debate, is concerned with the manner in which the Lord is present
at his Supper. Terms like 'transubstantiation,' 'consubstantiation,'
'receptionism,' 'virtualism,' and the rest, have been, and still are,
even in these ecumenical days, the most important concern of some
theologians. Yet need any of them have been coined?[5] As the
Comte d'Argenson said to the Abbé Guyot Desfontaines in
another connection, 'Je n'en vois pas la nécessité';[6] for Paul
solves the problem for us, if problem there be, in 1 Corinthians
10. 16–17, which may be paraphrased thus: 'We use one
cake of bread at the Lord's Supper to symbolize the fact that
although numerous, we form one personality (σῶμα), the
living corporate personality of the risen Lord, which is called

---

[1] E.g. A. Richardson, ITNT, pp. 378–9. Cf. J. Jeremias's interpretation of ἀνάμνησις as
God's remembrance of the Messiah (*The Eucharistic Words of Jesus*, pp. 162–3).
[2] *V. inf.*, pp. 176 ff., 192 ff.   [3] D. E. H. Whiteley, *The Theology of St. Paul*, p. 180.
[4] *V. inf.*, p. 131.
[5] 'In actual fact the differences between Roman Catholics and all but an extreme wing
of their fellow Christians in this matter is one of terminology, emphasis, and above all,
habits of devotion.' M. Goffin, in *Objections to Roman Catholicism*, p. 30.
[6] Voltaire, *Alzire, Discours Preliminaire.*

the Church. The action of breaking and distributing the broken pieces of the one cake symbolizes the fact that every one of us has a share in that corporate personality.' In fine, the personality of the risen, ascended Lord is present at the Supper, the Christian *ḥᵃbhûrāh* meal, in the shape of the κοινωνία (a word that is an adequate Greek rendering of *ḥᵃbhûrāh*), the Church.[1] This had been the experience of Jesus' followers ever since he died. It is the meaning of the Emmaus story; it was not until the two disciples ate together and repeated the actions of Jesus in a miniature *ḥᵃbhûrāh* meal that the Lord's presence became real to them (Lk. 24. 30–1, 35). Similarly Peter could say, 'We ate and drank with him after he rose from the dead' (Acts 10. 41). It is, therefore, not surprising that 'the breaking of the bread' (which was not strictly a liturgical act,[2] taking place in a building called a temple, but the weekly communal meal of the Christian κοινωνία, eaten in someone's house on the first day of the week, the day on which Christians commemorated the Lord's triumph),[3] with which phrase in Acts 2. 42 the word κοινωνία is closely linked, was one of the salient marks of apostolic Christianity (cf. Acts 2. 46; 20. 7, 11), for the Church was a communistic society and the κοινωνία or *ḥᵃbhûrāh* meal was one of the outward and visible expressions of its communism. 'Holy Communion was Holy Communism.'[4]

Yet there have been, and still are, communistic societies inspired by hatred. Indeed, a large part of the globe is governed by a communistic credo one of whose articles is, 'I believe in the class-conflict as the means of establishing a new order.' 'The history of all human society, past and present, has been the history of class-struggle. Freeman and slave, patrician and plebeian, lord and

[1] Cf. O. Cullmann, *Early Christian Worship*, Eng. tr. A. S. Todd and J. B. Torrance (London, 1953), p. 18.

[2] This is not to say that the Church was wrong to make the Lord's Supper a liturgical act. I believe that the liturgy of the Mass is a true development of the original Lord's Supper.

[3] There is no justification for thinking that the Lord's Supper was called the ἀγάπη at this time. The only place where the word occurs in this sense in the NT is Jude 12. *Vide* J. Moffatt, *Love in the NT* (London, 1929), pp. 246–8.

[4] J. Lewis, art. 'Communism the Heir to the Christian Tradition,' in *Christianity and the Social Revolution*, ed. J. Lewis, K. Polanyi, and D. K. Kitchin (London, 1935), p. 480.

K

serf, master and journeyman, in a word, oppressor and oppressed, stood in constant opposition to one another and carried on an uninterrupted, now hidden, now open, fight, that each time ended in a revolutionary reconstitution of Society at large, or in the common ruin of the contending classes.' Many will recognize those as the opening words of the first main section of the Communist Manifesto; and whether this be an accurate interpretation of history or not, the Marxist infers from it that the only method of building a just order is to continue the class-war until the proletariat is victorious and the State withers away for ever.[1] In contrast, as Paul emphasizes, the essential quality of the Christian κοινωνία is not hatred of its enemies, but ἀγάπη for all mankind.

The first two characteristics of the Church, then, are that it is a unity and a κοινωνία; and since it is the σῶμα τοῦ Χριστοῦ, the corporate personality of Jesus the Messiah and the risen Lord, its third characteristic is that it is willing to sacrifice itself to the uttermost even as he was; for Jesus was not only the Son of Man, but also the Suffering Servant of Deutero-Isaiah;[2] and since the Church is the corporate Son of Man, she too is the Suffering Servant.[3] Complete self-abnegation, even to the surrendering of life itself, is expected of its members; the Church is a sacrificial society. The good news publicly proclaimed by Paul is summed up in the words 'Christ crucified' (1 Cor. 1. 23; Gal. 6. 14); and since the Church's life is an *imitatio Christi*, its members carry in their personalities the dying of Jesus and 'are always being given up to death for Jesus' sake' (2 Cor. 4. 10). 'I have been crucified with Christ' (Gal. 2. 20). 'I bear on my body the stigmata of Jesus' (Gal. 6. 17). 'We are killed all day long for thy sake; we are regarded as sheep to be slaughtered,' quotes Paul.[4] The Church shares and completes the sufferings of Christ (Phil. 3. 10; Col. 1. 24). These are no mere rhetorical flourishes. The *nekrōsis*

[1] By 'class' the Marxist means a group of people who have a common economic interest.
[2] On Jesus as the Suffering Servant, *v. inf.*, pp. 180 ff.
[3] This is clearly implied by Jesus himself in Mk. 8. 31–7 = Mt. 16. 21–6 = Lk. 9. 21–5, etc. On the whole subject *vide* A. Richardson, ITNT, pp. 133 ff.; 250–1; 303–4.
[4] The quotation (in Rom 8. 36) is from Psalm 43. 22 (LXX).

of Jesus, his Passion and death, is to be emulated by the Church: she follows her Lord, the Suffering Servant, along the *Via Dolorosa*, which is the *Via Crucis*. Like the Church's communism this characteristic finds expression at the κοινωνία meal. This time it lies not in the breaking of the cake of bread, but in the pouring out of the wine and the drinking from the common cup into which it has been poured. Paul quotes the Lord's *ipsissima verba* recited over that cup: 'This signifies the new covenant established by the shedding of my blood. As often as you drink from this cup, do it (or you do it) to bring back my presence among you (εἰς τὴν ἐμὴν ἀνάμνησιν)'; on which the apostle comments: 'For as often as you eat from this cake of bread and drink from this cup, you proclaim the Lord's death till he comes' (I Cor. II. 25–6); and in the previous chapter he has written: 'When we bless God over the cup of blessing (*sc.* and distribute the wine), we signify that we share in the shedding of Messiah's blood' (I Cor. 10. 16). Analysing these passages, we discover that they contain two cardinal propositions. First, a new διαθήκη was being inaugurated through the instrumentality of Christ's death. As we have said, although the Last Supper could not have been either a Passover meal or an anticipated Passover or Passover *Kiddûš*, that the thought of the imminent Passover was certainly in the mind of Jesus is shown by his words: 'I had eagerly set my heart on eating this Passover with you before I suffered' (Lk. 22. 15). The significance of the Passover for Jesus and all his fellow-Jews was enormous; for whatever may have been its origins in the pastoral period of Semitic history, every Jew celebrated it, in accordance with the obligation laid on him by the Torah, as the memorial of the birth of the nation, when the Hebrew tribes were liberated from Egyptian oppression and the *b^e rîth* was established at Sinai according to which Yahweh chose Israel to be his own chosen race (Ex. 12. 3 ff., 26 f.; 13. 11–16; 24. 1–8). The whole concatenation of events was enacted through the Passover ritual and ceremonial, of which one of the most important elements was the sacrifice of the lamb. From time to time Hebrew prophets had anticipated the making of a new *berīth* (Jer. 31. 31–4; 32. 40; Ezek. 34. 25; 37. 26; Is. 55. 3). Now that moment had arrived. This was a new liberation from bondage, a new Exodus from captivity;[1] by a new covenant a new Israel, a new people of God, a new race of men, was being created; and as with the ancient covenant there must needs be a sacrifice. This time it was not an animal that was sacrificed, but Messiah himself, to whose sacrificial death the new people of God owed its very existence. It was this to which Jesus was referring when according to every account of the Last Supper he spoke of his 'covenant-blood.' Without the shedding of blood in sacrifice no covenant could be ratified. The new covenant was, to use Tertullian's fine phrase, *testamentum sanguine suo obsignatum.*[2] In short, before the Lord's corporate personality, the Church, the new Israel, could be born, he himself must needs die. To be a risen, victorious Lord he must first be a sacrificial victim. Thus Paul was right to describe the Messiah as the Christian Passover victim (1 Cor. 5. 7). There was no roast lamb on the table at the Last Supper; the Passover victim was presiding. Through his sacrifice the victim becomes the victor; but even though victorious, he continues to be a sacrificial victim; and his corporate personality, the Christian society, must resemble Jesus in this, as in every particular: it is a sacrificial body. It is this fact that its members proclaim when they drink the wine at the Lord's Supper; for the wine signifies his blood outpoured. By blessing God over the cup of blessing and drinking its contents, Christians signify that they share his sacrifice; they 'proclaim the Lord's death till he comes' (1 Cor. 10. 16; 11. 26). They show that the victorious, risen Lord, identical with his corporate personality (σῶμα), of which they are members, is a sacrificial, suffering servant; and when they drink the wine, it is in that sense that they re-present (εἰς τήν ἐμὴν ἀνάμνησιν) Messiah the sacrificed victim, the lamb of the Christian Passover, as well as Messiah the victorious Lord. In short, at the Lord's Supper the Lord in the

---

[1] For a list of works on the Exodus typology in the NT *vide* W. D. Davies in *Ecumenical Dialogue at Harvard. The Roman Catholic Protestant Colloquium*; ed. S. H. Miller and G. E. Wright (Cambridge, Mass. 1964), p. 128, n.

[2] *Adv. Marcion*, 4. 40.

form of his corporate personality, the Church, is present as the victorious, sacrificial victim.

It was for this reason—that the Lord's Supper was an expression of the sacrificial κοινωνία of the Church—that the behaviour of some of Paul's Corinthian converts was incompatible with participation in it. In the first place, they had a penchant for creating parties in the ecclesia. There were their doctrinal divisions, which Paul roundly condemned (1 Cor. 1. 10–17); and there were also their social divisions, which showed themselves at the Lord's Supper. As it was a communal meal, every participant brought his contribution of food and drink. The opulent contributed an ample supply; the poor brought little. The cleavage between the two classes was evident at the communal meal, when, as Paul puts it, 'each one eats his own supper before the rest, sc. instead of with them' (1 Cor. 11. 21). Apparently it was a case of 'every man for himself, his own ends, the devil for all.'[1] When this happened, when every man consumed his own comestibles before the meal began, the wealthy satiated themselves and even became inebriated, whereas the poor were left hungry. Such conduct was a grievous offence against Messiah's body and blood, i.e. against his corporate, sacrificial personality, the Church, where there was no place for any kind of selfishness (1 Cor. 11. 27). It sprang from a failure to discern the body (μὴ διακρίνων τὸ σῶμα) (1 Cor. 11. 29). These last Greek words, which have given rise to endless discussion, and have been used to support the doctrines both of transubstantiation and consubstantiation, mean that, as Dean Stanley says, it was 'the community and fellowship one with another which the Corinthian Christians were so slow to discern.'[2] To this selfish conduct Paul attributes the ill-health of many of them, and even the death of some, which he interprets as God's judgement on them, a conclusion that we should be very reluctant to draw today.[3] The remedy for the disorders is that everyone must examine himself to discover

---

[1] R. Burton, *The Anatomy of Melancholy*, Pt. 3, Sec. 1.
[2] A. P. Stanley, *Christian Institutions* (London, 1881), p. 111.
[3] Cf. D. E. H. Whiteley, *The Theology of St. Paul*, pp. 184–5.

whether he is in the appropriate frame of mind, i.e. whether he realizes what the Lord's Supper is, before he takes part in it (1 Cor. 11. 28).

Another sign that the Corinthian Christians did not understand its nature was their attendance at idolatrous feasts in the precincts of pagan temples. Paul tells them: 'You cannot drink from a cup that signifies fellowship with the Lord and from a cup that signifies fellowship with demons' (1 Cor. 10. 21). He well knew that where the Corinthians were concerned there was more in idolatry than taking part in a sacrificial feast in honour of Aphrodite Pandemos, goddess of sensual love and patroness of the city, whose shrine, standing on the Acrocorinthus 1,900 feet above the sea, was one of the most splendid temples of the Graeco-Roman world. A prominent feature of her cultus was sexual copulation with the ἱερόδουλοι, the sacred prostitutes, who numbered more than a thousand and on whose account, wrote Strabo, 'the city was frequented and enriched by the multitudes who resorted thither.'[1] There was always the danger that the members of the Corinthian ecclesia, who were still in their infancy as far as their knowledge of Christianity was concerned (1 Cor. 3. 1–3), would succumb to the seductions of Aphrodite; indeed, the present tense (πορνεύωμεν) in 1 Corinthians 10. 8 shows that they were in fact surrendering themselves to the delights that she offered her votaries. Earlier in the letter Paul had enjoined them not to give way to this temptation on the ground that a Christian belonged to his Lord alone. By copulating with a temple prostitute he gave himself to her, robbing the Lord of what was his rightful property (1 Cor. 6. 12–20). Now Paul was pointing out that idolatry, which was a participation in the κοινωνία of the pagan deity, was incompatible with participation in the Lord's Supper, which was an expression of the κοινωνία of the corporate personality of Christ, the Church. To emphasize his admonitions he referred to the idolatry and sexual immorality of the spiritual ancestors of Christians, the Israelites, during their wanderings after their liberation from oppression (1 Cor. 10. 5–11). He intends their

[1] Strabo, *Geographica*, 8, 6, 20.

conduct and its consequences to be a warning example (τύποι) to his readers.[1] Paul's Corinthian converts had been liberated from the bondage of sin as the Israelites had been freed from slavery in Egypt; by baptism they had been incorporated into Jesus the Messiah (i.e. into his corporate personality, the Church) as the Israelites had been incorporated into Moses (i.e. the congregation of Israel, which he embodied); and they had the bread and wine of the Lord's Supper as the Israelites had had the manna and the water from the rock (1 Cor. 10. 1–4). Yet the Israelites had lapsed into idolatry when they worshipped the golden calf, and into immorality when they had sexual intercourse with the Moabite women (1 Cor. 10. 7–9). Let the Corinthians be warned by the dire fate of the idolatrous and fornicating Israelites not to imitate their conduct.

The Church, the corporate personality of Christ, is, then, a sacrificial κοινωνία, a fact that shows itself prominently at the κοινωνία meal, the Lord's Supper. Yet although it is a sacrificial community, there is no cultus in the ancient sense. For a thousand years the focal point of Judaism had been the Temple, the central shrine, the home of the sacrificial cultus, the habitation of Yahweh; and although by the first century A.D. it was the regular worship and instruction in the Torah in the synagogue and the home, rather than the Temple cultus, that unified the Jews,[2] nevertheless it was still true that 'no matter where he had built his house or pitched his tent, every Jew lifted his eyes and his heart to this chosen spot, the holiest of all holy places sanctified by God's majesty,'[3] and if we can trust Josephus, the faithful still flocked thither in large numbers at the great festivals.[4] The suggestion that the Temple cultus was obsolete would have horrified most, if not all, Jews. Even the earlier prophets who attacked it (Mic. 6. 6–8; Am. 5. 21–5; Hos. 6. 6; 8. 13; Is. 1. 10–14; Jer. 7. 21–8) had never for one moment contemplated the destruction

<hr/>

[1] A. Robertson and A. Plummer (*Comm. on 1 Cor.* ICC, Edinburgh, 1911, pp. 202–3) and J. Moffatt (*Comm. on 1 Cor.* MNTC, London, 1938, p. 131) point out that τύποι in 1 Cor. 10. 6 means 'warning examples,' not types. However, there is typology in 1 Cor. 10. 1–4. *V. inf.*, p. 235.
[2] G. H. C. Macgregor and A. C. Purdy, *Jew and Greek: Tutors unto Christ*, pp. 77–8, 82.
[3] Ch. Guignebert, *The Jewish World in the Time of Jesus*, p. 61.   [4] *B.J.*, 6.9.3.

of the building in which it was practised; and their successors had
a vision of it as the place of worship of men of all nations (Is.
2. 2–3 = Mic. 4. 1–2; Is. 56. 1–8).[1] Some scholars believe that
because Jesus quoted the words of Isaiah 56. 7 (Mk. 11. 17) he
had the same vision. It is doubtful whether this was what he
meant. It is clear that he anticipated the time when the Temple
would be superseded by another kind of temple. At his trial he
was accused of having threatened to destroy it and build another
not made by human workmanship (Mk. 14. 58 = Mt. 26. 61. Cf.
Mk. 15. 29 = Mt. 27. 39–40); and although the evangelist states
that the evidence against him lacked consistency (Mk. 14. 59), in
the light of Mark 13. 2 and John 2. 19 it would seem that he made
some reference to the destruction of the sacred fane of Judaism
and its replacement by another. What that was is indicated
by the Fourth Evangelist: 'He spoke of the shrine of his body
(τοῦ σώματος αὐτοῦ). When therefore he was raised from the
dead, his disciples remembered that he had spoken thus; and they
believed the scripture, and the words which Jesus had said' (Jn.
2. 21–2). The temple of which Jesus was speaking was his corporate personality, the Church, which was founded at and by the
resurrection.[2] Evidently the original apostles failed to understand
that Jesus had advocated the abolition of the Jewish cultus as
decisively as he had abrogated the Torah, for they continued to
frequent the Temple like pious Jews (Acts 3. 1). It was left to two
Diaspora Jews to repeat and expound the teaching of Jesus concerning the cultus. One indictment against the former of these,
Stephen, was that he had stated that Jesus of Nazareth would
destroy the Temple (Acts 6. 14). Although the author of Acts
applies the same epithet—'false'—to those who gave evidence
against Stephen (Acts 6. 13) as Mark and Matthew do to the wit-
nesses at the trial of Jesus (Mk. 14. 57 = Mt. 26. 59–60), it would
seem that the accusation was true; for one theme of the proto-
martyr's apologia was that the presence of God was not to be

[1] Both Is. 2. 2–3 and Mic. 4. 1–2 are probably post-exilic. *Vide* D. W. Thomas, art.
'Micah,' PCB, p. 632.
[2] Cf. C. F. D. Moule, art. 'Sanctuary and Sacrifice in the Church of the N.T.' JTS,
N.S., Vol. 1 (1950), pp. 29–41.

found in man-made shrines (Acts 7. 48–50). His point was that 'the Temple was not intended, any more than the Tabernacle, to become a *permanent* institution, halting the advance of the divine plan for the people of God.'[1] The new temple, which had super-seded the old, was the Messiah, who was still alive in corporate form, viz. the Church. This was the implication of Stephen's speech; and it was grasped and developed by him who, if we accept the evidence of Acts, was present at Stephen's death, Paul of Tarsus, who, in one of his most celebrated speeches, repeated Stephen's statement that God 'does not live in places made with hands' (Acts 7. 48 = 17. 24), and who later spoke of that temple which 'was built on the foundation laid by the apostles and prophets, Jesus the Messiah himself being the chief corner-stone' (Eph. 2. 20–2); the temple that was Messiah's corporate personal-ity, the place of the divine activity ($\pi\nu\epsilon\hat{\upsilon}\mu\alpha$) (1 Cor. 3. 16–17; 6. 19; 2 Cor. 6. 16), where the only sacrifice was a rational ($\lambda o\gamma\iota\kappa\dot\eta\nu$) one, viz. the offering of men's living personalities to God, by which, as Paul explains, he means that transformed in nature, they live lives of absolute worth, nobility, and complete-ness (Rom. 12. 1–2).

The fourth characteristic of the Christian society is its unique-ness. In the salutations of five of his epistles Paul calls Christians $\dot\alpha\gamma\iota o\iota$ (Rom. 1. 7; 1 Cor. 1. 2; 2 Cor. 1. 1; Phil. 1. 1; Eph. 1. 1), the Hebrew equivalent of which, *ḳōdheš* (sing.), means 'separated' and is applied in the OT to anyone or anything that is set apart from what is profane. In the OT it is frequently used of Israel. 'You are a people holy to Yahweh your God, who has chosen you to be a people for his own special possession out of all the peoples that are on the face of the earth' (Deut. 7. 6) is a statement that sums up the OT doctrine of election. Paul could say the same about the new Israel. In one of the most beautiful of all his metaphors he describes the Church as the bride of Christ, who loved her and gave himself for her, his purpose being to set her apart ($\dot\alpha\gamma\iota\dot\alpha\sigma\eta$) as holy and unblemished ($\dot\alpha\gamma\iota\alpha$ $\kappa\alpha\iota$ $\ddot\alpha\mu\omega\mu\dot os$) (Eph. 5. 25–7). Similarly he tells the Corinthian Christians: 'I have

[1] W. Manson, *The Epistle to the Hebrews* (London, 1951), p. 34.

betrothed you to one husband, to present you as a chaste virgin to
Christ' (2 Cor. 11. 2). The Church is Christ's chosen spouse. The
question is: For what purpose has Christ chosen her and thus set
her apart? As we have pointed out earlier, the most advanced of
all the Jewish prophets had taught that the Jews had been chosen
to save other nations;[1] but this teaching had never been popular,
and in the days of Paul most Jews believed that God took no
interest in other races except to destroy them or make them
Israel's slaves if they opposed her.[2] This teaching Paul vehemently
combats. He has his doctrine of election, but it is the antithesis of
the prevailing Jewish doctrine. God's *modus operandi* in history
is still to choose his own people to carry out his purpose (ἡ κατ'
ἐκλογὴν πρόθεσις τοῦ θεοῦ) (Rom. 9. 11), but his choice is no
longer limited to Jews. Those who belong to Christ, whether
Jew or Gentile, constitute the new Israel, the new people of God
(Rom. 4. 16–17; 9. 24; Gal. 3. 29; 4. 28). Thus the Christian
society is a new kind of race, a new humanity that includes Jew
and Gentile, circumcised and uncircumcised, slave and freeman,
male and female (2 Cor. 5. 17; Gal. 3. 27–8; 6. 15; Eph. 2. 15;
Col. 3. 10–11). Furthermore, Paul asserts—what must have
sounded blasphemous to Jewish ears—that it does not include
'everyone who belongs to Israel; they are not all children of
Abraham because they are descended from Abraham' (Rom.
9. 6–7). Indeed, since they rejected Jesus the Messiah, the majority
of Jews do not belong to the new humanity. Another important
term used by Paul to describe the Christian society and signifying
its election is ἐκκλησία, the assembly of ἐκκλήτοι, 'those called
out, summoned' (1 Cor. 1. 2; 12. 28; 2 Cor. 1. 1; Eph. 1. 22;
3. 9–11; 5. 32; Col. 1. 18, 24; 1 Thess. 1. 1). The LXX uses the
word ἐκκλησία to translate the Hebrew word that describes the
old Israel, ḳāhāl = 'congregation.' Like the ḳāhāl of the old
Israel, the ἐκκλησία of the new Israel is a society of people called
out by God, i.e. God's people.[3] According to Paul, the difference

[1] *V. sup.*, p. 19. [2] *V. sup.*, pp. 20, 50.
[3] The LXX never uses ἐκκλησία to translate the Hebrew 'ēdhāh, which is a synonym
for ḳāhāl. It uses συναγωγή.

between the old Israel and the new Israel is that the latter is the one true Israel, the one true people of God (Rom. 8. 17; Gal. 3. 7, 9, 16, 29; 6. 16; Eph. 3. 6; etc.).

The purpose for which the new Israel has been called out from mankind is the liberation of men from the bondage of all forms of evil, legalism, evil forces, sin and death. This purpose it carries out by proclaiming to them the Lordship of Jesus the Messiah, uniting them with him in his corporate personality, the Church, and thus building itself (1 Cor. 14. 5, 12, 26; 2 Cor. 12. 19; Eph. 4. 12, 16, 29). To this end its whole diverse activity (πνεῦμα) is directed. More than once Paul gives a comprehensive list of the various functions performed by the σῶμα τοῦ Χριστοῦ (Rom. 12. 6–8; 1 Cor. 12. 28; Eph. 4. 11). It is important to note that in Paul's figure of the Church as the σῶμα τοῦ Χριστοῦ, the organs (μέλη) represent not functionaries, not orders of ministry, but functions (διακονίαι) (Rom. 12. 4 ff.; 1 Cor. 12. 5–31). First and foremost, there is Paul's own chief function, apostleship.[1] Next in rank to it or perhaps even on a par with it (Eph. 2. 20; 3. 5) stands that prominent feature of primitive Christianity, prophesying, the essence of which was that it was interpretative. Like the Greek Διὸς προφήτης and the Hebrew nābhi', when a Christian prophesied, he was a proxy of the deity, God's inspired mouthpiece, explaining the divine message to men. Although prediction finds a place in prophetic communications (Acts 11. 28; 21. 11), it is not properly a part of prophesying, the purposes of which are to build up, to stimulate, and to encourage the believer (1 Cor. 14. 3), and by stirring the unbeliever to search his conscience, to convert him (1 Cor. 14. 24–5). Third in Paul's list in Ephesians comes the evangelistic function, which was carried out by men like those who dispersed after the martyrdom of Stephen, of whom one, Philip, is mentioned by name (Acts 8. 5). As Acts 8 shows, they were itinerant missionaries, travelling far and wide to proclaim the good news. The difference between this and the apostolic function can be most succinctly expressed by saying that every apostle was also an evangelist, but that not

[1] V. sup., Chap. III.

every evangelist was also an apostle. The evangelistic task was to pave the way for those who performed the function mentioned next in Ephesians 4. 11, but third in 1 Corinthians 12. 28, the pastors or teachers. After the evangelist had proclaimed his message, the teacher or pastor (synonymous words in this context) systematically instructed, trained, and nurtured the newly-won converts. In performing these three last functions the Church showed itself to be the σῶμα τοῦ Χριστοῦ, the personality of the Messiah, for they were aspects of his activity (πνεῦμα) when he had been on earth; his had been a ministry of evangelization, interpretation, and instruction. It had also been a ministry of δυνάμεις, works of power, i.e. what were regarded as miraculous cures. This service, too, his corporate σῶμα continued to give to men. When Paul makes a distinction between healings and δυνάμεις (1 Cor. 12. 28), he probably means by the latter, exorcisms. What does he mean by 'helpings (ἀντιλήμψεις)' and 'governings (κυβερνήσεις)'? The former probably refers to the function of giving assistance to all who needed it: the poor, the sick, the widows, the orphans and the strangers. It is a ministration that figures prominently in the life of the Apostolic Church (Acts 3. 1–10; 5. 15–16; 6. 1–6; etc.; 1 Cor. 16. 15) being an essential element of the κοινωνία. The word κυβερνήσεις, derived from the conception of piloting a ship (Acts 27. 11), undoubtedly refers to the function of guiding and superintending the affairs of the ecclesia. Those who performed this function were et οἱ προισταμένοι (Rom. 12. 8; 1 Thess. 5. 12); in short, the elders (οἱ πρεσβύτεροι) or overseers (ἐπίσκοποι) (Acts 20. 28). Finally, Paul mentions that curious phenomenon of primitive Christianity called glossolalia, speaking with tongues.[1] At the Christian meetings some believers would utter meaningless syllables, which indicated to those who listened that the speakers were divinely inspired. Although Paul regarded this function as important (1 Cor. 14. 2), and, indeed, claimed that he himself possessed the ability to perform it (1 Cor. 14. 18), he realized that it had its risks:

---

[1] It has recurred and still recurs at times. *Vide* W. Sargant, *Battle for the Mind*, p. 101; R. Knox, *Enthusiasm* (Oxford, 1950), pp. 360, 366, 553–7.

it could be too individualistic, it tended to induce pride, and it was liable to cause unbelievers to ridicule Christians (1 Cor. 14. 4, 23). It was for those reasons that he believed that speaking with tongues must be controlled and interpreted (1 Cor. 14. 6–20, 27–8, 39–40). The interpreting of tongues, i.e. the reading of the minds of those who in their ecstasy poured out gibberish, was yet another function in the Church (1 Cor. 12. 10, 30; 14. 28).[1]

To enable them to carry out these functions Christians were endowed with χαρίσματα, gifts bestowed by the divine activity, the πνεῦμα, Christ's activity in the Church, which Paul enumerates in Romans. 12. 6–8 and 1 Corinthians. 12. 8–10. In the latter passage, which is the earlier of the two, he gives a detailed list of these endowments. The words of familiar Whitsuntide hymns express the view which has become traditional and is derived from the LXX version of Isaiah 11. 2, that the Spirit's gifts were sevenfold;[2] but Paul mentions nine χαρίσματα in 1 Corinthians 12. 8–10, and even this is not an exhaustive list, for the Christian virtues must be included among the gifts of the Spirit.[3] The first group of the nine χαρίσματα given to the Church to enable her to carry out her functions consists of the intellectual gifts needed and supplied to carry out the apostolic, prophetic and teaching functions: the gifts of being able to expound the gospel with insight (λόγος σοφίας) and to impart a knowledge of it (λόγος γνώσεως). Secondly, there is the gift of faith, which in this context cannot mean the faith that every Christian possessed, but probably refers to the faith necessary to those who perform the four gifts mentioned next: the ability to effect cures, to exorcize, to prophesy and to discern whether prophetic utterances were true or false. Lastly, there is the spectacular, but suspect, ability to speak with tongues, with which Paul couples the capacity to explain the thoughts behind

---

[1] On the subject of the glossolalia vide J. Moffatt, Comm. on 1 Cor., MNTC, pp. 206–31.
[2] E.g. Bishop Cosin's couplet based on the Veni Creator Spiritus:
'Thou the anointing Spirit art,
Who dost thy sevenfold gifts impart.'
Also Dryden's lines derived from the same source:
'Plenteous of Grace, descend from high,
Rich in thy sev'nfold Energy.'
Examen Poeticum (1693)
[3] V. inf., Chap. 8 passim. Paul is as fond of listing virtues as he is of listing vices.

the meaningless utterances. His treatment of the χαρίσματα in Romans 12. 6–8 is more general. He mentions the faith that a prophet must have; the ability to teach; the capacity to encourage; the will to serve; the singleness of purpose, and the cheerfulness that those who perform acts of beneficence, such as almsgiving, require; and the zeal which is a *sine qua non* for those in authority.

To these extraordinary χαρίσματα of the Spirit must be added its other operations. Conversion and admission into the σῶμα τοῦ Χριστοῦ do not automatically and magically change the essential character of the convert, who is still prone to sin. As we have said, that is merely the first step of a long journey towards the goal of complete liberation from sin and its consequences. How can he, weak and fallible creature as he is, reach his goal? Paul's answer, which was also the answer of the Johannine Christ, is that the Spirit, the divine activity in the Church, helps him. Once a man has been converted he is no longer ἐν σαρκί, in the sphere of the old, unredeemed human nature, but ἐν πνεύματι, in the sphere of the divine activity (Rom. 8. 9). No longer is he ruled by law, sin, and death, but by the πνεῦμα (Rom. 7. 5–6; 8. 5–9). No longer is his thinking (φρόνημα) dominated by the σάρξ, thinking that is hostile to God and can only result in death, but by the divine activity (πνεῦμα), whence come life and peace (Rom. 8. 6, 11). No longer is he ψυχικός, an unredeemed, animal creature, but a man possessing the divine activity (1 Cor. 2. 13–15); not only is he in the Spirit, but the Spirit inhabits him (Rom. 8. 11; 1 Cor. 2. 13–15; 3. 16; 6. 19; 2 Cor. 6. 16), and he cannot

> guess its grace,
> Till he become the place
> Wherein the Holy Spirit makes his dwelling.[1]

How does the Spirit assist him in the continuing struggle with the σάρξ within his personality (Gal. 5. 17)? First, the πνεῦμα, the Christ-like activity of the Church, unifies its members. It was Paul's wish that every one of them might have a share (κοινωνία) of the Spirit (2 Cor. 13. 14; Phil. 2. 1). He emphasizes that there is but one

---

[1] Bianco da Siena (*ob.* 1434), tr. R. F. Littledale.

Spirit (1 Cor. 12. 4, 13; Eph. 2. 18; 4. 4), from which springs the unity (ἑνότης) of the σῶμα. As Wheeler Robinson says, κοινωνία is 'the most characteristic and comprehensive work of the Holy Spirit.'[1] Secondly, the πνεῦμα is the source of the Christian virtues, the χαρίσματα that Paul calls 'the fruit of the πνεῦμα' (Gal. 5. 22), the chief of which is ἀγάπη (1 Cor. 12. 31—13. 13).[2] The third way in which the πνεῦμα helps the Christian convert is to come 'to his side and take hold of him to support him' (συναντιλαμβάνεται[3]) (Rom. 8. 26) when in his weakness he finds difficulty in putting his longing for deliverance into words; all he can do is to groan and sigh (Rom. 8. 23). His sighing for liberation is the operation of the divine activity, which Paul describes as interceding for him; and God, who searches the mind of man thus learns his longings, and understands them (Rom. 8. 26–7). In all these ways the divine πνεῦμα operates to lead the Christian to the glorious freedom which he enjoys as a son of God, whom he addresses as 'Father,'[4] a warm intimate approach indicating that the Spirit is giving evidence that he is genuinely God's son and an heir to his rightful inheritance, liberation, which he shares with Messiah himself (Rom. 8. 15–17; Gal. 4. 1–7; 5. 13, 18). Thus liberated, he enjoys a new kind of life (Rom. 6. 4; 8. 11), which the divine activity creates within him (πνεῦμα ζωοποιοῦν) (1 Cor. 15. 45. Cf. Rom. 8. 2, 11; 2 Cor. 3. 6). This life (ζωή) is the gift of God (Rom. 2. 7; 5. 17, 21; 6. 23); but to enjoy it a man must sow the right seed, i.e. he must co-operate with the divine activity (Gal. 6. 8). If he is to enjoy it, his thinking (τὸ φρόνημα) must accord with the Spirit, and not with his unredeemed self (σάρξ) (Rom. 8. 6). What kind of thinking is the φρόνημα τοῦ πνεύματος? It is that which leads a man to live a life of sacrifice, a continuous self-crucifixion, what Paul calls 'bearing in our personalities the putting-to-death (τὴν νέκρωσιν) of Jesus'

---

[1] H. W. Robinson, *The Christian Experience of the Holy Spirit*, pp. 123–4.

[2] *V. sup.*, pp. 198 ff.

[3] The only other place in the NT where this word occurs is Lk. 10. 40.

[4] Paul uses the colloquial Aramaic word *Abba* with which Jesus began the pattern prayer (Lk. 11. 2) and his supplication in Gethsemane (Mk. 14. 36), and adds the Greek equivalent (Rom. 8. 15).

(2 Cor. 4. 10), of which baptism (Rom. 6. 3–4) and participation in the Lord's Supper (1 Cor. 10. 16) are outward and visible signs. Although the Christian possesses this life in this age,[1] it is essentially ζωὴ αἰώνιος (Rom. 2. 7; 5. 21; 6. 22, 23; Gal. 6. 8), eternal life, 'aionian life,' the life of the age to come. Thus it is an eschatological concept, this concept of eternal life; and it is to Paul's ideas concerning the eschaton, the final consummation, that we shall turn in the next chapter.

[1] In this particular, as in certain others, Paul's thinking resembles that of the author of the Fourth Gospel.

6

THEOLOGIAN

PART III. CONSUMMATION

That God, which ever lives and loves,
One God, one law, one element,
And one far-off divine event,
To which the whole creation moves.

TENNYSON, In Memoriam, Conclusion

IN SACRIFICIAL living the members of the Body of Christ must persevere till the consummation of the liberation of man and, indeed, of all creation. This subject of the final consummation is the theme of the third movement (which is in a major key) of the Pauline symphony. Like millinery, tailoring, and many other things, NT scholarship has its vogues. As George Crabbe wrote,

> Fashion . . .
> Rules e'en the wisest, and in learning rules.[1]

A glance at any current theological catalogue will suffice to show that one of our present fashions is eschatology. Like George Whitefield's 'blessed word Mesopotamia' the term has great power: it is freely bandied about in the study and the lecture-room, and is occasionally heard in the pulpit, for it is, to use Professor Barr's phrase, one of the 'rather good words' of biblical theology.[2] Although most of the effusions on this subject are concerned with the statements in the Gospels concerning the eschaton, Paul's forecasts about the ultimate destiny of the universe can hardly be said to have been neglected. As we ponder the various interpretations of them, like those who in *Paradise Lost* 'apart sat on a hill retir'd,' we sometimes find ourselves 'in wand'ring mazes lost.'[3] It is hard to see the wood because the

---

[1] G. Crabbe, *The Library*, line 167.   [3] John Milton, *op. cit.*, Book 2, lines 557, 561.
[2] J. Barr, *The Semantics of Biblical Language* (Oxford, 1961), p. 281.

forest contains so many trees. Yet amid the complexity and obscurity and while we may agree with the 'distinguished theologian' quoted by Dr. Kennedy as saying that 'a man may have several Eschatologies' simultaneously,[1] one conclusion seems to stand out clearly: that with the passing of time Paul's thinking about the final consummation changed substantially.[2] It is as long ago as 1899 that R. H. Charles distinguished four stages in this development: (a) 1 and 2 Thessalonians; (b) 1 Corinthians; (c) 2 Corinthians and Romans; (d) Philippians, Colossians, and Ephesians.[3] We concur with Charles that it is possible to discern four stages of development, but our arrangement differs from his: (a) 1 and 2 Thessalonians; (b) 1 Corinthians and Philippians;[4] (c) 2 Corinthians 1—9 (with the omission of 6. 14—7. 1)[5] and Romans; (d) Colossians and Ephesians.

What is the trend of Paul's eschatological development? In a comparatively recent, stimulating work an *avant-garde* theologian describes Paul's progress as 'a shift from an apocalyptic to a non-apocalyptic form of eschatology,' by which he means that in his earlier epistles the apostle was expecting a second coming of Jesus the Messiah from heaven, whereas by the time when he wrote his later epistles he had relinquished that expectation, and instead was awaiting 'the certain reduction of all things to the Christ who had come, and whose "coming to his own," alike in victory and in visitation, was *from now on* the ultimate and most pressing reality with which man must reckon.' In fine, Paul moved from a futurist apocalyptic eschatology to an inaugurated non-apocalyptic eschatology; and in so doing came into line with the teaching of Jesus himself and with that of his earliest apostles, in neither of

---

[1] H. A. A. Kennedy, *St. Paul's Conception of the Last Things* (London, 1904), p. 25.

[2] C. H. Dodd, *New Testament Studies* (Manchester, 1953), pp. 108–28.

[3] R. H. Charles, *A Critical History of the Doctrine of the Future Life* (London, 1913), Chap. 11. The book was first published in 1899.

[4] Professor T. W. Manson's arguments for an early date for the writing of Philippians are most persuasive (*Studies in the Gospels and Epistles*, Manchester, 1962, pp. 149–68).

[5] I accept the hypothesis that 2 Corinthians is made up of one epistle (2 Cor. 1—6.13 and 7. 2—9. 15) and fragments of two others (2 Cor. 6. 14—7. 1 and 2 Cor. 10—13). Since neither of these fragments contains any eschatological statements, we can ignore them here, and the same applies to Galatians.

which is there any reference to a second coming of the Messiah.[1] Is this an accurate judgement? Our scrutiny of the Pauline epistles in what we believe to be their chronological order will show that while it contains much truth, it is an over-simplification.[2]

No-one could join issue with Dr. Robinson on his description of the eschatology of Paul's earliest writings, the Thessalonian epistles, as apocalyptic. It needs no more than a superficial reading of them to convince us that we are in the realm of that futurist eschatology that we find in apocalyptic writings, both Jewish and Christian. The picture that Paul paints resembles that of the apocalyptic passages in the Synoptic Gospels (Mk. 13; Mt. 24—25; Lk. 21), and, as Dr. Robinson says, both Paul and the Synoptists 'draw at points upon a common stock of established eschatological symbolism.'[3] When he wrote the Thessalonian Epistles, Paul was expecting the Parousia of Jesus the Lord in his glorious majesty[4] (1 Thess. 2. 19; 3. 13; 4. 15; 5. 23; 2 Thess. 2. 1, 8). Using a familiar OT term, he equates this event with 'the Day of the Lord' (1 Thess. 5. 2; 2 Thess 1. 10; 2. 2), the day when the current order would be brought to an end and the new order established. A command will be given by God for the denouement of the cosmic drama, the archangel's voice and the trumpet-blast will be heard,[5] and Jesus the Lord will descend from the heavens, accompanied by his mighty attendants in blazing fire (1 Thess. 4. 16; 2 Thess. 1. 7). Dead Christians, who are asleep in their graves, will be awakened by the sound of the trumpet and, in company with Christians who are alive, be snatched up on the clouds to meet the Lord as he is descending (1 Thess. 4. 13–17). The Lord with his attending angels will then execute the retributive, final judgement on all God's enemies, who will suffer ὄλεθρος, a strong word meaning 'destruction,' 'ruin,' but not necessarily

[1] J. A. T. Robinson, *Jesus and his Coming* (London, 1957), pp. 160–1, 160 n. and *passim*.
[2] As A. N. Whitehead used to say, 'Simple solutions are nearly always bogus solutions.'
[3] J. A. T. Robinson, *ibid.*, p. 107. We believe, however, that Paul's picture of Jesus in the Thessalonian Epistles differs from that of 'the Son of Man' of the Synoptic apocalypses. V. *inf.*, p. 153 n. 2.
[4] In the *Koine* the word παρουσία was used to describe the visit of a royal or noble personage. *Vide* VGT, p. 497.
[5] These are what a musician might call the Wagnerian accompaniments of the Christian *Götterdämmerung!*

'annihilation.' Its meaning here (2 Thess. 1. 9) is probably exclusion from the presence of Christ. Nor does the adjective that qualifies it, αἰώνιος (= aeonian), mean 'everlasting,' but 'belonging to the coming age.' The punishment, therefore, which will be meted out to Christ's enemies is exclusion from his presence in the coming age. In contrast, his followers will enjoy his presence in the age to come (1 Thess. 4. 17). Like the sword of Damocles these events are impending: so imminent is the snapping of the thread that Paul himself and his converts will still be alive when it occurs (1 Thess. 4. 15, 17; 5. 23). When it does take place, the catastrophe will catch men unawares 'like a thief in the night' (1 Thess. 5. 2, 4). Yet before it happens, there will be a last rebellion (ἀποστασία) of the forces of evil against God. An anonymous human embodiment of wickedness, the tool of Satan, will appear and attack every cultus, and even seat himself in God's temple, claiming that he himself is a deity. Temporarily he is being restrained by someone who is as anonymous as he himself is. Nevertheless, he is working secretly and will appear when the restraining power ceases to operate. After his final fling he and all those whom he has duped with his signs and wonders will be destroyed when Jesus the Lord gives them the *coup de grâce* at the Last Judgement (2 Thess. 2. 3–12).

When we examine the components of this description of the end seriatim, we find that they all belong to the stock-in-trade of apocalyptic writers. First, there is the prelude to the parousia. While there is no reference in the Thessalonian epistles to the grim portents that, according to the apocalypses, must precede the end, and which became known as the birth-pangs of the Messiah (Is. 13. 6 ff.; Zeph. *passim*; Joel 1–2; Dan. 12; Or. Sib. 3. 796–808; Jub. 23. 13, 18–24; 2 Bar. 27; 48. 31–41; 70. 2–8; 4 Ez. 5. 1–13; 6. 18–24; 9. 3; 13. 29–31; Mk. 13. 7–25; Mt. 24. 6–22, 29; Lk. 21. 9–27), Paul does, as we have seen, devote a section of 2 Thessalonians to that commonplace of apocalyptic, the prophecy of the last onslaught of the forces of evil on God.[2] As students of

[1] In the *Koine* it means 'the loss of all that gives worth to existence' (VGT, p. 449).
[2] What an American would call 'the show-down,' a term taken from the game of poker.

the Pauline Epistles know, Paul's neglect to name both God's adversary, whom he calls 'the man of lawlessness' (2 Thess. 2. 3) or 'the lawless one' (2 Thess. 2. 8), and the power restraining him has given rise to much speculation concerning their identity. It is the kind of passage that is meat and drink to exegetes, and it would seem that not a single one of their hypotheses lacks some degree of plausibility. As it was in the caucus race, so it is here: 'everybody has won, and all must have prizes.'[1] It is possible that the adversary represents Jewish opposition to Christianity or is some actual Jewish messianic claimant who is attacking it, and that the restraining power is the Roman *imperium*, which Paul saw as the guardian of law and order (Rom. 13. 1 ff.). On the other hand, he may be alluding to Caesar-worship, which is being held in check by God himself, or even by the reigning emperor, Claudius, who is known to have discouraged it,[2] or by Jewish opposition to it. Then there is the interesting suggestion that he has in mind some military commander stationed in the provinces whose name has not yet been revealed (2 Thess. 2. 3, 8) and who will seize power by force when Claudius, the restraining authority, dies and there is a struggle for the succession.[3] Yet another possibility, suggested by the use of Paul's word ἀποστασία (2 Thess. 2. 3), is that he was thinking of a rebellion within the Christian ecclesia. Finally, there is the view, urged by Cullmann and by Munck, that Paul is referring to the final attack of Satanic forces without having any particular individual or set of individuals in mind, and that he is thinking of his own proclamation of the Gospel to the Gentiles as the restraining power, the removal of which refers to his death.[4] Only Paul and, presumably, his Thessalonian converts could tell us which of these hypotheses is the right one; but the student of Paul's theology need not worry on that account because his primary concern is with the fact that

---

[1] Lewis Carroll, *Alice in Wonderland*, Chap. 3.
[2] M. Cary, *History of Rome* (London, 1949), p. 588.
[3] C. Ryder Smith, *The Bible Doctrine of the Hereafter* (London, 1958), p. 149.
[4] O. Cullmann, *Christ and Time*, Eng. tr. F. V. Filson (London, 1951), pp. 164–6; J. Munck, *Paul and the Salvation of Mankind*, pp. 36 ff. For a criticism of this view *vide* D. E. H. Whiteley, *The Theology of St. Paul*, p. 239.

at the root of the passage lies the apocalyptic interpretation of history. This belief that before the end of the age there must needs be a final decisive struggle between good and evil seems to have originated in Ezekiel's prophecy of the invasion of Israel by an evil host, almost certainly the Scythians, led by a powerful figure named Gog, who would be definitively defeated by Yahweh (Ezek. 38–9).[1] Thereafter the theme recurs again and again in Jewish literature. In Daniel 7–9 and 11–12[2] and Jubilees[3] the wicked adversaries with whom the final battle must be fought are the Seleucid hosts commanded by Antiochus Epiphanes; in the Zadokite Fragments (CD) and the Qumran War Scroll (IQM) they are either those same Seleucid armies or more probably the Romans;[4] and in the later Jewish apocalypses they are certainly the Romans (Or. Sib. 3. 46;[5] Pss. Sol. 2. 30 ff; 17; 2 Bar. 40; and 4 Ez. 5. 1 ff.). It is this apocalyptic notion of the last battle between the old Israel and her enemies that Paul adopted and applied to the final struggle between the new Israel, the Christian ecclesia, and the forces of Antichrist.

Paul's belief that the end was imminent was yet another typically apocalyptic notion. 'The age is hastening fast to pass to its end' (4 Ez. 4. 26; cf. 4. 46–50; 14. 10–12; 2 Bar. 23. 7; 83. 1), and we find the same belief expressed in Mk. 9. 1 = Mt. 16. 28 = Lk. 9. 27, Mk. 13. 30, and Mk. 14. 62 = Mt. 26. 64 = Lk. 22. 69. Furthermore, the incidentals of the Parousia mentioned in 1 and 2 Thessalonians are all derived from apocalyptic thinking: the trumpet-blast (4 Ez. 6. 23); the clouds of heaven on which the Lord comes (4 Ez. 13. 3; Mk. 13. 26 = Mt. 24. 30; Mk. 14. 62 = Mt. 26. 64); the angelic attendants (1 En. 1. 9; 61. 10; 4 Ez. 7. 28; Mt. 16. 27; 25. 31); and the assembling of the Lord's chosen

[1] On the identity of Gog *vide* H. H. Rowley, *The Relevance of Apocalyptic* (London, 1947), pp. 33 f., 40; and S. H. Hooke, art. 'Gog and Magog,' ET, Vol. xxvi (1914–15), pp. 317–19.

[2] The identity of the Seleucid kingdom is cloaked under the title of 'the little horn' of a beast (Dan. 7. 8, 20–1).

[3] *Op. cit.* 10. 8; 11. 5, 11; 17. 16; etc. Both here and in the Zadokite Fragments the adversary is called 'Mastema' and 'Beliar,' both of which are names for Satan.

[4] In IQM they are called the 'Kittim,' originally the Hebrew name for the Cypriots, but later applied to any enemies of the Jews.

[5] In the Sibylline Oracles the enemy is called 'Beliar'. Cf. sup., p. 79 n. 1.

ones on the earth, who with their resurrected brethren are taken up into the clouds to meet the Lord and accompany him on the last stage of his return to earth (4 Ez. 14. 9; Mk. 13. 27 = Mt. 24. 31). These details serve to clothe the returning Jesus with what Vincent Taylor calls 'the glittering apocalyptic robe';[1] and it is hard to resist the conclusion that Paul had in mind (although for the reason which we have stated previously he did not use the designation) the supernatural Son of Man figure of the Similitudes of Enoch (1 En. 37–71) together with the similar Messianic figure of 4 Ezra 13 (Cf. 2 Bar. 30).[2]

The doctrine of the resurrection of the dead (1 Thess. 4. 16) is another product of the apocalyptic mind, the earliest explicit statement of it[3] being found in the first Jewish apocalypse, which was written by one of the *ḥᵃsîdîm*, the forbears of the Pharisees. Thereafter it became one of the fundamental articles of the Pharisaic faith. Like the apocalyptic writers (Dan. 12. 2; 1 En. 100. 5; 4 Ez. 7. 32) Paul spoke of the dead as being asleep (1 Thess. 4. 15). Although they are what men call 'dead,' they are still alive and can be awakened. In the Thessalonian Epistles Paul does not say in what form he expected the dead to be raised. There is no justification for applying his description of the living in 1 Thessalonians 5. 23 to the dead, and so inferring that he believed, as many, perhaps the majority of Jews, held that the corpse would rise from the grave to be reunited with the nepheš (Greek, ψυχή), which since death had been sojourning in Sheol, the sub-terrestrial realm of darkness, gloom, silence, and forgetfulness (Job 10. 21–2; Is. 14. 9–12; 38. 18–19; Pss. 39. 12–13; 88. 9–12; 115. 17–18). According to 1 Thessalonians 4. 17 it is Christians alone who will be raised from the dead. Paul makes no reference to the unconverted dead. This is his version of what seems to have been the prevailing Jewish apocalyptic belief (1 En. 90. 33;

[1] *The Gospel according to St. Mark* (London, 1952), p. 644.
[2] He may have had in mind the words of Jesus about 'the Son of man' in Mk. 13 = Mt. 24–5 = Lk. 21 as well; but in my opinion, if he interpreted them in terms of the Enochene Son of Man, he differed from Jesus, who (I believe) always used the phrase in the Danielic sense of the faithful remnant.
[3] *V. sup.*, p. 16.

92, 3; Pss. Sol. 3. 16; and 2 Bar. 30. 2), that only righteous Israelites would be raised to enjoy the blessings of the age to come.

The resurrection of the dead will be followed by the judgement, which according to the Thessalonian Epistles will be executed on God's enemies (presumably only those that are still alive, since Paul has not mentioned the resurrection of dead enemies) by Jesus the Lord. As we have seen, the fate of the former will be ὄλεθρος αἰώνιος (1 Thess. 5. 3; 2 Thess. 1. 9), 'aeonian ruin,' which according to the next phrase in 2 Thessalonians 1. 9 means exclusion from the Lord's presence in the age to come. Here again there is a resemblance to current Jewish apocalyptic thinking, although there the ultimate fate of the foes of the Jews is complete annihilation (Pss. Sol. 2. 35; 1 En. 37–71 passim; Ass. Moses 10; 4 Ez. 13. 37, 38, 49). To sum up our examination of Paul's eschatology in the earliest of his Epistles, it is clear that it is a Christianized version of Jewish apocalyptic.

This futurist apocalyptic thinking was still influencing Paul's mind to some extent when he wrote the next Epistle in our chronological sequence, 1 Corinthians. He can still speak of the Parousia of Christ (1 Cor. 15. 23) and while admittedly this is the sole occurrence of the term in this Epistle, the same concept is expressed by such phrases as 'the revealing of Jesus our Lord and Messiah' (1. 7), 'the coming of the Lord' (4. 5), 'the day' (3. 13), and 'the day of the Lord' (5. 5). Furthermore, he still believes that this event is imminent; so imminent that it will take place before he dies (15. 51). Then there is his teaching about the resurrection of the dead, which occupies the whole of the longest chapter of the Epistle and which (except in one important respect, to which we shall refer later) is a Christianized form of apocalyptic doctrine. The circumstance that provoked Paul to devote so much space to the subject was that some of his converts were questioning his teaching on it. It is highly likely that in their pre-conversion days, as Greeks, they had learnt to believe either that at death a man ceased to exist or that, as Plato taught, the soul was naturally immortal. In either event there is no resurrection:

when a man dies, his body decomposes and eventually becomes dust. Typical of the Greek view are the words of Aeschylus:

ἀνδρὸς δ'ἐπειδὰν αἷμ' ἀνασπάσῃ κόνις
ἅπαξ θανόντος, οὔτις ἔστ' ἀνάστασις.[1]

Evidently some of the Corinthian Christians, while, in order to become Christians, they must have accepted the proclamation that Christ had been raised from the dead, found it hard to credit that they themselves would be raised (1 Cor. 15. 12). In the Thessalonian Epistles Paul had had no need to produce any argument to support his apocalyptic conviction that the dead would be raised, presumably because none of his converts in Thessalonica threw doubts upon it. Now, addressing the sophisticated, sceptical Corinthians, he was compelled to give reasons for holding it. It was one of the basic tenets that, long before his conversion to Christianity, Paul had been taught by his Pharisaic instructors, this apocalyptic doctrine that the dead would be raised. This hope he retained after he became a Christian (Acts 23. 6; 26. 8); and it is the foundation of his argument in 1 Corinthians 15. He begins by reminding the Corinthians that they have accepted the belief that had been proclaimed to them that Christ had been raised from the dead (verse 1); a fact authenticated by his appearances to the apostles, including Paul himself, and a host of other Christian believers (verses 3–8, 15), and by the Corinthians' own conversion, which would not have taken place if Christ had not been raised from the dead (verse 17). Thus the fact that Christ had been raised proves the truth of the Pharisaic, apocalyptic doctrine that dead men can, and will, be raised. To drive the point home Paul presents the Corinthians with what is virtually the negative form of a syllogism:

Major premise (what some Corinthians were saying)—Dead men are not raised (verses 12–13, 16).
Minor premise—Christ was a dead man.
Conclusion—Christ was not raised (verses 13, 16).

[1] *Eum.*, lines 647–8.

Yet the Corinthians accepted the opposite conclusion. How, then, could they logically deny the major premise on which it depended: that dead men are raised? As an afterthought Paul later adds two further implications of the denial that the dead will be raised: both the Corinthians' practice of vicarious baptism on behalf of deceased kinsfolk and friends who had died without baptism[1] and Paul's own self-exposure to dangers, including death itself, are absurd (1 Cor. 15. 29–32). Furthermore, for good measure he throws at them the thought that if there is to be no resurrection of the dead, then men would do well to emulate the Jews of seven centuries ago who during Sennacherib's siege of Jerusalem said: 'Let us eat and drink, for tomorrow we shall be dead' (Is. 22. 13; 1 Cor. 15. 32). Whether or not Paul's argument convinced his doubting converts no-one can say. What we can say is that he himself wrote as one who was utterly convinced that the dead would be raised at the final consummation. This was no mere apocalyptic hope, as it seems to have been in his pre-conversion Pharisaic days. 'If, enjoying the kind of life (ζωή) that we who are members of Christ's Body, the Church (ἐν Χριστῷ), possess, we have nothing more than an expectation (sc. that the dead will be raised), then we are more deserving of pity than anyone else' (verse 19); but we do not need that pity, for the dead will be raised even as Christ has been raised. 'Christ,' writes Paul triumphantly, 'has been raised from the dead as the first-fruits of those who are asleep' (verse 20). The metaphor of the first-fruits, an allusion to the offering of the first sheaf of barley in the Temple at the Passover, signifies that Christ's resurrection 'is the anticipation and the realization of new life after death for the new humanity of believers.'[2] As he had said earlier in the Epistle, 'God both raised the Lord and will raise up us through his power' (1 Cor. 6. 14. Cf. Rom. 8. 11; 2 Cor. 4. 14).

Having attempted to prove to the Corinthians the reasonableness of his conviction that the dead will be raised, Paul then deals

[1] There have been more than sixty interpretations of 1 Cor. 15. 29! This seems to be the most plausible of them.
[2] J. Moffatt, *Comm. on 1 Cor.*, MNTC, p. 245.

with a question that someone in the Corinthian Church was almost sure to ask: If the dead are to be raised, what form will they assume at the resurrection? (verse 35). As we have mentioned, it is probable that the majority of Jews, including the Pharisees, believed that the physical bodies of the dead would be raised to be reunited with the *nepheš*, which since death had been sojourning in Sheol, and thereafter the resurrected ones would enjoy a blissful existence in a sensuous world where food, drink, and the pleasures of the marriage-bed abounded. There were those Jews, however, who could no longer accept this materialistic view of the age to come. Influenced by Hellenism, they had come to realize that the *bāśār*, the physical organism, decomposed and turned to dust; and some of them, e.g. the author of Wisdom, seemed to be moving even towards the Greek doctrine of the immortality of disembodied souls. Others there were who found a compromise between the materialistic view and the Greek view: at the resurrection, they were saying, the *nepheš* would be united with a new kind of organism, a transformed physical organism (1 En. 62. 15; 2 Bar. 51. 1 ff.). Jesus himself appears to have held this view (Mk. 12. 25 = Mt. 22. 30 = Lk. 20. 36); and whatever he may have believed previously, this was also Paul's opinion when he wrote 1 Corinthians. Thus his teaching was 'not an innovation, but an able and developed exposition of ideas that were current in the Judaism of the time.'[1] He saw that 'flesh and blood can never possess the privileges of membership of the realm ruled by God, and the perishable cannot possess immortality' (1 Cor. 15. 50). In what form, then, is man to be resurrected if he has to shed his physical organism? Paul's answer is that God will provide him with a new kind of organism, a σῶμα πνευματικόν (verse 44). Using the Adam-Messiah typology, he cites Genesis 2. 7 to show that into the first Adam God breathed life, making him a living ψυχή, the human animal; but the first Adam sinned, through which act sinfulness and mortality gained a footing in the human race, making man's σῶμα, his personality, corruptible; a personality of weakness and disgrace, subject to

[1] R. H. Charles, *The Apocalypse of Baruch* (London, 1896), p. 82.

death. The situation was restored when God sent the second and
eschatic Adam, Jesus the Messiah, who by his victory over sin
and death ensured that those who accepted him as Lord would be
raised from the dead. Thus Paul describes Jesus as a πνεῦμα
ζωοποιοῦν, 'a life-creating activity,' i.e. he creates the new, divine
life in man (verse 45); and at the resurrection, those who have this
life in them, i.e. those who are ἐν Χριστω will receive a new organism, a σῶμα πνευματικόν, which in contrast with the ignominious,
inglorious, corruptible σῶμα, the animal organism, will be honour-
able, glorious, and incorruptible (verses 42-4). Nor is it only the
dead who will be provided with this new organism. As the
σῶμα ψυχικόν is corruptible, every Christian who is alive at the
final consummation will be given a σῶμα πνευματικόν, the animal
organism being transformed into a new organism (verse 51-2).
To show his converts that a man can have two different kinds of
organism Paul points out that in creation there are different kinds
of flesh (of men, beasts, birds, and fish) and different kinds of
bodies, those on earth and those in the heavens (the sun, the moon,
and the stars); and when he wants an analogy to demonstrate how
the σῶμα ψυχικόν becomes the σῶμα πνευματικόν, he goes to the
natural world again: before it can be given the life that will
enable it to become wheat, the grain of corn must be sown in the
ground and decompose (verses 35 ff.). So must man's σῶμα
ψυχικόν decay and die before it can become a new organism.

From Paul's statements can we describe the nature of the σῶμα
πνευματικόν more precisely? It should be remembered that the
word σῶμα means the whole psycho-physical organism, the nearest
English equivalent of it being 'personality.' Thus what Paul is
saying is that at the resurrection the old personality is replaced
with a new personality, which Paul describes as πνευματικός.
Since adjectives ending in -ικος mean 'like'[1] and since πνεῦμα
means 'divine activity,' πνευματικός means 'like the divine
activity.' Thus the new personality that man is given at the
resurrection is a personality whose activity resembles God's
activity. This seems to accord with Cave's interpretation: Paul's

---

[1] GGNT, Vol. 2, p. 378.

conception of the spiritual body (he says) 'is free from all materialistic conceptions, and yet, at the same time, asserts, not a mere continuation of existence, but the full affirmation and expression of perfected personality.'[1] The penultimate word in that quotation is the most important one: the new personality that every individual Christian is given is 'perfected' because it is πνευματικός, i.e. its activity is like God's own. It is a conception that would have satisfied even a Greek.

There is one other question to be answered concerning Paul's teaching in 1 Corinthians 15 about the resurrection of the dead. Does he limit it to Christians? It is a moot point. According to Schweitzer he nowhere teaches that there will be a general resurrection.[2] On the other hand, J. Weiss and H. Lietzmann hold that τὸ τέλος in 1 Corinthians 15. 24 means 'the rest (sc. of the dead)';[3] i.e. Paul is enumerating three stages in the resurrection: (1) Christ has been raised; (2) dead Christians will be raised at the Parousia; and then (3) the rest of the dead (τὸ τέλος) will be raised. Whether we accept this interpretation of τὸ τέλος or not, the Adam-Christ typology of verse 22, with its contrast between the dire effects of Adam's sin and the beneficial consequences of Christ's saving work, demands that πάτνες refer to all mankind in both clauses; it was through Adam's sin that all men became sinful and mortal; it is through being 'in Christ,' i.e. through their membership of Christ's Body, the Church, that all men will be made immortal and enjoy the life of the age to come.[4] In this word πάντες the unconverted dead must be included. Further support for this interpretation of verse 22 is to be found in verses 25-8 and in 1 Corinthians 3. 13-15. In the former passage Paul prophesies the destruction of all evil by Christ and the subjection of the whole universe to God. Obviously an essential element in this process is the conversion of the

---

[1] S. Cave, The Gospel of St. Paul (London, 1928), pp. 252-3.
[2] A. Schweitzer, The Mysticism of Paul the Apostle, p. 67.
[3] Referred to and refuted by W. D. Davies, Paul and Rabbinic Judaism, pp. 293-4.
[4] As the phrase ἐν τῷ 'Αδὰμ in the first clause is not adjectival, qualifying πάντες, but adverbial, modifying ἀποθνήσκουσιν, i.e. indicating the sphere in which all men sin and so die, likewise the phrase ἐν Χριστῷ in the second clause modifies ζωοποιηθήσονται, indicating the sphere in which all men are quickened.

unconverted dead. In the latter passage, speaking of the condemnation of sinners at the final judgement, Paul emphasizes that
the fires of judgement will be purgative, destroying the evil that is
in them, but preserving their personalities. This suggests that the
conversion of the unconverted dead will take place at the final
consummation.

The fourth element of futurist apocalyptic to be found in
1 Corinthians is the doctrine of the final judgement. Although
there is no allusion to it in 1 Corinthians 15, there are references
to it elsewhere in the Epistle; in 1. 8 Paul promises his readers
that Jesus, Messiah and Lord, will guarantee (βεβαιώσει) that they
will not be called to account (ἀνεγκλήτους) at the judgement; in
4. 4–5 he says that the Lord himself will be the chief judge; in
6. 2 he states that Christians will share the judging with Christ;
in 3. 13–15, speaking of the condemnation of sinners, he says
that the fire of judgement will be purgative, destroying the
evil that is in them; and in 11. 32 he speaks of the judgement of
non-Christians.

In Paul's teaching on the eschaton in 1 Corinthians the Parousia,
its imminence, the resurrection of the dead, and the final judgement
—all these features of futurist eschatology—are to be found there.
Yet there are indications that his eschatological thinking was
beginning to change. First, there is an almost complete lack of
that incidental detail that is an essential part of apocalyptic, and
some of which is found in the Thessalonian Epistles. In fact, in
1 Corinthians it is limited to one item, the trumpet-blast (15. 52).
Secondly, there is no reference in this Epistle to the Messianic
woes, regarded by apocalyptic writers as an essential prelude to
the end of the age. To those who hold that the word ἀνάγκην,
usually translated 'distress,' in 7. 26 is a reference to the Messianic
woes, we would reply that a sounder rendering is 'necessity'; i.e.
it is on account of the nearness of the end of the age that it is
necessary that men should remain single. Thirdly, and most
important, it is apparent in 15. 25 that Paul was beginning to
modify his futurist eschatology; here he states that the Christ
must continue to reign (βασιλεύειν, present infinitive) until he

has conquered evil in all its forms, after which he will abdicate and hand over the raj to God the Father. Thus Christ had begun to reign and was at that moment reigning. Had Paul been asked—'When did he begin to reign?' presumably he would have replied, 'When he was raised from the dead.'[1] Although he had been put to death, evil was powerless to destroy him: he had conquered, and he continued to live and was still living and reigning *de jure*, if not *de facto*. To the further question, 'How is he reigning?' Paul's answer is that he is reigning in the form of his corporate personality, his body, the Church (1 Cor. 12). This means that Christians are already living in the end-time, that interim period whose *terminus a quo* was the resurrection of Jesus and *terminus ad quem* will be the final consummation. In short, the Rule of God had been (to use Robinson's word) 'inaugurated.' Combined with this concept is the apocalyptic notion of the final conflict, which was, according to Paul, being waged there and then. Although Christ was the *de jure* ruler of men, he was not yet their *de facto* ruler. The forces of evil did not yet acknowledge his sovereignty, and until they were overcome by the corporate Christ there was a struggle to be waged.[2] Fourthly, consonant with this conception of the present reign of Christ in the form of his corporate personality, the Church, is Paul's modification of yet another tenet of traditional apocalyptic, the belief that the dead would be raised at the final consummation. As we have seen, he devoted a comparatively large amount of space to this doctrine, and what he has to say is a Christianized form of the ancient apocalyptic hope. At the same time, side by side with what might be called the orthodox doctrine of the resurrection

[1] Or even 'When he began to proclaim the Gospel.' As the Synoptic Gospels show (Mk. 1. 15, etc.), Jesus believed that the eschaton had arrived with his own mission, withal in an inaugurated form.

[2] Although a conception of a temporary Messianic reign is to be found in certain passages, in the pseudepigraphic writers, viz. 1 En. 91. 12–17, 2 En. 33. 1–2 (it will last 1,000 years, i.e. it is literally a millennium), 4 Ez. 7. 28 (it will last 400 years), and possibly 2 Bar. 27–30. 1; 30. 36–40, 53–74, there is a fundamental difference between Paul's picture of the Messiah's reign and theirs: in the pseudepigrapha it is a true millennium, an era of complete peace and bliss, whereas in 1 Cor. 15. 24–5 it is a period of conflict between Jesus the Messiah and his foes.

of the dead he introduces an important new idea. By his resurrection Christ had become the ruler of men and was now reigning
in the form of his body, the Church; therefore since every
individual Christian had been incorporated into the corporate
Christ, the Church, and was thus, to quote a characteristic Pauline
phrase, ἐν Χριστῷ, he had been raised with Christ and was already
living in the new age. As we have seen, in 1 Corinthians 15, Paul
proclaims that the resurrection of Jesus guarantees that those who
acknowledge his Lordship will rise from the dead at the eschaton.
The question is, How does it guarantee it? Paul answers that it is
because the Christian is 'in Christ,' i.e. he is a member of Christ's
body, the Church, that he has already risen from the dead and is
enjoying the life of the age to come, which he cannot lose even if
he experiences physical death. To refer again to words that we
have already quoted, this is the meaning of 1 Corinthians 15. 19:
'If, enjoying the kind of life (ζωή, which means 'the life of the
age to come,' the ζωή αἰώνιος) that we who are members of the
Church (ἐν Χριστῷ) possess, we have nothing more than an
expectation (sc. that the dead will be raised), then we are more
deserving of pity than anyone else in the world.' Paul means that
it is more than a mere hope; that it is a certainty that Christians
will be raised from the dead at the final consummation because
they are already living the risen life, the kind of life that belongs
to the new age and must continue into the new age.

The eschatology of Paul's next Epistle, Philippians, differs little
from that of 1 Corinthians. Although he does not use the word
'Parousia' to describe it, he shows that he is still expecting the
return of Jesus the Messiah (Phil. 1. 6, 10; 2. 16; 3. 20) in the very
near future (4. 5);[1] and although the apocalyptic details of the
Thessalonian Epistles and (to a lesser degree) of 1 Corinthians,
e.g. the trumpet-blast, the attending angels, and the clouds, are
missing, he still pictures him as one who comes from the heavens
like the Son of Man of Jewish apocalyptic (Phil. 3. 20). As to the

[1] C. H. Dodd thinks that Phil. 4. 5 is not a reference to the Parousia, but an echo of
Ps. 145. 18, which refers to the nearness of the Lord to those who are praying (*New Testament Studies*, Manchester, 1953, p. 112).

resurrection of the dead, in the first place, 3. 9–11 means that while it is an objective to be attained at the final consummation, Paul can know its power in the present age; thus it is inaugurated here and now. Secondly, he repeats the idea expressed in 1 Corinthians 15 of the transformation of the physical organism (3. 21). His one new eschatological statement in this Epistle is that if he were to die, he would be 'with Christ' (1. 23), a thought that, as we shall see in the next paragraph, is elaborated in 2 Corinthians 1–9. Possibly he had relinquished the idea that at death a man fell asleep.

In the next two letters in our sequence, 2 Corinthians 1–9 and Romans, the emphasis on inaugurated eschatology has increased, although it is not so pronounced as some scholars would have us believe; there is still a certain amount of futurist eschatology. Although he never uses the term 'Parousia'—as in Philippians—he is still expecting 'the day of Jesus our Lord' (2 Cor. 1. 14), 'the day of wrath' (Rom. 2. 5), when all men will be judged at God's, which is at the same time Messiah's, tribunal (2 Cor. 5. 10; Rom. 2. 16; 14. 10). Furthermore, he still thinks that the end is imminent (Rom. 13. 11–12); nor does the belief, apparently implied in 2 Corinthians 4. 14, that he will be in his grave before the final consummation imply the contrary, because, as the context shows, he wrote those words when his sufferings were bringing home to him his frailty, and his thoughts were turning to the possibility of having to face death in the very near future (2 Cor. 4. 7–12). In addition, there now appears in his writings for the first time another current apocalyptic idea. In Romans 8. 18–22 he says that man is not alone in looking forward to the final consummation: the rest of the natural creation shares his expectation because it, as well as man, will be liberated from its bondage to decay.' There is frustration in nature, which 'sighs and throbs with pain';[1] but all this will be rectified when the consummation comes. Paul had implied this conviction in an earlier Epistle (1 Cor. 15. 28); here he states it explicitly. It

[1] For a most illuminating exegesis of this passage *vide* C. H. Dodd, *Comm. on Rom.*, MNTC, pp. 133–5.

M

accords with the Jewish idea that Adam's fall adversely affected not only mankind, but the whole of the natural creation, and that when the Messiah came, this wrong, like all the others, would be righted. There is an early hint of this belief in Isaiah 11. 6–9, and an expanded statement of it in Isaiah 65. 17–25; but the place where it figures most prominently is the pseudepigrapha (e.g. 1 En. 45. 4 f.; 51. 4; 4 Ez. 7. 75; 2 Bar. 29. 5; Or. Sib. 3. 620–3, 744 ff.). The main difference between Paul's treatment of the theme and that of the pseudepigraphic writers is that whereas they portray the renovation of nature as something executed for the benefit of the Jews alone, Paul 'sympathizes with nature itself, and looks forward to a truly universal regeneration in which inanimate nature will have its share.'[1]

Yet simultaneous with this futurist eschatology there is, in these Epistles, an increasing emphasis on inaugurated eschatology. It is, for the most part, a development of his teaching in 1 Corinthians about the Christian's experience of resurrection here and now. Those who have been baptized into the death of the Messiah, i.e. who have accepted him as Lord, putting the old self to death, and become members of his corporate σῶμα, experience the resurrection life, the life of the age to come, in this age (Rom. 6. 3–4, 11). 'If a man is living in the Messiah's corporate personality, the Church, he is a new creature: for the old order has gone, and lo and behold! the new order has come into being' (2 Cor. 5. 17). The life of the risen Lord is to be observed in the personalities of Christians, even in their mortal organisms (2 Cor. 4. 10–11). The conclusion drawn from this, already mentioned in 1 Corinthians 15, that it is because they are living the risen life that Christians will be raised from the dead at the eschaton, is now amplified at this next stage of Paul's thinking. The same divine activity (πνεῦμα) that raised Jesus from the dead dwells in Christians now and will therefore make their personalities alive at the final resurrection (Rom. 8. 11).

It is here that we notice another inference which Paul draws from his belief that Christians are now living under the new

[1] H. St. J. Thackeray, *The Relation of St. Paul to Contemporary Jewish Thought*, p. 40.

order, having resurrection life in them here and now: that they will not be forced to wait for the transformation of their personalities until the resurrection of the dead at the eschaton; the metamorphosis is a continuous process, now taking place. On the one hand, the Christian's external, visible frame (ὁ ἔξω ἄνθρωπος), which resembles a fragile, earthenware jar (2 Cor. 4. 7), is being destroyed (2 Cor. 4. 16). Yet he does not lose heart, because 'the inward man' (ὁ ἔσω ἄνθρωπος), the essential personality, is being renewed all the time (2 Cor. 4. 16); and the suffering that accompanies the process of decay is momentary and vastly outweighed by the glory which he will experience in the age to come and which is being brought to its completion by the suffering (2 Cor. 4. 17). The Christian does not fix his gaze on the objects that he can see, like his physical body, which are transitory (πρόσκαιρα), but on those that he cannot see, like the essential personality, which are aeonian, i.e. they belong to the Age to Come (2 Cor. 4. 18). Man's physical body resembles a tent,[1] a temporary habitation, whereas his personality in the Age to Come, provided by God, will resemble a house, a permanent habitation (2 Cor. 5. 1).[2]

From this fact that the renewal of his essential personality is proceeding *pari passu* with the decay of his physical organism it follows that the conclusion of the two processes will coincide; and it is indeed this conclusion that Paul seems to be drawing in 2 Corinthians 5. 2–4. When he wrote 1 Corinthians, he believed that the σῶκα ψυχικόν would not be changed into the σῶμα πνευματικόν until the resurrection of the dead at the Parousia; but now he seems to be hoping (he does not say that it will) that the completion of the change that is (since Christians are living in the Age to Come and enjoying resurrection life in this present age) now proceeding all the time will take place at death (2 Cor. 5. 2–4). This interpretation of 2 Corinthians 5. 1 ff. has been challenged by H. A. A. Kennedy,[3] L. S. Thornton,[4] and H. L.

---

[1] Was Paul thinking of his own craft? *V. sup.*, p. 8.
[2] Paul says that it is ἐν τοῖς οὐρανοῖς. What does he mean? *V. inf.*, p. 167.
[3] *St. Paul's Conception of the Last Things* (London, 1904), pp. 263–5.
[4] *The Common Life in the Body of Christ* (Westminster, 1941), p. 284, note A.

Goudge,[1] who maintain that Paul still thinks, as he did when he wrote 1 Corinthians 15, that the transformation will not take place until the Parousia.[2] Goudge argues that Paul's subject is still that of 1 Corinthians 15—what will happen to Christians at the Parousia—and that he is merely making more explicit what he wrote then. Most Christians will be in the land of the living at the Parousia: they will be (Paul introduces a new metaphor here) wearing the clothes of the physical frame, and they are earnestly hoping that at the Parousia they will have the new clothing of the σῶμα πνευματικόν to put on over (ἐπενδύσασθαι— note the two prepositions, ἐπι and ἐν = 'on over') the old organism. They hope (this is the force of the phrase εἴ γε καί) that they will not be in a state of nakedness, i.e. without any kind of body, in a disembodied state like the *nepheš* in Sheol. Thus, to summarize this interpretation, 'these words give a hint of Paul's earnest desire and hope of surviving to the Parousia, and so escaping the terrifying experience of death.'[3] As W. D. Davies says, it is hard to accept this view, for 'there is nothing in the text to suggest Paul's hope of surviving to the Parousia.'[4] More-over, it is obvious from 2 Corinthians 1. 8–9, 2. 13, 4. 8–11, 6. 4–10 and 7. 5, that his trials and tribulations were causing his thoughts to turn more and more to what would happen to him and his fellow-Christians at death. Particularly significant in this respect is his statement, 'I want you to know, brothers, about the distress that I experienced in Asia. It was a burden that I found much too heavy to bear so that I despaired of my life. Indeed, I thought that sentence of death had been passed upon me' (2 Cor. 1. 8–9).[5] In his previous writings he had said that the resurrection of the dead would probably take place before his death;[6] now bitter experiences were forcing him to face the possibility that his

---

[1] *Comm. on* 2 *Corinthians*, WC (London, 1927), *ad loc.*
[2] R. H. Charles says that Paul believed that the change would take place at death when he wrote 1 Cor. 15, and that he made this explicit in 2 Cor. 5. 1 ff. (*A Critical History of the Doctrine of the Future Life*, pp. 394 f.).
[3] H. A. A. Kennedy, *St. Paul's Conception of the Last Things*, p. 265.
[4] *Paul and Rabbinic Judaism*, p. 311.
[5] No-one knows what this trouble was. Perhaps the most plausible suggestion is that it was illness coupled with the rebellious attitude of the Corinthian Christians.
[6] *V. sup.*, pp. 154, 163.

own decease would precede it. What, then, would happen to
him if he died in the near future? He replies that if the tent of his
physical form were destroyed, i.e. if he died, he would be provided by God with his permanent home, the σῶμα πνευματικόν.
Using the other metaphor (which he mingles with the domiciliary
metaphor), he likens the physical form to a garment over which
at death the new garment, the σῶμα πνευματικόν, is drawn on;
he shrinks from the thought of being naked, i.e. in a disembodied
state. Thus Paul takes courage from the knowledge that if he
were to die, he would be in the Lord's presence. Indeed, he
would prefer to be with his Lord than to be in his physical body
(verses 6–8).

   We have discussed two interpretations of this passage. Before
we leave it, we must glance at a third theory, that of Dr. J. A. T.
Robinson, who argues that for Paul the term σῶμα πνευματικόν
means the body of Christ, the Church.[1] He bases his case on two
Greek words, ἔχομεν and οἰκοδομή (2 Cor. 5. 1). He claims that
the present tense of the verb proves that Paul could not have been
thinking of the σῶμα πνευματικόν of the individual Christian; but,
as we shall show, this passage teems with Hellenistic ideas, and
this is one of them. Paul says that the σῶμα πνευματικόν exists
now ἐν τοῖς οὐρανοῖς, by which he means that (to use the Platonic
term) the ἰδέα[2] of the σῶμα πνευματικόν in which all particular
σώματα πνευματικά participate and which makes them what they
are, exists now in the eternal world, and it is in this sense that 'we
have' it ἐν τοῖς οὐρανοῖς (in addition to the fact that each Christian
has it while he is still on earth because he has already risen from
the dead by incorporation into Christ's body, the Church). As
for the noun οἰκοδομή, Dr. Robinson asserts that on every other
occasion when Paul uses it (he supplies four references, 1 Cor.
3. 9; Eph. 2. 21; 4. 12, 16; though in the last two it does not
mean a building, but the act of building = the classical οἰκοδομήσις,

---

[1] *The Body* (London, 1952), pp. 76–8. Cf. his *In the End, God* . . . (London, 1950),
pp. 96–7.
[2] *Republic*, 596A.

which does not occur in the NT), it refers to the Church. The answer to this argument is that because Paul uses it in 1 Corinthians 3. 9 and Ephesians 2. 21 to describe the Church, it does not follow that it must mean the same in 2 Corinthians 5. 1.

In the previous paragraph we stated that 2 Corinthians 5. 1 ff. contains an unusually large number of Greek ideas. The comparison of the physical organism to an earthenware vessel occurs frequently in Stoic writings, e.g. Seneca described man as 'a cracked vessel, which will break at the least fall.'[1] The contrast between the transient visible world and the permanent invisible world is pure Platonism, and is also found in Seneca, who says that worldly objects 'are unreal, and only for a time make a show. Not one of them possesses stability or substance. . . . Let us direct our minds to the objects that are eternal.'[2] Both the Pythagorean school of philosophers and Plato likened the body to a tent, a temporary home, which man, yearning for his eternal dwelling-place, is longing to quit.[3] Like Paul, Plato uses the adjective γύμνοι, in the sense of 'stripped,' to describe disembodied personalities.[4] Finally, to repeat what we have already said, in 1 Corinthians 5. 1 there is an echo of the Platonic doctrine of ideas. It is possible, as St. John Thackeray, basing his case on close verbal parallels, holds, that Paul derived these Greek ideas from that product of Hellenistic Judaism, written in Alexandria, the Book of Wisdom.[5] There is, however, this essential difference between Paul's picture of the condition of the dead and that portrayed by Hellenism. He can go so far with the author of Wisdom, agreeing that after death 'the souls of the righteous are in the hand of God' (3. 1); but his ingrained Jewish ideas prevent him from conceiving of disembodied souls. Plato and some Hellenistic Jews could see the post-mortem condition of man as γυμνός, stripped of the burdensome clothing of the physical body; but Paul could not picture man, even after death, as thus 'unclothed'; he could not be γυμνός (2 Cor. 5. 2–4).[6] Thus what

---

[1] *Ad Marc.* 11. [2] *Ep.* 59.
[3] A. Robertson and A. Plummer, *Comm. on 1 Cor.*, ICC, p. 142. [4] *Gorgias*, 523.
[5] H. St. J. Thackeray, *The Relation of St. Paul to Contemporary Jewish Thought*, pp. 131–2.,
[6] Cf. 1 En. 62. 15–16; 2 En. 22. 8; 4 Ez. 2.39.

we have in these verses is a repetition of the doctrine of the spiritual organism already found in 1 Corinthians 15. However much he has been influenced by Hellenism, Paul has not abandoned his Jewish belief that after death men will be clothed in some kind of body.

When we reach the last phase of Pauline eschatology with Colossians and Ephesians, we still find futurist and inaugurated eschatology side by side,[1] although the emphasis is placed much more on the latter. Paul still divides time into two ages (Eph. 1. 21), this present evil age (Eph. 2. 2; 5. 16) and the age to come, the age of glory (Col. 1. 27). Although he never mentions the word 'Parousia,' he says that the Messiah will be revealed (φανερωθῇ) (Col. 3. 4) and that Christians will share his glory (Col. 3. 4). He can still speak of the execution of a future judgement on apostates (Eph. 5. 6). On the other hand, his inaugurated eschatology, found in small measure in 1 Corinthians, and to an increasing degree in 2 Corinthians and Romans, has developed enormously. Christians, who have been buried with Christ and raised to new life with him (Col. 2. 12; 3. 1; Eph. 2. 6), are living under the rule of the Messiah (Col. 1. 13), who by his death and resurrection has triumphed over all the powers of evil (Col. 2. 15; Eph. 1. 19–23). All this has taken place in accordance with the divine plan. Two of the most significant words in Ephesians are πρόθεσις (1. 11; 3. 11) and οἰκονομία (1. 10; 3. 9). The former means 'a deliberate plan'; the latter, whose primary meaning is 'household or estate management,' is used here of God's execution of his πρόθεσις for the universe. This predetermined plan was kept secret until, when the time was ripe, it was disclosed in Jesus, Messiah and Lord (Eph. 1. 9–10; 3. 9–11. Cf. 1 Cor. 2. 7). Yet the advent of Jesus was only the inauguration of the οἰκονομία, which is now in process of being worked out (Eph. 1. 11), and its consummation is still to come. The powers of evil still

[1] For a convincing, lucid, and elegantly written investigation of the tension caused by the coexistence of the two *vide* C. F. D. Moule, art. 'The Influence of Circumstances on the Use of Eschatological Terms,' JTS, N.S., Vol. 15, Pt. 1, April, 1964, pp. 1–15.

operate, and Christ's body, the Church, must continue to combat them (Eph. 6. 10 ff.) until the time when the whole universe is at one with the Christ (Eph. 1. 10), the cosmic Christ (Col. 1. 15–17; 2. 10), until his *de jure* sovereignty becomes a *de facto* sovereignty.

7

THEOLOGIAN

Thou cam'st from Heaven to Earth, that we
Might go from Earth to Heaven with thee:
And though thou found'st no welcom here,
Thus didst provide us mansions there.

HENRY VAUGHAN, The Nativity, ll. 17-20.

WE HAVE examined Paul's theology of the liberation of man and, for that matter, of all creation. There remains for consideration his conception of the personality of the liberator, Jesus, through whom and in whom God carries out his saving work of liberation. What manner of man was and is Jesus? 'Who do you say that I am?' (Mk. 8. 29 = Mt. 16. 15 = Lk. 9. 20). 'You are the Messiah, the Son of the living God,' replied Simon Peter. What was Paul's answer to the question? The last movement (needless to say, written in a major key)[1] of our imaginary Pauline symphony supplies it; but before we apply ourselves to the task of discovering what it was, we are impelled to make three preliminary observations. In the first place, theologians are wont to write profound, lengthy excursuses on, what they call Paul's 'Christology.' It is a somewhat inappropriate term to apply to Paul's statements about the personality and work of Jesus because, as its suffix (-ology) implies, it denotes a formal science, and therefore to attribute to Paul a Christology means that he used the scientific method of collecting, verifying, comparing, and classifying data about Jesus, finally stating certain hypotheses about him as if he were the subject of a research project! A cursory reading of the Pauline Epistles shows that Paul's 'Christology,' far from being a formal science, consists of a number of

---

[1] Lest a musical pundit should read this, let me point out that I realize that the last movement of my symphonic parallel, Brahms's First Symphony (*v. sup.*, p. 76), begins in C minor; but it ends in C major.

scattered affirmations concerning the divine activity in Jesus (some of them being almost *obiter dicta*), and the frequent usage of various epithets and titles that exemplify the significance of Jesus for the groaning and travailing creation. If we must call this 'Christology,' then let us realize that we are not using the word in the sense in which we speak of Nicene or Chalcedonian Christology, or the Christology of Bishop Gore, P. T. Forsyth, Emil Brunner, D. M. Baillie, or Rudolf Bultmann.

Nevertheless—and this is our second preliminary point—although we may be reluctant to call Paul's 'Christology' a science, we must recognize that he was an empiricist to the extent that his conceptual image of Christ was the fruit of experience; his intense, personal experience of what God had achieved, and was still achieving in and through Jesus. H. R. Mackintosh warns us of 'the temptation to explain the Pauline Christology either as the product of mere theological reflection or as a mosaic of fragments borrowed from the traditions of Jewish apocalyptic':[1] or, we would add, as the fulfilment of Paul's desire to reconcile Jewish Messianic notions with the concepts of Alexandrian philosophy or those of the Mystery religions. It is true that Paul used the conceptual categories of contemporary Judaism (most of which are derived from the OT) and, to a far less extent, those of his Hellenistic environment, but this does not alter the fact that his Christology is, as Mackintosh says 'the offspring of creative religious intuition, working upon the felt realities of experience';[2] and it is this last phrase, 'the felt realities of experience,' that we would emphasize. As to the nature of that experience, although Paul himself no doubt regarded it as one and indivisible, it is analysable into two distinct parts, the direct and the indirect. Obviously the former consisted in his visionary personal encounter with the risen Jesus near Damascus, which was the *causa quod* of his conversion to Christianity; and the latter was mediated to him through the apostolic community, of which he became a baptized member. However vehemently

[1] H. R. Mackintosh, *The Doctrine of the Person of Jesus Christ* (Edinburgh, 1913), p. 59.
[2] *Ibid.*

and justifiably Paul insisted that the good news about Christ crucified yet risen, which he was proclaiming, had not been imparted to him by any human agent (Gal. I. 11–12), it is impossible to believe that the new convert knew the full story of the life and death of Jesus; that he lacked the desire to know it; and that the lacunae in his knowledge of it were not filled in by those who had consorted with Jesus. John Knox expresses the point admirably: Paul 'entered into the shared remembrance of Jesus which lay, has always lain, and lies still, near the center (*sic*) of the life of the Christian community.'[1] Nor was it only factual information about the earthly Jesus that the Church gave him: in and through its life and activity, its κοινωνία, he apprehended what God in Christ was still doing.

The third preliminary point is a warning that formal Christological assertions, whether they be primitive like Paul's, or recent like Bultmann's or Cullmann's, can *never* do full justice to what God in Christ has done, and does, for man. To think that they can is tantamount to believing that when a professor of music informs his pupils that in the finale of the 'Jupiter' Symphony Mozart uses five themes fugally and imitatively, at times treating them separately, at others inversively, and in the end in cleverly contrived combinations, he has conveyed to them the essence of what is one of the most remarkable pieces of music ever written; or that when an expert on Renaissance painting has anatomized for us in the minutest detail Fra Filippo Lippi's Madonna and Child, he has said the last word on it; or that when a literary scholar, dissecting John Donne's poetical gem, 'The Canonization,' tells us that 'the colloquial outburst of line 1, the heavy stress on "palsie" and "gout," the contemptuous alliteration of line 3, above all the play of an exasperated splutter of short phrases across the intricate stanza form, all impose on the reader the desired emphasis, tone, and mood,'[2] he is giving us a full explanation of the poem.

[1] *Jesus: Lord and Christ* (New York, 1958), p. 70.
[2] R. G. Cox, art. 'The Poems of Johne Donne' in *The Penguin Guide to English Literature* (London, 1954–61), Vol. 3, p. 99.

Yet although language has its limitations when it tries to express the significance of the Christ, Paul of Tarsus comes as near to telling us the whole truth about him as anyone does. His conception of Christ comprises seven salient motifs. First, there is the motif of sovereignty. Jesus is the Messianic King. As a result of his conversion experience Paul was convinced that those whom he had been persecuting were right and he was wrong: Jesus the crucified had indeed risen from the dead, and was therefore God's true anointed Messiah, whose coming was expected by all Jews, and furthermore (as Stephen's speech had implied) he was the Messiah, the deliverer, not only of Jews, but also of Gentiles. Thereafter, whenever he was addressing Jews, the Messiaship of Jesus was the burden of his message (Acts 9. 22; 13. 16–41; 17. 3; 18. 5; 26. 23; and 28. 23). Moreover, when we turn to his Epistles, we find the word χριστός applied to Jesus any number of times. To Paul himself, to the Jews and the proselytes of the gate who listened to his proclamation of the Gospel, and to any Jewish Christians who heard his Epistles read, the term was full of meaning. They would understand what he meant when he said that the Messiah by natural descent sprang from Jewry (Rom. 9. 5), and that he had been born, on a purely human level, of the stock of David (Rom. 1. 3). They would recognize, when Paul spoke of the execution of justice by Jesus Christ at the Parousia (2 Thess. 2. 8; Rom. 2. 16; 2 Cor. 5. 10), that this was a Messianic function. A Jew or anyone familiar with Judaism, then, knew what was meant by the term ὁ Χριστός; but had it any meaning for a Gentile Christian as he heard it again and again during the reading of Paul's Epistles? The general opinion of modern NT scholars is summed up in this sentence: 'In the Gentile world the term "Messiah" was meaningless, unless explained, and when explained was felt to be strange';[1] and, it is urged, since Paul obviously knew this, he always or nearly always used it as a personal name like 'Jesus.'[2] Ought we, however, to

---

[1] V. Taylor, *The Names of Jesus* (London, 1953), p. 22.
[2] V. Taylor, *ibid.*; also his *The Person of Christ in NT Teaching* (London, 1958), pp. 41–2; and A. E. J. Rawlinson, *The NT Doctrine of the Christ* (London, 1926), pp. 74–5.

dismiss lightly the exhaustive examination of the evidence made by Burton, who concludes that, broadly speaking, while Paul often uses Χριστός as a proper name, indicated by his omission of the definite article, he frequently uses it to designate the Messiah, which he achieves by placing the definite article in front of it? As to the argument that the Gentiles must have had difficulty in understanding the word, Burton goes on to point out that, although Paul never defines Χριστός, he supplies an important clue to its meaning: he almost always uses ὁ Χριστός in preference to Χριστός after terms that relate to salvation (e.g. τὸ εὐαγγέλιον in 1 Thess. 3. 2; Gal. 1. 7; 1 Cor. 9. 12; 2 Cor. 2. 12; 9. 13; 10. 14; Rom. 15. 19; and Phil. 1. 27; ὁ σταυρός in 1 Cor. 1. 17 and Phil. 3. 18; and ἡ ἀγάπη in Rom. 8. 35; 2 Cor. 5. 14; and Eph. 3. 19). Thus Burton's conclusion is that in the Pauline Epistles ὁ Χριστός means the divinely appointed Saviour and deliverer[1] or, to use the term that we prefer, liberator. This argument is reinforced by Cullmann's contention that Paul's 'occasional practice of putting "Christ" before "Jesus" shows that he was still clearly aware that the title is not a proper name.'[2] Admittedly there is no evidence that Paul gave his converts any detailed instruction on the meaning of the term; but it is more than likely that he did. After all, he must have been compelled to explain to them a large number of Jewish terms found in their bible and his own if they were to understand the message that he was proclaiming. As we Gentiles today cannot comprehend the meaning of the Christian kerygma without a knowledge of Judaism and the Hebrew scriptures, so it must have been for those Gentiles whom Paul evangelized; and we can be fairly certain that he taught them what their Jewish brothers already knew: Jesus was ὁ Χριστός, God's anointed Saviour, deliverer, liberator, of men. Now although the technical term 'the Messiah' does not appear in the OT, Mowinckel has conclusively demonstrated that 'both the content and the form of the conception of the Messiah are derived from the Israelite

[1] E. de W. Burton, *Comm. on Gal.*, ICC (Edinburgh, 1921), p. 396.
[2] O. Cullmann, *The Christology of the New Testament*, Eng. tr. S. C. Guthrie and C. A. M. Hall (Philadelphia, 1959), p. 134.

(and, ultimately, the oriental) conception of kingship *found in the OT.*[1] Fundamental to the understanding of the Messianic idea is 'that whatever applies to the Israelite ideal of kingship also applies to the Messiah, but in a still greater measure. The Messiah is the future, eschatological realization of the ideal of kingship.'[2] Thus, when Paul described Jesus as ὁ Χριστός, he meant that he was the fulfilment of the Jewish expectation of the advent of the ideal ruler.

To emphasize his conviction that Jesus is the sovereign ruler of men Paul describes him as ὁ Κύριος, a title which he applies to him far more frequently than any other. 'We proclaim Jesus Christ as Κύριος,' he writes (2 Cor. 4. 5). 'Jesus is Κύριος' summarizes Paul's credo (Rom. 10. 9, 12; 1 Cor. 12. 3; Phil. 2. 11). The purpose of the sacrificial life and death of Jesus was that the whole creation should acknowledge him as κύριος (Phil. 2. 9–11). With these references we must couple 1 Corinthians 15. 25, where Paul speaks of the Son as 'ruling' (βασιλεύειν), and Colossians 1. 13, where he refers to 'the sovereignty (βασιλείαν) of the Son.' That the term Κύριος, which, although it is always used in the NT as a noun, is properly an adjective equivalent to ὁ ἔχων κῦρος, having power or authority,[3] denoted in the vocabulary of the primitive Church and in Paul's (although, as we shall maintain, its meaning cannot be limited to this)[4] the Messianic kingship of Christ is proved by three pieces of evidence. In the first place, there are those passages where, speaking of the sovereignty of Jesus, Paul appears to be echoing the words of Psalm 110. Christ is seated on God's right hand, the position of delegated authority (Rom. 8. 34; Eph. 1. 20; Col. 3. 1), destined 'to reign until he has put all his enemies under his feet' (1 Cor. 15. 25; Eph. 1. 22). The allusion to Psalm 110. 1 is patent: 'The Lord says to my lord: "Sit at my right hand till I make your enemies your footstool".' It is highly probable that this was a Royal Psalm, recited at the enthronement of the Hebrew kings.[5] The author imagines

---

[1] S. Mowinckel, *He that Cometh*, p. 156.   [2] *Ibid.*

[3] W. Foerster and G. Quell, *Lord*, BKW, Eng. tr. H. P. Kingdon (London, 1958), pp. 1 ff.; MGLNT, p. 261.

[4] *V. inf.*, pp. 192 ff.   [5] *Vide* G. W. Anderson, PCB, pp. 411, 437.

Yahweh as bestowing the raj on the ruler, thus making him his vicegerent, and as promising him victory over his foes and the expansion of his *imperium* (cf. Ps. 2. 6; 89. 18 ff., also Royal Psalms). Later, the Jews,[1] possibly Jesus himself, and certainly his earliest followers interpreted it as a prophecy concerning the ideal king, the Messiah, and his rule. It is used in this manner by Peter in his first recorded speech, in which he argues that Psalm 110. 1 expressed King David's prevision that one of his royal descendants, whom he calls 'my Lord,' would be the Messiah (Acts 2. 30, 34). According to Peter this forecast came true when Jesus appeared, whom God made 'both Lord and Messiah' (Acts 2. 36). As Karl Adam puts it, 'In Peter's demonstration, this very position as ruler is the decisive characteristic of the Christ.'[2] Jesus the Κύριος is God's royal Messiah, his vicegerent, born of Davidic lineage and reigning until the final consummation. Obviously this Messianic interpretation of Psalm 110. 1 was an important article in early Christian thinking and preaching, and it is not surprising to find it in the Epistles of Paul, who seemingly assimilated it as an item in the paradosis that he received.[3] Secondly, there is Paul's use of the Aramaic word *marana* (or *maran*) in the formula 'Our Lord, come!' or 'Our Lord comes' (or 'has come,') (1 Cor. 16. 22),[4] which must have originated in the Aramaic-speaking Jewish community in Jerusalem.[5] What the word *marana* means has been shown by Cerfaux as a result of his exhaustive researches: 'The Aramaic *Marana* . . . has a technical sense of royal prerogative.'[6] Thus, if as Cullmann, following Lietzmann, suggests, Paul is quoting in 1 Corinthians 16. 22 a petition used at the Lord's Supper,[7] he is expressing the desire of the

[1] A. E. J. Rawlinson, *Comm. on St. Mark*, WC (London, 1925), pp. 174–5.

[2] K. Adam, *The Christ of Faith*, Eng. tr. J. Crick (London, 1957), p. 76.

[3] Cf. 1 Cor. 15. 3–5.

[4] Probably 'Our Lord, come' is the correct translation of *maranatha*. *Vide* O. Cullmann, *The Christology of the NT*, p. 209.

[5] This was what Rawlinson described as the Achilles' heel of Bousset's celebrated theory concerning the origin of the Christian use of the word κύριος (*The New Testament Doctrine of the Christ*, p. 235), a somewhat infelicitous description since it suggests that the theory has only one vulnerable point! On the theory *v. inf.*, p. 194 n. 3.

[6] L. Cerfaux, *Christ in the Theology of St. Paul*, Eng. tr. G. Webb and A. Walker (New York, 1959), p. 465 n.

[7] O. Cullmann, *The Christology of the New Testament*, pp. 208 ff.

primitive Church, including his own, that Jesus, the eschatic Messianic king, will soon return.[1] Obviously what has been said about the meaning of *marana* applies also to the meaning of its Greek equivalent, κύριος, and here again we are indebted to Cerfaux, who points out that 'the custom of calling a ruler "Lord" (Kurios) was an oriental one. ... As used by Greco-Romans in the East *it* (italics mine) was applied to kings.'[2] Thirdly, there is Paul's use of the word παρουσία to describe the eschatic arrival of Jesus Christ (1 Cor. 15. 23; 1 Thess. 2. 19; 3. 13; 4. 15; 5. 23; 2 Thess. 2. 1, 8). The significance of this word in this context is that it was a technical term for the official visit of a royal personage.[3] Complementary to it is the term ἀπάντησις, found in 1 Thessalonians 4. 17 and meaning the formal welcome given to a ruler on his arrival.[4] It is clear that this cumulative argument adds up to the conclusion that Paul used the word κύριος of Jesus in the sense of David's royal descendant, the ideal Messianic king, the sovereign ruler of men.

The second motif in Paul's conception of the personality of Jesus the ideal Messianic king, is that he was truly a human being, possessing all the characteristics of humanity. Those who write on the subject of Paul's Christology never fail to point out that he makes few references to the human life of Jesus of Nazareth. For example, John Knox says that 'whatever else the first reader of the Pauline letters may miss, he is certain to be struck by what would appear to be an almost complete lack of interest in the words and acts of Jesus.'[5] Yet this paucity of allusion to the doings of the earthly Jesus does not mean that Paul omits to tell us that Jesus was a human being. Although his statement that Jesus had the ὁμοίωμα (the simulacrum) and the σχῆμα (the outward

---

[1] Cf. 1 Cor. 11. 26: 'For as often as you eat this bread and drink this cup, you proclaim the Lord's death until he comes.'

[2] L. Cerfaux, *ibid*. Examples of the application of Κύριος to rulers, e.g. Ptolemy XIII, Ptolemy XIV, Cleopatra, Herod the Great, Herod Agrippa I, and in the East only, the Emperors Claudius and Nero, are to be found in A. Deissmann, *Light from the Ancient East*, Eng. tr. L. R. M. Strachan (London, 1910), pp. 353 ff. Augustus and Tiberius disclaimed the title (VGT, p. 365). In Acts 25. 26 Porcius Festus calls Nero ὁ Κύριος, i.e. the supreme ruler. Cerfaux denies that both *Marana* and *Κύριος*, when applied to rulers contained any cultic meaning. To this we shall return later. *V. inf.*, p. 192.

[3] VGT, p. 497.   [4] *Ibid*., p. 53.   [5] *Jesus: Lord and Christ*, p. 38.

shape) of a human being (Phil. 2. 7–8. Cf. Rom. 8. 3) has a
Docetic ring, elsewhere he dispels this impression by asserting
the real humanity of Jesus, who was a physical descendant of
King David (Rom. 1. 3), was born of a human mother (Gal.
4. 4),[1] and lived the life of a genuine human being (1 Cor. 15. 21).
The Jews emphasized that, like their ancient kings, the ideal
Messianic ruler would be truly human.[2] Jesus was truly a human
being, and thus the ideal was realized in this particular as in most
others. Withal his was a sinless humanity (2 Cor. 5. 21),[3] which, as
Taylor suggests, probably explains why in Philippians 2. 7–8, which
is part of a passage concerned with the essentially divine nature
of Christ, he describes the humanity of Jesus as a simulacrum.[4]

Thirdly, the essential nature of the man Jesus, the ideal Messianic
king, is that he is the slave of God and of humanity. This is yet
another particular in which the ideal was realized. The ancient
kings of Israel were regarded as Yahweh's servants (1 Kgs. 3. 7–9;
Hag. 2. 23; Zech. 3. 8; Ps. 89. 3, 20; etc.), and Messiah, the ideal
ruler, must resemble them (4 Ez. 7. 28; 13. 32, 37, 52; 14. 9;
2 Bar. 70. 9).[5] Jesus the ideal Messianic king in the flesh was a
man of gentleness (πραΰτης) and sweet reasonableness (ἐπιείκεια)
(2 Cor. 10. 1), did not please himself (Rom. 15. 3); and for a
comprehensive picture of him we have but to read Galatians
5. 22–23, where Paul enumerates the fruits of his activity, and
1 Corinthians 13, where he analyses in detail the first and foremost
of them, ἀγάπη. He gives us the conclusion of this whole matter
when he says that Jesus took the μορφή (Phil. 2. 7) of a slave. In
the NT this Greek word means 'a form which truly and fully
expresses the being which underlies it.'[6] Thus what Paul means

---

[1] Few of those who write on Paul's theology omit to remind us that he does not mention
the virginal conception.

[2] S. Mowinckel, *He that Cometh*, pp. 69, 76, 162, 284, 286, 323.

[3] Paul does not mean that he was incapable of sinning, but that in fact he did not sin.

[4] V. Taylor, *The Person of Christ in NT Teaching*, p. 40.

[5] I assume that 'the Son of Man' of the pseudepigrapha was regarded as the Messiah
(*vide* S. Mowinckel *ibid.*, pp. 360–2) and that the correct translation of the passages cited
is 'my servant' and not 'my son' (*vide ibid.*, p. 294).

[6] H. A. A. Kennedy, (*Comm. on Philippians* London, 1903, EGT, Vol. 3, p. 43). J. B.
Lightfoot (*Comm. on Philippians*, London, 1888, pp. 110, 127–33), J. H. Moulton and G.
Milligan (VGT, p. 417), J. H. Michael (*Comm. on Philippians*, MNTC, London, 1928,
p. 86); and V. Taylor (*The Person of Christ in NT Teaching*, p. 75) all agree with Kennedy.

here is not only that the actions of Jesus made him look like a slave, but also that he was essentially a slave, the slave of God and humanity. In the next verse and elsewhere (Rom. 5. 8; 1 Cor. 15. 3; 2 Cor. 5. 14) Paul shows us the extent of the self-enslavement of Jesus; and here, as we shall see, is one respect, the most important of all, in which Jesus differs from the Jewish image of the ideal Messianic king: voluntarily Jesus suffered the death of a criminal on humanity's behalf.[1] This was the character of the activity of Jesus. God's and humanity's slave, he served them throughout his life and crowned that life of sacrifice on man's behalf with his sacrificial death. *Finis coronat opus.*

This conception of Jesus as the suffering, executed δοῦλος, inevitably reminds us of Deutero-Isaiah's portrait of the Suffering Servant; and in spite of the persuasive thesis of Miss Morna Hooker,[2] it is difficult to resist the traditional opinion that Jesus himself and the early Church interpreted his mission in the light of that portrait, and that Paul followed them. We grant that Miss Hooker may be right in claiming that when Paul quoted from the fourth Servant Song in Romans 10. 16, and again in Romans 15. 21, he was not thinking of the remainder of the Song;[3] on the other hand, it is equally possible that he was. She may be right also when she says that the various echoes of the vocabulary of the Servant Songs in the Pauline Epistles do not necessarily mean that Paul identified Jesus with the Servant,[4] and that the phrase κατὰ τὰς γραφάς in 1 Corinthians 15. 3 is not a reference to any particular passages of Scripture, viz. Isaiah 53, but to OT prophecy in general;[5] but we must still account for the close parallels between the Songs and what used to be called 'the Kenotic passage,' but what it has now become fashionable to describe as a translation of a Christian Aramaic psalm[6] or a

---

[1] It seems, however, that the innocent sufferer of the Psalms of humiliation is the king (*vide* S. Mowinckel, *He that Cometh*, p. 235).

[2] M. D. Hooker, *Jesus and the Servant* (London, 1959), *passim*.

[3] *Ibid.*, pp. 116–17.   [4] *Ibid.*, pp. 121–3.

[5] *Ibid.*, pp. 117–20. J. Héring (*The First Epistle of St. Paul to the Corinthians*, Eng. tr. A. W. Heathcote and P. J. Allcock, London, 1962, pp. 158–9) agrees with her.

[6] E. Lohmeyer, *Kyrios Jesus*, Eine Untersuchung zu Phil. 2. 5–11 (Sitzungsberichte der Heidelberger Akademie der Wissenschaften, phil.-hist. Klasse), 1927–8.

Pauline adaptation of a Jewish-Gnostic hymn,[1] viz. Philippians 2. 5–11.[2] In her enthusiasm for demolishing the hypothesis that Paul related the two Miss Hooker erroneously states that the Hebrew 'ebhedh in the Servant Songs is always translated παῖς in the LXX, never δοῦλος, the word used by Paul in Philippians 2. 7.[3] In the third of the Songs δοῦλος is used twice to represent 'ebhedh (Is. 49. 3, 5). In any case, in the Koine παῖς and δοῦλος were synonymous.[4] Cerfaux's judgement shared by many others, seems ineluctable: 'It is in the songs of the servant in the book of Isaias that we must look for the most likely source of inspiration for this hymn. What is the story of Christ obedient and humbled, and then exalted, if not the mysterious experiences of "the servant of God" whose life is described by the prophet?'[5]

This Christian conception of a suffering Messiah was completely original, not being found anywhere in pre-Christian Jewish literature.[6] Claims that the Qumran sectaries regarded their founder or leader, 'the Teacher of Righteousness' (or, as he was called in the Damascus Document, 'the Interpreter of the Law'), as a suffering, martyred, and indeed (according to Allegro) crucified Messiah,[7] modelled (according to Brownlee) on Deutero-Isaiah's Suffering Servant, whose vicarious death possessed redemptive efficacy and who would rise from the dead,[8] seem to have been conclusively refuted by Millar Burrows, Abbé Carmignac, and Matthew Black.[9] The fact is that, as Paul insists,

[1] P. Bonnard, L'Épître de S. Paul aux Philippiens, CNT (Paris, 1950), p. 49.
[2] The parallels are tabulated by W. D. Davies, Paul and Rabbinic Judaism, p. 274. Cf. W. Zimmerli and J. Jeremias, The Servant of God (London, 1957), p. 97.
[3] M. D. Hooker, ibid., p. 120. She contradicts herself: on p. 184, n. 4, she admits that δοῦλος translates 'ebhedh in Is. 49. 3, 5.
[4] VGT, p. 475.   [5] L. Cerfaux, Christ in the Theology of St. Paul, p. 377.
[6] S. Mowinckel, He that Cometh, pp. 325 ff. Cf. O. Cullmann, The Christology of the NT., pp. 52–60.
[7] J. M. Allegro, The Dead Sea Scrolls (London, 1956), p. 100; and The Treasure of the Copper Scroll (New York, 1960), p. 72. In fairness to Allegro he explained in a letter to The Times, 20th March, 1956, that 'his theory remains only an inference, claiming only probability.'
[8] W. H. Brownlee, The Servant of the Lord in the Qumran Scrolls, BASOR, 132, Dec. 1953, pp. 8–15; 135, Oct. 1954, pp. 33–8. Cf. his Messianic Motifs of Qumran and the NT, NTS, 3, 1936–7.
[9] M. Burrows, More Light on the Dead Sea Scrolls (London, 1958), Chaps. 6 and 7; J. Carmignac, Christ and the Teacher of Righteousness (Baltimore, 1962), pp. 48–56; and M. Black, The Scrolls and Christian Origins (London, 1961), pp. 160–3.

the notion of a crucified Messiah, which was the pith and marrow of the Christian proclamation (1 Cor. 1. 22–3; 2. 2; Gal. 3. 1), was to the Jew a σκάνδαλον (Rom. 9. 32; 1 Cor. 1. 23; Gal. 5. 11), a trap that drew him into error.[1] No doubt during his debates with fellow-Jews (Acts 9. 22; 17. 2–3; 18. 4–6; 28. 23 ff.) they had hurled at him the words of Deuteronomy 21. 23: 'Everyone who is hanged on a gibbet is accursed in God's sight'; words that, with the omission of the last phrase, he himself deliberately applied to Jesus in order to show that he willingly became accursed to liberate men from the curse that the Torah pronounced on them for failing to keep its every ordinance (Gal. 3. 13).[2]

To the Jews, then, the proclamation of Christ crucified was a snare. What did the Gentiles think of it? To them it was silliness (1 Cor. 1. 23). Yet, as Paul and all others, both Jews and Gentiles, who had been converted, knew from their experience it was neither the one nor the other: they had found in it a demonstration of God's power, wisdom and love. It was on account of Christ's slave-like obedience to God's will, which involved his voluntary submission to crucifixion, that God showed his power by raising him from the dead and exalting him to his royal throne. Just as the Scriptural law ordained that the firstborn must be consecrated to Yahweh's service (Ex. 13. 2, 12), so, as 'the firstborn among many brothers' (Rom. 8. 29), Jesus was consecrated to God's service, which meant that he was perfectly obedient 'even to the extremity of death, even death on a cross' (Phil. 2. 8). Then Paul wrote one of the key-words of the whole passage: διό. It was for that reason that God 'exalted him on high and bestowed on him the name that is above every name, that at the name of Jesus every knee should bow, in heaven and on earth and under the earth, and every tongue confess that Jesus Christ is Lord' (Phil. 2. 9–11).[3] His crucifixion was followed by his exaltation (his Resurrection and Ascension), and the latter is the consequence of the former. How could it happen otherwise?

---

[1] On the meaning of σκάνδαλον vide VGT, p. 576.
[2] On this passage vide J. B. Lightfoot, Comm. on Galatians, pp. 136–40, 152–4.
[3] For a further examination of this passage v. inf., pp. 193–4.

For the Cross was a demonstration of God's love as well as his power and wisdom. Indeed, the very power by which he conquered was the power of love. 'God proves his own love towards us in that while we were still sinners Christ died for us' (Rom. 5. 8). God 'did not spare his own Son, but surrendered him on behalf of us all' (Rom. 8. 32). In saving mankind this was his *modus operandi*. Such love could not be otherwise than invincible. The slave is a Sovereign, and it is through his slavery that he is enthroned. 'To this end Christ died and lived again, that he might be the Lord (κυριεύσῃ) both of the dead and of the living' (Rom. 14. 9).

Yet although Jesus was humanity's true sovereign Lord, his sovereignty was acknowledged by a very small number of his subjects. How was he to extend it now that he was no longer present in the flesh? Paul's answer was that he was present pneumatically: his personal πνεῦμα, his activity,[1] was continuing through his body, the Church. Of this we have already written when dealing with Paul's doctrine of the Church;[2] what needs to be stressed here in the Christological context is that the personality of Christ, the σῶμα τοῦ Χριστοῦ, on earth after his Resurrection and Ascension, was (and still is) a corporate one; and that, in our opinion, this was Paul's version of—here we have the fourth motif of his Christology—the Danielic Son of Man concept. As Son of Man Jesus Christ the Lord is a corporate figure, representative, and inclusive, of all his followers, who constitute his σῶμα, the Church. As Richardson succinctly puts it, 'Paul's Christology and his doctrine of the Church meet in the conception of Christ as *Ben Adam*.'[3] In 1 Corinthians 12 we hear Paul expounding in detail his majestic conception of the σῶμα τοῦ χριστοῦ, and three chapters later we read his description of Christ as 'the eschatic Adam' (ὁ ἔσχατος Ἀδαμ), the eschatic 'man (= Son of Man) from heaven,' who resembles the Danielic Son of Man, and whom he describes also as the life-creating πνεῦμα of his σῶμα, the Church (1 Cor. 15. 45–7), by being incorporated into

---

[1] On the meaning of πνεῦμα v. sup., pp. 112-13.
[2] V. sup., pp. 113 ff., 132.   [3] A. Richardson, ITNT, p. 139.

which all will be made alive (1 Cor. 15. 22). Christ is the Christian version of the Danielic Son of Man, a corporate, representative figure, into whom 'the saints of the Most High,' viz. Christian converts, are incorporated. We have the same conception in 2 Corinthians 3. 17 and Romans 8. 9–10, where Christ is described again as the πνεῦμα of his corporate σῶμα, his *alter ego*, the Church; and it reaches its climax in Ephesians, where Christ is portrayed as the fully mature man (= Son of Man), the completed humanity, the body of all mankind, into which the Church will eventually grow (Eph. 1. 22–3; 4. 12–16).

Recapitulating, we see that Paul thought of Jesus as the ideal Messianic sovereign who was also God's slave, who through the humiliation of his passion and death was enthroned, and who as Son of Man continued his activity in the shape of his corporate personality, the Church. Turning to his fifth motif, we find that Paul believed that all this happened according to a plan. Two of the most important words in his vocabulary are πρόθεσις, 'purpose' or 'plan,' and μυστήριον, 'a secret.' God's plan for the world, which he had had in mind from all eternity, even before the creation, was to gather up and present as a unity (ἀνακεφαλαιώσασθαι) the whole creation in Christ (Eph. 1. 10).[1] This plan was a μυστήριον, a secret, unrevealed until the time was ripe (Eph. 1. 9, cf. Gal. 4. 4) and God acted, making the secret known in Christ.[2] Thus God's eternal purpose was realized in Christ Jesus our Lord' (Eph. 3. 11). Since his plan had existed from all eternity, it follows that Christ had existed in the mind of God from all eternity. There is, however, more to Paul's thinking about Christ's pre-existence than merely that he was the content of the divine plan, a thought in the mind of God from all eternity. If that were the sum total of it, then it would differ not one whit from current Rabbinical ideas concerning the pre-existence of other persons and of certain objects: Moses, the Torah, the Temple, the people of Israel—all these were regarded as pre-existent in the sense that they had always been important elements

---

[1] On the meaning of ἀνακεφαλαιώσασθαι *vide* J. A. Robinson, *Comm. on Ephesians*, p. 145.
[2] On the meaning of μυστήριον *vide* J. A. Robinson, *ibid.*, pp. 30–1; and GEL, p. 253.

in the divine plan for Israel. As Mowinckel says, 'That any expression or vehicle of God's will for the world, his saving counsel and purpose, was present in his mind, or his "word," from the beginning, is a natural way of saying that it is not fortuitous, but the due unfolding and expression of God's own being.'[1] To the list must be added the Messiah, who was thought of as pre-existent in this sense in some circles.[2] Paul, however, seems to have regarded Christ, not merely as a thought in God's mind, but as really existing, from all eternity. We find this doctrine implied in the statement that 'when the time was ripe, God sent out his son' (Gal. 4. 4). The same inference can be drawn when he speaks of God's sending his Son in the likeness of sinful human nature (Rom. 8. 3), of Christ's exchanging for the sake of men the wealth (*sc.* of his pre-existent nature) for the poverty of human nature (2 Cor. 8. 9), and of his emptying himself of his divine nature to become incarnate (Phil. 2. 6–7).[3] The doctrine is no longer merely implicit in the fully developed Christology of Colossians: it is unequivocally stated in Colossians 1. 15–17, where Paul describes the Son as πρωτότοκος πάσης κτίσεως, which does not mean, as the Arians interpreted it, that the Son was a created being,[4] but which, as Bethune-Baker says, should be translated 'born before all creation (*or* every creature).'[5] That this was Paul's meaning is placed beyond doubt by what follows: 'in him all things were created . . . all things were created through his agency . . . he exists before all things' (cf. 1 Cor. 8. 6).[6]

The source of this Pauline doctrine of the pre-existence of Christ has been discussed at some length. Paul may well have had in mind that mysterious, apocalyptic figure, prominent in the pseudepigrapha, the Son of Man, whose salient features were

[1] S. Mowinckel, *He that Cometh*, p. 334.   [2] *Ibid.*, p. 285.
[3] This interpretation of this last passage does not depend on whether or not the word ὑπάρχων in verse 6 means 'existing originally.' In fact, the verb had almost lost that meaning in the *Koine. Vide* VGT, pp. 650–1.
[4] They coupled with it Rom. 8. 29 ('the first-born among many brothers'). *Vide* J. N. Kelly, *Early Christian Doctrines* (London, 1958), pp. 229–30.
[5] J. F. Bethune-Baker, *An Introduction to the Early History of Christian Doctrine* (London, 1933), p. 162 n.
[6] On whether or not these verses are an interpolation *vide* W. D. Davies, *Paul and Rabbinic Judaism*, pp. 150–1.

transferred by some rabbis to the expected Messiah,[1] one of them being his pre-existence (1 En. 39. 3–7; 48. 3–6; 49. 2; 62. 7). After all, the Jesus of Paul's earliest Epistles bears a resemblance to this Son of Man. Like him the Jesus of the Thessalonian Epistles will descend from heaven to judge mankind at the Parousia, and to punish his enemies (1 Thess. 4. 16; 2 Thess. 1. 7–10; 2. 8). Nor is the same idea entirely absent from two later Epistles (1 Cor. 15. 52; Phil. 3. 20). There is also the view skilfully put forward by W. D. Davies, who maintains that Paul derived his doctrine of the pre-existent Christ from the idea, found in Proverbs 8. 22–31 and Ecclesiasticus 24. 3–9, of the pre-existence of the Wisdom of God and, since Jewish thinking, on the basis of such statements as Deuteronomy 6. 6 and Ecclesiasticus 24. 23, identified it with Wisdom, of the Torah. Davies argues that because Paul believed that Jesus had superseded the Torah, he transferred all its attributes, including pre-existence, to him.[2] Undoubtedly Davies makes out an excellent case for this view, being able to point to Paul's own explicit description of Christ as the Wisdom of God (1 Cor. 1. 24, 30). It was, however, another of Paul's titles for Jesus that, in our opinion, caused him to think of Jesus as pre-existent; but before we consider this, we must allude very briefly to two other explanations of Paul's use of the concept. The one, put forward by J. B. Lightfoot, Weiss, and E. F. Scott, is that Paul was in this matter indebted to the Logos doctrine of Philo;[3] the other finds the origin of Colossians 1. 15–17 in Stoicism.[4] Yet, as we have said, there is another possible source, much nearer home as it were than Alexandrian Judaism and Stoicism and much more prominent in his Epistles than either the Enochene Son of Man concept or the Wisdom concept. After all, there are only two explicit references to the latter, and those obviously *ad hoc*, elicited by the

---

[1] S. Mowinckel, *He that Cometh*, pp. 333 ff.
[2] W. D. Davies, *Paul and Rabbinic Judaism*, pp. 150–75.
[3] J. B. Lightfoot, *Comm. on Colossians and Philemon* (London, 1882), pp. 144 ff.; J. Weiss, *The History of Primitive Christianity*, Eng. tr. R. Knopf, completed by four friends, ed. F. C. Grant (London, 1937), Vol. 2, pp. 482 f.; E. F. Scott, *Comm. on Colossians, Philemon and Ephesians* (London, 1923), pp. 20 f.
[4] A. E. J. Rawlinson, *The NT Doctrine of the Christ*, p. 162.

interest of his Corinthian converts in σοφία, who prided themselves on their possession of it (1 Cor. 1. 18–31; 2. 6–16). This other source to which we refer—here we reach the sixth salient motif of Paul's Christology—is his conception of Christ's divine Sonship. This description of Christ as 'the Son of God' and its equivalents occur numerous times in the Pauline Epistles (Rom. 1. 3, 4; 5. 10; 8. 3, 29, 32; 1 Cor. 1. 9; 15. 28; 2 Cor. 1. 19; Gal. 1. 16; 2. 20; 4. 4, 6; 1 Thess. 1. 10; Eph. 4. 13; Col. 1. 13; etc.), to which references we must add those passages where Paul speaks of God as the Father of our Lord Jesus Christ (2 Cor. 1. 3; 11. 31; Eph. 1. 3; Col. 1. 3). To call someone 'son of God' was not a novelty in Judaism. After all, it was Scriptural enough. Some OT writings spoke of the whole Hebrew race as Yahweh's son (Ex. 4. 22–3; Deut. 32. 6, 18; Jer. 31. 9, 20; Hos. 11. 1); others called Israelite kings Yahweh's sons (2 Sam. 7. 14; 1 Chron. 17. 13; 22. 10; Ps. 2. 7; 89. 26–7); and certain of the apocryphal and pseud-epigraphic works informed their readers that the righteous were God's sons (Ecclus. 4. 10; Wisd. 2. 18; Pss. Sol. 13. 8; 17. 30; 18. 4). Similarly Paul himself could speak of all Christians as sons of God (Rom. 8. 14; Gal. 4. 5–7). As to the divine sonship of the Messiah, whilst orthodox Judaism shrank from calling him the Son of God, the rabbis sometimes used the title of him in their citations of Psalm 2. 7,[1] and also there is evidence that in some quarters (though not in the pseudepigrapha) it was given to the Son of Man.[2] Likewise the term was well-known in the Gentile world, where rulers, philosophers, priests, and worthy men were regarded as physical descendants of gods. For example, the progenitor of the ancient kings of Egypt was believed to be the god Ra and the Ptolemies were regarded as the sons of Isis and Osiris. It was in this same sense that the Roman emperor was named *divi filius*.[3] The Stoics widened the concept to include all men, whom they looked upon as the physical offspring of the

---

[1] S. Mowinckel, *He that Cometh*, pp. 293–4. [2] *Ibid.*, pp. 368–9.

[3] E.g. Augustus, Caligula, etc. It should be noted that this title 'as applied to the Roman emperor of the first Christian century, was not, however, a characterization of the emperor himself as divine, or of divine origin, but referred to the fact that his predecessor had been deified at death' (E. de W. Burton, *Comm. on Gal.*, p. 407).

universal divine force.[1] The important point here is that Paul's conception of the divine sonship of Jesus differed essentially from all these other conceptions of divine sonship. His Sonship was unique, and lest there should be any quibbling about the meaning of the adjective, let the oracle speak: 'It is applicable only to what is in some respects the sole existing specimen, the precise like of which may be sought in vain.'[2] In what respects was Jesus 'the sole existing specimen' of divine sonship? It is well-known to Biblical students that the Semitic expression 'son of,' when used metaphorically means 'being connected with' or 'belonging to' or 'having the quality or qualities of' what follows it; e.g. 'son of peace' (Lk. 10. 6), 'sons of disobedience' (Eph. 2. 2; 5. 6), etc.. Therefore to call someone 'son of God' meant that he shared a divine quality or divine qualities. As Paul depicts him, Jesus shared God's nature completely. He is 'the Lord of glory' ($\tau\hat{\eta}s$ $\delta\delta\xi\eta s$) (1 Cor. 2. 8). The glory of God shines in his face (2 Cor. 4. 4, 6). This word $\delta\delta\xi\alpha$, the LXX equivalent of the Hebrew $k\bar{a}bh\bar{o}dh$, 'is shown by a study of its Septuagintal background to evoke ideas of the brightness of God's presence and his saving activity as displayed in his "wonderful acts" performed on behalf of his people.'[3] The $\delta\delta\xi\alpha$ of God's presence, which, according to the OT, dwelt in the midst of Israel (Ex. 16. 10; 24. 16; 40. 34 f. Cf. Rom. 9. 4) and which the rabbis called the Shekhinah, 'that which dwells,' was now visible in Jesus Christ. He is also God's $\epsilon\imath\kappa\omega\nu$ (2 Cor. 4. 4; Col. 1. 15), God's image, a term that in the former passage is closely linked with the concept of Christ's $\delta\delta\xi\alpha$. It means more than mere likeness, denoting an expression of the reality that it portrays.[4] The $\epsilon\imath\kappa\omega\nu$ of God, in which Adam was created (Gen. 1. 27; 5. 1), was lost when he transgressed, only to reappear in all its glory in the face of Christ (cf. Col. 3. 10).

---

[1] Paul himself quoted the line from the Stoic poets, Cleanthes and Aratus: 'For we are indeed his offspring' (Acts 17. 28); but he did not mean thereby that men were physical descendants of God. He meant that God created them.

[2] H. W. Fowler, *A Dictionary of Modern English Usage* (Oxford, 1954), p. 681. Cf. E. Gowers, *The Complete Plain Words* (London, 1962), p. 232.

[3] D. E. H. Whiteley, *The Theology of St. Paul*, p. 101. Cf. A. Richardson, ITNT, pp. 64–7.

[4] J. B. Lightfoot, *Comm. on Colossians and Philemon*, pp. 144–6.

Paul's Christological statements reach their climax in Philippians 2. 6 and Colossians 2. 9. Jesus is the μορφή of God (Phil. 2. 6), which if we retain the meaning of the word μορφή that we accepted when we were discussing the phrase μορφὴ δούλου, viz. 'the form which truly and fully expresses the being which underlies it,'[1] means that Jesus not only resembled God, but also essentially was God. The conviction that this was Paul's meaning is strengthened by his use of the phrase, τὸ εἶναι ἴσα Θεῷ, the state of being equal in quality to God. Then there is Colossians 2. 9, where with the need of correcting the false speculations of some form of Gnosticism in mind, he says that the totality of the divine nature (πᾶν τὸ πλήρωμα τῆς Θεότητος) took pleasure in making its home in the person of (σωματικῶς) Jesus.

To reiterate what we have said, the basis of these assertions was Paul's experience of what God had done for man: 'God in Christ was reconciling the world to himself' (2 Cor. 5. 19). Nowhere in Paul's Epistles is his experience of Christ summed up more succinctly than in the phrase κατὰ πνεῦμα ἁγιωσύνης (Rom. 1. 4). What Paul experienced in Christ was πνεῦμα ἁγιωσύνης. As we have said, the word πνεῦμα means 'activity';[2] and the comparatively rare word ἁγιωσύνη is derived from the adjective ἅγιος, which, when applied to God, denotes what is characteristic of him, his essential nature. This includes an ethical content, which Paul refers to in 2 Corinthians 5. 21, where he declares that Jesus was sinless; but, as Otto has shown, there is more to the meaning of holiness than goodness: it is what he calls 'the numinous,' from the Latin word numen.[3] Mysterium tremendum, majestas, the wholly other—these are the terms that Otto uses in his attempt to define God's holiness.[4] Perhaps the last is the most satisfactory, although it is no more than a synonym for the word 'transcendence.' Whichever term we prefer, it was, according to Romans 1. 4, the activity of the all-holy God that Paul experienced in Jesus Christ. It may be that, as Otto says, we today are able to apprehend more easily what God in Christ achieved than did

---

[1] V. sup., p. 179.   [2] V. sup., p. 112.
[3] R. Otto, The Idea of the Holy (Oxford, 1924), pp. 6–7.   [4] Ibid., Chaps. 4 and 5.

Christ's own contemporaries, because 'not only is our historical insight more keen, but we can also see the whole in better perspective at our greater distance.'[1] Nevertheless, is not the conclusion that, according to Otto, those of us who contemplate the development of the faith of Israel and, above all, 'the personality that is its fulfilment, his firm, unfaltering hold upon God, his unwavering, unfailing righteousness, his certitude of conviction and assurance in action so mysterious and profound, his spiritual fervour and beatitude, the struggles and trustfulness, self-surrender and suffering, and finally the conqueror's death that were his,' must inevitably reach, an adequate summary of Paul's own? 'That is god-like and divine; that is verily Holiness. If there is a God, and if he chose to reveal himself, he could do it no otherwise than this.'[2]

Thus in Paul's opinion Christ was the unique Son of God, God's own Son (τοῦ ἰδίου ᾽Υιοῦ) (Rom. 8. 32), 'the Son of his love' (Col. 1. 13), the eternal Son, existing with his Father from all eternity, existing not only in the historical process, but also before it, beyond it, and outside it. To revert to those other conceptions of divine sonship,[3] not one of them reaches this height. At a point in time, viz. when the Sinaitic bᵉrîth was created, the Hebrew race was adopted as Yahweh's son, and it was in this sense alone that Yahweh 'gave birth to' Israel (Deut. 32. 6, 18; Mal. 2. 10). Likewise, the king of Israel was adopted as Yahweh's son at his accession, when the basic event 'was the incorporation of David's descendant into a filial relationship with Yahweh.'[4] The words in a royal Psalm, recited on that occasion and addressed by Yahweh to the king, 'You are my son, today I have begotten you' (Ps. 2. 7), as the word 'today' shows, are the formula of adoption of the ruler as Yahweh's son at that point in time. This is confirmed by the words of another royal Psalm: 'I will *make* him (the king) my first-born' (Ps. 89. 27): he is not Yahweh's son before his accession, but is given that status at that

---

[1] R. Otto, *The Idea of the Holy*, p. 174.   [2] *Ibid.*   [3] *V. sup.*, pp. 187-8.
[4] G. von Rad., *OT Theology*, Eng. tr. D. M. G. Stalker, 2 vols. (Edinburgh and London, 1963), Vol. 1, p. 320.

moment. Then there is the divine sonship of righteous Jews: in what sense were they regarded as sons of Yahweh? Although there is no statement in Hebrew writings that they were adopted as his sons at a moment of time, it is implied in the passages from the apocrypha and pseudepigrapha previously mentioned,[1] in that their sonship is conditional upon their observance of the Law. Similarly in his statements about the adoption of Christians as sons of God Paul implies that it is conditional: it depends upon their conversion (Rom. 8. 15–17; Gal. 4. 5; Eph. 1. 5). As for the divine sonship of Gentile rulers, philosophers, priests, and worthy men, since they were regarded as divine sons by physical descent, the implication is that they acquired this status at birth, i.e. like the various Hebrew 'sons of Yahweh,' at a point in time, but unlike Christ, who was the pre-existent, eternal Son of God.[2]

To sum up Paul's Christology, in accordance with God's plan he sent his pre-existent Son to earth to live as a human being whose essential quality was that of a Suffering Servant, who through his sacrificial death was raised to the throne that was rightfully his, the throne of the Sovereign Messiah of all mankind, and who continued his personal, saving activity as the corporate Son of Man, his body, the Church, of which he is the head. Pre-existent Son of God, Suffering Servant, Sovereign Messiah, and Corporate Son of Man—all these Jewish concepts (together with traces of that of the apocalyptic Son of Man of the pseudepigraphic writers and that of the divine Wisdom) are used by Paul and transformed by him in giving his portrait of him who was their fulfilment. There remains one final point before we leave the subject. Cullmann rightly says that 'all Christology is *Heilsgeschichte*, and all *Heilsgeschichte* is Christology.'[3] What Cullmann means by this German term, which, emanating from the

---

[1] *V. sup.*, p. 187.

[2] Obviously some comment on the phrase τοῦ ὁρισθέντος υἱοῦ θεοῦ ἐξ ἀναστάσεως νεκρῶν in Rom. 1. 4 is demanded here. It has been interpreted in an Adoptianist sense; viz. Jesus was appointed or adopted as Son of God as a result of the Resurrection. It is true that ὁρισθέντος can be translated 'appointed'; but equally well it can be translated 'declared'; i.e. Jesus was already Son of God and his resurrection merely declared that fact to men. In view of Paul's other statements about Christ's pre-existence the latter meaning is to be preferred.

[3] O. Cullmann, *The Christology of the NT*, p. 326.

Erlangen School, has become one of the jargon words of current theology, is 'redemptive history,'[1] i.e. the action of God in saving (or in our vocabulary, liberating) mankind. Thus in his statement that we have just quoted he is saying that the personality of Jesus Christ can be understood only by examining the function that he performed in that divine, saving action. We venture to say that this sums up Paul's own attitude. One of the sentences in his Epistles that deserves to be printed in the largest possible capital letters is: 'God in Christ was reconciling the world to himself' (2 Cor. 5. 19). Never at any time does he allow men to forget that in the life and work of Jesus there God was at work, liberating men from their bondage. Thus it follows that it is in Christ that God is revealing his nature to men or, to put it in Cullmann's words, *Jesus Christ is God in his self-revelation.*[2] As we have already pointed out, one way of saying that is, as Paul frequently does, to describe Jesus as the Son of God. It is claimed by most NT scholars that another way in which Paul expresses it is to give him the title κύριος. We have argued that one meaning conveyed by the term as it is applied to Jesus by Paul is that of Christ's royal sovereignty. The question is whether or not that exhausts its meaning. On the basis of his scrutiny of the evidence Cerfaux reached the conclusion that when it was applied to rulers, including Roman emperors, it connoted no more than royal dignity, having no cultic significance. There is, he says, a distinction between κύριος and θεός, and between their Aramaic equivalents *marana* and *elaha*.[3] Cullmann, on the other hand, dissents from this position, arguing that where the ruler was worshipped as a god, κύριος must inevitably appropriate to itself the meaning of divinity.[4] On the whole, Cerfaux seems to be right; if κύριος implied divinity it seems strange that men, when speaking of rulers whom they deified, should have thought it necessary to add the word θεός to κύριος to indicate that they were gods.[5]

---

[1] O. Cullmann, *Christ and Time*, Eng. tr. F. V. Filson (London, 1951), p. 27.
[2] O. Cullmann, *The Christology of the NT*, p. 325.
[3] L. Cerfaux, *Christ in the Theology of St. Paul*, p. 465 n.
[4] O. Cullmann, *The Christology of the New Testament*, pp. 198–9.
[5] For examples of the collocation of the two terms *vide* VGT, p. 365.

The truth is that we should always bear in mind that the word κύριος is basically an adjective meaning 'having κῦρος, authority'; therefore the kind of authority that it is describing in a particular instance depends not on κύριος itself, but on the status of the person to whom it is applied: when it is applied to a king, it means 'having the authority of a king'; when it is applied to a god, as it was in the oriental mystery religions, e.g. Osiris, Sarapis, Isis, Artemis of Ephesus, and Cybele,[1] then it means 'having the authority of a god.' Applying this to Paul's descriptions of Jesus Christ, we have already argued that since he regarded him as the royal Messianic ruler, when he speaks of him as a κύριος, he is referring to his royal authority. Likewise, if Paul believed him to be divine, then κύριος contains the idea of divine authority. That Paul believed him to be uniquely divine, we have already shown in our consideration of his application of the title 'Son of God' to him; and that alone would suffice to prove the case. There is, however, a much more powerful piece of evidence: Philippians 2. 9–11. Although in some of his Epistles 'there are some things hard to understand' (2 Pet. 3. 16), here he does not leave us in much doubt about what he means. As we stated in an earlier reference to this decisive passage, it asserts that the consequence of the crucifixion of Jesus Christ was his exaltation by God to his royal throne. The king is crowned as a result of his suffering. 'Therefore (διό), viz. on account of his obedience, his life of slavery, his humiliation, which ended with his death on a gibbet, God highly exalted him.' That, however, is not Paul's final word on the subject: he continues, 'and bestowed on him the name which is above every name, that at the name of Jesus every knee should bow, in heaven and on earth and under the earth, and every tongue confess that Jesus Christ is Lord.' Is the uniquely divine sovereignty of Jesus the royal, Messianic king more explicitly declared anywhere than it is here? One of the principal ideas in the ancient Israelite conception of the king, and therefore, of the ideal Messianic king, was that they were divine

---

[1] For examples of the application of κύριος and κύρια to these deities vide VGT, p. 365.

beings;[1] but neither of them is ever described or addressed in terms such as those of Philippians 2. 9–11.[2] God bestows on Jesus 'the name that is above every name.' What is that name? In view of his statement that God's intention was that the whole creation should bow the knee to Jesus in adoration, the name that Paul had in mind can have been only *Adonai-Yahweh*, the sacred name of God himself, of which κύριος, which he applies to Jesus in verse 11, was the LXX equivalent.[3] He has a vision of the entire universe prostrate before the throne of Jesus, its rightful, royal ruler, and uttering its credal confession that he is κύριος, the divine ruler whose sovereignty is that of *Adonai-Yahweh* himself. After reading the rhapsodical utterance of Philippians 2. 9–11, it is almost an anti-climax to find that Paul 'transfers to Christ not only the title *Kyrios* but some of the most striking attributes which had been associated with it in the Old Testament.'[4] After all, it is only what we expect to hear. Nevertheless, it serves to confirm the conclusion that the term κύριος contains the idea, not merely of a royal authority, but of a uniquely divine royal authority.

Yet although Paul regarded Jesus as uniquely divine, he nowhere makes the categorical assertion that Jesus is God. The weight of scholarly opinion is against the application of the doxology of Romans 9. 5 to Christ,[5] while the phrase τοῦ Θεοῦ ἡμῶν καὶ

[1] S. Mowinckel, *He that Cometh*, pp. 62, 175.

[2] Mowinckel claims that in Ps. 45. 6 the king is addressed as a god: but the verse is notoriously obscure. *Vide* G. W. Anderson, *ad loc*, in *Peake's Commentary*, new edn., p. 422.

[3] It is much more likely that this was the source of Paul's conception of the divine sovereignty of Jesus than that, as Bousset (*Kyrios Christos*, 2nd edn., Göttingen, 1921, pp. 90, 99) and Bultmann, who has recently given Bousset's hypothesis a new lease of life (*Theology of the NT*, Vol. 1, pp. 51, 124), claim, he assimilated it from the Greek-speaking Christian communities in centres like Syrian Antioch, Tarsus, and Damascus, who had adopted it from the oriental mystery religions with which they were familiar, thus making Jesus an imitation of the κύριοι and κύριαι of those cults, e.g. Osiris, Sarapis, Isis, Artemis of Ephesus, and Cybele (for examples of the application of κύριος and κύρια to these deities *vide* VGT, p. 365). The most notable attacks on Bousset's theory are to be found in A. E. J. Rawlinson's *The NT Doctrine of the Christ*, pp. 39 f. 92–107, 231–7, V. Taylor's *The Names of Jesus*, pp. 47–9, and R. Fuller's *The Mission and Achievement of Jesus* (London, 1954), pp. 111–14.

[4] C. A. A. Scott, *Christianity according to St. Paul*, p. 252. There is no need for me to give instances of this transference; Scott does it (*ibid.*, pp. 252–3).

[5] C. H. Dodd, *Comm. on Rom.*, MNTC, *ad loc*; L. Cerfaux, *Christ in the Theology of St. Paul*, pp. 517–20.

Κυρίου Ἰησοῦ Χριστοῦ in 2 Thessalonians 1. 12 is highly ambiguous. Furthermore, in 1 Corinthians 8. 5–6, where he is contrasting the one God and Jesus Christ the one Lord with the θέοι and κύριοι of the pagan world, he seems to make a distinction between God and Jesus. The same can be said of Philippians 2. 11, where the purpose of the establishment of the sovereignty of Jesus is the glorification of God the Father. The issue is placed beyond doubt when we read the subordinationist passages, 1 Corinthians 3. 23; 11. 3; and 15. 28,[1] 'Christ is God's; the head of Christ is God.' Paul is too sound a monotheist to be guilty of the heresy of identifying the two.

Jesus Christ is the pre-existent Son of God; the Suffering Servant; the Sovereign Ruler of mankind; the Son of Man; and finally, the Divine Lord; and the sum total of all this is (to repeat Cullmann's italicized sentence) that 'Jesus Christ is God in his self-revelation.' In the Heilsgeschichte God in Christ liberates man; the end, the final outcome, the consummation of the redemptive history, when the Son hands over his authority to God the Father will be that state in which God is 'everything to everyone' (1 Cor. 15. 28).

[1] Cf. V. Taylor, The Person of Christ in NT Teaching, p. 56.

8

MORALIST

Conduct is three-fourths of our life and its largest concern.
MATTHEW ARNOLD, Literature and Dogma, Chapter 1, par. 3.

Dilige et quod vis fac.
AUGUSTINE, In Ioann, 7. 8

IF WE hope to discover in the Pauline epistles a formal science of
ethics, we shall be disappointed. As L. H. Marshall says, 'Paul is
not to be regarded in any sense as an ethical philosopher, for he
entered into no discussion of ethical theories.'[1] At the same time,
the title that we have bestowed upon him at the head of this
chapter is justified: a moralist is one who teaches morality, and a
large proportion of Paul's writings are concerned with telling
Christians how they ought to behave. As we saw when we were
considering his theology, he taught that the acceptance of Jesus
as Lord was only the beginning of the life of the Christian.
When the convert becomes a member of Christ's corporate
personality ($\sigma\hat{\omega}\mu\alpha$), the Church, he is immersed in Christ's $\pi\nu\epsilon\hat{\nu}\mu\alpha$,
Christ's activity; a process described by Paul as a crucifixion of
the $\sigma\acute{\alpha}\rho\xi$, the old ego, and a resurrection to the new life led by a
new ego (Rom. 6. 3–4; Gal. 3. 27; Col. 2. 12; 3. 1).[2] When a
man is united with Christ's activity ($\pi\nu\epsilon\hat{\nu}\mu\alpha$), i.e. becomes a
member of the Christian society, there is a new act of creation
(2 Cor. 5. 17). This does not mean, however, that he is suddenly,
and as it were magically, changed from sinner into saint. To
profess with their lips that Jesus was Lord and to become members
of the Christian society did not automatically ensure that Paul's
converts would forthwith cease to live as they had been living
before their conversion. On the contrary, they were still liable
to sin, and therefore needed ethical guidance. For example,
although the Corinthian Christians had been washed, sanctified,

[1] *The Challenge of N.T. Ethics* (London, 1947), p. 21. [2] *V. sup.*, p. 122.

196

and vindicated (1 Cor. 6. 11), they were still immature 'infants in Christ' allowing themselves to be governed by their unredeemed human nature (σαρκίκοι); a fact that showed itself in their jealousy and wrangling (1 Cor. 1. 10–12; 3. 2–3), their fondness for litigation (1 Cor. 6. 1–7), their sexual immorality (1 Cor. 5. 1; 6. 12–20), and their idolatry (1 Cor. 10. 1–22). Likewise the Christians of Colossae and of the province of Asia in general were by their immoral conduct (Col. 3. 5–9; Eph. 4. 25–31; 5. 4) showing that they had not yet outgrown adolescence. Indeed, Paul himself was still immature, pressing towards the goal like an athlete (Phil. 3. 12–14).

What that goal was Paul indicates in Ephesians 5. 1, where he urges his readers to become 'imitators of God' (μιμηταὶ τοῦ Θεοῦ), which, as he explains in the next verse, means that they must try to live as the Jesus of history did (cf. Rom. 15. 7; Phil. 2. 5; Eph. 4. 32). In earlier letters he had bidden his readers imitate his own conduct (2 Thess. 3. 7, 9; 1 Cor. 4. 16; 11. 1; Gal. 4. 12; Phil. 3. 17; 4. 9), an injunction that may to some sound inexcusably arrogant, although he strives to remove that impression by stating in 1 Corinthians 11. 1 that his own model, and by implication theirs as well, is Christ himself, and by changing in Philippians 3. 17 the first person singular (μου) to the first person plural (ἡμᾶς) to include his colleagues, Epaphroditus and Timothy. The imitatio Christi, according to Paul, is the life of the Christian. Christian thinking, the Christian attitude to life, is that of Jesus Christ himself (Phil. 2. 5). It is this which shows that the Christ is still alive in the world, that the Church is his corporate personality (τὸ σῶμα τοῦ Χριστοῦ), whose activity (πνεῦμα) continues his own. Therefore, if this claim is to be believed, it is essential that the conduct of Christians shall exactly resemble Christ's own (Rom. 8. 9, 12–14; Gal. 5. 16, 25). We discover what the broad pattern of Christ's activity was when we examine passages like Romans 14. 15; 15. 3; 2 Corinthians 5. 14–15; 8. 9; and Philippians 2. 4–8, whose leitmotiv is that, as the Suffering Servant, he sacrificed himself to the utmost in the service of mankind.[1] For

---

[1] V. sup., pp. 180 ff.

Paul's more detailed portrait of Christ's activity and therefore of the activity of the mature Christian disciple, we turn to some of the best known passages in his epistles: Ephesians 4. 1–3; Colossians 3. 12–14; the list in Galatians 5. 22–3 of the products of Christ's activity in the Church, the last eight of which are, when all comes to all, manifestations of the first; and above all the paean of 1 Corinthians 13, lauding ἀγάπη, a word translated 'charity' by the makers of King James's version, and 'love' in the RV and the modern translations.

In the first century A.D. there existed three Greek words to denote the various kinds of love. First, there was ἔρως, with its related verb ἐράω, used to describe sexual love and implying sexual attraction. Then, there was the φιλία group: φιλία, φιλέω, and φίλος. The nearest English translation of φιλία is probably 'friendship'; of φιλέω, 'to love as a relative or friend'; and of φίλος, 'friend.' It is significant that the noun φιλία occurs only once in the NT, in James 4. 4, where it is applied to friendship with the corrupt system of the age. The verb φιλέω is frequent in the Fourth Gospel,[1] but Paul uses it only once, in 1 Corinthians 16. 22, where curiously enough he applies it to love for the Lord. Like the verb φιλέω the adjective φίλος is found in numerous NT verses, but none of them were written by Paul. The truth is that Christianity preferred the third group of words: ἀγάπη, 'love'; ἀγαπάω, 'to love'; and ἀγαπητός, 'beloved.' There should be no need to point out that the Christians did not manufacture these words to describe what they believed to be, and indeed what was, a new phenomenon. The verb and the adjective are found in the classical writings and the LXX, but the noun occurs in pre-Christian literature only in the *Epistula ad Philocratem* of Aristeas (2nd–1st cent. B.C.), the Herculaneum papyri of Philodemus the Epicurean (1st cent. B.C.), and the LXX. In the last it denotes any kind of love (except, of course, what the Christian meant by the word), including, as in the *Song of Songs*, sexual passion.[2] As the

---

[1] There are places in the Fourth Gospel where φιλέω may be synonymous with ἀγαπάω. *Vide* J. H. Bernard, *Comm. on St. John*, ICC (Edinburgh, 1928), Vol. 2, pp. 702–4.

[2] For references *vide* VGT, p. 2. Possibly Philo used it once (VGT, *ibid.*), but we can hardly call him 'pre-Christian,' his dates being 20 B.C.–A.D. 50

most comprehensive word for love that there was in the Greek vocabulary, it was the most appropriate term to describe Christian love. That Paul, whatever he may have believed about sexual relations when he was writing 1 Corinthians,[1] included ἔρως in ἀγάπη when he was inditing Ephesians is shown by his injunction to husbands (Eph. 5. 25), where the verb is ἀγαπάω.[2] Ἀγάπη also included and transcended mere φιλία, 'friendship.' The fact that the OT contains no fewer than nine words that can be accurately translated 'friend' suggests that the Hebrews knew what the nature of genuine friendship was. Although there is no abstract treatise on friendship in their canonical literature, they have given to the world something better, namely a picture of an ideal friendship: "The soul of Jonathan was knit to the soul of David, and Jonathan loved him as his own soul' (1 Sam. 18. 1). What is more majestically poignant than David's lament over his dead friend? 'I am distressed for you, my brother Jonathan; very pleasant have you been to me; your love to me was wonderful, passing the love of women' (2 Sam. 1. 26). It is small wonder that the Hebrews described even the transcendent, all-holy Yahweh himself, far removed from humanity as he was, as the friend of man. 'Yahweh used to speak to Moses face to face, as a man speaks to his friend' (Ex. 33. 11). Likewise Abraham was known as Yahweh's friend (2 Chron. 20. 7; Is. 41. 8; cf. Jas. 2. 23). Like the Hebrews the Greeks had their prototype of friendship: Pylades and Orestes of Homeric legend. As for the Romans they could point to a David and Jonathan who were not at all legendary, the Pythagorean philosophers of Syracuse, Damon and Pythias. Furthermore, unlike the Jews, Gentile writers produced theoretical disquisitions on friendship.[3] According to Xenophon and Plato, Socrates expatiated on its nature;[4] but it was Aristotle and his successor as head of the Lyceum, Theophrastus, who wrote on the

---

[1] V. inf., pp. 199 ff.   [2] V. inf., p. 211.

[3] Although there is no Jewish treatise on friendship, there are apophthegms about it in Prov. 13. 20; 17. 17; 27. 6, 10.

[4] Xenophon, Memorabilia, 1, 2, 55; 2, 4, 6; Plato, Lysis, 210–21.

topic at the greatest length.[1] The Romans had their say as well, the classic Latin treatise on it being Cicero's *Laelius vel de Amicitia*, and some of the most magnificent passages in the writings of Paul's celebrated contemporary, Seneca, being concerned with it. Thus both the OT and the classical writers provide us with concrete examples of friendship, and the latter also define it, analyse it, and express noble sentiments about its essential qualities; but all their examples and their ideas were to be excelled by the Christian conception and practice of love. David and Jonathan, Pylades and Orestes, Damon and Pythias, are devoted each to the other; Aristotle defines a friend as 'one who wishes, and promotes by action, the real or apparent good of another for that other's sake,'[2] friendship consisting in loving rather than in being loved;[3] Cicero in the *de Amicitia* describes it as 'agreement on all subjects sacred and secular, coupled with goodwill and affection,'[4] and in an earlier work as 'the willing good things to another person for his own sake, together with the same will on his part towards you';[5] and Seneca says that you ought to want a friend, not 'that you may have somebody to sit by your bedside when you are sick and to help you when you are in prison or poor,' but that you may have someone by whose bedside you may sit and whom you may rescue from the enemy's dungeon.[6] All these sentiments sound most exalted; yet we cannot fail to notice that none of these writers succeeds in painting friendship as entirely selfless. Socrates stresses the usefulness of friends, even advising the wealthy to purchase them when their price is low![7] Although there is none of such cynicism in Aristotle's long dilation on the subject, and although, indeed, he condemns 'the friendship of utility' as 'a thing for sordid souls,'[8] our approval of his lofty thoughts diminishes somewhat when we see that he denies the possibility of unconditional friendship between persons of

---

[1] Aristotle, *Eth. Nic.*, Bks. 8 and 9; *Eth. End.*, Bk. 7, chs. 1–12. Theophrastus wrote a work on it, περὶ φιλίας, no longer extant, but referred to by Diogenes Laertius (*De Vitis Philosophorum*, 5, 2, 45) and quoted by Aulus Gellius (*Noctes Atticae*, 1, 3).
[2] *Eth. Nic.*, 9, 4, 1.   [3] *Ibid.*, 8, 8, 3.   [4] *Op. cit.*, Ch. 6.
[5] *De Inventione*, 2, 166.   [6] *Epistles*, 9, 8.
[7] Xenophon, *Memorabilia*, 1. 2. 52; 2. 10. 4.   [8] *Eth. Nic.*, 8, 6, 4.

unequal rank.[1] The truth is that Aristotle was an early sample of
an intellectual gentlemanly snob, whose analysis of friendship as
if it were a corpse in a dissecting-chamber both leaves us unmoved
and also shows us that he had not begun to understand the meaning of genuine friendship! When we turn to the Roman writers,
the picture is much the same. Cicero, however high-minded
some of his statements may seem, makes friendship depend on
intellectual affinity,[2] while in one of his maxims even the noble
Seneca suggests that the motive of loving is the desire to be loved.[3]

It was Christianity that metamorphosed the Jewish and the
Graeco-Roman conception of friendship. Taking over the LXX
word ἀγάπη, the Christians used it to describe the love that they
experienced within their own community; a love that, unlike
ἔρως and φιλία, contained no trace of self-regard, and, since it did
not depend on the attractions of the beloved, was neither emotional nor irrational. It stemmed from the major premise that
the all-embracing attitude of God to man was comprehensively
described by this word ἀγάπη; or, to put it in the familiar terminology of Jesus, that he was the Father who loved all men equally,
from which the inference was that men 'ought also to love one
another' (1 Jn. 4. 11). There we have the consummation of
friendship. Whether a man is unattractive or repulsive is im-
material: Esmeralda shows that she can love the hideously
grotesque Quasimodo, offering him a cup of water.[4]

> All must love the human form
> In heathen, Turk, or Jew.[5]

In a nutshell that expresses what the NT means by ἀγάπη; for
'the law of God which was of universal obligation was the law
of universal love, the law which regards every other human
being as of equal intrinsic importance to oneself, as equally
entitled to have his true good promoted by every other rational

---

[1] *Eth. Nic.* 8, 6, 6.   [2] *Vide* his definition of friendship on p. 200, *sup.*
[3] Seneca quotes a saying of Hecaton, a pupil of Panaetius: 'I will show you a love-
potion without drug or herb or any witch's spell: if you wish to be loved, love' (*Epistles*,
9, 6). He is speaking of friendship, not sexual love.
[4] Victor Hugo, *Notre Dame de Paris*, Bk. 6, ch. 4.
[5] William Blake, *Songs of Experience, The Divine Image.*

being. The most certain thing about the teaching of Jesus is that He did teach this doctrine of universal love.'¹ Christian ἀγάπη, says Paul, is the consummation of all moral law. 'Be in debt to no-one except for the debt of love to one another; for he who loves his fellow-man has consummated the law. These command-ments, "You must not commit adultery," "You must not kill," "You must not steal," "You must not covet," and if there is any other, it is summed up in the sentence, "You must love your fellow-man as you love yourself." He who is possessed by love does no ill to his neighbour: therefore love is the consummation of law' (Rom. 13. 8–10. Cf. Gal. 5. 14). Ἀγάπη is superior even to faith and hope (1 Cor. 13. 13). Without it the dithyrambics of the revivalist orator resemble the din made by a noisy gong or a clanging cymbal. Without it the inspired proclamation of the good news of God, the comprehension of the divine purpose, and the possession of omniscience or of a wonder-working faith produce nothing of value (1 Cor. 13. 1–2). All these, which appertain to the immature stage of human growth, when man can see truth only as a distorted reflection in a metal mirror, are transient; ἀγάπη alone will remain into the new age that has already begun with the advent of the Messiah. When the con-summation comes, men will understand as completely as God has understood them all along that ἀγάπη alone is sempiternal (1 Cor. 13. 8–12). Without ἀγάπη the surrender of all a man's goods and chattels to enable him to mete out food doles to the indigent and even the sacrifice of his life itself will avail him not one whit (1 Cor. 13. 3).²

Ἀγάπη is a cut gem with many facets. As we have seen, Paul is fond of listing the virtues that it comprises and the vices rife among the Gentiles whom he evangelized, that it excludes.³ One of the most prominent qualities of him whose life is ruled by ἀγάπη is humility (Rom. 12. 10; Phil. 2. 3–4; Eph. 4. 2; Col. 3. 12). 'Love does not play the braggart, is not puffed up with

¹ H. Rashdall, *Conscience and Christ* (London, 1916), p. 108.
² On 1 Cor. 13 *vide* A. Nygren, *Agape and Eros*, Eng. tr. A. G. Hebert, Pt. I (London, 1932), pp. 98–106; and J. Moffatt, *Love in the N.T.* (London, 1929), pp. 178–85.
³ *V. sup.*, pp. 85, 143 n. 3.

pride' (1 Cor. 13. 4). There is no place for arrogant, haughty braggadocio in the life of the Christian (Rom. 1. 30). Humility is, in the words of Gregory of Nyssa, 'the mother of the habit of meekness.'[1] This last word is the customary English translation of the penultimate in Paul's list of the products of Christ's activity (πνεῦμα, Gal. 5. 23. Cf. Eph. 4. 2; Col. 3. 12). It is a pity that the word 'meekness' and its synonym 'gentleness' have come to have a derogatory meaning.[2] The origin of the conception represented by Paul's word πραΰτης is to be found in the OT conception of those who are afflicted and oppressed, but who still trust in their God alone to vindicate and deliver them, and who therefore refrain from asserting themselves. They are the ᶜᵃnāwîm, the righteous remnant, 'the poor in spirit' (Is. 66. 2; Ps. 37. 11; Mt. 5. 3, 5), who quietly and patiently endure opposition, tyranny, and persecution. Their motive is neither fear of destruction nor pride nor scorn. Far from being timid and compliant, proud and scornful, the πραεῖς are heroic, conquering their own self-assertiveness and desire for vengeance. This attitude is described by Paul as μακροθυμία (2 Cor. 6. 6; Gal. 5. 22; Eph. 4. 2; Col. 1. 11). Perhaps the most fitting translation of this Greek noun is a word rarely used nowadays but not entirely obsolete, 'longanimity,'[3] or a coined word, 'long-temperedness.' What it amounts to is that, whatever the provocation, the Christian stores up no resentment when he is wronged (1 Cor. 13. 5) and forbears to return evil for evil (Rom. 12. 17). His angry impulse (ὀργή) must be restrained so that there are none of those ireful outbursts (θυμοί) (2 Cor. 12. 20; Gal. 5. 20) typical of the unredeemed man. Enmity (Gal. 5. 20), whether it be an inward malicious disposition (κακία) (Rom. 1. 29; 1 Cor. 5. 8; 14. 20; Eph. 4. 3; Col. 3. 8) or the external expression of that disposition (πονηρία) (Rom. 1. 29; 1 Cor. 5. 8; Eph. 6. 12) like killing (φόνος) (Rom. 1. 29), has no place in the life of the Christian. If Paul

[1] *The Lord's Prayer and the Beatitudes*, tr. H. C. Graef (London, 1954), p. 104.
[2] As in the popular interpretation of the words 'Gentle Jesus, meek and mild.'
[3] Although modern dictionaries contain this word, the most recent use of it, as far as I know, is to be found in the *Spectator* for 11th Jan., 1890: 'His longanimity under the foolishness of the young woman is really marvellous.'

tells his converts to restrain their anger, why then in Ephesians 4. 26 does he apparently order them to be angry? Even if, as some interpret, he is here speaking of anger against evil—righteous anger some would call it—his injunction still seems to be inconsistent with his absolute prohibition of anger in the other passages to which we have referred. The charge ceases to be valid, however, when we realize that he is quoting the LXX version of Psalm 4. 4, where the construction is the literal equivalent of a Hebraism. Frequently when we find two imperatives connected by *waw* in the Hebrew OT, the first represents the protasis, and the second, the apodosis, of a conditional sentence.[1] The literal translation, 'Be provoked to anger (ὀργίζω means 'to provoke to anger') and do not continue to sin (μή with the present imperative means 'Do not continue an action') is the equivalent of: 'If you are provoked to feel angry, stop sinning, i.e. do not give way to your anger.' What follows supports this interpretation: 'Never let the sun set on your exasperation; give the devil no room'; i.e. if a man harbours anger, he is yielding to sin. If Paul had left it there, recommending a mere passivity in the face of injustice and oppression, we could call it a negative attitude. He goes further, however, urging his readers to return good for evil. Echoing the very words of Jesus (Mt. 5. 44), he writes: 'Bless those who persecute you. . . . If your enemy is hungry, feed him; if he is thirsty, give him a drink, for by so doing you will heap burning coals on his head' (Rom. 12. 14, 20). Ἡ ἀγάπη μακροθυμεῖ, he writes (1 Cor. 13. 4); and his next sentence is, χρηστεύεται ἡ ἀγάπη.

Those last three words bring us to another aspect of ἀγάπη, viz. χρηστότης (2 Cor. 6. 6; Gal. 5. 22; Col. 3. 12), which is usually translated 'kindness.' The basic conception here is that of 'humaneness'; it is the attitude of him who does not insist on having his own way (οὐ ζητεῖ τὰ ἑαυτῆς) (1 Cor. 13. 5), who is not ruled by ἐριθεία, 'self-seeking' (Rom. 2. 8; 2 Cor. 12. 20; Gal. 5. 20; Phil. 1. 17), and whose sole concern is the welfare of his fellows. Obviously χρηστότης excludes a wide range of vices:

[1] GNTG, pp. 391–2.

envy (φθόνος) (Rom. 1. 29; Gal. 5. 21; Phil. 1. 15) and jealousy (ζῆλος) (Rom. 13. 13; 1 Cor. 3. 3; 13. 4; 2 Cor. 12. 20; Gal. 5. 20); wrangling (ἔρις) (Rom. 1. 29; 13. 13; 1 Cor. 3. 3; 2 Cor. 12. 20; Gal. 5. 20; Phil. 1. 15) and factiousness (αἱρέσεις) (Gal. 5. 20); bad faith (ἀσυνθεσία) (Rom. 1. 31), deception (δόλος) (Rom. 1. 29; 2 Cor. 12. 16; 1 Thess. 2. 3), plotting (ἐφεύρεσις κακῶν) (Rom. 1. 30), and lying (ψεῦδος) (Eph. 4. 25; Col. 3. 9); abusive speech (λοιδορία) (1 Cor. 5. 11; 6. 10) and slandering, whether secret (ψιθυρισμός) (Rom. 1. 29; 2 Cor. 12. 20) or coram populo (καταλαλιά) (Rom. 1. 30; 2 Cor. 12. 20); every form of lust (ἐπιθυμία) (Rom. 7. 17; Gal. 5. 24; Col. 3. 5; 1 Thess. 4. 5), whether it be aggressive cupidity (πλεονεξία) (Rom. 1. 29; Eph. 4. 19; 5. 3; Col. 3. 5), leading to the violent seizure of other men's personal property (1 Cor. 5. 10; 6. 10) or petty pilfering (1 Cor. 6. 10; Eph. 4. 28) or the various kinds of sexual depravity. As to this last, it comes as no surprise to those who have read descriptions of Graeco-Roman society of the first century A.D.[1] that its sexual immorality comes in for a major share of Paul's denunciation. Three terms used by him to describe sexual sins in general are πορνεία (Rom. 1. 29; 1. Cor. 5. 1; 6. 13, 18; Eph. 5. 3; Col. 3. 5)—which originally meant only 'prostitution' or 'fornication';[2] ἀκαθαρσία (Rom. 1. 24; 6. 19; 2 Cor. 12. 21; Gal. 5. 19; Eph. 4. 19; 5. 3; Col. 3. 5; 1 Thess. 2. 3; 4. 7)—'impurity'; and πάθος (Col. 3. 5; 1 Thess. 4. 5)—'sexual lust.' Particularizing, he mentions ἀσέλγεια (Rom. 13. 13; 2 Cor. 12. 21; Gal. 5. 19; Eph. 4. 19)—open wantonness that shocks public decency; fornication (πορνεία) (1 Cor. 5. 9; 6. 9; Eph. 5. 5); adultery (μοιχεία) (1 Cor. 6. 9; 1 Thess. 4. 6); sodomy (Rom. 1. 27; 1 Cor. 6. 9–10); lesbianism (Rom. 1. 26); and incest (1 Cor. 5. 1). What it amounts to is that in sexual matters χρηστότης involves complete self-control (ἐγκράτεια) (Gal. 5. 23), which is to be extended to the other appetites as well, especially drinking. Drunken carousals (κώμοις καὶ μέθαις) (Rom. 13. 13; 1 Cor. 5. 11; 6. 10; Gal. 5. 21; Eph. 5. 18; 1 Thess. 5. 7), another feature of the age, are

[1] V. sup., p. 85.   [2] VGT., p. 529. Κοίτη in Rom. 13. 13 has the same meaning.

condemned by Paul as yet another manifestation of the σάρξ, unredeemed human nature.

Obviously χρηστότης must be especially prominent within the Christian κοινωνία; otherwise this last word would be a misnomer. Quarrelling and the creation of cliques (1 Cor. 1. 10–12; 11. 17–34; 2 Cor. 12. 20) must cease, and there must be no litigation among Christians (1 Cor. 6. 1–8). Believers are to respect the scruples of other believers where vegetarianism (Rom. 14. 1–4), the observance of holy days (Rom. 14. 5), and participation in feasts where meat that has been used in idolatrous sacrifices is consumed (Rom. 14. 13 ff; 1 Cor. 8. 1–13; 10. 23–33). On the positive side, χρηστότης in the Christian community involves the provision of hospitality (φιλοξενία) (Rom. 12. 13). On the meaning of this Greek word Sanday and Headlam comment, 'The Christians looked upon themselves as a body of men scattered throughout the world, living as aliens amongst strange people, and therefore bound together as the members of a body, as the brethren of one family. The practical realization of this idea would demand that whenever a Christian went from one place to another he should find a home among the Christians in each town he visited.'[1] Thus Paul commends his messengers, most prominent of whom is Titus, to the Corinthian Christians, presuming that they will show their ἀγάπη by their hospitality (2 Cor. 8. 23–24). Another important manifestation of the χρηστότης of the κοινωνία was the contributing of financial aid by the wealthier Christian communities to the indigent church in Jerusalem. Liberal giving was the mark of a Christian (Rom. 12. 8); and Paul spent much time and energy on organizing the collection for the poverty-stricken believers in Jerusalem. He directed the members of the churches in Galatia and of the church in Corinth to put aside and save a sum of money each week for this purpose (1 Cor. 16. 1–2. Cf. Gal. 2. 10). Rightly he stresses the importance of the frame of mind of the giver (2 Cor. 9. 7). It was their willingness to contribute as well as the generosity of

[1] W. Sanday and A. C. Headlam, *Comm. on Rom.*, ICC, p. 363.

the contribution of the Christians of Macedonia that delighted him (2 Cor. 8. 1–4).

Finally, Paul gives guidance to his converts on four subjects of vital concern to the Christian community: marriage, the family, slavery, and their attitude towards the State. We shall consider the apostle's opinions on them *seriatim*. It has been said that Paul's attitude to marriage was 'that of one who might be described as naturally celibate.'[1] The author of that judgement has in mind 1 Corinthians 7, most of which seems, as the late Bishop Kirk said, to be 'devoted to a steady vindication of celibacy as against marriage.'[2] Not only does Paul advise those who have never married and widows to remain single (verses 7–8, 26–7, 37–38,[3] 40), but also he expresses the wish that everyone was, like himself, unmarried (verse 7). Yet before we endorse the opinion of Anderson Scott and Bishop Kirk, we must ask the question— Why does Paul advocate this course? Was it the outcome of a conviction that celibacy was, on account of the sexual relationship that matrimony involved, a higher moral state than the latter? Here as everywhere else we must consider the context of Paul's statements. The opening words of the chapter are, περὶ δὲ ὧν ἐγράψατε, καλὸν ἀνθρώπῳ γυναικὸς μὴ ἅπτεσθαι, which we translate thus: 'I am now turning to the particular matters which you mention in your letter to me. You say, "The proper course for a man is to discontinue sexual intercourse with his wife." '[4] Evidently some of the Corinthian Christians, living as they were in the extremely licentious environment of one of the most depraved cities of the Empire, thought that they ought to go to the extremes of asceticism and forswear the pleasures of the marriage bed altogether. Obviously in their minds all sexual intercourse, now that they had become Christians, was associated with the promiscuity

---

[1] C. A. A. Scott, *Christianity according to St. Paul*, p. 225.

[2] K. E. Kirk, *The Vision of God* (London, 1931), p. 76.

[3] It makes no difference to this argument whether in verses 36–8 Paul is referring to (*a*) father and daughter or (*b*) a man and his fiancée or (*c*) a man and his spiritual bride. For an adequate discussion of the various views *vide* D. E. H. Whiteley, *The Theology of St. Paul*, pp. 218–22.

[4] ἅπτεσθαι governing the genitive case means here 'to have sexual intercourse with' and, being a present infinitive, expresses the idea of continuing action.

that surrounded them and in which some of them had perhaps indulged in their pre-Christian days. Does Paul applaud their attitude? Does he either explicitly state or imply that the sexual act is *per se* obscene? Certainly, as we have already seen, he advises the unmarried and widows to remain single, and even goes so far as to say that he wishes that everyone were unmarried; but his reason is not the belief that sexual intercourse is sinful, but his conviction that the age is drawing to a close (verses 29 and 31). Obviously in such a situation there was no point in marrying, for marriage was meaningless. Therefore it was best if everyone remained as he was (verse 26). With what he calls 'the impending distress' (verse 26) in mind, he urges the Corinthian Christians to live lives of 'non-attachment' (to use Aldous Huxley's word);[1] they should not allow themselves to be distracted by thoughts of marriage, with which in this connection Paul links any cause of grief or happiness, business deals, the slave's craving for emancipation, and the desire of the Jewish Christian to have the marks of his circumcision removed,[2] and of the Gentile Christian to be circumcised (verses 27–33, 17–24). The married are so busy trying to please each other that they forget the Lord's business, which demands singlemindedness, whereas the unmarried are spared this distraction (verses 32–5). Thus we must reiterate that Paul's reason for advocating celibacy was his belief that the present age was nearing its end and that the age to come was dawning. He neither states nor implies that sexual intercourse is shameful. Yet the erroneous opinion that he did is, like Charles II, 'an unconscionable time dying.'[3] For example, the author of the introduction to a recent edition of that classic of erotica, Sir Richard Burton's translation of *The Perfumed Garden*, after quoting with approval Havelock Ellis's description of Paul as 'morbid,' a 'neuropath,' having a 'twisted suffering nature,' and one who 'trampled on nature when it came in his way, and for the rest never saw it,' traces the unhealthy attitude of many Christian

---

[1] *Ends and Means* (London, 1937), pp. 3–6.
[2] As certain Jews had done during the Maccabaean struggle (1 Macc. 1.15).
[3] Macaulay, *History of England*, Vol. 1, ch. 4.

theologians, e.g. Augustine, to the sexual relationship back to Paul's often quoted statement in 1 Corinthians 7. 9: 'It is better to marry than burn with the flame of sexual passion.' From this (it is held) stems their belief that sexual intercourse is indecent.[1] Likewise one of the exponents of the so-called 'new morality,' within the Christian fold, lays the blame at Paul's door.[2] The truth is that later theologians have perverted the apostle's dicta on the sexual relationship as monstrously as they have some of his other statements.[3] What Paul is saying is that, although in view of the imminence of the final consummation, it is advisable for Christians not to be preoccupied with, *inter alia*, marriage, there are those Christians whose sexual instinct is so powerful that for them the best course is to marry. 'It is better for them to marry than to burn with the flame of sexual passion.' It is better to satisfy the natural god-given sexual desire within marriage than either to suppress it[4] or to satisfy it with extra-marital coitus as many inhabitants of Corinth did. There is no suggestion that the marital relationship is morally inferior to celibacy or that it is shameful. On the contrary, Paul explicitly says that it is not sinful (verses 28 and 36), and that the desire to marry and the ability to make a satisfactory marriage is a divine χάρισμα (verse 7). Moreover, to revert to the statement in the letter from Corinth that it is best for married couples to abstain from sexual intercourse completely (1 Cor. 7. 1), Paul shows his disapproval of such asceticism, emphasizing that without sexual copulation no marriage is genuine. It is in this mutual self-surrender that each shows that he or she belongs to the other (verses 3–5). Even if the partners agree to abstain from sexual intercourse for a time in order to concentrate on prayer, the period of abstinence ought

[1] A. H. Walton, *op. cit.* (London, 1963; Panther edn.), pp. 49–51. Mr. Walton praises the Cambridge contributors to *Soundings*, ed. A. Vidler (Cambridge, 1962), especially H. A. Williams.
[2] D. Rhymes, *No New Morality* (London, 1964), pp. 10–15.
[3] E.g. his assertions concerning predestination in Rom. 9. 6–29. The Exhortation in the 1662 Prayer Book Marriage Service has played its part in distorting Paul's statements about the sexual relationship.
[4] I can think of no better pictorial illustration of the suppression of sexual desire than Thomas Hughes's exquisite painting, 'The Long Engagement,' in Birmingham Art Gallery. He who has eyes to see can feel the agony of the lovers.

not to be too long lest they be tempted to find satisfaction outside marriage (verse 5). The conclusion that emerges from this discussion is that 1 Corinthians 7 is not an attempt to demonstrate that celibacy is essentially a superior state to matrimony, and that Anderson Scott's opinion that Paul's attitude to marriage was 'that of one who might be described as naturally celibate,'[1] which is shared by Bishop Kirk and others, is erroneous.

This conclusion is strengthened when we examine Paul's other principal passage dealing with marriage, Ephesians 5. 22–33; for when he no longer believed that the end of the age was near, he never once mentioned celibacy. The picture of marriage painted in these verses is, apart from one item in it, idyllic. Seeking an analogue that will adequately describe the complete oneness of Christ with his Church, Paul can find none more fitting than the old, familiar metaphor of the Jewish prophets, who frequently thought of Israel as the bride of Yahweh (Am. 3. 2; Hos. 2. 7; Is. 54. 5–7; 62. 4 f.; Ezek. 16. 15–43), and of Jesus himself, who portrayed his own relationship with his followers in those same terms (Mk. 2. 19–20 = Mt. 9. 15 = Lk. 5. 34–5; Mt. 25. 1–6). The union of Christ and his Church resembles the union of husband and wife, who says Paul (quoting Gen. 2. 24), in sexual intercourse remain no longer separate beings, but become one personality (Eph. 5. 31). It is important to stress that Paul regards sexual coition not merely as a physical union, but a fusion of personalities. He who has sexual intercourse with a prostitute becomes, through this the most intimate of all human relationships, one personality with her (1 Cor. 6. 16). Similarly husband and wife united in sexual copulation become completely identified with each other. Christian marriage is, to use Shakespeare's timeless phrase, a 'marriage of true minds.' The love on which it is based is not that love

> which alters when it alteration finds,
> Or tends with the remover to remove.
> O, no! it is an ever-fixed mark.

[1] He himself seems to have thought that there was always the possibility that he might marry (1 Cor. 9 5).

It is

> not Time's fool, though rosy lips and cheeks
> Within his bending sickle's compass come.[1]

It is 'the kind of loving to carry us through' that Victor Brown in Stan Barstow's powerful novel hoped eventually to find:[2] the kind of loving in which the husband's personality is surrendered to his wife and hers to him so that the two melt into one whole.[3] It is this fusion that Paul has in mind when he says that 'he who loves his wife loves himself' (Eph. 5. 28), and that the personality (σῶμα) of each partner belongs to the other (1 Cor. 7. 4). The most important word in the passage in Ephesians is the verb ἀγαπάω. Christian marriage is a relationship governed by ἀγάπη from start to finish. The ideal is summed up in Paul's words: 'Husbands, love (ἀγαπᾶτε) your wives, as Christ loved the Church and gave himself up for her' (verse 25). Christian marriage is a complete, loving self-surrender of each partner to the other. This implies the equality of the two partners: 'a perfect union of love and affection, and entire community of aims and interests, as also of worldly possessions, and a perfect mutual understanding.'[4] How, then, can this be squared with the words of Ephesians 5. 22–4 and 1 Corinthians 11. 3, which categorically state that the husband is the wife's superior[5]? In spite of the attempts to water down this statement,[6] it is difficult to rid our minds of the suspicion that with all his idealistic statements about marriage Paul had not entirely shed the Jewish attitude to woman, which placed her in a position inferior to her husband's. We say this in spite of the fact that his primary concern in Ephesians 5 is to show how the union of Christ and the Church resembles Christian marriage in every way, and therefore because Christ is the head of his body, the Church, the Jewish conception of the husband's superiority to, and control of, the wife suits his argument.

[1] *Sonnets*, 116.   [2] *A Kind of Loving* (Penguin Books, London, 1962), p. 272.
[3] It is the kind of love that Robert Browning and Elizabeth Barrett knew. For a beautiful treatment of this theme *vide* Dallas Kenmare, *Ever a Fighter* (London, 1952).
[4] W. M. Foley, art. 'Marriage (Christian)', ERE, Vol. 8, p. 434.
[5] I exclude 1 Cor. 14. 34, which together with the next two verses is probably a later interpolation. *Vide* C. A. A. Scott, *Christianity according to St. Paul*, pp. 227–8.
[6] E.g. D. E. H. Whiteley, *The Theology of St. Paul*, p. 223.

P

Marriage between Christians is, according to Paul, indissoluble (1 Cor. 7. 10–11. Cf. Rom. 7. 2–3). It was easy for Paul to make this assertion because, as he said, he was merely repeating the teaching of Jesus.[1] Yet when dealing with the practical difficulties of his Corinthian converts, he was forced to take into account the lingering habits of their former mode of living. According to Roman Law, by which Corinth was governed, divorce was permitted. Either party could divorce the other even without giving a reason for ending the union. Faced with the possibility that a Christian might take this step,[2] Paul orders him or her not to marry again, but either to remain single or to seek a reconciliation (1 Cor. 7. 11). There was also the problem of giving advice to the Christian convert who was married, not to a Christian, but to a heathen, partner; and there he had no saying of Jesus to guide him. It may be that in their letter to him the Corinthian Christians had inquired whether such converts ought to continue to cohabit with their partners. His answer was that provided the heathen partner wished the marriage to continue, it must not be dissolved (1 Cor. 7. 12–13). To prove it, Paul used the curious argument that since the offspring of such a union were ἅγια (i.e. regarded as Christians) because the one partner was a Christian, they had been born of Christian marriage (1 Cor. 7. 14). What, however, was to be a Christian's action if his or her heathen spouse wanted to end the marriage? Paul's answer—οὐ δεδούλωται —is that the believer, although he or she accepts the Christian ideal of the indissolubility of marriage, is under no obligation to resist the divorce. Wisely Paul was thinking of the consequences of that course; it would only cause contention; the peace of mind of the Christian would be lost, and in such circumstances there would be little hope of converting the heathen spouse (1 Cor. 7. 15–16). Whether, as Luther maintained, Paul meant by οὐ δεδούλωται that the divorced Christian partner was free to marry again is not certain. Even if Luther was wrong, it does not mean that Paul condemned all second marriages: he did not object to them where one of the partners had died, although here again he says

[1] Mk. 10. 9–12 = Lk. 16. 18.   [2] Possibly one had.

that on account of the imminence of the Parousia, it is better to remain unmarried. If, however, a widow earnestly desires to re-marry, his only stipulation is that she ought to marry a Christian (1 Cor. 7. 39–40), a decision that presumably applied to widowers as well.

After his emphasis on ἀγάπη in his teaching on marriage, it is strange to find that he never explicitly mentions it in his brief references to the relationship between parents and children, although it seems to be implied. He enjoins on Christian children obedience to parents by appealing, as a good Jew would, to the third commandment of the Decalogue, which he quotes somewhat freely from a LXX text of Exodus 20. 12 or Deuteronomy 5. 16.[1] This, he says, is δίκαιον, i.e. in accordance with the norm of behaviour laid down by God (Eph. 6. 1–3). He cites the divine ordinance in full, not omitting the purpose clause referring to the material rewards promised by Yahweh to those children who keep it. Commenting on Paul's citation of the third commandment, we should notice, first, that the translation of τίμα by 'honour' does not convey the full meaning of the word. Basically the verb means 'to treat as valuable or precious' ('treat your father and mother as precious' would be an accurate rendering of the command). Secondly, the conjunction ἵνα can here mean only 'in order that'; i.e. the purpose of obedience to parents is to gain the reward of long life and prosperity in the age to come, a statement which falls below the Christian level of behaviour. When we turn to Colossians, which was almost certainly written before Ephesians, we find the same injunction to children to obey their parents in everything (Col. 3. 20), but the reference to the third commandment is missing. Here its justification is that it is εὐάρεστον ἐν Κυρίῳ, which probably means: 'It is the way in which we treat parents in the Church,' the phrase ἐν Χριστῷ being interpreted as 'in the Lord's corporate personality.' Obedience to parents is a Christian duty. The disobedience to them common among Gentiles is a sin to be condemned (Rom. 1. 30). Obviously in all this we hear the Jew, with his knowledge, and approval, of

[1] On the LXX text of this passage *vide* J. A. Robinson, *Comm. on Ephesians, ad loc.*

the marked Old Testament emphasis on paternal supremacy over the rest of the family; and we may well ask, 'Is, then, ἀγάπη entirely absent from Paul's conception of the right relationship between father and child?' When we reach the conclusion of his remarks on the subject, we see that it is not: Christian parents are enjoined to reciprocate their children's obedience by refraining from provoking them and by educating and training them (Eph. 6. 4; Col. 3. 21). Moreover, love of parent for child and child for parent are implied in Romans 13. 9, which states that all the commandments, including the third, are included in ἀγάπη.

The third social relationship that Paul refers to is that which Gibbon euphemistically calls 'an unhappy condition of men who endured the weight, without sharing the benefits, of society.'[1] Those who know their *Decline and Fall* will recognize this description as an allusion to slavery. None of those who write on the attitude of the primitive Church to this basic institution of Graeco-Roman society neglect to inform us that Paul did not explicitly condemn it. They can quote to us Paul's dicta in 1 Corinthians 7. 17 and 20–1: 'Let each man order his life according to the gift that the Lord has granted him and according to his condition when God called him to become a Christian. . . . Let every man remain in the condition in which he was when he was converted. Were you a slave when you were converted? Do not let that worry you.' In short, the Christian slave is not to change his status. Then, by way of a footnote as it were,[2] in the next sentence Paul says: 'But if you actually have before you the possibility of becoming free, avail yourselves of it by preference.'[3] Possibly what Paul means is this: 'Do not take the initiative yourselves; but if the chance of gaining your freedom comes through the initiative of someone else, take it.' The precise action

[1] E. Gibbon, *The History of the Decline and Fall of the Roman Empire*, 12 Vols. (London, 1791), Vol. 1, p. 63.
[2] J. H. Moulton says that in a modern work it would be a footnote (GGNT, Vol. 2, p. 49).
[3] This seems to me to be the meaning of this ambiguous *crux criticorum*, on which *vide* A. Robertson and A. Plummer, *Comm. on 1 Cor.* ICC, pp. 147–8; J. B. Lightfoot, *Notes on the Epistles of St. Paul* (London, 1895), pp. 229–30 and *Comm. on Colossians and Philemon*, pp. 324–5 n.; GGNT, Vol. 2, pp. 49, 165; VGT, pp. 690–1; GNTG, pp. 554–5.

that Paul is recommending the Christian slave in the former of those injunctions not to take seems to be either to escape or—what was done by many slaves in the reign of Claudius, one of whom was Claudius Lysias (Acts 22. 28)—to buy his freedom, either by paying his *peculium* (his savings) to his owner or to a third party, who used it to buy him from his owner and then freed him, or by persuading a friend to lend him the purchase-price. As to the second injunction, Paul must have had in mind the two customary methods of manumission initiated by someone other than the slave himself: *vindicta*, which consisted in a legal action brought by an *adsertor liberatis*, who was usually a lictor and who claimed the slave before a magistrate; and—what was more common—*testamento*, the liberation of a slave in accordance with the terms of the will of a deceased master. It was presumably Paul's opinion that Christian slaves should not seek to free themselves which prompted him to send Onesimus, the fugitive slave who had sought asylum of him, back to his owner, Philemon (Philem. 10–14).

If Christian slaves remain in their enslaved state, they are to serve their owners obediently and with single-mindedness. Their motive in fulfilling their obligations to their owners should not be a lickspittle toadyism, but the realization that as Christians they are Christ's slaves, and must therefore carry out his will by completing their appointed tasks (1 Cor. 7. 22–4; Eph. 6. 5–7; Col. 3. 22–4). At the same time Paul points out that the Christian slave-owner has reciprocal obligations to his human chattels: he is to treat them humanely (Eph. 6. 9; Col. 4. 1; Philem. 15–17). Various reasons have been suggested why Paul did not launch a frontal assault on slavery. It is clear that when he was writing 1 Corinthians, he believed that because the end of the age was near (1 Cor. 7. 26, 31), the best course for every Christian to pursue was to remain as he was (1 Cor. 7. 17, 20, 24). Furthermore, it has been pointed out that the condition of the domestic slave was not so unbearable as the English word 'slavery' implies.[1]

---

[1] J. A. Robinson, *Comm. on Eph.*, pp. 129–30.

This last argument seems to have some force when we remember that under the early Emperors there was a marked amelioration of the slave's lot.[1] A third suggestion, not lacking evidence to support it, is that Paul shrank from directly attacking what was, after all, one of the foundations of the social system because he had a distaste for violence. It has been urged also that as a Roman citizen he believed that he must be loyal to the imperial power; and finally, that he realized what disastrous consequences for the Church any criticism of this fundamental institution of the Roman social system would have had. Nevertheless, although he did not openly denounce slavery, its abolition was implied by his teaching. If 'we were all brought into one body by baptism in the one Spirit, whether we are Jews or Greeks, whether slaves or free men' (1 Cor. 12. 13), if 'there is neither slave nor free . . . for you are all one in Christ Jesus' (Gal. 3. 28. Cf. Col. 3. 11), then owner and owned within the Church, if nowhere else, are on the same footing: God is the master of both and 'there is no partiality with him' (Eph. 6. 9). It is because Philemon and Onesimus are Christians, acknowledging the same Father, that Paul can appeal to the former 'for love's sake' to treat the slave on his return as a 'beloved brother' i.e. a Christian (Philem. 16).

Finally, there was the question of the Christian attitude to the State. Paul's teaching on the subject is compactly expressed in Romans 13. 1–7. Unlike a large number of Jews, viz. the Pharisees and the Zealots, who, believing that there could be only one ruler of Jewry, Yahweh, refused to acknowledge the Roman imperium,[2] he enjoined upon Christians obedience to it on the ground that all human government was derived from God (Rom. 13. 1–2). This last belief had been frequently expressed in Jewish writings (e.g. Wisd. 6. 1–3; 1 En. 46. 5), although only to remind rulers that they were responsible to God for their actions or that his power was superior to theirs. Paul says that the State was created for a beneficial purpose, the welfare of the

[1] M. Cary, *History of Rome* (London, 1949), p. 562.
[2] Ch. Guignebert, *The Jewish World in the Time of Jesus*, pp. 40, 167–8.

whole community, which end it achieves by curbing and punishing evil;[1] therefore it is the duty of Christians to honour and respect the ruler, and pay their taxes. It is obvious that, although he does not quote the well-known words of Jesus, 'Pay back to Caesar the things that belong to Caesar, and to God the things that belong to God' (Mk. 12. 17 = Mt. 22. 21 = Lk. 20. 25), he had them in mind when he wrote Romans 13. 7. Yet he goes much further in his allegiance to Caesar than Jesus does. There is no evidence to show that Jesus thought of the Roman Empire or any other state as the creation of God. Indeed, in the light of his all-consuming theocratic obsession it is highly probable that he did not. What, then, impelled Paul to write in this vein? In the first place, there was his obvious pride in his Roman citizenship, which served him in good stead on more than one occasion when he was in danger of suffering at the hands of the authorities (Acts 16. 37–9; 22. 25–9; 25. 11–12). Secondly, no-one who was unprejudiced could deny that the Roman *imperium* provided its subjects with impartial justice, security, and a measure of prosperity. This was true of the State even under the emperor who was reigning when Paul wrote the Epistle to the Romans and whom the traditional judgement has damned to all eternity as one of the blackest monsters of history. As Dr. Glover puts it, Nero 'has few apologists.'[2] The trouble is that, in the words that Shakespeare put into the mouth of another celebrated Roman, who preceded Nero by approximately a century:

> the evil that men do lives after them,
> The good is oft interred with their bones.[3]

So it has been with Nero. Posterity has been so engrossed with the record of his admittedly paranoiac exhibitionism and his unmitigated profligacy and cruelty that it has forgotten the benefits that he conferred on his subjects. At the time when Paul wrote the Epistle to the Romans the emperor was wisely allowing himself to be guided by those two sages, Seneca and

---

[1] Cf. 2 Thess. 2. 7–8. *Vide* inf., p. 151.
[2] T. R. Glover, *The Ancient World* (Pelican edn., London, 1944), p. 320.
[3] *Julius Caesar*, Act 3, Scene 2.

Burrus, with the result that his dominions were more settled and prosperous than they had been at any time since the death of the first occupant of the imperial throne.[1] The legions preserved the *Pax Romana*, without which Paul would almost certainly have been unable to make his long evangelistic journeys. It was not for nothing that Paul spoke of the imperial government as 'the restraining power' (2 Thess. 2. 7);[2] for its officials intervened to protect him from the wrath of his fellow-Jews (Acts 18. 12–16; 21. 30–2; 23. 16–30). Hand in hand with the peace ensured by the might of the legions, justice and comparative prosperity walked, both at home and in the provinces. Nero showed that he would not tolerate abuses, stamping out corruption wherever it was found. Thus, to sum up, when Paul speaks in laudatory language of the Roman State, he is 'thinking of a great and beneficent power which has made travel for him possible, which had often interfered to protect him against an angry mob of his own countrymen, under which he had seen the towns through which he passed enjoying peace, prosperity and civilization.'[3]

We have completed our sketch of Paul's picture of ideal Christian behaviour; of what he called ἀγαθωσύνη, which is yet another of the words in the list of the fruits of the Spirit (Gal. 5. 22). In the NT the adjective ἀγαθός is applied *inter alia* to soil (Lk. 8. 8), a tree (Mt. 7. 18), treasure (Mt. 12. 35), a work (Phil. 1. 6) and man's personality (Lk. 8. 15). Both in Greek thought and in the OT (LXX) the noun ἀγαθωσύνη was used to express the concept of absolute moral excellence; in short, perfection, which, so Paul believed, was to be found in the man whose activity was Christ-like. Such a man has yet another attribute that is found among the products of the πνεῦμα: εἰρήνη, an attribute of God himself (Rom. 15. 33; 16. 20; 2 Cor. 13. 11) and a sign of his rule (Rom. 14. 17). Where men have peace in

---

[1] It is uncertain whether this was the *Quinquennium Neronis* referred to by Trajan. *Vide* J. G. C. Anderson, art. 'Trajan on the *Quinquennium Neronis*,' JRS, Vol. 1 (London, 1911), pp. 173–9; F. A. Lepper, art. 'Some Reflections on the *Quinquennium Neronis*,' JRS, Vol. 47 (London, 1957), pp. 95–103.

[2] *V. sup.*, p. 151.

[3] W. Sanday and A. C. Headlam, *Comm. on Rom.*, ICC, p. xvi.

themselves and are living peaceably with their neighbours, there God is reigning. In Galatians 5. 22 Paul is thinking primarily of the former, although the latter is a concomitant of the former. He who imitates Christ's activity, who has the φρόνημα (frame of mind) τοῦ πνεύματος (Rom. 8. 6), possesses εἰρήνη. He is in this frame of mind because he is convinced that his sins have been forgiven through the saving, liberating work of Jesus, Lord and Messiah (Rom. 5. 1). If we wish to grasp the full meaning of this word εἰρήνη we must go to the LXX, where it translates the Hebrew šālôm, which means 'wholeness,' 'soundness,' or, to use a word popular in some modern psychological circles, integration. The εἰρήνη which is a product of Christ's activity in the Church is simply integration of personality. Nor is εἰρήνη the only reward of Christian living: with integration comes joy, χαρά, yet another of the fruits of Christian activity (πνεῦμα) (Gal. 5. 22). It is an emotion that the popular mind rarely associates with Christianity. The vulgar picture of the disciple of Christ shows one who resembles Don Quixote, 'El Caballero de la Triste Figura.'[1] How different is the portrait of the Christian painted by Paul, who expects his converts to be in a permanent state of exultation (Phil. 4. 4; 1 Thess. 5. 16)! Indeed, like peace χάρα is one of the signs of God's rule (Rom. 14. 17). Christian joy is the lasting joy that comes from the Christocentric life, the life of self-abnegation. Even suffering for Christ's sake ought to bring joy. The Thessalonians rejoiced because they had suffered for their acceptance of him (1 Thess. 1. 6). Paul himself faces the prospect of martyrdom with joyfulness, which he asks his Philippian converts to share (Phil. 2. 17–18). Above all, it is an attitude consonant with that of Jesus himself, who bade his disciples rejoice and exult whenever men reproached, persecuted, and slandered them (Mt. 5. 11–12).

---

[1] Cervantes, *Don Quixote*, Pt. I, ch. 19.

9

WRITER

Proper words in proper places make the true definition of a style.
JONATHAN SWIFT, Letter to a Young Clergyman, 9th Jan., 1720.

Quand on voit le style naturel, on est tout étonné et ravi, car on s'attendait de voir un auteur, et on trouve un homme.

PASCAL, Pensées, I. 29.

IF WE were to call Paul a *littérateur*, there are no doubt those who would take exception to that description of him on the ground that it implies that his writings were factitious creations whereas, in fact, they were spontaneous effusions, *pièces de circonstance*, written *ad hoc* to solve the problems of the infant Christian communities. Scholars have been eager to point out that they were not imitations of those Greek and Roman epistles written by the erudite for the purpose of giving instruction, defending opinions that the writers held, or debating interesting philosophical problems. Among the Greeks the epistles of Epicurus and Polemon of Ilium, and among the Romans the *Hortationes ad Philosophiam* of Augustus and the epistles of Capito, Seneca, and Varro, indisputably belong to this category. It was a characteristic of this genre of writing that although it was epistolary in form, the language used was literary because the authors intended their works for publication, i.e. to be recited aloud to an audience as a modern formal lecture would be. It is not surprising, therefore, that they paid attention to the finer points of linguistic style, striving to observe certain laws of rhythm, cadence, and diction and thus giving an impression of artificiality. Therein these literary products differed from private letters, which, since they were never meant to be read orally to a large audience, but were intended only for the eye of the recipient or recipients, were written in a natural, colloquial, unstudied style.

---

[1] G. H. Putnam, *Authors and their Public in Ancient Times* (New York, 1894), pp. 78 f.

We are indebted to Deissmann for pointing out and emphasizing
the difference between these two kinds of epistolary art, which
he distinguished by the names of 'epistle' and 'letter' respectively.[1]
Do Paul's writings fall into either of these categories? Using
Deissmann's terminology, shall we call them 'epistles' (as the
AV and the RV do) or 'letters' (as Deissmann himself,[2] the RSV
and NEB do)? The answer seems to be that they were a combination of the two, a new genre of epistolary art. On the one
hand, they were private letters in that their author intended them
for the recipients alone, in that they were written to solve various
concrete problems, and in that the writer had a personal interest
in the recipients, loving and caring about them, and so writing
to them as a father to his children (1 Cor. 4. 15). In keeping with
this character is their form. Like any contemporary private letter
every Pauline Epistle begins with an address and ends with a
farewell salutation. The difference between Paul's addresses and
conclusions and those of contemporary letters lies in language.
Paul never uses the conventional opening of a letter, the epistolary infinitive χαίρειν.[3] Instead, he created a new mode of
address for Christian letter-writers: χάρις ὑμῖν καὶ εἰρήνη ἀπὸ Θεοῦ
Πατρὸς ἡμῶν καὶ Κυρίου Ἰησοῦ Χριστοῦ (Rom. 1. 7; 1 Cor. 1. 3; 2
Cor. 1. 2; Gal. 1. 3; Eph. 1. 2; Phil. 1. 2; 2 Thess. 1. 2; Philem. 3.[4] As
it was with the beginning, so it was with the ending: he created a
new kind of farewell salutation for Christian letter-writers. He never
uses the customary formulae: ἔρρωσθε or ἐρρῶσθαι ὑμᾶς εὔχομαι; at
the end of every one of his epistles he expresses his wish that χάρις
may come to his converts from Jesus, the Lord and Messiah, and
in 1 Corinthians he sends them his ἀγάπη as well. Another mark
of the private letter, found in the Pauline epistles, is the tendency
to use expressions that resemble stock epistolary phrases: παρακαλῶ
ὑμᾶς) (Rom. 12. 1; 2 Cor. 2. 8; Eph. 4. 1. Cf. Phil. 4. 2), γινώσκειν
δὲ ὑμᾶς βούλομαι (Phil. 1. 12), οὐ θέλω δὲ ὑμᾶς ἀγνοεῖν (Rom.
1. 13; 2 Cor. 1. 8; 1 Thess. 4. 13), θέλω δὲ ὑμᾶς εἰδέναι (1 Cor.

---

[1] G. A. Deissmann, *Bible Studies*, Eng. tr. A. Grieve (Edinburgh, 1903), pp. 4 ff.
[2] *Ibid.*, p. 43. [3] As in Acts 15. 23; 23. 26; and James 1. 1.
[4] Colossians has the same address without the words, 'and the Lord Jesus Christ' (Col. 1. 2).

11. 3; Col. 2. 1), and ἐχάρην (Phil. 4. 10). At the same time they had certain characteristics of the literary epistle. Although they were spontaneous, their author frequently paid some heed both to the words that he was using and to the manner in which he was using them. Again, although his purpose was to deal with particular problems, he enunciates general principles, applicable on a wide scale, in which respect the Pauline Epistles resemble imperial edicts and rescripts. Furthermore, like the literary epistles they were intended to be read aloud to audiences, the Christian communities to which they were addressed (1 Thess. 5. 27; Col. 4. 16); and it was probably for this reason that, as the evidence shows, Paul did not entirely disregard the finer points of literary style.[1]

For example, he makes skilful use of that weapon popular among the Stoics (e.g. Epictetus) and the Cynics, the diatribe; a dialogue conducted between the writer and an imaginary opponent. Instances of this are easily found in several of the Pauline epistles; but it is in Romans that it is most marked. One example from that epistle will suffice. In chapter 3 Paul is arguing that the Jews are as much in need of forgiveness as the Gentiles are. The dialogue runs thus:

OBJECTOR—If the Jews, the chosen race, are as guilty of sinning as the Gentiles are, what is the point of being a Jew? What is the value of circumcision?

PAUL—There is much point in being a Jew. To the Jews was entrusted a divine revelation.

OBJECTOR—(this is not expressed, but it must have been in Paul's mind)—But if the Jews are sinners, and therefore lost, God has broken the covenant that he made with the race.

PAUL—That does not follow. If some Jews, those who have not recognized Jesus as Messiah, have not fulfilled their covenant obligations, we must not infer that God has broken his word. We must always believe that God has kept his word even though it means that all men are liars.

---

[1] What Quintilian calls 'tropes' and 'figures.' *Institutio Oratoria*, Bk. VIII, ch. 6 and Bk. IX.

OBJECTOR—For the sake of the argument I concede that the Jews are sinners. If their sinfulness causes God's justice to stand out clearly, they are doing him a good turn, and therefore to punish them would be unjust.

PAUL—God is the judge and cannot be unjust.

OBJECTOR—That is no answer to my argument. If the failure of the Jews to carry out their covenant obligations establishes the fact that God is faithful to his, then their sinfulness adds to his prestige, and they ought not to be condemned for sinning. Indeed, why should we not continue to sin in order that good may come from it?

PAUL—That is the calumny of which I have been accused by my opponents, who deserve to be condemned for their misrepresentation.

We are not concerned here with the validity of Paul's argument, which, as Dodd rightly says, is 'obscure and feeble,'[1] and which could profitably be omitted. We merely quote the passage in full to illustrate the apostle's use of the diatribe (other examples are Rom. 4. 1–2; 9. 14—11. 32; Gal. 3. 19–22; and 1 Cor. 6. 12–13).

Of the literary devices found in his epistles Paul uses none more tellingly than the metaphor. Our attention has been drawn by more than one writer to the contrast between the tropology of Jesus the countryman, who went to the rural scene for his figures, speaking mainly of pastoral and agricultural objects and pursuits, and that of Paul the townsman, who drew most of his illustrations from the activities of urban society.[2] For example, the apostle makes effective use of architectural ideas. The Church, the corporate personality of Christ, was an edifice, God's shrine, the new temple that had superseded the old Jewish temple[3] (1 Cor. 3. 9, 16; 6. 19; 2 Cor. 6. 16; Eph. 2. 14, 19–22). The foundation-stone of this building is Jesus the Messiah (1 Cor. 3. 11; Eph. 2. 20; Col. 2. 7), a metaphor that Paul takes a stage further when he calls him the ἀκρογωνιαῖος (Eph. 2. 20), an adjective that has been discussed by exegetes at some length. Since the literal meaning of the word is 'at the extreme angle,'

[1] C. H. Dodd, *Comm. on Romans*, MNTC, p. 46.
[2] T. R. Glover, *Paul of Tarsus*, p. 8.   [3] *V. sup.*, pp. 137-9.

Paul cannot be thinking, as some commentators hold, of the copestone at the top of a building,[1] or, as others suggest, of the keystone of an arch,[2] or of the angular stone placed at the corner formed by the bases of two walls to bind them together, an example of which Layard saw at Nineveh.[3] Clearly what Paul had in mind was 'the primary foundation-stone at the angle of the structure by which the architect fixes a standard for the bearings of the walls and cross-walls throughout.'[4] It was the kind of massive, straight stone to which Menenius draws the attention of Sicinius in Shakespeare's *Coriolanus*:

> See you yond' coigne o' the Capitol,—yond' corner-stone.[5]

Apart from this, the only place in the whole of Greek literature where the word ἀκρογωνιαῖος occurs is Isaiah 28. 16 (LXX), so that it is probable that Paul had that verse in mind: 'I am laying for Zion's foundations a very costly tested stone, a precious corner-stone (ἀκρογωνιαῖον).' As the writer was probably referring to the Messianic king, Paul, in calling Jesus the ἀκρογωνιαῖος, meant that as Messiah he was the foundation standard in relation to which (as he says in the next verse) the edifice of the Church was being, and would be, built in order to become the divine dwelling-place (Eph. 2. 21). If, however, Jesus Christ her Lord is 'the Church's one foundation,' what does Paul mean when in Ephesians 2. 20 he writes ἐποικοδομηθέντες ἐπὶ τῷ θεμελίῳ τῶν ἀποστόλων καὶ προφητῶν? The words can mean only, 'built upon the foundation *laid by* the apostles and prophets.' That this was Paul's meaning is confirmed by his statement in 1 Corinthians 3. 10: 'In accordance with the commission given to me by God, like a skilled master-builder I laid a foundation.' As one of the apostles and prophets Paul helped to lay the

---

[1] E.g. J. Jeremias, art. Ἀκρογωνιαῖος, TWNT, 1, pp. 792 ff.

[2] E.g. E. Best, *One Body in Christ*, p. 166. *Vide* also a *varia lectio* in NEB, Eph. 2. 20.

[3] H. Layard, *Nineveh and its Remains* (London, 1850), Vol. 2, p. 254.

[4] VGT, p. 19, quoting W. W. Lloyd, CR, 3, p. 419a (1889). R. J. McKelvey wrongly thinks that this stone and the angular stone to which I have referred in my previous sentence were one and the same. Art. 'Christ the Cornerstone,' NTS, Vol. 8, No. 4 pp. 352–9. The primary foundation-stone was straight, not angular.

[5] *Op. cit.*, Act 5, Scene 4.

ἀκρογωνιαῖος of the Church, the personality of Jesus the Messiah. On it others would have the task of erecting the superstructure, the Christian Society, God's shrine (I Cor. 3. 10). At this point the metaphor becomes more detailed. In the erection of buildings men use various kinds of material: gold, silver, costly stones (like marble and granite), wood, dried grass, or stubble, which represent the varying degrees in the quality of the work done by those who are building the Church on the foundation laid by the apostles. It will be tested by the fire of judgement at the final consummation, what is sound surviving and what is unsound being consumed (I Cor. 3. 12–15).

Almost as prominent as architectural figures in Paul's writings are military metaphors. If in his travels he was seldom far from a building, he was just as frequently within sight and sound of the Roman soldiery. Indeed, if Acts is to be believed, he spent many hours in their company. In Jerusalem he was arrested by Claudius Lysias, the *tribunus militum* in command of the garrison stationed in the Antonia fortress, where he spent some time in custody (Acts 21. 33 ff.). On his journey to Antipatris he had a guard of 400 infantrymen and 70 cavalry soldiers (Acts 23. 23 ff.). During the whole of his two years' imprisonment in Caesarea (Acts 23. 33—26. 32) he must have been in close proximity to Roman soldiers. On his voyage by sea from Caesarea to Puteoli, and thence by land to Rome, one of his closest companions was Julius, the humane centurion of the Augustan cohort, in whose charge Paul was placed (Acts 27. 1). Finally, during his imprisonment in Rome he was chained to a Roman soldier (Col. 4. 18). We are therefore not surprised to hear him speak of the soldier's armour: 'The night is far advanced, the day is at hand; therefore let us put off the deeds of darkness and put on the armour of light; let us conduct ourselves becomingly as in the daylight; not in revelling and drunkenness' (Rom. 13. 12–13). As he wrote those vivid words, was he thinking of the armour of the Roman soldiers as they changed the guard at dawn, with the first light glinting on it? What the armour represents Paul tells us immediately: the personality of Jesus, Messiah and Lord. In 2 Corinthians 6. 7 he refers to two kinds of arms: 'for the right hand and for the left,' which presumably means the offensive weapon, the sword, wielded with the right hand, and the defensive piece of armour, the shield, held by the left hand. He specifies two pieces of armour in 1 Thessalonians 5. 8, where he speaks of the Christian as being armed with faith and love as his breastplate and with the hope of salvation for his helmet. It is, however, in that vivid passage, Ephesians 6. 10–20, that he particularizes in greater detail the pieces of the Christian's panoply, to be donned in his struggle with the forces of evil (verses 12–13). It has been suggested that the source of Paul's metaphor was not, as it is customary to believe, so much the armour of the Roman legionary as Isaiah 11 and 59 and, possibly, Wisdom 5.[1] It may be that he had these passages in mind; but that does not mean that as he was dictating the words he was not looking at a Roman soldier either with the eye of the mind or, perhaps, even in the flesh. The fact that he does not give us a complete description of Roman armour as Polybius does is irrelevant.[2] Paul was not trying to find a Christian virtue to fit every piece of Roman armour. He knew his *Isaiah* and his *Wisdom*; he was familiar with the accoutrements of the Roman soldier; and he used all this knowledge in painting his picture of the Christian warrior. We see him standing firm (as the NEB so aptly translates it) 'when things are at their worst' like a Praetorian guardsman, with his six pieces of armour. Fastened firmly around his waist is the leather belt covered with metal plates; it represents truth (cf. Is. 11. 5). Protecting his chest is the cuirass, the bronze coat of mail; it represents δικαιοσύνη, which means here the conviction of the Christian that he has been vindicated, i.e. liberated from the bondage of evil forces[3] (cf. Is. 59. 17; Wisd. 5. 18). On his head is the bronze, crested helmet; it represents the hope of salvation, by which, according to 1 Thessalonians 5. 8, Paul means the Christian's hope of complete liberation at the final consummation (cf. Is. 59. 17; Wisd. 5. 18). On his feet he wears the sandals, which enable him to march

---

[1] J. A. Robinson, *Comm. on Ephesians*, pp. 133–5.
[2] Polybius, *Histories*, 6. 22–3.   [3] *V. sup.*, pp. 78 ff.

rapidly; they represent the alacrity of the Christian in proclaiming the good news of peace. Most important of all his defensive arms is the huge, arc-shaped *scutum*, $2\frac{1}{2}$ feet broad, 4 feet long, and 3 inches thick. It was made by gluing two pieces of wood together, covering it first with linen and then with hide, binding it with iron at the top and the bottom, and fitting an iron boss to it.[1] So large and substantial was it that it protected the whole body from the violent blows of all missiles, including, as Paul says, those tipped with flame; it represents the faith of the Christian, the complete surrender, and devotion, to Jesus, Messiah and Lord, that enables his followers to repel all the attacks of evil (cf. Wisd. 5. 19). Last of all comes the sole offensive piece of armour, the powerful, two-edged *gladius* called 'the Spanish sword';[2] it represents the weapon that the Christian uses to attack evil; the proclamation of the good news, which is the Church's main activity (πνεῦμα, cf. Is. 11. 4; Wisd. 5. 20).

These are not the only places where Paul uses military phraseology. In 2 Corinthians 10. 3–6 he describes his altercation with the Judaizers who are attacking his apostolic authority, in terms of a military campaign. He speaks of weapons sufficiently powerful to demolish the fortresses of the sophistical arguments used by his opponents, of forcing the thoughts of men to capitulate to Christ, and of punishing rebellion. In two places he refers to the familiar, picturesque spectacle of the victorious procession of a Roman general as he led his captives in triumph. In the earlier of these passages, 2 Corinthians 2. 14–16, Christ is the conqueror and Christians are his captives; in the other, Colossians 2. 15, Christ is still the victor, but the vanquished are now the cosmic powers. This does not exhaust Paul's allusions to military affairs. He describes the inner conflict of his pre-Christian days as a war between the Torah and his unredeemed self, with the latter victorious and taking him prisoner (Rom. 7. 23). He promises his Philippian converts that the peace of God, which is beyond man's power to comprehend, will garrison their personalities (Phil. 4. 7). Finally, he prophesies that at the general resurrection

---

[1] Polybius, *Histories*, 6, 23.   [2] *Ibid.*

the military trumpet will sound and every Christian soldier will be raised to take his place in his own army division (1 Cor. 15. 23, 52).

Architecture and armies were prominent features of Paul's urban environment; just as prominent were the athletic games, which took place wherever there were Greeks, i.e. throughout the whole of the Eastern Mediterranean world. In every city of any size, e.g. Corinth, Ephesus, Athens, and Tarsus itself, the gymnasium or place of training and the stadium or racecourse were as conspicuous and popular as any other public building. While we are not willing to go so far as to suggest, as one scholar does, that in his younger days Paul himself probably took part in the games at Tarsus, especially the foot-races,[1] we need not be surprised (as Dr. Glover is[2]) that he refers to them so frequently. Surely with its emphasis on struggle and the necessity for self-discipline it was an obviously fruitful source of telling images for anyone who was writing about Christian living. Of all the Greek games the most exciting, and therefore the most popular, was the foot-race, which Paul often mentions. In his first recorded sermon, at Pisidian Antioch, he speaks of John the Baptist as completing the race ($\delta\rho\acute{o}\mu os$) that he was running (Acts 13. 25), and later, in his farewell speech to the Ephesian elders at Miletus, he applies the same figure to his own career (Acts 20. 24). In 2 Thessalonians 3. 1 he pictures the good news as the runner who, he hopes, will run swiftly and successfully. In all the other passages where he uses the metaphor, it is of himself or his converts that he speaks, and very vivid passages they are to boot. To the leaders of the Jerusalem ecclesia he had given an account of the good news that he was proclaiming lest 'the race I had run, and was running, should be to no purpose' (Gal. 2. 2); and again, writing to his beloved Philippian converts, he employs the same phrase (Phil. 2. 16).[3] It is in the next chapter of this same letter and in 1 Corinthians 9 that the metaphor occurs in rich detail.

[1] H. A. Harris, *Greek Athletes and Athletics* (London, 1964), pp. 133–5.
[2] T. R. Glover, *The Ancient World*, p. 124.
[3] H. A. Harris suggests that we should translate $\epsilon\grave{\iota}s$ $\kappa\epsilon\nu\acute{o}\nu$ $\check{\epsilon}\delta\rho a\mu o\nu$: 'I should be an also ran.' *Greek Athletes and Athletics*, p. 132.

He has not yet reached the winning-post (σκόπον) of full resurrection, but straining every sinew, he presses forward (διώκω) towards
it to win the prize of full maturity, not looking back over the
part of the course of his life that he has already covered (τὰ
ὀπίσω) (Phil. 3. 12–14).[1] In 1 Corinthians 9. 24–7 Paul is
obviously thinking of the Isthmian games, which were
held every three years in the vicinity of Corinth. He points out
that in a foot-race there is only one prizewinner, by which he
means the Church. Therefore, his readers, who are the Church,
must run to win the wreath of eternal life, which, unlike the
wreath of pine-leaves bestowed on the victors in the Isthmian
games, never dies. Like Paul himself they must have a clear
knowledge of the course. The main emphasis in this particular
passage, however, is not on the prize or a knowledge of the
course, but on the athlete's need of ἄσκησις, strict training, if he
is to be victorious. 'Everyone who enters for a contest, practises
complete self-control (πάντα ἐγκρατεύεται)'; i.e. he goes into
rigorous training for a period of ten months. So must the Church
practise self-discipline if it is to win the prize in life's race. In
this same passage Paul alludes to yet another popular item in
Greek athletics, boxing. 'I resemble a boxer who does not beat
the air'; i.e. he plants his blows accurately on the enemy, evil.
Cleverly, in his next clause, he uses this notion of beating to
stress the boxer's as well as the runner's need of strict training;
'I bruise my body black and blue (ὑποπιάζω)[2] and so lead it as a
slave (δουλαγωγῶ)'; for having proclaimed the good news (κηρύξας)
to men, he has no wish to be disgraced because he fails to practise
what he preaches. It would seem that when he uses the word
κηρύξας there, he has in mind another figure prominent at the
athletic games, this time not a competitor, but the κῆρυξ, who
announced the contest, summoned the contestants, and read the
rules. Nor does Paul omit to mention an official of the games

[1] An alternative suggestion is that the source of this metaphor was the chariot races in
the Circus Maximus; but it is more probable that Paul was thinking of the foot-race of
the Greek games.
[2] H. A. Harris points out that Paul seems to have been the first Greek author to use
this word metaphorically. *Greek Athletes and Athletics*, p. 132.

more important than the κῆρυξ, viz. the umpire. In Colossians
3. 15 we have the interesting verb βραβενέτω, from βραβεύειν, 'to
act as umpire': 'Let Christ's peace act as umpire in your personalities'; i.e. wherever there is friction in the Church, the peace that
Christ gives must be allowed to act as the umpire, settling all
disputes. There are several other places where Paul uses the
metaphor of the games. In 1 Thessalonians 2. 19 and Philippians
4. 1 he describes his converts as his victory wreath, and in Philippians 2. 16 we have the same idea when he tells them that they
are the proof that he has not run the race to no purpose. Finally,
in the Pauline fragment 2 Timothy 4. 6 ff. he speaks of the race,
the course, the prize, and the judge.[1]

Yet although Paul derived the major part of his imagery from
features of urban life like buildings, the armed forces, and the
Greek games, he did not entirely neglect the rural scene. For
example, he describes his first evangelization of Corinth as a
planting of the seed, and the work of Apollos, who succeeded
him, as the irrigation of the land; but—what is the all-important
point—it is God alone who makes it grow. The Corinthian
ecclesia is the result neither of Paul's nor of Apollos's cultivation
(γεώργιον), but God's (1 Cor. 3. 6–9). Later in the same epistle
he finds a different use for the metaphor of sowing and the
growth of the seed. Seeking to find convincing answers to the
questions how the dead will be raised, and what the nature of the
resurrection body will be, he refers his readers to the facts of
nature known to every gardener; first, before there can be
germination, the seed must decay and dissolve; and secondly, the
plant that appears is a new creation, the work of God (1 Cor.
15. 35–8). The resurrection will be analogous to the natural
process: the physical body must decompose in the ground before
there can be a spiritual body, which is a new kind of organism,
raised by God (1 Cor. 15. 42–4). We find ourselves once again
in the world of agriculture in several passages where Paul is enjoin-
ing on his converts the duty of liberal almsgiving. In 1 Corinthians
9. 10–12 he argues that as the farmer ploughs the land, sows the

[1] V. inf., p. 251.

seed, and threshes the crop, in the hope of obtaining an abundant yield, so he who has sown the seed of the gospel among Christians has a right to expect a harvest of material gifts from them. Although in Galatians 6. 6–10 the theme is the same—the pupil's obligation to give liberal support to his teachers—the metaphor of sowing and reaping is used somewhat differently. It is a divine law of nature that a man reaps what he sows: if he sows inferior seed, he will reap a rotten crop. Then suddenly he changes his application of the metaphor: as in Jesus' parable of the sower (Mk. 4. 3–9 = Mt. 13. 3–9 = Lk. 8. 5–8), a plentiful harvest depends on the quality of the soil as well as upon sound seed. The explanation of the metaphor is that if the Galatian Christians plant the seed of their unredeemed human nature, the harvest will be rotten; but if they sow their seed in the πνεῦμα, i.e. take part in Christian activity, which in this instance means beneficent giving, they will reap the harvest of ζωή αἰώνιος, the kind of life that men live in the age to come. A third passage is 2 Corinthians 9. 6–10, where the context is Paul's directions for the organization of the collection for the poverty-stricken ecclesia in Jerusalem. His words are: 'He who sows sparsely will reap sparsely; but he who sows bountifully will reap bountifully' (verse 6). Four verses later the metaphor recurs: God, who in the natural world supplies the seed and the bread that comes from it, will supply the Corinthians with the figurative seed for them to sow, i.e. the spirit of generosity, and will make it produce an abundant harvest, i.e. he will increase their benevolence. In one other reference to the collection he uses this same metaphor of the harvest yet again: in Romans 15. 28 he describes the contribution of the Christians of Macedonia and Achaia as the fruit (sc. of their generosity) that he is planning to take to Jerusalem. Finally, we have those passages where he applies the metaphor of the harvest to the results of conversion, and of evangelization.[1] For example, in Romans 6. 22 he speaks of the fruit of conversion, i.e. a consecrated life; and similarly in Romans 7. 4 a reformed life is the fruit of being wedded to Christ. He refers also to 'the fruits of

[1] For one instance of this previously mentioned (the first-fruits) v. sup., p. 125.

δικαιοσύνη,' i.e. the conduct of those who have been vindicated, liberated, by Jesus the Messiah (2 Cor. 9. 10; Phil. 1. 11). As to the results of evangelization he refers to the fruit of his own work (Rom. 1. 13; Phil. 1. 22) and, what is the same, of the fruit that the proclamation of the good news yields (Col. 1. 6). Perhaps the best known of all his allusions to fruit is to be found in Galatians 5. 22–3, where he lists the various kinds of it produced by the activity (πνεῦμα) of Christ in men. Similar to this passage is Ephesians 5. 8–9, where he urges his readers to lead the life of those who are enlightened, and who consequently produce the fruits of enlightenment, viz. goodness, just dealing, and truthfulness. Evidently, although Paul, as far as we know, had never heard of photo-synthesis, he knew that growth depended on light as well as on heat and water. In contrast, he speaks of the 'unfruitful deeds of darkness,' to which there is a parallel in Romans 6. 21, where he refers to the fruit borne by his Roman converts when in their pre-conversion days they were enslaved by sin.

Of all Paul's agricultural metaphors none has been subjected to more comment than that contained in Romans 11. 16–24. The context of this section of the 'Theodicy ad Judaeos' is Paul's attempt to show that God's rejection of the Jews is only temporary, and there is, so he believes, every ground for hope that they will be received into the Kingdom. The second of the two metaphors (the first is the metaphor of the heave-offering) used by Paul to convince his readers depicts Israel as a tree that has for its roots the patriarchs and for its branches individual Israelites. Paul's argument is that if the roots are holy, then the whole tree must be holy, since it derives its sap from the roots; i.e. Israel derives its holiness from the patriarchs. His arboreal metaphor then brings to his mind a particular kind of tree, the olive; a figure that had been employed by the prophets to depict Israel (Jer. 11. 16; Hos. 14. 6). The true Israel, by which Paul means the Christian society, is like the olive tree, whose roots represent the patriarchs, and which has two kinds of branches: the original ones, which represent the Jews and some of which have been lopped off, and the branches of wild olive that have been grafted into the cultivated tree and that represent the Gentile Christians. Later, the branches of the cultivated tree that have been cut off, viz. the Jews who have rejected Jesus the Messiah, will be re-engrafted into the tree, the new, true Israel, the Christian society. Few exegetes have failed to expose Paul's ignorance of gardening. 'A truly remarkable horticultural experiment! Paul had the limitations of the town-bred man,' comments Dr. Dodd.[1] His point is that no expert gardener would graft a branch of a wild olive-tree into a cultivated one; the correct process is diametrically opposite. Nor would he graft a cultivated branch into a cultivated tree. Yet Paul knew as well as the commentators do that what he was describing was extraordinary. Does he not say so in verse 24? As Karl Barth observes, 'the incomprehensible occurrence with which Paul is concerned defies every correct and natural analogy.'[2] He intended that it should, for he was trying to show that the liberation of the Gentiles and their admission into the Kingdom was, and that the future return of the Jews into it would be, unaccountable except as the consequence of the divine operation. The last two agricultural metaphors in Paul's writings which we note occur in a passage to which we have already referred, 1 Corinthians 9. 3–12. The first is a passing allusion to the vineyard, some of whose produce, says Paul, the cultivator takes for his own use (verse 7). The second occurs in a quotation from Deuteronomy 25. 4: 'You must not muzzle an ox when it is treading out the grain' (verse 9). Both metaphors are intended to show that Paul's converts are under an obligation to support him. In this same context we have one other metaphor, rural but not agricultural, which has the same meaning as the two to which we have just referred: the shepherd takes some of the milk of the flock that he tends (1 Cor. 9. 7).

In addition to the urban metaphors and the rural metaphors there are those that come under both headings since they concern the activities both of townsmen and countrymen. Many of these have been mentioned in earlier chapters: marriage laws, wills, the

[1] C. H. Dodd, *Comm. on Romans*, MNTC, p. 180.
[2] K. Barth, *Comm. on Romans*, Eng. tr. E. C. Hoskyns (Oxford, 1933), p. 408.

sealing of documents, payment of the first instalment, adoption, the process of trial, the cultus, liberation from slavery, dwellings, ceramics, clothing, birth, death and burial—they cover the whole range of human experience. To them we add two others, both of them financial and both striking. First, in Colossians 4. 5 and Ephesians 5. 16 Paul advises his converts to buy out for themselves (ἐξαγοραζόμενοι) the critical time (τὸν καιρόν), which is in the wrong hands. The καιρός is the eschaton, the last time, in which they are living and which is (as Paul continues in Ephesians 5. 16) evil, i.e. it is like property in the possession of evil, which has no right to it. It is for the Christian by his conduct to buy it out of the hands of evil.[1] The second metaphor is to be found in Colossians 2. 14, where Paul says that Christ has 'blotted out (ἐξαλείψας) the written bond (χειρόγραφον)' on which man's debt is certified, taken it away, and nailed it to the Cross. It is a picture of an oriental custom: when a man had settled a debt, his creditor cancelled the certificate, the I.O.U., and nailed it above the door of the debtor's house to make public that the debt had been paid. Sinful man is in debt to God; and it is only through the suffering and crucifixion of Christ that the debt is cancelled.[2]

No consideration of Paul's use of metaphor would be complete without some reference to his allegorizing. The original meaning of the word ἀλληγορία, which belongs to the terminology of Greek rhetoric, is supplied by Cicero: 'Iam cum fluxerunt continuae plures tralationes, alia plane fit oratio. Itaque genus hoc Graeci appellant ἀλληγοριαν.'[3] As employed by Jewish and Christian writers, however, allegorizing was far more than the mere use of a series of metaphors: it was a method of interpreting the Scriptures. When we remember the addiction of Jewish writers, especially those of the Diaspora, to allegorizing, we should be surprised if it were absent from the epistles of Paul. Nevertheless, unlike that other celebrated Diaspora Jew, Philo of Alexandria, he was not obsessed with it. Indeed, Dean Farrar

---

[1] The customary translation of ἐξαγοραζόμενοι is 'redeeming,' i.e. buying back (RV). Another rendering is 'making the most of' (RSV. Cf. NEB).
[2] Another interpretation sees this as a reference to the custom of hanging the written indictment (χειρόγραφον) above the head of a crucified prisoner.   [3] *Orator*, 27, 94.

could discover only one allegory in Paul's writings, Galatians 4. 21–7, which he calls 'a passing illustration.'[1] The good dean erred here: there are the allegorical interpretation of Deuteronomy 25. 4 in 1 Corinthians 9. 9–10, and of the Passover in 1 Corinthians 5. 6–8.[2] The allegorizing of the story of Sarah and Hagar in Galatians 4. 21–7 is an example of how Paul cleverly combats the Judaizers with their own weapon, using their own beloved Torah to prove that they are wrong in requiring Gentile Christians to be circumcised and keep the Jewish Law. It is important to notice that, as K. J. Woollcombe points out, in contrast with Philo's allegorism, in which the historical pattern is ignored, 'St. Paul's allegorism was firmly anchored to history, and thereby preserved from extravagance.'[3] This same contrast is observable when we place the typology (which is a development of allegorism) of the two writers side by side. In fact, it is doubtful whether there is any typology whatsoever in Philo's writings, for 'typological exegesis is the search for linkage between events, persons or things within the historical framework of revelation'[4] and Philo ignores history. There are two outstanding examples of typology in the Pauline epistles: in Romans 5. 14 and 1 Corinthians 15. 22 we see Adam as τύπος τοῦ μέλλοντος, the type of which Christ is the antitype; and in 1 Corinthians 10. 1–13 the events of the Exodus are treated as τύποι ἡμῶν (1 Cor. 10. 6. Cf. verse 11), types of which the events of the Christian dispensation are the antitypes.

Of the other rhetorical devices found in the Pauline Epistles we notice, first, asyndeton—the lack of any copulative particle between clauses or between words within a sentence. It is a contrivance that Greek and Latin writers used most effectively. Winer says of it: 'As the language receives from it terseness and swiftness of movement, it serves to render the style lively and forcible.'[5] The first kind of asyndeton—the lack of any connecting particle between clauses—takes three forms, all of which

---

[1] F. W. Farrar, *History of Interpretation* (London, 1886), p. xxiii.
[2] We can forgive him for this inaccuracy, but not for writing 'Eric, or Little by Little'!
[3] G. W. H. Lampe and K. J. Woollcombe, *Essays on Typology* (London, 1957), p. 56.
[4] *Ibid.*   [5] GNTG, p. 674.

appear in the Pauline Epistles. First, there is the omission of the copula between parallel clauses that lead up to a climax. As examples we have 1 Corinthians 4. 8: ἤδη κεκορεσμένοι ἐστέ, ἤδη ἐπλουτήσατε, χωρὶς ἡμῶν ἐβασιλεύσατε; 1 Thessalonians 5. 14: παρακαλοῦμεν δὲ ὑμᾶς, ἀδελφοί, νουθετεῖτε τοὺς ἀτάκτους, παραμυθεῖσθε τοὺς ὀλιγοψύχους, ἀντέχεσθε τῶν ἀσθενῶν, μακροθυμεῖτε πρὸς πάντας; and 2 Corinthians 7. 2: οὐδένα ἠδικήσαμεν, οὐδένα ἐφθείραμεν, οὐδένα ἐπλεονεκτήσαμεν. Secondly, we have the asyndeton used to emphasize a contrast; e.g. 1 Corinthians 15. 42-3: σπείρεται ἐν φθορᾷ, ἐγείρεται ἐν ἀφθαρσίᾳ· σπείρεται ἐν ἀτιμίᾳ, ἐγείρεται ἐν δόξῃ· σπείρεται ἐν ἀσθενείᾳ, ἐγείρεται ἐν δυνάμει· σπείρεται σῶμα ψυχικόν, ἐγείρεται σῶμα πνευματικόν. Thirdly, Paul sometimes omits the copula between a sentence and an explanation of it, or a warning deduced from it: e.g. Romans 6. 9: Χριστὸς ἐγερθεὶς ἐκ νεκρῶν οὐκέτι ἀποθνῄσκει, θανατος αὐτοῦ οὐκέτι κυριεύει; and 1 Corinthians 6. 17: ὁ δὲ κολλώμενος τῷ Κυρίῳ ἓν πνεῦμά ἐστιν. φεύγετε τὴν πορνείαν (cf. 1 Cor. 7. 4, 23, 27). Of the second kind of asyndeton—the omission of the copulative particle within clauses—there are many examples in the Pauline writings. The most striking instances of it are to be seen in his enumerations (e.g. Rom. 1. 29 ff.; 2. 19; 1 Cor. 13. 4-8; 14. 26; Phil. 3. 5; etc.); and very occasionally it occurs in contrasts (e.g. 1 Cor. 3. 2: γάλα ὑμᾶς ἐπότισα, οὐ βρῶμα). Our comment on all these instances of asyndeton is: How much less forcible the clauses and words would have been, had Paul joined them!

From asyndeton we move to a consideration of Paul's frequent use of ellipsis, which Hermann defined thus: 'Ellipseos propria est ratio grammatica, quae posita in eo, ut oratio, etiamsi aliquid omissum sit, integra esse censeatur, quia id quod omissum est, necessario tamen intelligi debeat, ut quo non intellecto sententia nulla futura sit.'[1] It takes two main forms: the omission of the copulative verb and of the subject. Of the many examples of the former in Paul's writings we cite πιστὸς ὁ Θεός (1 Cor. 1. 9; 10. 13), εἰ δυνατόν (Rom. 12. 18), ὁ Κύριος ἐγγύς (Phil. 4. 5), and δῆλον ὅτι (1 Cor. 15. 27). As to the omission of the subject, we

[1] J. G. T. Hermann, *Opuscula*, 7 vols. (Leipzig, 1827-39), Vol. 1, p. 153.

find it where the writer can reasonably assume that the reader knows what it is; e.g. ὅταν δὲ εἴπῃ ὅτι πάντα ὑποτέτακται (sc. ὁ θεός) (1 Cor. 15. 27), (in which verse, as we have seen, there is also an ellipsis of the copulative verb), and ἄρα οὖν ὃν θέλει ἐλεεῖ, ὃν δὲ θέλει σκληρύνει (again sc. ὁ θεός) (Rom. 9. 18). There is a kind of ellipsis in the figure of speech known as zeugma or synizesis: the use of two nouns with one verb where only the first fits the verb; e.g. in 1 Corinthians 3. 2 only γάλα and not βρῶμα suits the verb ἐπότισα. Before we leave this subject, we must mention the quasi-ellipsis whereby a word or phrase written in a clause needs to be repeated in a connected clause, but is omitted to avoid repetition. Of this there are many occurrences in Paul's Epistles; e.g. in 2 Corinthians 1. 6 θλιβόμεθα is understood in the second clause (cf. Rom. 3. 27; 8. 4; 11. 6; 1 Cor. 11. 25; 15. 27; 2 Cor. 11. 11).

Since Paul's writings are often highly rhetorical, we expect to find in them instances of that figure of speech related to ellipsis and known as aposiopesis. Winer defines it as 'the suppression of a sentence or a part of a sentence in consequence of excited feeling (e.g. of anger, sorrow, fear, etc.), the member omitted being supplied by the gesture of a speaker.'[1] It is disappointing to discover that the whole Pauline corpus contains but three possible instances of it—Romans 7. 24, Philippians 1. 22, and 2 Thessalonians 2. 3–4.

Of the other figures of speech found in the classical writers Paul makes scant use. There are few instances of metonymy in his Epistles: in 1 Corinthians 11. 25 the cup stands for its contents; in 2 Corinthians 3. 14 'covenant' might be said to equal 'the book of the Covenant'; and in Galatians 5. 11; 6. 12, and 14, and elsewhere 'the Cross' represents the death of Christ and all that it signified. Here and there synecdoche can be found: in Romans 13. 1 and 1 Corinthians 15. 45 ψύχη stands for 'man'; similarly in Galatians 1. 16 'flesh and blood' means 'a human being'; and in 1 Corinthians 15. 50 and Ephesians 6. 12 the same phrase means

[1] GNTG, pp. 749–50.

'humanity' as opposed to God and supernatural beings. Occasionally Paul wields the weapons of sarcasm and irony. There is an example of the former in Philippians 3. 2, where Paul refers to Judaizers, not as τὴν περιτομήν, those who advocate circumcision for Gentiles, but as τὴν κατατομήν, those who want to mutilate them! Apart from the gentle irony of Galatians 4. 18, where Paul is chiding his converts for their fickle treatment of him, his use of this figure is confined to the epistles that he wrote to the ecclesia which gave him the most trouble (1 Cor. 1. 21; 4. 8; 2 Cor. 12. 11; 11. 5, 19; 12. 13). Euphemism finds little place in his writings: we find the word ἅπτεσθαι in 1 Corinthians 7. 1, meaning 'to copulate with,' and two verses later the expression τὴν ὀφειλὴν ἀποδιδότω, meaning 'let him have sexual intercourse with.'[1] We expect an impassioned person like Paul to make use of hyperbole, especially when he is waxing hot in debate; and we are not disappointed. For example, in Galatians 1. 8 he writes: 'But if anyone, if we ourselves or an angel from heaven, should proclaim a gospel not consonant with the gospel that we proclaimed to you, let him be anathema.' The exaggeration is obvious again three chapters later: 'You would have plucked out your very eyes and given them to me if that had been possible' (Gal. 4. 15). We have an instance of the opposite of hyperbole, meiosis, in Galatians 5. 23: having enumerated the fruits of the πνεῦμα Paul tersely observes: 'There is no law where these are concerned'—a masterpiece of understatement! In the previous chapter there is an effective use of litotes: referring to the Judaizers, he writes: 'Those to whom I have referred are envious of you, but not with honest intentions' (Gal. 4. 17). To have written, 'with dishonest intentions,' would have been far less effective. Finally, a most arresting figure of speech that occurs in the Pauline writings is the rhetorical question (Rom. 8. 35; 1 Cor. 9. 1–8 (eleven of them in all), Gal. 1. 10, and 3. 1–5).

---

[1] There is a euphemism in the English translations (except possibly NEB) of Gal. 5. 1 ; but in the Greek we have the exact opposite: the verb ἀποκόψονται is a blunt word meaning 'they would castrate themselves' (sc. like the priests of Cybele).

From figures of speech we pass to a consideration of word-order.[1] Because it was a highly inflected language, Greek had no need of hard and fast rules for the regulation of the relative positions of the various syntactical components (verb, subject, object, etc.) of clauses. The most that we can say is that (*a*) more often than not, especially in narrative writing, the verb tends to precede the subject, and the subject, the object; (*b*) grammatically closely related words, e.g. an adjective used attributively and the noun that it qualifies, an adverb and a verb or an adjective or another adverb that it modifies, a preposition and the word that it governs, a qualifying genitive and the word that it qualifies, are placed in immediate juxtaposition; and (*c*)—what is the most significant fact of all when we are considering the word-order of a rhetorical writer like Paul—words and phrases that the writer wishes to emphasize are placed mostly at the beginning of a sentence or clause, and occasionally at the end. Whilst a consideration of the first of these three points as it concerns Paul would no doubt be academically interesting, it would not be particularly profitable. Much the same can be said about the second. Professor Moule has drawn our attention to the curious displacements of the adverb καί meaning 'in fact' in 1 Thessalonians 2. 13; 3. 5, Romans 3. 7, and Philippians 4. 15, the negative adverb οὐ in Romans 3. 9, 1 Corinthians 2. 2, and 15. 51 (a well-known crux interpretum), the pronoun ἡμᾶς in Romans 9. 24 and ὑμᾶς in Colossians 2. 8, the article τοῦ in Galatians 2. 12, and the adjective μέλλουσαν in Romans 8. 18 and Galatians 3. 23.[2] Yet in every case except that of Romans 3. 9 (where in any case there is a dispute about the reading[3]) Paul's meaning is clear.[4] We cannot, however, neglect the third point because on almost every page of his Epistles it is possible to find instances of Paul's skilful,

[1] On the subject of word-order in the NT *vide* GNTG, pp. 684 ff.; F. Blass, *Grammar of of NT Greek*, Eng. tr. H. St. J. Thackeray (London, 1905), pp. 295 ff.; and C. F. D. Moule, *An Idiom Book of NT Greek* (Cambridge, 1963), pp. 166–70.
[2] C. F. D. Moule, *ibid.*, pp. 167–70. [3] Some manuscripts omit οὐ.
[4] This applies even to 1 Cor. 15. 51 in spite of all the discussion. One reading has οὐ. in the right place, before πάντες.

significant positioning of words and phrases that he wants to emphasize, at the beginning of sentences and clauses. We shall select one or two examples of this practice. In Romans 5. 6 there are the strikingly emphatic positions of the word Χριστός and the phrase ὄντων ἡμῶν ἀσθενῶν. In Romans 8. 18 the negatived predicative adjective οὐκ ἄξια, in Romans 14. 1 the direct object τὸν δὲ ἀσθενοῦντα τῇ πίστει, and in Romans 11. 13 the indirect object ὑμῖν, are in each instance placed in this same position.[1] If we want an instance of an emphatic phrase at the end of a clause, we have only to look at 1 Corinthians 13. 1, where καὶ τῶν ἀγγέλων follows λαλῶ. We should expect it to be closely linked with τῶν ἀνθρώπων and so to precede λαλῶ. What Paul is saying is: 'If I speak in tongues of men and *even of angels.*'

When we remember that the Pauline Epistles were meant to be read aloud, it is not surprising that their author pays attention to euphony, to secure which he employs various devices. Paronomasia occurs uncommonly often. Thus we find that in lists of words Paul puts together those of similar sound; the assonance is obvious in Romans 1. 29, where we have φθόνου and φόνου, and again two verses later when ἀσυνθέτους follows ἀσυνέτους immediately. Again, in 1 Corinthians 2. 13 (here the words are derived from a common root) πνεύματος, πνευματικοῖς and πνευματικὰ, in 2 Corinthians 8. 22 πολλοῖς and πολλάκις, in 2 Corinthians 9. 8 παντί, πάντοτε, and πᾶσαν, and in 1 Corinthians 15. 39 κτηνῶν and πτηνῶν occur in close proximity. Related to paronomasia, but not the same, is the play on words: viz. we have words of a similar sound, and in addition there is a play on their meaning. We have an instance of it in the antithesis of Romans 5. 19, where there is obviously a play on the words παρακοῆς and ὑπακοῆς. Other instances are not hard to discover: ἀόρατα and καθορᾶται (Rom. 1. 20), κατατομήν and περιτομή (Phil. 3. 2–3), ἀπορούμενοι and ἐξαπορούμενοι (2 Cor. 4. 8. Cf. Phil. 3. 12; 2 Thess. 3. 11; 2 Cor. 5. 4), ἄχρηστον and εὔχρηστον

---

[1] There is another curious displacement, which must have been deliberate, in this same sentence: the qualifying genitive ἐθνῶν is placed before ἀπόστολος.

(Philem. 11), ὀναίμην (Philem. 20) and Ὀνήσιμον (Philem. 11), the name of the fugitive slave, and finally μὴ ὑπερφρονεῖν παρ' ὃ δεῖ φρονεῖν, ἀλλὰ φρονεῖν εἰς τὸ σωφρονεῖν (Rom. 12. 3). Another creator of euphony is the repetition of words and phrases (called anaphora by the grammarians). For example, πάντα μοι ἔξεστιν, ἀλλ' οὐ πάντα συμφέρει. πάντα μοι ἔξεστιν, ἀλλ' οὐκ ἐγὼ κ.τ.λ. (1 Cor 6. 12) is an effective piece of rhetoric, as is the reiteration of μὴ οὐκ ἔχομεν ἐξουσίαν in 1 Corinthians 9. 4–5. Still more effective are the quintuple occurrence of πάντες in 1 Corinthians 10. 1–4, the quadruple writing of νήπιος at the end of each clause in 1 Corinthians 13. 11, and the repetition of εἰσιν and κἀγώ in 2 Corinthians 11. 22. Another impressive rhetorical device is to begin one sentence and to conclude the same or the next sentence with the same word; e.g. ἐλπίς in Romans 8. 24 and χαίρετε in Philippians 4. 4. Under the heading of euphony we must subsume parallelism, which, since it was a characteristic of Hebrew poetry, we expect to find in the writings of Paul. Hebrew poetry contained two kinds of parallelism: synonymous and antithetic. We find an example of the former in 1 Corinthians 15. 54: ὅταν δὲ τὸ φθαρτὸν τοῦτο ἐνδύσηται ἀφθαρσίαν καὶ τὸ θνητὸν τοῦτο ἐνδύσηται ἀθανασίαν; and another in Romans 11. 33: ὡς ἀνεξεραύνητα τὰ κρίματα αὐτοῦ καὶ ἀνεξιχνίαστοι αἱ ὁδοὶ αὐτοῦ (cf. Rom. 9. 2; 11. 12). Of antithetic parallelism there is an example in Romans 2. 7–8: τοῖς μὲν καθ' ὑπομονὴν ἔργου ἀγαθοῦ δόξαν καὶ τιμὴν καὶ ἀφθαρσίαν ζητοῦσιν ζωὴν αἰώνιον· τοῖς δὲ ἐξ ἐριθείας καὶ ἀπειθοῦσι τῇ ἀληθείᾳ πειθομένοις δὲ τῇ ἀδικίᾳ, ὀργὴ καὶ θυμός (cf. Rom. 8. 10). In 1 Corinthians 15. 42–4 synonymous and antithetic parallelism are interwoven to form a terse, vivid piece of poetry, which, when recited aloud, must have stirred the hearers with its matchless euphony. It is possible to find an example of that third kind of parallelism known as chiasmus (frequent in the OT)[1], the inversion in a second clause or second series of clauses of the order followed in the first clause or first series of clauses: e.g. in 1 Corinthians 7. 3 we have:

[1] Vide N. W. Lund, Chiasmus in the New Testament (University of North Carolina, 1942).

(A) τῇ γυναικὶ
(B) ὁ ἀνήρ
(B) ἡ γυνὴ
(A) τῷ ἀνδρί

A more elaborate example (this time it is a different kind of chiasmus) is found in 1 Corinthians 11. 8–12:

(A) ἀνὴρ
(B) ἐκ γυναικός
(B) γυνὴ
(A) ἐξ ἀνδρός

(A) ἀνὴρ
(B) διὰ τὴν γυναῖκα
(B) γυνὴ
(A) διὰ τὸν ἄνδρα

(B) γυνὴ
(A) χωρὶς ἀνδρὸς
(A) ἀνὴρ
(B) χωρὶς γυναικὸς

(B) γυνὴ
(A) ἐκ τοῦ ἀνδρός
(A) ὁ ἀνὴρ
(B) διὰ τῆς γυναικός

(cf. 1 Cor. 5. 2–6; Col. 3. 3–4; Phil. 3. 10–11).

The heights of euphony are scaled in 1 Corinthians 13 and Romans 8. 31–9, Norden's comment on which sums up all that we have said about Paul's rhetoric: 'How such language of the heart must have penetrated the souls of people who were accustomed to listen to the silly rigmaroles of the Sophists! In such passages the diction of the apostle rises to the heights of Plato in the *Phaedrus*.'[1]

Before we leave our discussion of Paul's literary style, we would glance at two other points: his solecisms and (what some purists would subsume under the same heading) his so-called Semitisms. There are few obviously flagrant grammatical blunders in the Pauline Epistles. In Romans 2. 8 we find two direct objects of

[1] E. Norden, *Die antike Kunstprosa* (Leipzig, 1898), Vol. 2, p. 506.

the verb ἀποδώσει in the nominative case, ὀργὴ καὶ θυμός. In Ephesians 5. 5 the relative pronoun whose antecedent is a masculine noun is ὅ, neuter in gender, and similarly in Colossians 3. 14 the neuter of the relative pronoun has for its antecedent a feminine noun, ἀγάπην. Classical pundits would regard as a solecism the use of the accusative and infinitive construction instead of the nominative and infinitive construction after a main verb of saying, believing, thinking and the like when the subject of the finite verb and of the infinitive are the same (e.g. Phil. 3. 13: ἀδέλφοί, ἐγὼ ἐμαυτὸν οὔπω λογίζομαι κατειληφέναι); yet, as J. H. Moulton points out, this development in the *Koine* was perfectly natural.[1] Pedants would probably deem Paul's fairly frequent anacolutha to be his most culpable syntactical errors, and admittedly some of them are inexcusable (e.g. the interposition of the relative pronoun ᾧ between σοφῷ θεῷ and ἡ δόξα in Rom. 16. 27 and the grammatically notorious rhetorical question in 2 Cor. 12. 17: μή τινα ὧν ἀπέσταλκα πρὸς ὑμᾶς, δι' αὐτοῦ ἐπλεονέκτησα ὑμᾶς;). Ought we to include in the category of solecism also the anacoluthon caused by the use of a participle for an indicative? In one form of this construction Paul continues a clause with a participle (not being part of a genitive absolute) that is not in agreement with any noun or pronoun in the clause, but seems to be the equivalent of a finite verb co-ordinate with the finite verb in the clause; e.g. οὐδεμίαν ἔσχηκεν ἄνεσιν ἡ σάρξ ἡμῶν, ἀλλ' ἐν παντὶ θλιβόμενοι (2 Cor. 7. 5; cf. 2 Cor. 1. 7; 9. 10–11; 9. 13; Phil. 1. 29–30). At other times the participle does agree with the subject of the verb, but is still obviously a substitute for a finite verb in the indicative mood; e.g. σωθησόμεθα ἐν τῇ ζωῇ αὐτοῦ· οὐ μόνον δέ, ἀλλὰ καὶ καυχώμενοι ἐν τῷ Θεῷ (Rom. 5. 10–11); and οὐ ˀπάλιν ἑαυτοὺς συνιστάνομεν ὑμῖν, ἀλλὰ ἀφορμὴν διδόντες· (2 Cor. 5. 12). Some have suggested that this use of the participle for the indicative is a Semitism on the ground that the construction is common in Biblical Hebrew.[2] Even if it is, it does not

[1] GGNT, Vol. 1, pp. 212–13. Occasionally Paul uses the nominative and infinitive construction; e.g. Rom. 9. 3 and 2 Cor. 10. 2.
[2] C. F. D. Moule, *An Idiom Book of NT Greek*, pp. 179–80.

R

exonerate Paul from the charge of perpetrating a solecism. On the other hand, if the construction had become as common in the *Koine*, as J. H. Moulton claims that it had,[1] then only those who regard Attic Greek as the grammatical norm for all time could convict Paul on this count. As Turner points out, we should not call the use of a participle for an imperative, so frequent in the *Koine* an anacoluthon because 'as ἐστέ (imper.) never occurs in NT we must presume that it is understood as a copula with all these ptcps.'.[2] An outstanding illustration of this construction is to be found in Ephesians 4. 1–2: Παρακαλῶ οὖν ὑμᾶς ἐγὼ ὁ δέσμιος ἐν Κυρίῳ ἀξίως περιπατῆσαι τῆς κλήσεως ... ἀνεχόμενοι ἀλλήλων ἐν ἀγάπῃ; and another in Colossians 3. 16: ὁ λόγος τοῦ Χριστοῦ ἐνοικείτω ἐν ὑμῖν πλουσίως, ἐν πάσῃ σοφίᾳ διδάσκοντες καὶ νουθετοῦντες ἑαυτούς (cf. the succession of imperatival participles in Rom. 12. 9–13). Comparatively infrequent in the Pauline Epistles is the anacoluthon caused by the transition to a finite verb after a participle; e.g. ὃς δὲ ἕστηκεν ἐν τῇ καρδίᾳ αὐτοῦ ἑδραῖος, μὴ ἔχων ἀνάγκην, ἐξουσίαν δὲ ἔχει (instead of ἔχων) (1 Cor. 7. 37; cf. Col. 1. 26). Occasionally we observe the casus pendens anacoluthon: a sentence begins with a nominative unconnected with what follows; e.g. τὸ γὰρ ἀδύνατον τοῦ νόμου, ἐν ᾧ ἠσθένει διὰ τῆς σαρκός ὁ Θεὸς τὸν ἑαυτοῦ Υἱὸν πέμψας ... κατέκρινεν τὴν ἁμαρτίαν (Rom. 8. 3).[3] We can describe as another kind of anacoluthon the use of μέν without a following contrasting clause marked by δέ; e.g. ἅτινά ἐστι λόγον μὲν ἔχοντα σοφίας ἐν ἐθελοθρησκίᾳ καὶ ταπεινοφροσύνῃ ... οὐκ ἐν τιμῇ τινι πρὸς πλησμονὴν τῆς σαρκός (Col. 2. 23). As to the misuse of the genitive absolute, which is common enough in the *Koine*[4] and which is a sort of anacoluthon, Paul errs only twice: μὴ πάλιν ἐλθόντος μου ταπεινώσῃ με ὁ Θεός μου πρὸς ὑμᾶς (2 Cor. 12. 21); and τὸ γὰρ παραυτίκα ἐλαφρὸν τῆς θλίψεως καθ᾽ ὑπερβολὴν εἰς ὑπερβολὴν αἰώνιον βάρος δόξης κατεργάζεται ἡμῖν, μὴ σκοπούντων ἡμῶν τὰ βλεπόμενα ἀλλὰ τὰ μὴ βλεπόμενα (2 Cor. 4. 17–18). Lastly, there is the anacoluthon

---

[1] GGNT, Vol. 1, pp. 222–3.   [2] GGNT, Vol. 3, p. 343.
[3] C. F. D. Moule thinks that this is an accusative in apposition to the whole sentence (*An Idiom Book of NT Greek*, p. 35). *Vide* Sanday and Headlam, *in loc.*
[4] E.g. in the NT Mt. 1. 18; 8. 1; 9. 18; Mk. 13. 1; Lk. 12. 36; Acts 21. 34; 22. 17; etc.

where the length of his sentence causes a writer to lose his thread and so to land himself in some impossible grammatical situation. The most flagrant instances of this in the Pauline Epistles are to be found in succession in Galatians 2. 4–6. In verse 5 after καταδουλώσουσιν Paul discontinues the sentence that he has begun, leaving it without a main verb, and launches into a relative clause introduced with οἷς.[1] Seemingly the long parenthesis, consisting of two relative clauses and a final clause, was the cause of this anacoluthon. The parenthesis ὁποῖοί... λαμβάνει in verse 6 has the same effect, and the opening phrase ἀπὸ δὲ τῶν δοκούντων εἶναι τι is abandoned and a new construction begun.[2] Almost as culpable as these two anacolutha is that which occurs in Romans 5. 12, where the adverbial clause of comparison beginning Διὰ τοῦτο ὥσπερ is left in the air without a main clause.

Finally, there is the question of Paul's 'Semitisms'; and to forestall queries about the meaning of this term let it be understood that we accept J. H. Moulton's definition of it: 'a deviation from genuine Greek idiom due to too literal rendering of the language of a Semitic original.'[3] Exhaustive research seems to have established that on the rare occasions when Paul does strain Greek idiom, his Semitisms are secondary, i.e. he has acquired them through the media of his bible, the LXX, and other translations of Hebrew writings. We have already referred to a construction used by Paul that is considered to be a Semitism by some: the use of the participle instead of the indicative or the imperative. Classifying his other 'Hebraisms,' we find, first, two infinitival constructions. There is the use of ἐν τῷ with the infinitive in what seems to be a temporal sense in 1 Corinthians 11. 21 and Galatians 4. 18, which resembles the Hebrew bᵉ with the infinitive; and the obvious explanation is that Paul learnt it from the LXX, where it occurs regularly. On the other hand, when we read this line from Sophocles, ἐν τῷ φρονεῖν μηδὲν ἥδιστος βίος,[4] we should not be too hasty to call the construction

---

[1] οἷς is omitted by D etc.
[2] Obviously when Paul wrote this, he was in an agitated state of mind, which may explain the atrociously bad syntax.
[3] GGNT, Vol. 2, p. 14.   [4] *Ajax*, line 554.

a Semitism. We should be even less ready to apply that description to his use of the construction τοῦ with the infinitive, found thirteen times in his Epistles. In Classical Greek τοῦ with the infinitive is either adnominal, i.e. dependent on a noun, or it is used after a verb governing the genitive case or, thanks to the influence of Thucydides, it expresses purpose[1]. All three of these uses appear in Paul's Epistles: adnominal (Rom. 1. 24; 15. 23; 1 Cor. 9. 10; 10. 13; 16. 4; 2 Cor. 8. 11; Phil. 3. 21);[2] after a verb governing the genitive case (Rom. 15. 22; 2 Cor. 1. 8); and telic (Rom. 6. 6; Phil. 3. 10).[3] This leaves only two instances: Romans 7. 3 and 8. 12, where the construction appears to be used in a consecutive sense, which is certainly foreign to Classical Greek, and may well be due to the influence of the LXX. Secondly, there are several instances in Paul's Epistles of the so-called 'Hebraic Genitive,' viz. the genitive of a noun used instead of an adjective to qualify another noun (Rom. 1. 26; 2. 5; 6. 6; 7. 24; Phil. 3. 21; Eph. 1. 14; 4. 22; Col. 1. 22; 2. 11; etc.). Before we declare these to be Hebraisms, we should remember that there is a genitive of definition in Attic poetry[4] and in the Koine,[5] and that 'it is a mistake to claim a Semitic Genitive where a good Greek Genitive makes better sense.'[6] In fact, only one of the Pauline instances mentioned, ἡμέρα ὀργῆς (Rom. 2. 5), could be called a Hebraism, and that is a phrase common in the LXX.[7] In this same category of the 'Hebraic Genitive,' but meriting separate treatment because it is particularly Semitic, must be included the metaphorical use of υἱός or τέκνον followed by a genitive of origin or definition; e.g. τὰ τέκνα τῆς σαρκὸς, τέκνα τοῦ Θεοῦ, τὰ τέκνα τῆς ἐπαγγελίας (Rom. 9. 8); υἱοὶ φωτός, υἱοὶ ἡμέρας (1 Thess. 5. 5); ὁ υἱὸς τῆς ἀπωλείας (2 Thess. 2. 3); τοῖς

---

[1] We exclude as irrelevant to this argument the use of τοῦ with the infinitive governed by a preposition.

[2] If we wish, we can call the construction in Rom. 13. 24 and 1 Cor. 10. 1 epexegetic.

[3] As Moulton says, these could well be interpreted in a consecutive sense (GGNT, Vol. 1, p. 218).

[4] E.g. Μέλαινά τ'ἄστρων ἐκλέλοιπεν εὐφρόνη (Sophocles, Electra, line 19).

[5] GGNT, Vol. 1, pp. 74, 235.

[6] C. F. D. Moule, An Idiom Book of NT Greek, p. 175.

[7] I have not included ἡμέρᾳ σωτηρίας (2 Cor. 6. 2) because it occurs there in a quotation from the LXX.

υἱοῖς τῆς ἀπειθείας (Eph. 2. 2); τέκνα φωτός (Eph. 5. 8). Deissmann's judgement on Paul's use of these expressions is that 'in no case whatever are they un-Greek; they might quite well have been coined by a Greek who wished to use impressive language. Since, however, similar terms of expression are found in the Greek bible, and are in part cited by Paul and others, the theory of analogical formations will be found a sufficient explanation.'[1] Thirdly, it has been claimed that on eight occasions Paul follows the LXX in using the preposition ἐν to translate the Hebrew causal b^e = 'because of,' 'by reason of' (Rom. 1. 21, 24; 5. 3; 1 Cor. 4. 6; 7. 14; 2 Cor. 12. 5, 9; Phil. 1. 13).[2] Our first comment on this assertion is that in four of these instances (Rom. 1. 21, 24; 2 Cor. 12. 9; Phil. 1. 13) the most appropriate meaning of ἐν is 'in the sphere of,' and in two others (1 Cor. 4. 6; 7. 14), 'through the agency of.' In the remaining two it could be causal: καὶ καυχώμεθα ἐν ταῖς θλίψεσιν = 'let us even exult because of our sufferings' (Rom. 5. 3); and ὑπὲρ δὲ ἐμαυτοῦ οὐ καυχήσομαι εἰ μὴ ἐν ταῖς ἀσθενείαις = 'I shall not boast on my own account unless my weaknesses cause me to boast' (2 Cor. 12. 5). On the other hand, in both cases ἐν could bear the meaning 'about.' Thus we cannot be certain that Paul ever uses ἐν causally. Our second comment is that there is evidence for the causal use of ἐν in the *Koine*, which means that even if Paul did use this construction, he need not necessarily have been influenced by LXX usage. Fourthly, it is pointed out that when in Ephesians 4. 29 Paul writes πᾶς . . . μή and in Ephesians 5. 5, πᾶς . . . οὐκ, he is giving us a literal translation of the Hebrew and Aramaic kōl . . . lō', instead of which he ought to have written μηδείς in Ephesians 4. 29 and οὐδείς in Ephesians 5. 5. Winer's comment on this suffices to show that it is not a Hebraism: 'This Hebraism should in strictness be limited to the expression οὐ (μή) . . . πᾶς; for in sentences with πᾶς . . . οὐ (μή) there is usually nothing that is alien to Greek usage.'[3] Finally, very occasionally we hear in Paul's Epistles echoes of Hebrew phrases; e.g. ἀναβαίνειν ἐπι τήν καρδίαν (1 Cor. 2. 9) is the literal translation in the LXX of the Hebrew

---

[1] *Bible Studies*, p. 161.   [2] *Vide* GGNT, Vol. 2, p. 463.   [3] GNTG, p. 215.

'ālāh 'al lēbh (LXX, 4 Kings 12. 4, Hebrew, verse 5; Jer. 3. 16); the expression ἐν χειρί (Gal. 3. 19) is a literal Greek reproduction of the Hebrew *bᵉyadh*, meaning 'through the agency of'; and possibly ἡμέρᾳ καὶ ἡμέρᾳ (2 Cor. 4. 16) may be a literal Greek version of the Hebrew *yōm wāyôm* as in Esther 3. 4, although it should be noted that the LXX translates this καθ' ἑκάστην ἡμέραν.[1] What conclusion is to be drawn from this study of Paul's Semitisms? The answer is that they amount to very little; and although, as we have suggested, the arguments of those who are currently reacting to the position taken up by Deissmann and J. H. Moulton carry some weight,[2] especially where the language of the Gospels and that of the Apocalypse are concerned, Moulton's judgement on the Semitic element in the language of the Pauline Epistles still stands: 'The most patriotic Jew of the Dispersion could not get on without Greek. It need not be added that for Paul's missionary work in the West, Greek had no possible alternative except Latin. A man thus accustomed to use the language of the West was not likely to import into it words and constructions that would have a foreign sound. The LXX had no such supreme authority for Paul that a copying of its language would strike him as natural. And if Greek was an alternative mother-tongue to him, he would use it too unconsciously to drop into Aramaisms, defective renderings of a language he could correct as well as any one. The *a priori* view thus sketched tallies satisfactorily with the observed facts. Paul very rarely uses phrases which come from a literal rendering of the Semitic. His Semitisms are secondary at most—defensible as Greek, and natural to a Greek ear.'[3]

[1] In Ps. 67. 20 the LXX version of the Hebrew *yôm yôm* (Ps. 68. 20) is ἡμέραν καθ' ἡμέραν.
[2] *V. sup.*, p. 22, n. 4.   [3] GGNT, Vol. 2, p. 21.

10

FINALE

For the journey is done and the summit attained,
And the barriers fall,
Though a battle's to fight ere the guerdon be gained,
The reward of it all.
I was ever a fighter, so—one fight more,
The best and the last!

R. BROWNING, Prospice

Καὶ οὕτως εἰς τὴν ῾Ρώμην ἤλθομεν (Acts 28. 14). Thus did Paul
c. A.D. 59 fulfil an ambition at least five years old (Rom. I. 10–11;
15. 23, 32; Acts 19. 21. Cf. Acts 23. 11); and there he remained
for two years, living under house arrest in a rented lodging,
situated, according to a tenth-century tradition, in the Via Lata,
where 'he welcomed all who came to see him, proclaiming God's
rule to them and teaching them about Jesus, Lord and Messiah,
with complete boldness and without let or hindrance' (Acts
28. 30–1). If we depend on Acts alone, 'the rest is silence.' Is
there any information about his other doings during those two
years? There seem to be no overwhelmingly decisive arguments
to destroy the hypothesis that it was the period during which he
indited the Epistle to the Colossians, the personal letter to Philemon, and the encyclical to the Christian communities of the
province of Asia, which we call the Epistle to the Ephesians and
which seems to be to some extent an expansion of the Epistle to
the Colossians.[1]

What happened to him at the end of the two years, viz.
c. A.D. 61? The stage is shrouded in obscurity. The usual theory
is that he was released either because at long last his appeal to
Caesar (Acts 25. 11–12; 26. 32) was heard and was successful or
because his accusers failed to appear within the period stipulated

[1] I do not include the Epistle to the Philippians among 'the Captivity Epistles' for reasons
already mentioned. *V. sup.*, p. 148 n. 4.

by law.[1] This hypothesis is based on the necessity of finding a place in his life for that period of evangelistic activity described in the frequently cited, equivocal words of Clement of Rome and implied by statements in the Pauline fragments of the Pastoral Epistles. Clement's assertion that the apostle reached 'the limits of the West' (ἐπὶ τὸ τέρμα τῆς δύσεως ἐλθών),[2] has been interpreted as a reference to that visit to Spain that Paul had long intended to pay (Rom. 15. 23, 28), which is a *non sequitur* if ever there was one.![3] Nor is Clement's phrase, as some would have us think, a description of Britain. Likewise it is difficult to believe that an inhabitant of Rome would have applied such an expression to the capital. Rather was he likely to think of it as the hub of the universe. The most that we can say about Paul's projected Spanish mission seems to be summed up by Lowther Clarke: 'We must conclude that tradition assumed the intention was carried out, the true facts having been forgotten, or that Clement refers to a matter of common knowledge, our ignorance of which is a salutary reminder of the limits of the NT evidence.'[4] We have, however, a source of information more valuable than Clement's Epistle to the Corinthians in the Pauline fragments of the Pastoral Epistles,[5] from which it is inferred that the apostle made a tour of Crete with Titus, whom he left there to build an ecclesia (Tit. 1. 5), returned to the province of Asia, visiting Miletus (2 Tim. 4. 20), Ephesus (1 Tim. 1. 3), and Troas (2 Tim. 4. 13), crossed once more to Macedonia (1 Tim. 1. 3), went to Corinth (2 Tim. 4. 20), possibly travelled to Nicopolis in Epirus (Tit. 3. 12), was arrested again, and incarcerated in Rome (2 Tim. 1. 17). It is in one of these same Pauline fragments that we catch

---

[1] H. J. Cadbury in *Beginnings*, Vol. 5, pp. 326–32. For a refutation of Cadbury's argument *vide* A. N. Sherwin-White, *Roman Society and Roman Law in the N.T.*, pp. 112 ff.

[2] Clement of Rome, *1 Cor.* 5. 7.

[3] *The Muratorian Fragment* (*c.* A.D. 190) speaks of 'the departure of Paul from the city on his journey to Spain' (H. M. Gwatkin, *Selections from Early Christian Writers*, London, 1937, p. 84).

[4] W. K. Lowther Clarke, Eng. tr. of *The First Epistle of Clement to the Corinthians* (London, 1937), p. 90.

[5] On the authorship of the Pastoral Epistles *vide* A. J. B. Higgins, art. 'The Pastoral Epistles,' *Peake's Commentary on the Bible* (1962 edn.), pp. 1001–2; F. F. Bruce, art. 'The Epistles of Paul,' *ibid.*, pp. 934–5; and J. N. D. Kelly, *Comm. on the Pastoral Epistles*, BNTC (London, 1963), pp. 1–34.

a glimpse of him in prison awaiting death. Using exquisite phraseology, he writes: 'Already my life-blood is being poured out as a libation, and the moment for me to strike my tent has come. I have finished playing my part in the great games, broken the tape, and observed the rules.[1] As for the future, what is waiting for me is the victor's wreath, the reward of having run according to the divine wish (τῆς δικαιοσύνης), which on that last day of judgement the Lord, the impartial judge in the games, will award me;[2] and not me alone, but all who have delighted in his appearance' (2 Tim. 4. 6–8). For approximately thirty years he had travelled the roads and seas of the Empire, striving to build the σῶμα τοῦ Χριστοῦ. To that end he had undergone all manner of trials and tribulations (2 Cor. 4. 8–9; 6. 4–5; 11. 23–8); to that end he had surrendered his Jewish privileges and come to reckon them as of less value than dung (σκύβαλα) (Phil. 3. 4–8); and to that end, like Jesus, Messiah and Lord, and like Stephen, whose death had played a seminal part in his career, he sacrificed his life.

Concerning the circumstances of his death tradition alone gives any detailed information. We do not know on what precise charge he was re-arrested. Chrysostom's story (which would seem to be suitable for inclusion in the script for a Hollywood epic) that he had incurred Nero's wrath by converting one of his mistresses, who thereupon refused to return to the emperor's embraces, must be taken *cum grano salis*.[3] It would appear that we must be content with Clement's statement that Paul 'bore witness before the rulers' before 'he passed from the world and went to the holy place, having shown himself the greatest pattern of endurance,'[4] words which suggest that he was put to death for being a Christian. Clement does not say even who 'the rulers' were. The apocryphal *Acta Pauli*, written probably *c.* A.D. 160,[5] states that Paul was executed in the Neronian persecution,[6] an

---

[1] The translation of the first and the last clause of this sentence is that suggested by H. A. Harris, *Greek Athletes and Athletics*, p. 131.

[2] The word κριτής is used here in the sense of the judge in the games, not in a court of law.

[3] *Adv. Vitup. Vit. Monast.*, 1. 4.   [4] Clement of Rome, *1 Cor.* 5. 7.

[5] *The Apocryphal New Testament*, ed. M. R. James (Oxford, 1924), p. 270.

[6] *Ibid.*, pp. 294–6.

assertion corroborated by Eusebius.[1] Conflicting with it is the statement of Sulpicius Severus (c. A.D. 363–c. 420/5) that Peter and Paul were executed after edicts had been published forbidding the profession of Christianity; but unless both of them lived to be centenarians, this cannot possibly be true, since the first formal proscription of Christianity did not take place until c. A.D. 112, when Trajan sent his rescript to the younger Pliny, Governor of Bithynia.[2] Thus it would seem that the traditional opinion that both apostles were put to death in the reign of Nero is the most tenable. How did Paul meet his death? Eusebius records that he suffered the capital punishment meted out to Roman citizens, decapitation;[3] to which information tradition adds the further details that he was led about three miles along the Via Ostiensis (mod. Via Ostiense) and then the Via Laurentina to a place named Aquae Salviae (mod. Tre Fontane), where he was executed under a stone pine;[4] and that his corpse was thrown into the charnel-house reserved for dead criminals, from which it was later recovered by a Christian lady named Lucina, who buried it in her own vineyard.[5] Another tradition has it that in A.D. 258 during the persecution under Valerian his remains, together with Peter's, were transferred to the Catacombs of St. Sebastian on the Via Appia, along which he had first travelled to Rome from Puteoli (Acts 28. 14–15). Approximately half a century later the Emperor Constantine is said to have encased his remains in a coffin of solid bronze, to which he attached a heavy golden cross. Whether this is true or not, it was Constantine who built the first basilica of San Paolo fuori le Mura over the supposed site of Paul's grave at the place where the Via Ostiensis met a by-way that led to the left bank of the Tiber. Later in the same century the Emperors Theodosius I (A.D. 378–95) and Valentinian II (383–92), supported by Arcadius, the son of Theodosius, set in

[1] H.E., 2. 25. 5.
[2] H. M. Gwatkin, *Selections from Early Christian Writers*, pp. 30–1.   [3] H.E. 2. 25. 5.
[4] Today the Abbey of the Three Fountains stands there among the eucalyptus trees. One of the three churches on the site is known as San Paolo alle Tre Fontane.
[5] There is a theory, based on a discovery in the catacombs, that she was Pompina Graecina, the wife of Aulus Plautius, who began the conquest of Britain during the years A.D. 43–7.

motion the reconstruction of Constantine's basilica, which in fact entailed its destruction. The process of building was completed by the Emperor Honorius (395–423), and this imposing edifice lasted until it was almost completely destroyed by fire in 1823. Thirty-one years later the present church of St. Paul Without-the-Walls, a reconstruction of the old, was consecrated by Pio Nono. Monarchs contributed to its building, the Tsar Nicholas I giving altars of malachite and lapis lazuli and even the Khedive Mehemet Ali sending six columns of Egyptian alabaster. There it stands today in a heavily industrialized quarter, the most magnificent of all Paul's architectural monuments. Those who have been privileged to visit it would echo H. V. Morton's verdict that 'no other building gives one a better idea of the majesty of Rome than St. Paul's Without.'[1] There are those who find it impossible to believe that Paul's bones are lying under the high altar. They point out that even if they ever rested there, the Saracens must have taken the sarcophagus when they sacked the city in A.D. 846. Reputable archaeologists, however, claim that the relics were saved.[2] Whether they are there or not, only those without imagination must fail to be thrilled as they gaze by the light of a torch at the fourth-century inscription on the stone, PAVLO APOSTOLO MART. . . .[3]; and again as they stand in another impressive Roman basilica, San Giovanni in Laterano, 'omnium urbis et orbis Ecclesiarum Mater et Caput,' with eyes fixed on its high altar, where, it is claimed, rest the heads of Peter and Paul. Yet, however majestic and solid a building may be, there is no guarantee that it will abide.

> The cloud-capped towers, the gorgeous palaces,
> The solemn temples, the great globe itself,
> Yea, all which it inherit, shall dissolve
> And, like this insubstantial pageant faded,
>   Leave not a rack behind.[4]

---

[1] H. V. Morton, *A Traveller in Rome* (London, 1957), p. 198.
[2] R. Lanciani, *Pagan and Christian Rome* (London, 1892), p. 149; and A. S. Barnes, *The Martyrdom of St. Peter and St. Paul* (Oxford, 1933), pp. 147 ff.
[3] For an illustration of this *vide* R. Lanciani, *ibid.*, p. 157.
[4] Shakespeare, *The Tempest*, Act 4, Scene 1.

St. Paul's Without-the-Walls, St. John in Lateran, London's St. Paul's, St. Paul's, any town—nobody can be certain that they will be standing a century, or for that matter a year, hence. Even if they are not, Paul will not lack an enduring monument. 'Si monumentum requiris, circumspice': so runs the inscription in St. Paul's Cathedral, London, written by the architect's son. Anyone in almost any part of the world could say the same of the man to whom the edifice is dedicated; for all around him he can see a building made of—to quote Peter's phrase, which Paul himself would in the light of Ephesians 2. 20–2 have applauded— 'living stones . . . a spiritual temple' (1 Pet. 2. 5), the Christian Church, the corporate personality of Jesus, Messiah and Lord, which, without the conversion of the Jew of Tarsus, would hardly have survived. Paul could appropriately have spoken a line from the writings of a pagan poet: 'Exegi monumentum aere perennius.'[1]

Saulus Paulus, Diaspora Jew, Roman citizen, Christian apostle, theologian, moralist, writer of epistles, and martyr: this is the portrait that we have tried to paint. There is one detail lacking, an aspect of his personality that we have omitted to mention: his outward appearance. In all the portraits of him painted on the walls of the catacombs (e.g. the fourth-century fresco in the Catacombs of Domitilla), in the third-fourth-century mosaic in what is possibly the oldest church in Rome, Santa Pudenziana in the Via Urbana, and in the gold leaf engravings on the *vetri cemeteriali*, he is depicted as thin and wiry, partly bald, and wearing a long, pointed beard. In the frequently quoted description of him as he was when he first arrived in Iconium, the apocryphal *Acta Pauli et Theclae* supplies additional details: he was 'a man little of stature, thin-haired upon the head, crooked in the legs, of good state of body, with eyebrows joining, and nose somewhat hooked, full of grace; sometimes he appeared like a man, and sometimes he had the face of an angel.'[2] Although Ramsay thinks that the *Acta* 'goes back ultimately to a document

---

[1] Horace, *Odes*, 3, 30, 1.
[2] *The Apocryphal New Testament*, p. 273. He certainly has the face of an angel in the noble painting by Pietr Van Lint of the seventeenth-century Flemish School, now in the British Museum.

of the first century,' and that 'this plain and unflattering account
of the Apostle's personal appearance seems to embody a very
early tradition,'[1] it is impossible to be sure that this portrait is
accurate and we should do well to be cautious.[2] Paul himself
supplies us with very little information about his physique. He
tells us that some of his opponents at Corinth described his
physical appearance as weak (2 Cor. 10. 10), which may have
been caused partly by the malady from which he is thought to
have suffered, and which he describes as 'a thorn for the flesh
(σκόλοψ τῇ σαρκί)',[3] a messenger of Satan to rack me and keep
me from being conceited on account of my visions' (2 Cor. 12. 7).
Thrice he had prayed that he might be cured of it, and received
the reply that he would be given the strength to bear it and that it
was in human weakness that the divine power was fully perceived
(2 Cor. 12. 8–9). He was probably referring to this same affliction
when he told the Galatian Christians that it had been 'on account
of a bodily weakness (δι' ἀσθένειαν τῆς σαρκὸς)' that he first
came to proclaim the good news of God to them. He reminded
them that they had not despised and loathed him for his frail
condition, but had welcomed him as they would have done a
divine messenger or even Jesus himself, the Messiah; indeed, they
would have dug out their eyes and given them to him (Gal.
4. 13–15). As we should expect, these two passages have been
a happy hunting-ground for the exercise of scholarly ingenuity,
the result of which has been a series of conjectures concerning the
nature of Paul's 'thorn for the flesh': spiritual temptations, lustful
stimuli, persecutions, obstruction of his evangelistic work, ear-
ache, headache, leprosy, Malta fever, chronic rheumatism,
erysipelas, haemorrhoids, malaria, some ophthalmic disease, and
epilepsy—all these have been suggested.[4] Yet we cannot be
certain what the weakness or ailment was; and the wisest course

---

[1] *The Church in the Roman Empire* (London, 1894), p. 32.
[2] Cf. M. Goguel, *The Birth of Christianity*, p. 207. Lanciani urges that the portraits in the catacombs are authentic (*Pagan and Christian Rome*, p. 212).
[3] Lightfoot suggests that σκόλοψ means 'stake' rather than 'thorn' (*Comm. on Gals.*, p. 189); but Moulton and Milligan show that 'thorn' is correct (VGT, pp. 578–9).
[4] Perhaps Le Père E. B. Allo's conclusion that it was malaria comes nearest to the truth (*Seconde Épître aux Corinthiens*, Paris, 1956, Excursus xvi, pp. 313–23).

seems to be to concur with Goguel's conclusion: 'All we know is that Paul was puny and unhealthy, extremely sensitive, and subject to alternating bouts of enthusiasm and despondency; his influence owes nothing to his physical make-up. His fiery soul had only a feeble body at its disposal.'[1] Paul is numbered among those who in spite of (or—here perhaps Goguel is wrong—on account of) their physical weakness, e.g. Julius Caesar, Napoleon, and Pius IX, have changed the history of mankind.

It is my belief that the essence of what he taught can still change it. Today a large number of men and women refuse to listen to the Christian evangel, not because they think that it is telling fairy-tales, but because they believe that it is no longer (even if it ever was) relevant to life. The Church says that they are mistaken; but can we blame them when Christians still expend a vast amount of time and energy (both of which are limited) on the nugae of religiosity, the minutiae of ecclesiastical legalism, and the sterile metaphysics of fourth- and fifth-century credal statements? What does a man who is not a Christian think as he scans (if he ever does) the counters and shelves in the theological section of a bookshop? If he knows his Gilbert, perhaps he likens the theologians to Bunthorne:

> You must lie upon the daisies and discourse in novel phrases of your complicated frame of mind,
> The meaning doesn't matter if it's only idle chatter of a transcendental kind.
> And everyone will say
> As you walk your mystic way,
> If this young man expresses himself in terms too deep for me,
> Why, what a very singularly deep young man this deep young man must be![2]

'Idle chatter of a transcendental kind' is not an unfair description of the contents of some theological works, which are not made any less irrelevant by being dressed up in gaily coloured paper covers. Can it be that their authors' intention (if we are charitable,

[1] M. Goguel, *Birth of The Christianity*, p. 207.   [2] W. S. Gilbert, *Patience*, Act 1.

we shall say that it is subconscious) is to provide themselves with the sand in which to bury their heads and so to escape the painful sight of man's present predicament? And all the time here is Paul of Tarsus speaking to us in our sorry plight, showing us what is radically wrong with the world and also how to put it to rights. We may no longer believe, as he did, that there exists (except in the realms of myth and poetry) a supernatural being called Satan, who heads an army of evil spirits and holds man in thrall; but it is not hard to see, as Paul saw, that humanity is enslaved by sin. Whether we call it ἁμαρτία, ἀνομία, ἀδικία, or any other appropriate name, matters little; what it is in its essence is self-deification, the worship of the creature rather than the Creator (Rom. 1. 25). We may no longer accept his account of the origin of human sinfulness, finding it impossible to believe that Adam was a historical person,[1] and that when he was created man was in some kind of unfallen state of moral perfection.[2] We who take an evolutionary view of man's origin find it 'difficult, if not impossible, to assign a particular epoch to the emergence of man as an embodied spiritual being; and consequently difficult to conceive of primitive man even for a short time as being in a state of innocence.'[3] If we accept the hypotheses of biology, the only possible explanation of what Paul calls sin—it is an explanation that also discloses the essential nature of sin—is that it arose, and arises, from the anti-social misuse of those innate impulses (or, to use a word that seems to be no longer acceptable in psychological circles, instincts) that man shares with the animals and have, therefore, been in him *ab initio*. Those impulses are not *per se* sinful; but they become so when they are used to inflict harm on a man's neighbour and thus break the divine law of love. It is a point of view succinctly summarized by Bishop Barnes: 'Those whose outlook has been transformed by modern biologists see, in selfishness and lust, by-products of instincts implanted to secure the continuance of the individual and the race. Man with

[1] We trust that we are not flogging a very dead horse when we say that today only the literalists would disagree with us.
[2] *V. sup.*, pp. 81, 90.
[3] G. D. Yarnold, *The Spiritual Crisis of the Scientific Age* (London, 1959).

his ethical conscience has moved far from the animals whence he
has sprung. Thus there has arisen a tension between moral duty
and inherited instinct.'[1] Is this picture completely irreconcilable
with Paul's account of the origin of human sinfulness? Provided
that we accept, with one reservation, the second of the two
interpretations of his teaching on the subject, outlined above,[2]
viz. that Adam is a typical (here is our demurrer), albeit a fictitious,
figure, representing humanity, which is in effect tantamount to
translating the Hebrew word 'ādhām, 'man,' then we can say
that all men are 'in Adam' in the sense that they all have common
characteristics, one of which is that they all possess animal impulses
which they misuse to the hurt of their fellows (with Paul we can
call it σάρξ), and another of which is mortality.

Thus humanity cries for deliverance. Whence is it to come?
Certainly our experience tells us that Paul was right in rejecting
legalism as a method of liberation. Far from leading men to
freedom, it is only another kind of bondage; in fact, as Paul said,
it is the tool of sin. The history of mankind shows that laws,
rules, ordinances, are impotent to free men from self-deification;
indeed, as Paul found to his utter misery when he tried to keep the
enactments of the Torah, they strengthen the fetters. Furthermore, it is psychologically unsound to contend that legalism can
liberate men from sin; for—this again was Paul's own experience
—the more we order men to keep off the grass, the more they
will be tempted to disobey us. The only way to liberate men is,
as Paul emphasized, the way of ἀγάπη, the way pointed out and
trodden by Jesus of Nazareth. It is that path, and that path alone,
the *Via Crucis*, that leads to 'the glorious liberty of the children
of God' (Rom. 8. 21). Because we believe that Jesus showed men
God's way of liberation and he himself trod it, and that he was
the incarnation of that sacrificial ἀγάπη which is consummated in
complete self-giving and is the quintessence of the divine nature,
we can subscribe to Paul's credo 'Jesus is Lord' (Rom. 10. 9;
Phil. 2. 11); with him we can say that Jesus is 'the image of the

[1] E. W. Barnes, *The Rise of Christianity* (London, 1947), p. 240.
[2] *V. sup.*, pp. 92-3.

invisible God' (Col. 1. 15), and that 'in his personality the fullness of God was pleased to dwell' (Col. 1. 19). We believe also that Paul's vision of the Church as the risen, victorious personality of Jesus Christ, who in this form continues his divine activity, is a magnificent and entirely rational concept, and that where the Church is true to that vision and continuously re-presents her Lord to the unliberated world through her κοινωνία in all its richness, through the daily living of her members, that rational service which consists in offering the personality as a living sacrifice, i.e. in living a life ruled by ἀγάπη, and through the drama of her central liturgical act, the Lord's Supper or the Mass—that where the Church acts in this way, she is carrying out God's eternal purpose of reconciling the world to himself.

Finally, can we still accept Paul's teaching concerning the consummation of the whole process? As Paul himself appeared to do, we would jettison any idea of a Parousia, a literal second advent of Jesus, and look for his return in

the one far-off divine event,
To which the whole creation moves,[1]

when (to quote Paul's own words) all things are reconciled to God (Col. 1. 20) and he is 'everything to every one' (1 Cor. 15. 28). And what shall we say to his teaching about 'the departed dead'[2]? He made a brave attempt to reconcile the Jewish belief that the bodies of the dead would be resuscitated with the ineluctable fact that the physical organism dies and decomposes. So he has given us the concept of a new organism. Is this so irrational? Yet even if it is not, the truth is that as John Baillie has stressed in a profound, exquisitely written work, although there is (to use his phrase) a 'logic of hope,' we *know* nothing of the nature of immortality.[3] As he says, 'We willingly leave to the Eternal Wisdom the whole economy of the future. "The souls of the righteous are in the hand of God," and we are content that there they should remain';[4] or as Paul himself put it, 'If we live, we

[1] Tennyson, *In Memoriam*, Conclusion.
[2] The phrase is Shelley's (*Hymn to Intellectual Beauty*, l. 51).
[3] *And the Life Everlasting* (Oxford, 1934), pp. 197–8.   [4] *Ibid.*, p. 198.

S

live to the Lord, and if we die, we die to the Lord; so then, whether we live or whether we die, we are the Lord's. For to this end Christ died and lived again, that he might be Lord both of the dead and of the living' (Rom. 14. 8–9). Through that same Lord Jesus Christ 'to the only wise God be glory for evermore! Amen' (Rom. 16. 27).

BIBLIOGRAPHY

BIBLIOGRAPHY

A. WORKS ON PAUL (excluding Commentaries)

Barclay, W. *The Mind of St. Paul.* London, 1958.

Barrett, C. K. *From First Adam to Last.* London, 1962.

Beare, F. *St. Paul and his Letters.* London, 1962.

Bruce, F. F. Art. 'The Epistles of Paul.' *Peake's Commentary on the Bible.* London, 1962.

Caird, G. B. *Principalities and Powers.* Oxford, 1956.

Cave, S. *The Gospel of St. Paul.* London, 1928.

Cerfaux, L. *Christ in the Theology of St. Paul.* Eng. tr. G. Webb and A. Walker. New York, 1959.

Cerfaux, L. *The Church in the Theology of St. Paul.* Eng. tr. G. Webb and A. Walker. New York, 1959.

Davies, W. D. *Paul and Rabbinic Judaism.* London, 1948.

Deissmann, G. A. *St. Paul. A Study in Social and Religious History.* Eng. tr. L. R. M. Strachan. London, 1912.

Deissmann, G. A. *Die Neutestamentliche Formel 'in Christo Jesu.'* Marburg, 1892.

Dibelius, M. and Kümmel, W. G. *Paul.* Eng. tr. F. Clarke. London, 1953.

Dodd, C. H. *The Meaning of Paul for To-day.* London, 1958.

Duncan, G. S. *St. Paul's Ephesian Ministry.* London, 1929.

Ellis, E. E. *Paul's Use of the Old Testament.* Edinburgh, 1957.

Findlay, G. G. Art. 'Paul.' HDB, Vol. 3. Edinburgh, 1900.

Glover, T. R. *Paul of Tarsus.* London, 1925.

Goudge, H. L. Art. 'The Theology of St. Paul.' *A New Commentary on Holy Scripture*, ed. C. Gore, H. L. Goudge, and A. Guillaume. London, 1928.

Guthrie, D. *New Testament Studies. The Pauline Epistles.* London, 1963.

Hamer, G. A. Art. 'Saul who is also called Paul.' HTR, Vol. 33.

Harrison, P. N. *The Problem of the Pastoral Epistles.* Oxford, 1921.

Howell, E. B. Art. 'St. Paul and the Greek World.' *Greece and Rome*, Vol. 11, No. 1 (2nd series). Oxford, 1964

Hunter, A. M. *Paul and his Predecessors.* Philadelphia, 1961.

Inge, W. R. 'St. Paul.' Chapter 8 of *Outspoken Essays*, Vol. 1. London, 1933.

Jackson, F. J. Foakes. *The Life of Saint Paul.* London, 1926.

Jeremias, J. Art. 'Ἀκρογωνιαῖος, TWNT, Vol. I, Stuttgart, 1933–.

Jones, M. *St. Paul the Orator.* London, 1910.

Kennedy, H. A. A. *St. Paul's Conception of the Last Things.* London, 1904.

Klausner, J. *From Jesus to Paul.* Eng. tr. W. F. Stinespring. London, 1944.

Knox, J. *Chapters in a Life of Paul.* London, 1954.

Knox, W. L. *St. Paul and the Church of Jerusalem.* Cambridge, 1925.

Knox, W. L. *St. Paul.* London, 1932.

Knox, W. L. *St. Paul and the Church of the Gentiles.* Cambridge, 1939.

Lake, K. *The Earlier Epistles of St. Paul.* London, 1927.

Lightfoot, J. B. *Notes on the Epistles of St. Paul.* London, 1895.

McKelvey, R. J. Art. 'Christ the Cornerstone.' NTS, Vol. 8, No. 4.

Manson, T. W. *On Paul and John.* London, 1963.

Mitton, C. L. *The Epistle to the Ephesians.* Oxford, 1951.

Mitton, C. L. *The Formation of the Pauline Corpus of Letters.* London, 1955.

Metzger, B. M. (ed.) *Index to Periodical Literature on the Apostle Paul* (NT Tools and Studies), Vol. I. Leyden, 1960.

Montefiore, C. J. G. *Judaism and St. Paul.* London, 1914.

Moulton, J. H. Art. 'The Gospel according to Paul.' *Expositor,* 8th series, Vol. 2.

Munck, J. *Paul and the Salvation of Mankind.* Eng. tr. F. Clarke. London, 1959.

Nock, A. D. *St. Paul.* London, 1938.

Pfleiderer, O. *Paulinism.* Eng. tr. E. Peters. 2 vols. London, 1877.

Ramsay, W. M. *St. Paul the Traveller and Roman Citizen.* London, 1895.

Ramsay, W. M. *The Cities of St. Paul.* London, 1907.

Ramsay, W. M. *The Teaching of Paul in Terms of the Present Day.* London, 1913.

Robinson, J. A. T. *The Body: a Study in Pauline Theology.* London, 1952.

Sabatier, A. *The Apostle Paul.* Eng. tr. A. M. Hellier. London, 1891.

Schoeps, H. J. *Paul.* Eng. tr. H. Knight. London, 1961.

Schweitzer, A. *Paul and his Interpreters.* Eng. tr. W. Montgomery. London, 1912.

Schweitzer, A. *The Mysticism of Paul the Apostle.* Eng. tr. W. Montgomery. London, 1931.

Scott, C. A. A. *St. Paul: the Man and the Teacher.* Cambridge, 1936.

Scott, C. A. A. *Christianity according to St. Paul.* Cambridge, 1961.

Sevenster, J. N. *Paul and Seneca*. Leyden, 1961.
Shedd, R. P. *Man in Community*. London, 1958.
Smith, D. *The Life and Letters of St. Paul*. London, 1919.
Stacey, W. D. *The Pauline View of Man*. London, 1956.
Stewart, J. S. *A Man in Christ*. London, 1935.
Stonehouse, N. B. *The Areopagus Address*. London, 1949.
Thackeray, H. St. J. *The Relation of St. Paul to Contemporary Jewish Thought*. London, 1900.
Thornton, L. S. *The Common Life in the Body of Christ*. Westminster, 1941.
Whiteley, D. E. H. *The Theology of St. Paul*. Oxford, 1964.
Wrede, W. *Paul*. Eng. tr. E. Luminis. London, 1907.
Zahn, T. Art. 'Paulus.' RE, Vol. 15.

B. COMMENTARIES ON PAUL'S EPISTLES AND THE ACTS OF THE APOSTLES

ROMANS

Barrett, C. K. BNTC. London, 1957.
Barth, K. Eng. tr. E. C. Hoskyns. Oxford, 1933.
Dodd, C. H. MNTC. London, 1932.
Manson, T. W. Peake's Commentary. London, 1962.
Nygren, A. Eng. tr. C. C. Rasmussen. Philadelphia, 1949.
Sanday, W. and Headlam, A. C. ICC. Edinburgh, 1900.
Williams, N. P. New Commentary on Holy Scripture. London, 1928.

I CORINTHIANS

Allo, E. B. Études Bibliques. Paris, 1956.
Héring, J. Commentaire du Nouveau Testament, Eng. tr. A. W. Heathcote and P. J. Allcock. London, 1962.
Moffatt, J. MNTC. London, 1938.
Plummer, A. and Robertson, A. ICC. Edinburgh, 1900.

2 CORINTHIANS

Allo, E. B. Études Bibliques. Paris, 1956.
Goudge, H. L. WC. London, 1927.
Robertson, A. and Plummer, A. ICC. Edinburgh, 1915.
Strachan, R. H. MNTC. London, 1933.

GALATIANS

Burton, E. de W. ICC. Edinburgh, 1921.
Duncan, G. S. MNTC. London, 1934.
Lightfoot, J. B. London, 1880.

266 BIBLIOGRAPHY

EPHESIANS, COLOSSIANS, PHILEMON

Abbott, T. K. Ephesians. ICC. Edinburgh, 1897.
Beare, F. W. Ephesians. IB, Vol. 10. New York, 1953.
Lightfoot, J. B. Colossians and Philemon. London, 1882.
Robinson, J. A. Ephesians. London, 1907.
Scott, E. F. Colossians, Philemon, Ephesians. MNTC. London, 1930.

PHILIPPIANS

Beare, F. W. BNTC. London, 1954.
Kennedy, H. A. A. EGT. London, 1903.
Lightfoot, J. B. London, 1883.
Meyer, H. A. W. London, 1876.
Michael, J. H. MNTC. London, 1928.
Vincent, M. R. ICC. (This includes Philemon.) Edinburgh, 1897.

1 AND 2 THESSALONIANS

Bicknell, E. J. WC. London, 1932.
Frame, J. E. ICC. Edinburgh, 1912.
Neil, W. MNTC. London, 1950.

THE PASTORAL EPISTLES

Kelly, J. N. D. BNTC. London, 1963.
Scott, E. F. MNTC. London, 1936.

THE ACTS OF THE APOSTLES

Bruce, F. F. London, 1951.
Bruce, F. F. NLC. London, 1954.
Dessain, C. S. Catholic Commentary. London, 1952.
Jackson, F. J. Foakes. MNTC. London, 1931.
Lampe, G. W. H. Peake's Commentary. London, 1962.
Loisy, A. Paris, 1920.
Rackham, R. B. WC. London, 1906.
Williams, C. S. C. BNTC. London, 1957.

C. OTHER WORKS

Abbott-Smith, G. *A Manual Greek Lexicon of the New Testament*, Edinburgh, 1937.
Adam, D. S. Art. 'Theology.' ERE, Vol. 12. Edinburgh, 1921.
Adam, K. *The Christ of Faith*. Eng. tr. J. Crick. London, 1957.
Allegro, J. M. *The Dead Sea Scrolls*. London, 1956.
Allegro, J. M. *The Treasure of the Copper Scroll*. New York, 1960.

Anderson, J. G. C. Art. 'Trajan on the Quinquennium Neronis.' JRS, Vol. 1. London, 1911.

Aristotle. *The Nichomachean Ethics.* Loeb edn., with Eng. tr. H. Rackham. London, 1956.

Baillie, D. M. *God was in Christ.* London, 1961.

Baillie, J. *And the Life Everlasting.* Oxford, 1934.

Barnes, A. S. *The Martyrdom of St. Peter and St. Paul.* Oxford, 1933.

Barnes, E. W. *The Rise of Christianity.* London, 1947.

Barr, J. *The Semantics of Biblical Language.* Oxford, 1961.

Bauer, W. *A Greek-English Lexicon of the New Testament and other Early Christian Literature,* trans. and ed. by W. F. Arndt and F. W. Gingrich. Cambridge, 1956.

Beasley-Murray, G. A. *Baptism in the New Testament.* London, 1962.

Bernard, E. R. Art. 'Sin.' HDB, Vol. 4. Edinburgh, 1909.

Bernard, J. H. *Commentary on St. John's Gospel.* ICC. 2 vols. Edinburgh, 1928.

Best, E. *One Body in Christ.* London, 1955.

Best, E. Art. 'Acts XIII. 1–3', JTS, N.S., Vol. 11.

Bethune-Baker, J. F. *An Introduction to the Early History of Christian Doctrine.* London, 1933.

Black, M. *The Scrolls and Christian Origins.* London, 1961.

Blass, F. *Grammar of New Testament Greek.* Eng. tr. H. St. J. Thackeray. London, 1905.

Blass, F. and Debrunner, A. *A Greek Grammar of the New Testament* (9th Edn.). Eng. tr. R. W. Funk. Chicago, 1961.

Bloch, M. *The Historian's Craft.* Eng. tr. P. Putnam. Manchester, 1954.

Bousset, W. *Kyrios Christos.* Göttingen, 1926 (3rd edn.). (1st edn., 1913.)

Bousset, W. *Die Religion des Judenthums in späthellenistischen Zeitalter.* Berlin, 1903.

Brandon, S. G. F. *The Fall of Jerusalem and the Christian Church.* London, 1957.

Brown, J. A. C. *Techniques of Persuasion.* London, 1963.

Bultmann, R. *Theology of the New Testament.* Eng. tr. K. Grobel, 2 vols. London, 1952–5.

Bultmann, R. Art. 'New Testament and Mythology' in *Kerygma and Myth,* ed. H. Bartsch, Eng. tr. R. H. Fuller. London, 1953.

Burkitt, F. C. *Christian Beginnings.* London, 1924.

Burrows, M. *The Dead Sea Scrolls.* London, 1956.

Burrows, M. *More Light on the Dead Sea Scrolls.* London, 1958.

Caird, G. B. *The Apostolic Age.* London, 1955.

Carmignac, J. *Christ and the Teacher of Righteousness.* Baltimore, 1962.

Carr, E. H. *What is History?* London, 1962.

Cary, M. *A History of Rome.* London, 1949.

Cave, S. *The Christian Estimate of Man.* London, 1944.

Charles, R. H. *A Critical History of the Doctrine of a Future Life in Israel, in Judaism and in Christianity.* London, 1913.

Charles, R. H. *The Apocalypse of Baruch.* London, 1896.

Charles, R. H. *Religious Development between the Old and New Testaments.* London, 1914.

Charles, R. H. (ed.) *The Apocrypha and Pseudepigrapha of the Old Testament,* 2 vols. Oxford, 1913.

Cicero. *Laelius vel de Amicitia,* ed. L. Laurand. Paris, 1942.

Cirlot, F. L. *The Early Eucharist.* London, 1939.

Clark, N. *An Approach to the Theology of the Sacraments.* London, 1956.

Clement of Rome. *Epistle to the Corinthians. The Apostolic Fathers,* ed. J. B. Lightfoot. London, 1907. Also translation of the same by W. K. L. Clarke. London, 1937.

Collingwood, R. G. *An Essay on Metaphysics.* Oxford, 1940.

Collingwood, R. G. *The Idea of History.* Oxford, 1946.

Cullmann, O. *Christ and Time.* Eng. tr. F. V. Filson. London, 1951.

Cullmann, O. *Early Christian Worship.* Eng. tr. A. S. Todd and J. B. Torrance. London, 1953.

Cullmann, O. *Christology of the New Testament.* London, 1959.

Daube, D. *The New Testament and Rabbinic Judaism.* London, 1956.

Davies, W. D. Art. 'The Apostolic Age.' Peake's Commentary. London, 1962.

Davies, W. D. Art. in Ecumenical Dialogue at Harvard. *The Roman Catholic-Protestant Colloquium,* ed. S. H. Miller and G. E. Wright. Cambridge, Mass., 1964.

Deissmann G. A. *Bible Studies.* Eng. tr. A. Grieve. Edinburgh, 1909.

Deissmann G. A. *Light from the Ancient East.* Eng. tr. L. R. M. Strachan. London, 1910.

Dewar L. *The Holy Spirit and Modern Thought.* London, 1959.

Dibelius M. *Studies in the Acts of the Apostles.* Eng. tr. M. Ling. London, 1956.

Dix G. *The Shape of the Liturgy.* London, 1945.

Dodd C. H. *The Bible and the Greeks.* London, 1954.

Dodd C. H. *History and the Gospel.* London, 1938.

Dodd C. H. *The Apostolic Preaching and its Developments.* London, 1936.

Dodd, C. H. *New Testament Studies.* Manchester, 1953.

Ehrhardt, A. *The Apostolic Succession.* London, 1953.

Ehrhardt, A. *The Framework of the New Testament Stories.* Manchester, 1964.

Eichrodt, W. *The Theology of the Old Testament.* 1961.

Farrar, F. W. *History of Interpretation.* London, 1886.

Farrer, A. M. *The Glass of Vision.* Westminster, 1948.

Fison, J. E. *The Blessing of the Holy Spirit.* London, 1950.

Flemington, W. F. *The New Testament Doctrine of Baptism.* London, 1948.

Flew, R. N. *Jesus and his Church.* London, 1938.

Foley, W. M. Art. 'Marriage (Christian).' ERE, Vol. 8. Edinburgh, 1918.

Friedlander, L. *Roman Life and Manners under the Early Empire.* Eng. tr. L. A. Magnus, J. H. Freese, and A. B. Gough. 4 vols. London, 1908–13.

Foerster, W. and Quell, E. *Lord* (BKW). Eng. tr. H. P. Kingdon. London, 1958.

Fuller, R. H. *The Mission and Achievement of Jesus.* London, 1954.

Fuller, R. H. *The New Testament in Current Study.* New York, 1962.

Gärtner, B. 'John 6 and the Jewish Passover.' Coniectanea Neotestamentica, XVII. Lund and Copenhagen, 1959.

Garvie, A. E. Art. 'Belial.' HDB, Vol. 1. Edinburgh, 1898.

Gavin, F. *The Jewish Antecedents of the Christian Sacraments.* London, 1928.

Gibbon, E. *The Decline and Fall of the Roman Empire.* 12 vols. London, 1791.

Goffin, M. Art. in *Objections to Roman Catholicism,* ed. M. de la Bedoyere. London, 1964.

Glover, T. R. *The Ancient World.* London, 1944.

Goguel, M. *The Birth of Christianity.* Eng. tr. H. C. Snape. London, 1953.

Gomme, A. W. *A Historical Commentary on Thucydides.* 3 vols. Oxford, 1954–6.

Graetz, H. *History of the Jews.* Eng. tr. B. Löwy. 5 vols. London, 1891–2.

Grant, M. *The World of Rome.* London, 1960.

Guignebert, Ch. *The Jewish World in the Time of Jesus.* Eng. tr. S. H. Hooke. London, 1939.

Gwatkin, H. M. *Selections from Early Christian Writers.* London, 1937.

Hanson, A. T. *The Wrath of the Lamb.* London, 1957.

Harris, H. A. *Greek Athletes and Athletics.* London, 1964.

Hatch, E. and Redpath, H. A. *A Concordance to the Septuagint and other Greek Versions of the Old Testament including the Apocryphal Books.* Oxford, 1897–1907.

Hendry, G. S. *The Holy Spirit in Christian Theology.* London, 1957.

Herford, T. R. *Pharisaism.* London, 1912.

Higgins, A. J. B. *The Lord's Supper in the New Testament.* London, 1952.

Higgins, A. J. B. Art. 'The Pastoral Epistles.' *Peake's Commentary.* London, 1962.

Higgins, A. J. B. *Jesus and the Son of Man.* London, 1964.

Holtzmann, H. J. *Lehrbuch der Neutestamentlichen Theologie,* 2 vols. Tübingen, 1911.

Homo, L. *Roman Political Institutions.* Eng. tr. M. R. Dobie. London, 1929.

Hooke, S. H. Art. 'Gog and Magog.' ET, Vol. 26. 1914–15.

Hooker, M. D. *Jesus and the Servant.* London, 1959.

Inge, W. R. *Christian Mysticism.* London, 1925.

Jackson, F. J. Foakes, Lake, K., Ropes, J. H. and Cadbury, H. J. *The Beginnings of Christianity,* 5 vols. London, 1920–33.

Jacob, E. *Theology of the Old Testament.* Eng. tr. A. W. Heathcote and P. J. Allcock. New York, 1958.

James, M. R. (ed.) *The Apocryphal New Testament.* Oxford, 1924.

James, W. *The Varieties of Religious Experience.* London, 1902.

Jarrett-Kerr, M. *The Secular Promise.* London, 1964.

Jaubert, A. *La Date de la Cène.* Paris, 1957.

Jaubert, A. Art. RHR (1954), pp. 140 ff.

Jeremias, J. *The Eucharistic Words of Jesus.* Eng. tr. A. Ehrhardt. Oxford, 1955.

Jerome. *Works,* ed. D. Vallarsi, 11 vols. Verona, 1734–42. Reprinted in J. P. Migne, PL, vols. 22–30.

Johnston, G. *The Doctrine of the Church in the New Testament.* Cambridge, 1943.

Jones, G. V. *Christology and Myth in the New Testament.* London, 1956.

Josephus. *Works.* Loeb edn. London, 1926.

Jung, C. G. *Collected Works,* 18 vols. London, 1953– .

Kautsch, E. Art. 'The Religion of Israel.' HDB. Extra vol. Edinburgh, 1904.

Kennedy, H. A. A. *The Theology of the Epistles.* London, 1919.

Kirk, K. E. *The Vision of God.* London, 1931.

Knox, J. *Jesus: Lord and Christ.* New York, 1958.

Knox, J. *The Church and the Reality of Christ.* London, 1963.

Knox, R. *Enthusiasm.* Oxford, 1950.

Knox, W. L. *Some Hellenistic Elements in Primitive Christianity.* London, 1944.

Laidlaw, J. Art. 'Psychology.' HDB, Vol. 4. Edinburgh, 1902.

Lampe, G. W. H. and Woollcombe, K. J. *Essays in Typology.* London, 1957.

Lanciani, R. *Pagan and Christian Rome*. London, 1892.

Laski, M. *Ecstasy*. London, 1961.

Layard, H. *Nineveh and its Remains*. London, 1850.

Lepper, F. A. Art. 'Some Reflections on the "Quinquennium Neronis",' JRS, Vol. 47, pp. 95–103. London, 1957.

Lloyd-Jones, D. M. *Conversions Psychological and Spiritual*. London, 1959.

Loewe, H. Essay 'Pharisaism' in *Judaism and Christianity*, Vol. 1, ed. W. O. E. Oesterley. London, 1937.

Lund, N. W. *Chiasmus in the New Testament*. North Carolina, 1942.

Macgregor, G. H. C. and Purdy, A. C. *Jew and Greek: Tutors unto Christ*. London, 1959.

Mackintosh, H. R. *The Doctrine of the Person of Jesus Christ*. Edinburgh, 1913.

Macquarrie, J. *Twentieth-Century Religious Thought*. London, 1963.

Macquarrie, J. *An Existentialist Theology*. London, 1955.

Manson, T. W. *Studies in the Gospels and Epistles*, ed. M. Black. Manchester, 1962.

Manson, T. W. *The Teaching of Jesus*. Cambridge, 1963.

Manson, W. *Commentary on St. Luke's Gospel*. MNTC. London, 1930.

Manson, W. *Jesus the Messiah*. London, 1943.

Manson, W. *The Epistle to the Hebrews*. London, 1951.

Marsh, H. G. *The Origin and Significance of New Testament Baptism*. Manchester, 1941.

Marshall, H. L. *The Challenge of New Testament Ethics*. London, 1947.

Moffatt, J. *Love in the New Testament*. London, 1929.

Moore, G. F. *Judaism*. 3 vols. Oxford, 1927–30.

Morton, H. V. *A Traveller in Rome*. London, 1957.

Moule, C. F. D. Art. 'Sanctuary and Sacrifice in the Church of the New Testament.' JTS, N.S., Vol. 1.

Moule, C. F. D. Art. 'The Influence of Circumstances on the Use of Eschatological Terms.' JTS, N.S., Vol. 15, Pt. 1.

Moule, C. F. D. *An Idiom Book of New Testament Greek*. Cambridge, 1963.

Moulton, J. H. and Milligan, G. *Vocabulary of the Greek New Testament*. London, 1949.

Moulton, J. H. *A Grammar of New Testament Greek*, Vol. 1. Edinburgh, 1906.

Moulton, J. H. and Howard, W. F. *A Grammar of New Testament Greek*, Vol. 2. Edinburgh, 1919–29.

Mowinckel, S. *He that Cometh*. Eng. tr. G. W. Anderson. Oxford, 1956.

Niebuhr, R. *The Nature and Destiny of Man*. 2 vols. London, 1941.

Nock, A. D. *Conversion*. Oxford, 1933.

Norden, E. *Agnostos Theos*. Leipzig and Berlin, 1913.

Norden, E. *Die antike Kunstprosa*, 2 vols. Leipzig, 1898.

Nygren, A. *Agape and Eros*. Eng. tr. A. G. Hebert and P. S. Watson, 3 vols. London, 1932–9.

Oesterley, W. O. E. *The Jewish Background of the Christian Liturgy*. Oxford, 1925.

Oesterley, W. O. E. and Robinson, T. H. *Hebrew Religion*. London, 1930.

Otto, R. *The Idea of the Holy*. Eng. tr. J. W. Harvey. Oxford, 1924.

Oulton, J. E. L. *Holy Communion and Holy Spirit*. London, 1951.

Pfeiffer, R. H. *History of New Testament Times*. New York, 1949.

Philo. *Opera*. Loeb edn., with Eng. tr. F. H. Colson. 10 vols. London, 1929.

Plato. *Lysis*. Loeb edn., with Eng. tr. W. R. M. Lamb. London, 1946.

Pliny. *Letters*. Loeb edn., with Eng. tr. W. M. L. Hutchinson. 2 vols. London, 1957–8.

Polybius. *The Histories*. Loeb edn., with Eng. tr. W. R. Paton. 6 vols. London, 1960.

Porter, F. C. Art. 'The Yeçer Hara.' Yale Bicentenary Volume, Biblical and Semitic Studies, 1901.

Putnam, G. H. *Authors and their Public in Ancient Times*. New York, 1894.

Quell, E. and Schrenk, G. *Righteousness* (BKW). Eng. tr. J. R. Coates. London, 1951.

Rad, G. von. *Theology of the Old Testament*, 2 vols. Eng. tr. D. M. G. Stalker. Edinburgh, 1962–3.

Ramsay, W. M. *The Church in the Roman Empire before* A.D. 170. London, 1894.

Ramsay, W. M. Art. 'Tarsus.' HDB, Vol. 4. Edinburgh, 1909.

Rashdall, H. *Conscience and Christ*. London, 1916.

Rashdall, H. *The Idea of Atonement in Christian Theology*. London, 1925.

Rawlinson, A. E. J. 'Corpus Christi' in *Mysterium Christi*, ed. G. K. A. Bell and G. A. Deissmann. London, 1930.

Rawlinson, A. E. J. *Commentary on St. Mark*. WC. London, 1925.

Rawlinson, A. E. J. *The New Testament Doctrine of the Christ*. London, 1926.

Rees, T. *The Holy Spirit in Thought and Experience*. London, 1915.

Rengstorff, K. H. *Apostleship* (BKW). Eng. tr. J. R. Coates. London, 1952.

Rhymes, D. *No New Morality*. London, 1963.

Richardson, A. *An Introduction to the Theology of the New Testament*. London, 1958.

Richardson, A. *History, Sacred and Profane*. London, 1964.

Ritschl, A. B. *De Ira Dei*. Bonn, 1859.

Ritschl, A. B. *The Christian Doctrine of Justification and Reconciliation*. Vol. 3. Eng. tr. H. R. Mackintosh and A. B. Macaulay. Edinburgh, 1900.

Robinson, H. W. *The Christian Doctrine of Man*. Edinburgh, 1926.

Robinson, H. W. *The Christian Experience of the Holy Spirit*. London, 1962.

Robinson, J. A. T. *In the End, God. . . .* London, 1950.

Robinson, J. A. T. *Jesus and his Coming*. London, 1957.

Rostovtzeff, M. *The Social and Economic History of the Roman Empire*, rev. by P. M. Fraser, 2 vols. Oxford, 1957.

Rowley, H. H. *The Relevance of Apocalyptic*. London, 1947.

Rowley, H. H. *The Biblical Doctrine of Election*. London, 1950.

Rowley, H. H. *The Faith of Israel*. London, 1956.

Sanctis, S. de. *Religious Conversion*. Eng. tr. H. Augur. London, 1927.

Sanders, J. N. *The Foundations of the Christian Faith*. London, 1950.

Sargant, W. *Battle for the Mind*. London, 1959.

Schecter, S. *Some Aspects of Rabbinic Theology*. London, 1909.

Schneider, J. Art. ʽΟμοίωμα, TWNT, Vol. 5. Stuttgart, 1933–.

Schürer, E. *A History of the Jewish People in the Time of Jesus*. Eng. tr. J. Macpherson, S. Taylor, and P. Christie, 5 vols. and Index. Edinburgh, 1885–91.

Schweizer, E. *Spirit of God* (BKW). Eng. tr. A. E. Harvey. London, 1960.

Scott, E. F. *The Spirit in the New Testament*. London, 1923.

Seneca. *Select Letters*, ed. W. C. Summers. London, 1910.

Sherwin-White, A. N. *Roman Society and Roman Law in the New Testament*. London, 1963.

Skinner, J. Art. HDB, Vol. 4. Edinburgh, 1909.

Smith, C. Ryder. *The Bible Doctrine of the Hereafter*. London, 1958.

Snaith, N. H. *The Distinctive Ideas of the Old Testament*. London, 1944.

Stanley, A. P. *Christian Institutions*. London, 1881.

Starbuck, E. D. *The Psychology of Religion*. London, 1901.

Stendahl, K. (ed.) *The Scrolls and the New Testament*. London, 1958.

Stevens, G. B. Art. 'Righteousness in NT.' HDB, Vol. 4. Edinburgh, 1902.

Strabo. *Geographica*, ed. G. Kramer, 3 vols. Berlin, 1847.

Strack, H. L. and Billerbeck, P. *Kommentar zum Neuen Testament aus Talmud und Midrasch.* 6 vols. München, 1928.

Suetonius. *De Vita Caesarum*, Loeb edn., 2 vols., with Eng. tr. J. C. Rolfe. London, 1950.

Tarn, W. W. *Hellenistic Civilization.* London, 1930.

Tasker, R. V. G. *The Wrath of God.* London, 1957.

Taylor, C. (ed.) *Sayings of the Jewish Fathers.* Cambridge, 1877.

Taylor, H. O. *Ancient Ideals*, 2 vols. New York, 1900.

Taylor, V. *The Gospel according to St. Mark.* London, 1952.

Taylor, V. *The Names of Jesus.* London, 1953.

Taylor, V. *The Person of Christ in New Testament Teaching.* London, 1958.

Tennant, F. R. *The Sources of the Doctrines of the Fall and Original Sin.* Cambridge, 1903.

Tertullian. *Opera*, 2 vols., ed. J. G. P. Borleffs, E. Dekkers, *et al.* (Corpus Christianorum). Turnholt, 1952– .

Thayer, J. H. *A Greek-English Lexicon of the New Testament* (Grimm's Wilke's *Clavis Novi Testamenti* tr. and enl.). Edinburgh, 1901.

Thomas, D. W. Art. 'Micah.' *Peake's Commentary.* London, 1962.

Thomson, G. *The Greek Language.* Cambridge, 1960.

Thouless, R. H. *Introduction to the Psychology of Religion.* Cambridge, 1924.

Thucydides. *Historiae.* 2 vols., ed. H. S. Jones. Oxford, 1942.

Tinsley, E. J. *The Imitation of God in Christ.* London, 1960.

Troeltsch, E. Art 'Historiography.' ERE, Vol. 6. Edinburgh, 1913.

Turner, C. H. Art. 'Chronology of the New Testament.' Vol. 1. Edinburgh, 1898.

Turner, N. *A Grammar of New Testament Greek*, by J. H. Moulton, Vol. 3 (Syntax). Edinburgh, 1963.

Turner, N. Art. 'The Language of the New Testament.' *Peake's Commentary.* London, 1962.

Turner, N. *Grammatical Insights into the New Testament.* Edinburgh, 1965.

Vidler, A. (ed.) *Soundings.* Cambridge, 1962.

Vriezen, Th. C. *An Outline of Old Testament Theology.* Oxford, 1960.

Walbank, F. W. *A Historical Commentary on Polybius*, Vol. 1. Oxford, 1957.

Weiss, J. *The History of Primitive Christianity*, Eng. tr. R. Knopf, completed by four friends and ed. F. C. Grant. London, 1937.

White, R. E. O. *The Biblical Doctrine of Initiation.* London, 1960.

Williams, N. P. *The Ideas of the Fall and Original Sin*. London, 1927.

Winer, G. B. *A Treatise on the Grammar of New Testament Greek*, Eng. tr. W. F. Moulton. Edinburgh, 1882.

Wood, H. G. *Jesus in the Twentieth Century*. London, 1960.

Xenophon. *Memorabilia*. Loeb edn., with Eng. tr. E. C. Marchant. London, 1923.

Yarnold, G. D. *The Spiritual Crisis of the Scientific Age*. London, 1959.

Zimmerli, W. and Jeremias, J. *The Servant of God*. London, 1957.

Zuckermandel, M. S. (ed.) *Tosephta Kiddushin*. Pasewalk, 1880.

T

INDICES

REFERENCE INDEX

OLD TESTAMENT

Genesis		7. 6	18, 139
1. 27	188	11. 13–21	7
2. 7	157	14. 2	19
2. 24	210	21. 23	42, 182
Chap. 3	28, 89	22. 12	7
3. 17–18	96	23. 1	52
3. 19	94	25. 4	233, 235
3. 22	94	31. 16 ff.	117
5. 1	188	32. 6	187, 190
6. 1–4	80, 89	32. 7	6
12. 3	19	32. 18	187, 190
15. 6	119	*Judges*	
32. 10	103	5. 11	102
35. 17	3	1 *Samuel*	
Exodus		14. 41	58
4. 22–3	187	18. 1	199
12. 3 ff.	133	2 *Samuel*	
12. 26–7	6, 133	1. 26	199
13. 1–10	7	2. 14	187
13. 2	182	1 *Kings*	
13. 11–16	7, 133	3. 7–9	179
13. 12	182	2 *Kings*	
13. 14–16	6	12. 4	248
15. 3	103	1 *Chronicles*	
16. 10	188	17. 13	187
19. 5	116	22. 10	187
20. 12	213	2 *Chronicles*	
24. 1–8	133	20. 7	199
24. 16	188	*Esther*	
25. 17	107	3. 4	248
33. 11	199	*Job*	
34. 7	103	10. 21–2	153
40. 34–5	188	*Psalms*	
Leviticus		2. 6	177
16. 11 ff.	107	2. 7	187, 190
16. 16	107	4. 4	204
20. 26	19	7. 11	103
26. 14 ff.	117	9. 4	103
Numbers		9. 8	103
15. 37–8	7	37. 11	203
Deuteronomy		39. 12–13	153
5. 16	213	43. 22 (LXX)	132
6. 4	6, 84	72. 11	20
6. 4–9	7	88. 9–12	153
6. 6	186	89. 3	179
6. 20–5	6	89. 18 ff.	177

279

U

AUTHOR INDEX

Abbott-Smith, G., 61, 124, 176
Adam, K., 75, 177
Aeschylus, 155
Allegro, J. M., 181
Allo, E. B., 255
Anderson, G. W., 176, 194
Anderson, J. G. C., 218
Aratus, 71, 188
Aristotle, 199, 200, 201
Arnold, Matthew, 85, 196
Augustine, 94, 196, 209
Aulus Gellius, 200
Austen, Jane, 23

Bainton, R. H., 77
Baillie, D. M., 110 f., 172
Baillie, J., 259
Barclay, W., 82
Barnes, A. S., 253
Barnes, E. W., 258
Barr, J., 101, 147
Barrett, C. K., 101, 112
Barstow, S., 211
Barth, K., 101, 233
Bauer, W., 3, 4, 184
Bernard, E. R., 83
Bernard, J. H., 198
Bengel, J. A., 101
Best, E., 92, 224
Bethune-Baker, J. F., 185
Black, M., 181
Blake, William, 201
Blass, F., 239
Bloch, M., 34
Bonnard, P., 181
Bousset, W., 88, 115, 195
Brandon, S. G. F., 24, 36, 52
Brown, J. A. C., 37, 44
Browning, Robert, 50, 249
Brownlee, W. H., 181
Bruce, F. F., 8, 67, 70 f., 77, 250
Brunner, E., 172
Bultmann, R., 46 f., 68, 87, 96, 111, 172, 195

Burrows, M., 181
Burton, E. de C., 37, 54, 88, 175, 188

Cadbury, H. J., 9, 250
Caird, G. B., 96, 112
Calvin, J., 113
Capito, 220
Carlyle, Thomas, 50
Carmignac, J., 181
Carr, E. H., 34
Carroll, Lewis, 1, 151
Cave, S., 41, 90, 159
Cerfaux, L., 177 f., 181, 192
Cervantes, M. de, 219
Charles, R. H., 16, 148, 157, 166
Chrysostom, John, 251
Cicero, 25 f., 82, 200 f., 220, 234
Cirlot, F. L., 129
Clark, N., 127
Clarke, W. K. L., 250
Cleanthes, 71, 188
Clement of Alexandria, 86
Clement of Rome, 250 f.
Cosin, J., 143
Cox, R. G., 173
Collingwood, R. G., 34, 37, 75
Cowper, William, 68
Crabbe, George, 147
Cullmann, O., 131, 151, 175, 177, 181, 191 f., 195

Davies, W. D., 5, 7, 24, 29, 45, 55, 77, 88, 91 f., 94, 122, 134, 159, 166, 181
Deissmann, G. A., 7, 22, 77, 114, 121 f., 178, 221, 247
Dessain, C. S., 67
Dibelius, M., 65 f.
Diogenes Laertius, 200
Dix, G., 128, 185 f.
Dodd, C. H., 27, 29, 50, 55, 68, 87, 89, 92 101, 102, 106, 108, 111, 162 f., 223, 233
Cary, M., 151, 216
Donne, John, 173
Dryden, John, 143
Duff, J. W., 85
Dunbar, William, 100

296

SUBJECT INDEX

Abraham, 2, 4, 19, 119, 140, 199
Adam, 28 f., 81–3, 89–96, 105, 111, 157–9, 164, 183, 188, 235
Adoption, 110, 191
Angels, 21, 78, 149, 152, 162
Anger, divine, 106–9
    human, 203–4
Antioch, Pisidian, 55, 69, 228
    Syrian, 52 f.
Anti-Christ, 79, 81, 151 f.
Appeals to Caesar, 25
Apostleship, 59–62
Aramaic, 2 f., 4, 21 f., 42, 72, 247, 248
Athens, 55, 69–71, 73, 86, 228
Atonement, Day of, 106 f.

Baptism, 123 f., 146
Barnabas, 53 f., 56, 70, 126
Birth, date of Paul's, 2
Body of Christ (the Church), 45, 77, 93, Chap. 5 passim, 156, 159, 161 f., 164, 167, 170, 183 f., 196 f., 216, 259
Bride of Christ (the Church), 138 f., 210

Caesar-worship, 151
Captivity Epistles, 148, 169, 249
Charismata, 64, 143 f.
Chiasmus, 241 f.
Christology, Chap. 5 passim
Colossae, 197
Conversion of Paul, 9, Chap. 2, 53, 56, 98, 112, 121
Corinth and Corinthian Church, 9, 35, 55–63, 72–4, 76, 79, 86, 123, 135–9, 155–7, 196, 209, 212, 228, 230, 250
Corporate Personality, 92 f., 115, 125, 141
Covenant, 19, 102 f., 116 f., 119, 133 f., 190
Cross of Christ, 47, 69, 73 f., 86 f., 100, 112, 116, 119, 132 f., 182 f., 193
Cultus (Christian), 137–9

David, King, 15 f., 174, 177, 179, 190, 199 f.
Dead Sea Scrolls, 119, 129, 152, 181
Death, 17, 78, 90, 94–6, 98 f.
Death, Paul's, 251–2

Deity of Christ, 194 f.
Demons, 21, 78–80, 99
Diaspora Judaism, 3, 5, 9, 22 f., 24, 42, 138, 168, 234
Diatribe, 222 f.
Divorce, 212
Docetism, 179

Education, Paul's, 4–9, 11
Election, 6, 14, 18 f., 21, 38, 102–4, 117, 139 f.
Ephesus and Ephesian Church, 55, 67, 228, 250
Epicureans, 71, 86
Epistolography, 220 f.
Eschatology, 14–16, 18, 20, 38, 76, 81, 107–9, Chap. 6 passim, 209, 259 f.
Exodus, 6, 69, 77, 101, 133 f., 235
Expiation, 106 f.

Faith, 118 f., 120 f.
Fatherhood of God, 84, 145, 161, 201, 216
Fall, doctrine of, 81 f., 89–94, 96, 101, 157, 164, 257 f.
Family, 213 f.
Flesh, 29, 87–9, 94, 122, 144, 196, 206
Formgeschichte, 65 f.

Galatian churches, 9, 206, 255
Gamaliel, 8–10, 24, 72
Gentiles, immorality of, 84 f., 197, 205, 208
    Jewish attitude to, 10 f., 19–21, 38, 50
    mission to, 45, 53–6
Glory, Christ the, 188
Glossolalia, 142
Gnosticism, 76, 189

Ḥᵃbhûrāh, 127–31
Hebrew Christians, 42, 52–5, 57 f.
Hebrew language, 21. See also Semitisms
Hellenism, Paul's attitude to, 29 f.
Hellenists, 42, 50, 51 f.
Heilsgeschichte, 191 f., 195
Holiness of God, 189, 199
    of the Church, 139 f.
Humanity of Jesus, 177 f.

300